SOCIAL CONTEXTS OF TRIBAL EDUCATION

About the Author

Vimal P. Shah obtained his M.A. (Sociology) degree from the Gujarat University and Ph. D. (Sociology) degree from the University of Wisconsin. He has worked as a Research Associate with Professor Wm. H. Sewell at the University of Wisconsin, and as a Programme Associate in the Ford Foundation, New Delhi. He is currently working as Professor and Head of the Department of Sociology of the Gujarat University. He has published several research papers/ monographs in the fields of educational aspirations/achievements, family and research methods.

Tara Patel obtained her M.A. (Gujarati & Sanskrit) degree from the University of Bombay, M.A. (Sociology) degree from Columbia University, and her Ph. D. from the University of London. She was Head of the Department of Sociology, Gujarat University, from its inception in 1954 till her retirement in 1978. She was a Fellow of the Agricultural Development Council Inc. at the University of Wisconsin for a year, and a Visiting Professor of Rural Sociology at the University of the Philippines, Los Banos. She was also a member of the Socially and Educationally Backward Classes Commission appointed by the Government of Gujarat. She has published several research reports/papers in the fields of family, social problems, educational aspirations, and educational attainment of the scheduled castes and scheduled tribes.

SOCIAL CONTEXTS
OF
TRIBAL EDUCATION

VIMAL P. SHAH
TARA PATEL

CONCEPT PUBLISHING COMPANY PVT. LTD.
NEW DELHI-110059

ISBN: 978-81-7022-100-5

Reprint 2023

Published and Printed by

Concept
Since 1974

Concept Publishing Company Pvt. Ltd.
A/15-16, Commercial Block, Mohan Garden,
New Delhi-110059 (India)
T: 91-11-41101460
E: publishing@conceptpub.com, *W*: www.conceptpub.com

ACKNOWLEDGEMENTS

ANY social science research, based on a large-scale survey spread over a vast geographical area, is of necessity a team work ; it requires the co-operation and assistance of several organizations and individuals. This monograph, based on a field survey conducted in 64 villages of the 32 talukas in the tribal sub-plan area of Gujarat, falls in this category of social research. We would like to gratefully acknowledge here the support and assistance received by us. The Government of Gujarat has extended the financial support for this study. We deeply appreciate the encouragement and co-operation extended to us in this regard by Shri P.B. Buch, Ex-Dircctor, Bureau of Economics and Statistics, Shri P.H. Bhatt, Ex-Secretary, Labour, Social Welfare and Tribal Development Department, and Shri G.S. Shah, Director, Bureau of Economics and Statistics. We thank Shri A.L. Barmeda, K.G. Chaudhari, N.B. Chaudhari, S.C. Chaudhari, U.G. Chaudhari, N.B. Gamit, K.R. Parmar, N.B. Patel, J.B. Patel and D. Orenkar all of whom worked as field investigators, and our colleague Shri D.B. Desai who helped us in supervising the field work. It is not possible to name the principals and the teachers of several ashramshalas who have extended very generous hospitality and other assistance in the field work. We thank all of them. We gratefully acknowledge the assistance of Smt. Amita R. Shah, Senior Research Officer, for her dilligent and willing assistance in coding, tabulation and other research operations ; Shri Ajay Patel, Kumari Meera Pathak and Shri Deepak Doctor, programmers in the Gujarat University Computer Centre for their assistance in programming and analysis of the data ; Shri G.F. Patel, Stenographer, for typing the drafts and final copy of the monograph ; and Shri S.N. Shah for looking after the accounts work of the project.

We gratefully acknowledge the assistance received from the

Government of Gujarat Computer Centre, the Gujarat University Computer Centre and the Physical Research Laboratory Computer Centre for the computerization and analysis of the data. Last but not the least, we thank Dr. I.P. Desai and Shri P.B. Buch for their comments and suggestions on the draft chapters of this monograph.

Ahmedabad
30 January 1984

VIMAL P. SHAH
TARA PATEL

CONTENTS

LIST OF TABLES

1

THE RESEARCH PROBLEM

INTRODUCTION

THE CONSTITUTION of India prescribes certain safeguards for the tribals (along with the scheduled castes and other backward classes), either specifically or by way of general rights of the citizens. The objective of such safeguards is to promote the educational and economic interests of the tribals and other backward classes, and to remove their traditional social disabilities.

For the past three decades, we have been attempting to direct and accelerate the process of economic and social development through planned programmes. We have accepted education as one of the key factors for the development not only of the tribals but also of the other communities. The government has launched various schemes to motivate the tribals (along with the scheduled castes and other backward classes) to obtain education. There are several programmes of the central and the state governments to extend financial and other assistance for obtaining education right from the primary to the university stage. The special programmes for the tribals provide for free supply of school uniform, slates, books, notebooks, etc. to primary school students ; mid-day meal ; payment of term, gymkhana and other compulsory fees to secondary school students ; pre-matric and post-matric scholarships ; facilities for additional coaching, vocational and pre-service training classes ; balwadis ; ashram-shalas and hostels with free lodging and boarding facilities ; reservation of seats in institutions of higher and technical education, and so on.

Since the tribal population is concentrated in certain areas, the government formulates a special sub-plan for accelerating, with intensive inputs, the development of the tribals in such areas. The tribal sub-plan area in Gujarat is spread over 32 talukas of seven districts. About 72 per cent (26.82 lakhs) of the total tribal population of the state resides in the tribal sub-plan area.[1]

For the purposes of planning, it is necessary to obtain a detailed picture of the educational development of the tribals in the tribal sub-plan area. There are three major sources of data in this regard, namely, the decennial censuses, records of the departments of education and social welfare, and social/economic sample surveys conducted by various government and research organizations. The 1971 Census gives only literacy data for the scheduled tribes, by sex, rural-urban areas, district, taluka and tribal groups. Although the 1961 Census gives detailed data regarding the levels of education attained by the scheduled tribes, no such data are available in the 1971 Census publication. We can, no doubt, obtain enrolment data for the scheduled tribes, the scheduled castes and the general population from the department of education. Such data fall short of providing adequate information, regarding the size and other characteristics of the sub-populations, which is necessary for examining the various factors associated with their educational development. Although numerous social/economic sample surveys have been conducted in the past, such surveys are limited in their coverage of study area and tribal groups. They are also limited by the extent to which they examine the relevant factors associated with the educational development of the tribals. The present study is an attempt to fill in some of the gaps in our knowledge concerning the educational development of the tribals as well as the factors associated with it. In view of the fact that about ninety per cent of the tribals residing in the tribal sub-plan area live in the rural areas, this study was conducted in the rural areas included in the tribal sub-plan.

Scheduled tribes

The term 'tribe' has not been defined in the Constitution of India. Under its provisions, the President specifies, from time to time, various tribes in the states and the union territories as scheduled tribes. According to the 1971 Census, the scheduled tribes constituted 6.9 per cent of the total population and numbered 38,015,162.

After the removal of certain area restrictions, as per the Scheduled Castes and Scheduled Tribes Orders (Amendment) Act 1976, the revised estimate of their population in 1971 was 4.11 crores or 7.5 per cent of the total population. According to the 1971 Census, the population of the scheduled tribes in Gujarat was 3,734,422 or 13.99 per cent of the total population, and the revised estimate, after the removal of area restrictions, was 37.57 lakhs or 14.07 per cent of the total population. Gujarat, with 9.82 per cent of the tribal population in the country, ranks fourth after Madhya Pradesh (22.06%), Orissa (13.34%) and Bihar (12.98%).

The 1971 Census lists 30 categories of the scheduled tribes or their groupings in Gujarat. Out of these categories, the population of four scheduled tribes [Barda (53), Pomla (300) Gond or Rajgond (402), Bharwad (531)] is very small, and that of ten others is less than 5,000. Of the remaining categories, the population of ten scheduled tribes or their groupings is more than a lakh each. Bhils (14.52 lakhs) constituting 38.9 per cent of the tribal population in the state form the largest group. They, though distributed all over the tribal belt, are concentrated mainly in Panchmahals, Bharuch, Vadodara, Dangs, Sabarkantha and Banaskantha districts. Dublas (3.89 lakhs), Dhodias (3.59 lakhs) and Gamits (2.77 lakhs) together constitute about one-fourth of the tribal population in the state, and reside mainly in Surat, Valsad and Bharuch districts. Nayakas or Naikdas (2.35 lakhs) are concentrated in Panchmahals and Valsad districts. The other major tribal groups are Chaudharis (1.77 lakhs) in Surat, Valsad, Bharuch and Dangs districts ; Dhankas (1.39 lakhs) in Bharuch, Vadodara and Surat districts ; Koknas (1.47 lakhs) in Valsad and Dangs districts ; Rathwas (1.39 lakhs) in Vadodara and Panchmahals districts ; and Varlis (1.26 lakhs) in Valsad, Dangs and Surat districts. The tribals are concentrated in 32 talukas of seven districts (Bharuch, Dangs, Panchmahals, Sabarkantha, Surat, Vadodara and Valsad), which are included in the tribal sub-plan area.

Education

Education is concerned with learning. Learning is the process of acquiring knowledge or skills by instruction, study or experience ; in this broad sense, learning is a life-long process. Education refers to the method by which a society attempts to direct and accelerate the learning process of its members. Formal education refers to schooling—an organized system of training for developing knowledge, skills, mind, character, etc. of individuals. Informal education emanates from an individual's own experience and continues throughout his life. However, with the development and use of organized sources of mass media for 'education', the distinction between formal and informal education hinges on enrolment, specified instructional programme spread over a period of time, examination and certification. In this monograph, the term 'education' is used in its narrower sense ; it refers to literacy and formal schooling.

It has been argued that the school, as envisaged under the conventional system, may not be in keeping with the cultural milieu of the tribal population. Ashram schools are, therefore, established in the tribal areas ; they provide free boarding and lodging facilities and aim at imparting, besides general education, craft-based education to students.

Theoretically, the strength of the ashram schools lies in imparting education which is relevant to tribal life, close student-teacher interactions and lower rates of absenteeism and dropouts. Apart from the question of an adequate functioning of the ashram schools, the major hurdle is their high cost. In a study of Dharampur taluka (Desai and others, 1976, Vol. II, 64-65), it was observed that "ashramshala education is a high cost process in the sense that an annual investment of nearly Rs. 6 lakhs could cover only 1.16 per cent of the eligible children of Dharampur taluka. At the same time, the prevailing poverty of local tribals and their general lack of interest in formal education (particularly among the poorest sections) make this high cost process an imperative need to attract tribal children to the school." However, it was further observed that "almost a 100 per cent government subsidy to run ashramshalas at such high cost and low coverage cannot be a permanent feature of the educational system." The present study does not take any special notice of the system of ashram schools. It aims to examine the educational development of the tribals, given the available educational facilities, including the ashram schools. We shall first examine the available data from the census reports regarding the educational development of the tribals in Gujarat.

Literacy in Gujarat

The educational progress of the tribals must be examined in relation to that of the scheduled castes (for whom similar programmes are in operation) as well as the non-scheduled caste/tribe (non-SCST) population. As there are differences in the educational accomplishments of males and females residing in rural and urban areas, it is necessary to control for sex and rural-urban residence while examining their progress. Also, we must examine the educational progress of the tribals in Gujarat in relation to that of the tribals in the country as a whole. Literacy rate is a general, albeit rather crude, indicator of education among the people. Let us, therefore, examine the available literacy data from the census reports.

We find from Table 1.1 that, in terms of literacy, the non-SCST population is at the top, the scheduled castes are in the middle, and the tribals are at the bottom. The differences by sex and rural-urban residence are found in all these sections of the population. The tribal females in the rural areas have the lowest level of literacy, and the non-SCST urban males show the highest level of literacy. Among the backward sections of the population, sex differences are greater in the urban than in the rural areas. Rural-urban differences are greater for the males than for the females in the backward sections, but they are greater for the females than for the males in the non-SCST population. The additive differences of sex and rural-urban residence are the lowest among the tribals and the highest among the non-SCST population. The pattern in the literacy rates of the three sections of the population is the same in Gujarat as in the country as a whole.

Between 1961 and 1971, the increase in the literacy rate of the tribals was lowest, but that of the non-SCST population was the highest. This increase was generally greater among the males than among the females in the backward sections, but it was greater among the females than among the males in the non-SCST population. In Gujarat, the scheduled castes (except the rural females) have registered almost the same increase in the literacy rate as that by the non-SCST population; but the

TABLE 1.1 : Literacy rates* of scheduled tribes, scheduled castes and non-SCST population in India and in Gujarat, in 1961 and 1971, by sex and rural-urban areas

	Rural			Urban			Total		
	Males	Females	Total	Males	Females	Total	Males	Females	Total
	1	2	3	4	5	6	7	8	9
INDIA									
Scheduled Tribes									
1961 Census	134	29	82	304	135	224	138	32	85
1971 Census	169	44	107	371	196	288	176	49	113
Scheduled Castes									
1961 Census	151	25	89	322	100	217	170	33	103
1971 Census	200	51	128	389	170	286	224	64	147
Non-SCST Population									
1961 Census	337	104	223	602	372	497	394	156	279
1971 Census	385	159	278	643	449	551	445	222	338
Total Population									
1961 Census	291	85	190	575	345	470	344	130	240
1971 Census	338	132	237	613	421	524	395	187	295
GUJARAT									
Scheduled Tribes									
1961 Census	185	39	113	287	78	188	191	41	117
1971 Census	211	57	135	336	138	242	219	62	142

TABLE 1.1 : (*Contd.*)

	1	2	3	4	5	6	7	8	9
Scheduled Castes									
1961 Census	301	93	198	449	152	308	339	107	225
1971 Census	354	118	238	514	238	384	399	150	277
Non-SCST Population									
1961 Census	384	157	273	615	390	509	453	224	342
1971 Census	435	205	324	659	474	571	508	290	403
Total Population									
1961 Census	345	132	241	596	368	488	411	191	305
1971 Census	390	172	284	640	448	549	462	248	359

*No. of literates per 1,000 persons.

Source : 1961 and 1971 Census Reports.

increase in the literacy rate of the tribals was the lowest. Further, while the 1961-71 increase was greater for the males than for the females of all the three sections in the rural areas of Gujarat, it was greater for the females than for the males in the urban areas.

The literacy rates are higher in Gujarat than in the country as a whole for all the sections, except the scheduled tribe urban males and females. In terms of the tribal literacy in 1971, Gujarat (142) ranks behind only Meghalaya (256), Nagaland (240) and Assam (207).

The literacy data indicate that as compared to the tribals in the country as a whole the tribals in Gujarat are in a slightly advantageous position ; however, they are at the bottom of the literacy pyramid in the state. There are considerable differences by sex and rural-urban residence in the literacy rates of the tribals. In 1971, while only 57 per 1,000 scheduled tribe rural females were literate, 336 per 1,000 scheduled tribe urban males were literate.

There is also a considerable inter-district variation in the literacy rates. We find from Table 1.2 that the literacy rate of the general population varies from 142 in Dangs to 488 in Ahmedabad. There are also significant differences in the literacy rates of the rural and the urban population ; the literacy rates vary from 129 for the rural population of Banaskantha to 616 for the urban population of Vadodara. Similar rural-urban and inter-district differences are found in the literacy rates of the tribals ; they vary from as low as 21 for the rural areas of Surendranagar to as high as 492 for the urban areas of Gandhinagar.

Since the proportion of the tribal population is very small in 12 of the 19 districts of the state, the variation in the tribal literacy rates of all districts does not seem to present a clear picture. It is, therefore, necessary to examine, in detail, the literacy rate of people in the tribal sub-plan districts. There is a considerable reduction in the variation in the tribal literacy rates ; their literacy rates vary from as low as 88 in the rural areas of Panchmahals to as high as 294 in the urban areas of Valsad. It should be noted that the tribal literacy rates in the rural areas vary from 88 in Panchmahals to 176 in Valsad.

TABLE 1.2 : **Literacy rates* of general population and scheduled tribes, by district and rural-urban areas.**

District	Percentage of ST Population in State	Percentage of SC Population in Dist.	General Population Rural	General Population Urban	General Population Total	Scheduled Tribes Rural	Scheduled Tribes Urban	Scheduled Tribes Total
Districts in tribal sub-plan area								
1. Bharuch	13.0	43.9	319	541	357	136	179	138
2. Dangs	2.4	93.5	142	—	142	113	—	113
3. Panchmahals	19.1	88.6	188	548	228	88	187	92
4. Sabarkantha	4.8	15.1	291	528	311	165	210	165
5. Surat	22.2	46.3	309	561	394	164	262	171
6. Vadodara	12.7	23.9	315	616	407	109	224	113
7. Valsad	20.8	54.3	332	575	376	176	294	186
Other districts								
1. Ahmedabad	0.6	0.7	314	574	488	177	284	262
2. Amreli	**	**	301	479	337	280	429	299
3. Banaskantha	2.1	6.2	129	429	158	36	144	40
4. Bhavnagar	**	**	238	517	327	394	322	335
5. Gandhinagar	**	0.2	399	555	418	117	492	239
6. Jamnagar	**	0.2	227	491	320	39	288	6
7. Junagadh	**	0.5	234	481	306	33	106	40
8. Kaira	0.7	1.0	385	589	425	126	181	135
9. Kuchchha	1.1	4.8	229	489	294	28	63	34
10. Mehsana	**	0.4	358	522	389	127	209	164
11. Rajkot	**	**	285	565	392	255	324	319
12. Surendranagar	**	0.6	221	509	299	21	114	22

*No. of literates per 1,000 persons.

**Negligible.

Literacy in the tribal sub-plan area

All the talukas of the seven districts are not included in the tribal sub-plan area ; therefore, it is necessary to examine the literacy rates of the tribals as well as the general population residing in the different talukas of the tribal sub-plan area. These data are given, by rural-urban areas and sex, in Table 1.3. It should be noted that 16 of the 32 talukas comprise of only rural areas and, therefore, the respective cells for the urban and the total population are blank in this table.

We find that the literacy rate of the general population is higher than that of the tribals in each of the talukas. This pattern continues even when we examine the literacy rates separately for males and females in the rural as well as the urban areas. For the tribal as well as the general population, the literacy rate is higher among the males than among the females of all talukas, except Bansda ; similarly, the literacy rate is higher for the urban population than for the rural population of all talukas except Bansda and Pardi. On account of such a pattern of differences by sex and rural-urban residence in the literacy rates of the tribal and the general population, we find that in each of these talukas the literacy rate of the tribal rural females is the lowest while that for the urban males in the general population is the highest. There is, however, a considerable variation in the literacy rates of different sections of the population across talukas. For example, the literacy rates of the tribal rural females vary from as low as 6 in Chhota Udepur and Khedbrahma to as high as 214 in Mahuva ; similarly, the literacy rates of the urban males in the general population vary from 488 in Songadh to 857 in Pardi.

It is also instructive to note the quantum of differences in the literacy rates of (a) males and females, (b) rural and urban population, and (c) tribal and general population in these talukas. The sex differences in the literacy rates of the tribal rural population vary from 69 in Chhota Udepur to 307 in Bhiloda ; such differences among the tribal urban population vary from 76 in Pardi taluka to 383 in Santrampur. Similarly, the sex differences in the literacy rates of the general population in the rural areas range from 87 in Chhota Udepur to 245 in Tilakwada, and those for the urban areas range from 115 in Bansda and Chikhli to

TABLE 1.3 : **Literacy rates* of scheduled tribes and general population in the tribal sub-plan area, by taluka, rural-urban areas and sex**

District/Taluka	Rural			Urban			Total		
	Males	Females	Total	Males	Females	Total	Males	Females	Total
	1	2	3	4	5	6	7	8	9
Vadodara District	172 (420)	40 (201)	109 (315)	326 (696)	103 (523)	224 (616)	179 (506)	43 (297)	113 (407)
Chhota Udepur	75 (116)	6 (29)	41 (74)	351 (634)	118 (392)	234 (518)	79 (158)	8 (56)	44 (107)
Naswadi	198 (270)	39 (91)	121 (183)	—	—	—	—	—	—
Tilakwada	295 (412)	87 (167)	194 (295)	—	—	—	—	—	—
Bharuch District	224 (428)	46 (204)	136 (319)	271 (635)	79 (441)	179 (541)	226 (464)	48 (245)	138 (357)
Sagbara	202 (229)	45 (59)	122 (144)	—	—	—	—	—	—
Dediapada	181 (206)	36 (55)	109 (131)	—	—	—	—	—	—
Valia	246 (361)	63 (160)	155 (257)	—	—	—	—	—	—
Jhagadia	220 (384)	49 (179)	136 (284)	—	—	—	—	—	—
Nandod	274 (356)	58 (133)	167 (247)	400 (667)	159 (471)	285 (574)	280 (411)	63 (191)	173 (303)

TABLE 1.3 : (*Contd.*)

	1	2	3	4	5	6	7	8	9
Valsad District	261	91	176	381	199	294	271	99	185
	(422)	(243)	(332)	(648)	(496)	(575)	(464)	(287)	(376)
Dharampur	148	42	95	319	101	216	152	43	98
	(154)	(47)	(101)	(550)	(377)	(465)	(179)	(67)	(124)
Bansda	248	72	160	236	282	259	247	77	162
	(435)	(241)	(336)	(734)	(619)	(676)	(—291)	(120)	(205)
Chikhli	339	141	239	440	223	331	340	142	239
	(435)	(241)	(336)	(734)	(619)	(676)	(443)	(251)	(346)
Pardi	342	114	227	311	235	275	338	126	232
	(456)	(224)	(339)	(857)	(465)	(528)	(482)	(268)	(375)
Umbergaon	196	30	110	382	113	256	202	32	114
	(374)	(163)	(266)	(656)	(442)	(553)	(394)	(180)	(285)
Panchmahals District	156	18	88	279	86	187	161	20	92
	(297)	(72)	(188)	(653)	(436)	(548)	(337)	(112)	(228)
Jhalod	169	26	99	—	—	—	—	—	—
	(234)	(73)	(155)						
Dohad	151	15	83	313	105	212	164	22	94
	(180)	(27)	(104)	(656)	(476)	(566)	(321)	(158)	(240)
Santrampur	195	23	110	522	139	352	198	23	112
	(257)	(55)	(159)	(679)	(415)	(585)	(272)	(67)	(172)
Limkheda	116	13	65	—	—	—	—	—	—
	(187)	(25)	(107)						
Devgadhbaria	115	11	65	313	56	197	121	12	69
	(241)	(34)	(141)	(648)	(454)	(555)	(266)	(59)	(166)

TABLE 1.3 : (*Contd.*)

Sabarkantha District	270	59	165	303	64	210	270	59	165
	(422)	(155)	(291)	(637)	(407)	(528)	(442)	(176)	(311)
Vijaynagar	383	94	233	—	—	—	—	—	—
	(410)	(111)	(258)	—	—	—	—	—	—
Khedbrahma	78	6	43	354	109	254	80	6	44
	(209)	(71)	(141)	(551)	(319)	(443)	(241)	(92)	(169)
Bhiloda	409	102	254	—	—	—	—	—	—
	(425)	(130)	(278)	—	—	—	—	—	—
Meghraj	268	41	155	—	—	—	—	—	—
	(310)	(72)	(194)	—	—	—	—	—	—
Surat District	**213	64	164	360	151	262	251	89	171
	(393)	(222)	(309)	(641)	(471)	(562)	(480)	(303)	(394)
Uchhal	156	30	94	—	—	—	—	—	—
	(171)	(37)	(105)						
Vyara	276	113	195	400	201	305	281	117	200
	(286)	(124)	(206)	(617)	(472)	(546)	(328)	(166)	(248)
Valod	329	134	233	—	—	—	—	—	—
	(484)	(254)	(344)						
Songadh	157	43	101	500	228	393	176	50	114
	(171)	(49)	(111)	(488)	(264)	(393)	(269)	(104)	(191)
Nijar	230	53	140	—	—	—	—	—	—
	(326)	(114)	(320)						
Mahuva	426	214	320	—	—	—	—	—	—
	(481)	(281)	(381)						

TABLE 1.3 : (*Contd.*)

	1	2	3	4	5	6	7	8	9
Mandvi	215	61	139	295	112	206	218	63	141
	(296)	(126)	(212)	(601)	(449)	(526)	(323)	(155)	(240)
Mangrol	238	64	152	263	90	179	238	64	152
	(363)	(194)	(279)	(558)	(398)	(481)	(375)	(206)	(291)
Bardoli	223	76	150	329	92	216	232	77	155
	(402)	(275)	(339)	(616)	(446)	(535)	(437)	(302)	(371)
Dangs District	176	47	113	—	—	—	—	—	—
	(208)	(71)	(142)						

Note : Figures in the parentheses indicate literacy rates of the general population.

*Literates per 1,000 persons.

**Based on total scheduled tribe population of Surat District according to 1961 Census.

Source : 1971 Census Reports.

392 in Pardi. It may be noted that the sex differences in the literacy rates are generally greater in the urban areas than in the rural areas of many talukas. This is presumably indicative of the fact that while a greater proportion of the males in the urban areas have made use of the expanding facilities for education the females are lagging behind.

The rural-urban differences in the literacy rates of the tribal males vary from 25 in Mangrol taluka to 343 in Songadh, and those for the tribal females vary from 16 in Bardoli to 210 in Bansda. Similar differences in the literacy rates of the males in the general population vary from 195 in Mangrol to 518 in Chhota Udepur, and those for the females in the general population vary from 171 iu Bardoli to 449 in Dohad. Further, the rural-urban differences are generally greater for the males than for the females in many talukas.

With regard to the differences in the literacy rates of the tribal population and the general population, the literacy rates of the rural males vary from 6 in Dharampur to 187 in Bansda, but those of the rural females vary from 5 in Dharampur to 199 in Bardoli. Similar differences among the urban males vary from 12 in Songadh to 546 in Pardi but those for the urban females vary from 36 in Songadh to 398 in Devgadh Baria.

Thus, there is a considerable variation in the literacy rates of the general and the tribal population residing in different talukas of the tribal sub-plan area. Similarly, there are considerable sex and rural-urban differences in their literacy rates. There is also a lot of inter-taluka variation in the literacy rates of the general as well as the tribal population in each category of sex and rural-urban areas. In view of the fact that different tribal groups are concentrated in different regions of the tribal sub-plan area, it seems necessary to examine inter-tribe and inter-taluka variations in their literacy rates. Since most of the tribals reside in rural areas, it will be adequate to examine the literacy rates of the major scheduled tribes residing in the rural areas of the tribal sub-plan. Further in view of the sex differences in the literacy rates of the tribals, it will also be necessary to examine such data separately for males and females. For this purpose, the major tribal groups have been defined as those whose population in the state is one lakh or more. It is considered adequate to examine the literacy of only those major tribal groups that reside in the rural areas and whose total population in the taluka is 5,000 or more. The relevant literacy data are given in Table 1.4. The average ($\bar{X}$) literacy rate, the range of inter-taluka variation in the literacy rates, and the standard deviation of the literacy rates of the males and the females in these major tribal groups are also given in this table. It reveals several important aspects of the literacy patterns among the tribals.

As previously mentioned, the tribals who have settled in the relatively more developed parts of the state, especially in the urban areas, indicate a relatively high literacy rate. As compared to the literacy rates of the general, the non-SCST and the scheduled caste population in the respective areas, the literacy rates of the tribals are the lowest. A majority of the tribal population is concentrated in the rural areas of the tribal sub-plan, and a more dismal picture of tribal literacy is revealed in this area. There are considerable inter-tribe and sex differences in the literacy rates of the tribals in this area. The average male literacy rate varies from 107.3 (Varlis) to 424.6 (Dhodias) and the average female literacy rate varies from 13.8 (Varlis) to 172.7 (Dhodias). Thus, among the major tribal groups, the Dhodia males and females are at the top of the literacy ladder, while the Varli males and females are at the bottom. The rank-order of different tribal groups, in terms of the male literacy rates, is (1) Dhodias, (2) Chaudharis, (3) Dhankas, (4) Gamits, (5) Koknas, (6) Bhils, (7) Dublas, (8) Naikdas, (9) Rathwas, and (10) Varlis. Their rank-order in terms of the female literacy rates is generally the same; only in the case of Dhankas and Koknas, and Bhils and Dublas, we find slight reversals. Among all the tribal groups residing in different talukas, the female literacy rate is considerably lower than the male literacy rate. However, the literacy rate of the Dhodia and Chaudhari females is higher than that of the Rathwa and Varli males. Such a pattern of literacy rates among different tribal groups suggests the need for examining the socio-economic and other background characteristics of different tribal groups that might be related to their literacy, albeit educational achievement.

There is an inter-taluka variation in the literacy rates of males and females in different tribal groups. Among males, the

TABLE 1.4 : **Literacy rates* of major tribes in the tribal sub-plan area by taluka and sex (for rural areas only)**

Talukas	Bhils		Dublas		Dhodias		Gamits		Naikdas	
	Males	Females	Males	Females	Males	Females	Males	Females	Males	Females
	1	2	3	4	5	6	7	8	9	10
Chhota Udepur	31	6	—	—	—	—	—	—	3	1
Naswadi	179	41	—	—	—	—	—	—	—	—
Tilakwada	289	87	—	—	—	—	—	—	—	—
Sagbara	208	47	—	—	—	—	213	46	—	—
Dediapada	177	34	—	—	—	—	—	—	—	—
Valia	236	54	—	—	—	—	—	—	—	—
Jhagadia	22	46	—	—	—	—	—	—	—	—
Nandod	252	69	—	—	—	—	—	—	—	—
Dharampur	—	—	—	—	381	146	—	—	—	—
Bansda	—	—	—	—	367	144	—	—	—	—
Chikhli	—	—	149	53	421	188	—	—	194	49
Pardi	—	—	204	45	424	151	—	—	191	45
Umbergaon	—	—	210	42	333	68	—	—	—	—
Jhalod	169	26	—	—	—	—	—	—	—	—
Dohad	97	10	—	—	—	—	—	—	—	—
Santrampur	197	23	—	—	—	—	—	—	—	—
Limkheda	108	11	—	—	—	—	—	—	—	—
Devgadhbaria	—	—	—	—	—	—	—	—	94	6
Vijaynagar	385	95	—	—	—	—	—	—	—	—
Khedbrahma	77	6	—	—	—	—	—	—	—	—
Bhiloda	409	102	—	—	—	—	—	—	—	—
Meghraj	269	41	—	—	—	—	—	—	—	—
Uchhal	165	30	—	—	—	—	146	27	—	—

TABLE 1.4 : (*Contd.*)

	1	2	3	4	5	6	7	8	9	10
Vyara	—	—	—	—	530	239	260	96	—	—
Valod	—	—	170	46	—	—	309	112	—	—
Songadh	127	25	—	—	—	—	155	45	—	—
Nizar	197	44	—	—	—	—	338	87	—	—
Mahuva	—	—	161	40	516	273	—	—	271	88
Mandvi	131	21	156	34	—	—	201	58	—	—
Mangrol	197	37	—	—	—	—	257	65	—	—
Bardoli	—	—	164	31	—	—	—	—	—	—
Ahwa	101	23	—	—	—	—	—	—	—	—
Average ($\overline{X}$) literacy rate	182.9	39.9	173.4	41.6	424.6	172.7	234.9	67.0	150.6	37.8
Range of inter-taluka variation in literacy rates	22 to 409	6 to 102	149 to 210	31 to 53	333 to 516	68 to 273	146 to 338	27 to 112	3 to 271	1 to 88
Std. Dev. of literacy rates	96.6	26.8	22.3	6.7	68.6	62.9	64.3	27.1	92.7	31.8

Talukas	Chaudharis		Dhankas		Konkas		Rathwas		Varlis	
	Males	Females	Males	Females	Males	Females	Males	Females	Males	Females
	1	2	3	4	5	6	7	8	9	10
Chhota Udepur	—	—	96	11	—	—	87	7	—	—
Naswadi	—	—	277	45	—	—	229	35	—	—
Tilakwada	—	—	305	89	—	—	—	—	—	—
Sagbara	—	—	—	—	—	—	—	—	—	—
Dediapada	—	—	—	—	—	—	—	—	—	—
Valia	—	—	—	—	—	—	—	—	—	—
Jhagadia	—	—	—	—	—	—	—	—	—	—
Nandod	—	—	310	47	—	—	—	—	—	—
Dharampur	—	—	—	—	134	21	—	—	57	9
Bansda	—	—	—	—	211	33	—	—	93	5
Chikhli	—	—	—	—	254	59	—	—	—	—

TABLE 1.4 : (*Contd.*)

Pardi	—	—	—	—	—	—	—	—	—	—
Umbergaon	—	—	—	—	—	—	—	—	127	7
Jhalod	—	—	—	—	—	—	—	—	—	—
Dohad	—	—	—	—	—	—	—	—	—	—
Santrampur	—	—	—	—	—	—	—	—	—	—
Limkheda	—	—	—	—	—	—	—	—	—	—
Devgadhbaria	—	—	—	—	—	—	73	2	—	—
Vijaynagar	—	—	—	—	—	—	—	—	—	—
Khedbrahma	—	—	—	—	—	—	—	—	—	—
Bhiloda	—	—	—	—	—	—	—	—	—	—
Meghraj	—	—	—	—	—	—	—	—	—	—
Uchhal	—	—	—	—	—	—	—	—	—	—
Vyara	321	112	—	—	149	185	—	—	—	—
Valod	406	164	—	—	—	—	—	—	—	—
Songadh	223	61	—	—	—	—	—	—	—	—
Nizar	—	—	—	—	—	—	—	—	—	—
Mahuva	495	264	—	—	—	—	—	—	—	—
Mandvi	245	73	—	—	—	—	—	—	—	—
Mangrol	291	131	—	—	—	—	—	—	—	—
Bardoli	369	164	—	—	—	—	—	—	—	—
Ahwa	—	—	—	—	259	74	—	—	152	34
Average ($\bar{X}$) literacy rate	335.7	138.4	247.0	48.0	201.4	74.4	129.7	14.7	107.3	13.8
Range of inter-taluka	223	61	96	11	134	21	73	2	57	5
variation in literacy	to	to	to	to	to	to	to	to	to	to
rates	495	264	310	89	259	185	229	35	152	34
Std. Dev. of literacy rates	88.3	63.4	88.1	27.7	51.9	58.4	70.4	14.5	35.6	11.7

lowest literacy rate (22) is among Bhils residing in Jhagadia and the highest literacy rate (516) is among Dhodias residing in Mahuva. Among females, the lowest literacy rate (2) is among Rathwas residing in Devgadhbaria and the highest literacy rate (273) is among Dhodias residing in Mahuva. It may be useful to study the factors associated with the top performance of Dhodias in Mahuva.

It is interesting to note that the inter-taluka variation in the literacy rates is higher for the males than for the females in all the tribal groups except Koknas. The range of the standard deviations of the male literacy rates is from 22.3 (Dublas) to 96.6 (Bhils), and the range of the standard deviations of the female literacy rates is from 6.7 (Dublas) to 63.4 (Chaudharis). This may partly be due to generally lower female literacy rates among all the tribal groups.

Educational achievement

Literacy is only a crude indicator of education. It is, therefore, necessary to examine the level of education attained by the tribals. Unfortunately, detailed tables of the 1971 Census regarding education among the tribals have not been published. We shall, therefore, examine the 1961 Census data so as to obtain a broad picture of the educational achievement of the tribals in 1961. We find from Table 1.5 that only 4 per 1,000 scheduled tribe urban males in Gujarat had completed high school education (matriculation) and only a negligible number of them had obtained some post-high school education. For the rural males as well as females and the urban females, the number in this category is very negligible. In the other categories of education, we find the usual differences of sex and rural-urban residence. The lowest level of education among the tribals in Gujarat is indicated by the fact that only 27 per 1,000 rural females and 201 per 1,000 urban males had obtained primary or junior basic education.

It can be argued that the above data are inadequate to reflect the changing picture of education in the younger generation. We, therefore, need to examine enrolment data; but here again the non-availability of adequate and up-to-date data presents a big hurdle. Naik (1971a, 1971b) has computed percentage enrolment

TABLE 1.5 : **Distribution of 1,000 tribal males and females, by rural-urban areas and educational level in Gujarat (1961 Census)**

Educational level	Rural		Urban	
	Males	Females	Males	Females
Illiterate	815	961	714	922
Literate (without educational level)	66	12	81	21
Primary or junior basic	119	27	201	57
Matriculation	N*	N*	4	N
Total	1000	1000	1000	1000

*Includes those with post-high school education.
N=Negligible.

ratios and coefficients of equality of the scheduled castes/tribes in different states. The extracted data for the tribals in Gujarat are given in Table 1.6. We find that the tribals are way behind the other communities in regard to enrolment at all levels of education. With regard to enrolment in primary and middle schools, the performance of the tribals in Gujarat is somewhat better than the tribals in the country as a whole. But at the high school and higher educational levels, the tribals in Gujarat are lagging behind. What is alarming is the fact that the tribals in Gujarat registered a sharp fall in the coefficient of equality for enrolment at all levels of education, from 56.9 in 1960-61 to 46.7 in 1965-66. Such a decline in the overall coefficient of equality seems to be largely due to a decrease in their enrolment ratios for primary and middle schools.

Further, with respect to enrolment in primary and secondary schools, there is a considerable inter-district variation in the coefficients of equality of the tribals. According to the Bureau of Economics and Statistics (1974), among the six tribal districts, the coefficients of equality for the scheduled tribe enrolment in primary schools in 1970-71 varied from 38.23 in Panchmahals to 82.10 in Sabarkantha, and those for their enrolment in secondary schools varied from 5.03 in Vadodara to 25.66 in Sabarkantha. (The coefficient of equality for Dangs were not calculated because of a negligible population of other communities in that district).

TABLE 1.6 : **Percentage enrolment ratios and coefficients of equality of the tribals in Gujarat, in 1960-61 and 1965-66, by levels of education**

Level of education	Percentage enrolment ratios		Coefficients of equality	
	1960-61	1965-66	1960-61	1965-66
Pre-primary schools*	0.2	1.6	1.2 (29.9)	9.6 (42.5)
Primary schools	15.2	14.1	91.0 (69.0)	84.4 (77.0)
Middle schools	8.7	7.4	52.1 (41.4)	44.3 (42.5)
High/Higher secondary schools	2.0	2.8	12.0 (14.9)	16.8 (19.5)
Vocational/Technical schools	N.A.	3.2	N.A.	19.2 (31.0)
Schools for other education	N.A.	13.1	N.A.	78.4 (124.1)
Universities/Colleges of general education	N.A.	0.7	N.A.	4.2 (13.8)
All levels of education	9.5	7.8	56.9 (54.0)	46.7 (57.5)

*Does not include data about Balwadis, etc. conducted by the Department of Social Welfare.

N.A.=Not available.

Note : Figures in the parentheses are for the whole of India.

Source : Naik (1971a, 1971b).

The 1973-74 data regarding the enrolment of the tribal children in Gujarat (Table 1.7) indicate that there was an impressive increase in their enrolment in primary schools; 560 tribal children (against 886 children from the total population) per 1,000 in the corresponding age-group were enrolled in classes I to V. They still lagged behind the general population, especially with regard to their enrolment at the higher levels of education. Only 174 and 58 tribal children per 1,000 in the corresponding age-groups were enrolled in classes VI-VIII and classes IX and above, respectively, as against the respective figures of 440 and 264 children from the total population. The ratio of enrolment in classes VI to VIII to that in classes I to V as well as the ratio of enrolment in classes IX and above to that in classes

TABLE 1.7 : **Enrolment of children per 1,000 persons in the corresponding age-group, separately for the scheduled tribes and total population, Gujarat, 1973-74**

Educational level	Scheduled tribes	Total population
Classes I—V	560	886
Classes VI—VIII	174	440
Classes IX and above	58	264

Source : Report of the Commissioner for Scheduled Castes and Scheduled Tribes, 1975-76 and 1976-77, Part II : 32-33.

VI to VIII is higher for the general population than for the tribal population. This indicates that the dropout rate is higher in the tribal population than that in the total population. In other words, inequality in educational attainment increases sharply as they move to higher levels of education.

This brief review of the available data regarding literacy, enrolment and educational attainment of the tribals in Gujarat indicates very clearly that they are at the lowest level of the educational pyramid. There is a considerable variation, in terms of sex, rural-urban residence and district, in their literacy rates. An examination of the literacy rates of the rural people in the tribal sub-plan area brings out a more dismal picture of literacy among the tribals. We also find considerable inter-taluka and inter-tribe variations in the male and the female literacy rates of the tribals in this area. Such an uneven educational progress of different tribes in various parts of the country has also been documented in several studies (for example, Bose (1969), Shah and Patel (1977), Chitnis (1978).)

The research problem

Several studies have been undertaken to assess the impact of the government policy of protective discrimination for the scheduled castes/tribes. They show that the spread of education, as measured in terms of literacy and levels of education, has been very slow among these groups as compared to the non-SCST population. Karuna Ahmed (1979: 159-160) points out serious drawbacks, despite the phenomenal quantitative expansion of education in the post-Independence period. Although this expansion has undoubtedly benefited almost all sections of our society, the extent of benefit differs according to the location (rural or urban), sex and socio-economic stutus. The chief beneficiaries of this expansion have been the middle sections of our society in the urban areas. In the rural areas, the landowning groups and the middle castes have taken a great advantage of the new opportunities. At present, in the hierarchy of educational achievement, the non-scheduled castes are at the top, the scheduled castes are in the middle, and the tribals are in the bottom category. The differences by sex and rural-urban residence persist in all groups, although they become very sharp in the case of the most disadvantaged. Inequality in educational attainment increases sharply as we move to the higher levels of education. Further, the spread of education has not been uniform among them.

Attempts have been made to identify individual, familial and community contextual characteristics that are responsible for such a differential response to utilization of the facilities and assistance for education extended to them by the government (see, Shah. 1975 ; Shah and Patel, 1977 ; Chitnis, 1978). In general, socio-economic background, type of community of residence and lack of adequate facilities for education in it, absence of guidance from parents and significant others, lack of aspirations, motivation and conducive environment for educational attainment have been pointed out as responsible factors in this regard.

The present study aims to examine, in detail, the educational development of the tribals residing in the rural areas of the tribal sub-plan in Gujarat. In view of the uneven educational development of the tribals, it aims further to examine various factors associated with their educational development.

The factors associated with the educational development of the tribals can be grouped into two broad categories. In the first category, we may consider the physical facilities that are available for education in their community of residence as well as the financial and other assistance that the government extends to them. That is, in the first category, we include those variables that constitute educational opportunities available to them. It seems that these variables can be manipulated rather easily by the government. In the second category, we may consider individual, familial and other contextual characteristics that determine the use of available opportunities for education by individuals. More specifically, ability, interest and aspirations of individuals, socio-economic background of their family and social-psychological support provided to them by their family and significant others, and the community-contextual environment may be considered in this category. Thus, in the second category, we include those individual, socio-economic and social-psychological variables which determine the use of available opportunities for education by individuals and which are, by and large, difficult to be brought into the ambit of planning.

In view of the fact that the state has already provided facilities for primary education to 97.7 per cent of the school-going population either in their own habitation or within one mile from it, and further that, the government provides financial and other assistance to the tribals without any restriction as to the place of study, the scope of the present study is restricted to an examination of certain individual, familial and community contextual aspects of the educational development of the rural tribal population which has been provided facilities and opportunities for post-primary education in its own community of residence. It is felt that such an approach would provide an insight into the factors associated with the utilization of available facilities and opportunities for education.

The focus of the present study is, however, on an examination of the social contexts of the educational development of the tribals. The study aims to examine the educational development of the tribals in relation to four categories of social contexts. For this purpose, we shall first compare the educational progress of the tribals with that of the other castes/communities residing in the same area. We shall also examine the educational progress of different tribal groups. Then, we shall examine the relationship between caste/community/tribe and occupation on one hand, and that between occupation and education on the other hand. Finally we shall examine the relationship between occupation and education within different tribal groups.

Secondly, we shall examine whether the normative climate, generated by the non-tribals in the village community, is positively related to the educational development of the tribals. For this purpose, we shall first demonstrate that the categories of villages based on the proportions of the non tribal households and development scores of the villages are also indicative of their corresponding composition in terms of caste/community, occupation and educational development. Then, we shall examine the relationship between the community contexts of the village and the educational development of the tirbals.

Thirdly, it is often mentioned, even in the case of the weaker sections such as the scheduled castes and the tribals, that the benefits of the government programmes of financial and other assistance for education accrue most to the children of the more privileged among them. We shall, therefore, examine the relationship between social class and educational attainment of different tribal groups.

Finally, we shall examine whether and to what extent (a) the tribals are aware of the various types of facilities as well as the programmes of special assistance to the tribals for education/jobs, (b) they are exposed to mass media and urban influences, and (c) they perceive the importance of acquiring education. Then, we shall examine the relationship between awareness and educational development of the tribals.

Throughout the analysis, we shall attempt to examine various indicators of educational development and control, separately as well as simultaneously, for sex, age-group and tribe. Such an approach will make it possible for us to examine the relationships of different categories of social contexts of the tribals to the educational development of males as well as females, in the younger as well as the older generation, from different tribes.

REFERENCE

1. The 1981 Census data regarding education among the tribals have not as yet been published. We have, therefore, used the 1971 census data in this monograph.

2

METHODOLOGY

SAMPLE DESIGN

THERE were three major considerations in delimiting the study area and devising an adequate sample design for the study. First, it was deemed necessary to conduct the study in a predominantly tribal area. The tribal sub-plan area fulfilled this objective. In Gujarat, it consists of 29 talukas in which the tribal population is 50 per cent or more of the total population and three talukas in which the tribal population is a little less than 50 per cent of the total population. About 72 per cent (26.82 lakhs) of the total tribal population of the state resides in the tribal sub-plan area. Secondly, less than 10 per cent of the tribal population resides in the urban areas of the tribal sub-plan. There are 60 urban areas. The population of these urban areas is predominantly non-tribal ; only in one area (namely, Abrama in Valsad taluka), the percentage of the tribal population is 51.39. In most of the urban areas in Valsad and Surat districts, the percentage of the tribal population varies between 20 and 40 per cent, but it is much less in the others. It was, therefore, decided to conduct the study only in the rural areas. Thirdly, since the major objective of this study was to examine the social contexts of the educational development of the tribals, given certain educational facilities in their community of residence, it seemed appropriate to select the sample from only those villages in which at least one secondary/*uttar buniyadi*/training school was located. The sample design of this study envisaged a two-stage sample selection, namely, selection of villages in the first stage and selection of households in the second stage.

Considering the limitations of the resources available for this study, it was decided to select two villages from each of the 32 talukas in the tribal sub-plan area. A taluka-wise list of villages with at least one secondary/*uttar buniyadi*/training school (as per the 1971 District Census Handbooks) was prepared. Prior to the decision regarding the selection procedure, the following information for all these villages was extracted from the 1971 District Census Handbooks :

1. Total population
2. Tribal population
3. Number of occupied households
4. Number of literates
5. Medical facilities (Hospital, Maternity Home, Child Welfare Centre, Health Centre, Dispensary, Family Planning Centre)
5. Availability of electricity (for agriculture, for all purpose)
7. Facilities for communication (pucca road, railway station, availability of bus service throughout the year or only during the fair season, posts/telegraphs office, telephone, distance from the nearest town, weekly market).

On examining the above information, it was found necessary to develop a simple overall measure of available infrastructural facilities in the villages. Accordingly, a simple summated score (development score) of the various facilities available in each of the villages was developed. For this purpose, arbitrary weights were assigned to different facilities as under :

Weight	*Item*
1	Hospital
1	Maternity Home
1	Child Welfare Centre
1	Health Centre
1	Dispensary
1	Family Planning Centre
4	Electricity (all purpose)
2	Electricity (for agriculture)
2	Pucca Road
2	Railway Station
4	Bus : Whole year
2	Bus : Fair season

1	Post Office
1	Telegraph Office
2	Post & Telegraphs Office
2	Telephone

While fixing even the abovementioned arbitrary weights, the distribution of the various types of facilities in the area and the often-noticed clustering of certain facilities were kept in mind.

It was observed that the villages differed considerably in terms of the number of occupied households, proportion of the tribal population and development score. It soon became clear that the development score was generally positively associated with the proportion of the non-tribal population. It seemed that a random sample might not obtain a sample of villages with a fair distribution of certain characteristics considered necessary for the study. It was, therefore, dec ded to select, from each taluka, one village with a relatively high development score and a relatively modest proportion of the tribal population (25% to 60%), and another village with a relatively low development score and a relatively high proportion of the tribal population (80% and above).

For this purpose, all the villages with less than 25 per cent tribal population were eliminated from the list. Then, the villages in each taluka were divided into two categories : (a) those with less than 60 per cent tribal population and (b) those with more than 60 per cent tribal population. Further, the villages in each category were arranged in a descending order of the development scores. The villages with an equal development score were arranged according to the proportion of the tribal population. Finally, it was decided to select from each taluka, the village with the highest development score in category (a) and the village with the lowest development score in category (b). However, certain modifications became necessary while executing this design. In certain talukas, where no village was found in either category (a) or (b), we included in the list the villages with ashram school and followed the above procedure. But, a village with a secondary/*uttar buniyadi*/training school was preferred to that with an ashram school. In certain talukas, where all villages were predominantly tribal (that is with more than 80 per cent tribal population), they were arranged accordingly to percentages of tribal population and then the list was divided into two categories using the median as a cutting point. In certain cases where two or more villages were located at the top of category (a) or at the bottom of category (b) (because of equal development scores) : one of them was selected at random. Finally, in a few cases, it was found during the field work, that a selected village was only a fringe of an urban area, or that the number of occupied households in a selected village was too low (less than 20), or that two adjoining villages were separated only by a road, or that a revenue village was spread over in several hemlets scattered over a vast area, or that the census information pertained to a group panchayat village. In all such cases, the next village in the list that satisfied the criteria laid down was selected.

Thus, the first-stage selection of the villages in the present study is based on certain criteria considered relevant for the objectives of the study. It is a purposive type of selection based on a systematic examination of the available data so as to obtain, from each taluka, two villages that have rather contrasting characteristics of (a) a modest proportion of the tribal population and a high development score, and (b) a high proportion of the tribal population and a low development score. In this sampling procedure, however, no personal bias was allowed to influence the selection of the sample villages. A list of the sample villages, together with information regarding total population, number of occupied households, percentage of the tribal population, percentage of the literate population, and development score is given in Appendix-I.

For the second-stage sampling plan, it was necessary to prepare an up-to-date sampling frame of all tribal households in the sample villages. Since the study is concerned with examining certain contextual factors related to the educational development of the tribals, it was deemed necessary to obtain certain information from the tribal as well as the non-tribal households in the sample villages. It was, therefore, decided to prepare a complete list of all, tribal as well as non-tribal, households in the sample villages.

On an examination of the distribution of different tribal groups in the house-lists, it seemed feasible to devise a sampling plan that would ensure inclusion, in the sample, of respondents belonging to different tribal groups and residing in different talukas. But, it was felt that any sampling plan involving a proportionate random selection of households from different tribal groups in the 32 talukas would increase the total number of interviews beyond the scope of the available resources for the present study. The distribution of the tribal population in different talukas, as given in the Census, showed a concentration of major tribal groups in certain talukas ; however, the Census does not give any information regarding the distribution of certain smaller tribes. Under these circumstances, it was decided to select households from (a) those tribal groups which were preponderent in different talukas, and (b) those tribal groups which were not found in the previous study (Shah and Patel, 1977) but appeared in the house-lists. For this purpose, the distribution of the population (1971 Census) of major tribal groups in each of the 32 talukas, vis-a-vis a similar distribution of the tribal households in the sample villages, was examined. On the basis of this examination, the tribal groups to be selected from the two villages in each of the 32 talukas were determined. Such a procedure ensured inclusion of different tribal groups which are relatively densely distributed in certain talukas and also those which are relatively scattered in various talukas.

The next question was regarding the number of households to be selected from each of the tribal groups in each of the sample villages. It was decided, rather somewhat arbitrarily, to select a minimum of ten households from each sample village and a minimum of ten households from each of the tribal groups in different talukas. This meant selection of five households of the required tribal groups from each of the two villages in the 32 talukas. If more than two tribal groups were represented in the house-list of a sample village, it was decided to select the tribal groups from different villages in the talukas of a district such that all major tribal groups of that district are included in the sample. In addition, care was taken to check that households from the smaller tribal groups were also included in the sample. In the event that the required minimum number of 5 households belonging to a tribal group (particularly in the case of the smaller tribal groups) were not found in the house-list of a sample village, the available households were included in the sample. Thus, the number of households to be selected from each of the tribal groups residing in the sample villages was fixed. The distributions of the total and the sample tribal households are given, by tribe, separately for each village, in Appendix-II.

The households from different tribal groups residing in the sample villages were then selected at random. The serial numbers of the households belonging to different tribal groups were written in the first column of the sample selection form. The total number of households and the number of households to be selected were written in the next two columns. The serial numbers were written on separate chits, well mixed, and then the required number of chits were selected through lots. If the serial number of a household selected in the sample was that of a household already covered in the pre-test, the investigators were required to draw another chit. The serial numbers thus selected were written in the last column of the sample form in the same order as of their selection. Keeping in mind the possible need for substitute households later on, it was decided to select one more household for every five households to be selected. The serial numbers of these additional households were marked with a prefix 'S' so as to indicate that the head of that household was to be interviwed only if a substitute was necessary. Thus, the households in this study have been selected by a stratified random procedure. The criteria used for stratification were (1) villages/talukas, and (2) tribal groupings. However, while the households belonging to smaller tribal groups not found in the previous study were selected with certainty, the probability of selection of the other households differed for different tribal groups in the 32 talukas of the tribal sub-plan area.

Data-collection instruments

Two data-collection instruments were used in this study, one for collecting certain information while preparing the list of households and another for interviewing the heads of the sample households.

A simple form was prepared in order to elicit information from each of the households in the sample villages. This house-listing form was devised to record information regarding serial number (identity) of the household, name of the head of the household, scheduled tribe/sub-tribe, scheduled caste/sub-caste, other caste/community, major occupation of the head of the household, the highest level of education attained by any male/female member in the household, the number of boys/girls currently studying in primary/middle/high school, and the number of illiterate/total boys/girls in the age group 5-17 in the household.

A detailed interview schedule was prepared for obtaining information from the heads of the sample households. The interview schedule was designed to collect information regarding (1) tribe, sub-tribe, religion, (2) sex, marital status, education, occupation of all members, (3) educational/occupational expectations for those going to school and reasons for those who dropped out of school, (4) annual income, landholding, cattle, type of housing, utensils and other household possessions, (5) knowledge of facilities/assistance for education, (6) exposure to mass media and urban influences, and (7) opinions regarding certain statements.

The interview schedule was pre-tested during the second round of data-collection. In all, 25 pre-test interviews were conducted from 22 villages in 19 talukas of 5 districts. The respondents in the pre-test belonged to 18 different tribes. In the light of the experiences in the pre-test and analysis of the pre-test data, certain minor modifications were made in the interview schedule.

In addition to these two data-collection instruments, we devised separate forms to collect certain information concerning (a) sample villages, (b) different tribes residing in the sample villages, and (c) enrolment in the schools located in these villages. The village information form aimed at collecting information regarding population composition, village location, surroundings and available means of transport, drinking water facilities, public institutions, major economic activities, and names of village headman and other formal/informal leaders. The tribe information form was devised to collect information regarding the distribution of different tribes in the area, economic activities, housing, food and drinking habits, dress and ornaments, festivals, marriage and death ceremonies, tribal panchayat, etc. The school enrolment form aimed at collecting aggregate enrolment of boys and girls in different standards by caste/tribe.

Field work

The field work for the study was carried out in three phases: collecting information concerning distribution of smaller tribal groups at the village level from knowledgeable persons (December, 1976 to January, 1977); preparation of up-to-date lists of households in the sample villages (February to March, 1977); and personal interviews of the heads of the sample households (March to June, 1977).

In the beginning, four investigators were recruited, and at the peak of the field work eight investigators were working. In all, ten investigators were recruited. It was also felt that the scheduled tribe investigators would be in a better position to communicate with the tribal respondents. We succeeded in recruiting five scheduled tribe, two scheduled caste and three other investigators to work on this project. Eight investigators held a post-graduate degree in social sciences; the other two were graduates with two to four years' experience in similar research projects. All the investigators were given training, ranging from two days to a week, at different stages of the research work. The objective of this approach was to train them for the tasks they were to carry out during the next phase of the study.

The starting point for this study was to cover about 50 scheduled tribes in Gujarat and find out the reasons for their total lack of higher education among them. Since most of these scheduled tribes are small, difficulty was faced in tracing them. Hoping that information concerning the distribution of these tribes at the village level might be available from the social workers and administrators, letters were written to all members of the Legislative Assembly and the parliament, project administrators, social workers, and principals of the ashram schools in the tribal sub-plan area of Gujarat. They were requested to supply information, in a proforma, regarding estimates of population and households of different scheduled tribes, areas/villages of their concentration, and names of local informants who could be contacted for further information. Stamped envelopes were also sent along with the letters of request to them. We wrote to 148 persons, but received replies from only about one-fourth of them. The non-respondents were contacted personally by the investigators, but they could collect information from additional 56 informants only.

An analysis of the information obtained from these persons indicated that it was of a very general nature ; sometimes it differed markedly from the Census information ; information was not available for all of the tribes in whom we were interested. Therefore, our approach to the problem had to be modified. It was felt that we should study not only the small tribes that seemed to be not using government assistance for higher education but also the other tribes residing in the same locality who might be using the available facilities for education. Our revised thinking was to aim at a comparative study of education among different tribes. Again, it was felt that a more fruitful approach would be to study factors related to education at all levels, and not only at the level of higher education. This however, should not mean that the focus of the study was shifted from higher education to primary and secondary education. What was becoming clear was the need to examine the nature of primary and secondary education among the tribals before examining the factors responsible for the non-utilization of government assistance for higher education by some of the scheduled tribes.

In the second phase of data collection, the investigators prepared complete lists of all households in the sample villages and obtained information in the village information form. Given the difficult travel and living conditions in the tribal area, the investigators were sent in pairs so that they may be able to help each other. Such an arrangement helped in maintaining their morale. In all, the house-listing information was obtained from 15,861 tribal and non-tribal households in the 64 sample villages.

In the third phase of data collection, a different pair of investigators was sent to the sample villages. Such a procedure was considered necessary and adequate for checking the house-listing data collected by the first team. The village information form came in handy in informing the new team about the villages to be visited by it. The investigators were required to first go round the village, house by house, and recheck the house list.

Then they selected at random the required number of households from different tribes for interview. Each of the investigators was asked to conduct interviews in turn. In other words, when one investigator was interviewing a respondent, the other was expected to listen and intervene only if he felt that the interviewer was missing some points or when there was the need for further probing. In all, 884 interviews were conducted. During this phase, the investigators collected information regarding (a) different tribes, and (b) enrolment in the schools located in the sample villages.

The investigators were given training at the head-quarters for the respective phases of data collection. They were adequately informed regarding the objectives of the study and were made familiar with all items of the data collection instruments. Further in order to ensure consistency in data collection, detailed guidelines for each item in the house-listing form and the interview scheduled were prepared. The investigators were instructed to refer frequently to these written guidelines. Each team of two investigators was assigned the villages to be visited. They prepared a detailed plan for travel and field work. Care was taken to see that each team of investigators had to spend about 10 to 15 days in one round of field work. The place of their overnight stay was fixed, as far as possible, in advance. The arrangements for their stay were made, as far as possible, in a government/panchayat guest house. Each team was required to mail a post-card every day from the village of its overnight stay and report to the headquarters about the work carried out, difficulties encountered, and the need, if any, for revising the field programme. The investigators were required to inform the headquarters telegraphically in the event of an emergency or the need for a drastic departure from their scheduled programme. Each investigator was provided with a light travel bag to carry the field-work material. Between two field visits, the investigators spent about a week at the headquarters. During this period, they checked each other's data and planned for the next field visit. Also, a research officer scrutinised their data. If any error or deficiency was noticed, necessary and possible corrective mechanisms were carried out.

The project director and another faculty member supervised

the field work. They paid a surprise visit to each team at least once during each of its scheduled programmes of field work. Sometimes, they visited the same team more than once during the same field programme. During his visit, the supervisor checked the field work, observed the investigators while conducting interviews, and settled their queries. He also tried to keep up the morale of the investigators. The major concern in supervising the field work was to ensure reliability of the data collected by different investigators. In the beginning, it was observed that some investigators finished their work earlier than planned, and took off for a day or two in the nearby taluka headquarters. One of the problems in employing the scheduled tribe investigators was that they were tempted to take off for a few days to visit their native place. Later on, the field work plan of each team was, therefore, drawn in such a way that the investigators would get the necessary leave during their field visits.

There were the usual problems of field work in backward/tribal areas. Some of the sample villages were located in the interior and required a day's journey by train or bus to reach there from Ahmedabad. Delays in bus service often upset the schedule. In some places, there was only one bus service a day, and sometimes it would so happen that the bus would arrive earlier than the scheduled time and leave. In such circumstances, one had to walk long distances to get alternative transport facilities. Although we were permitted to stay overnight in government/panchayat guest houses at the taluka headquarters which had relatively adequate facilities, at times it was impossible to find accommodation there since they gave priority to government employees. Moreover, all guest houses did not provide food and we had to fend for ourselves with great difficulty. However, the ashram schools, whenever found in the sample villages or nearby area, provided adequate facilities. Some villages did not have any transport facilities. The investigators managed to stay in the nearby places and walked back and forth for collecting data. Sometimes, a revenue village was spread over several scattered hamlets and, therefore, the investigators had to cover long distances on foot.

Most of the interviews had to be conducted either early in the morning or late in the evening to suit the convenience of the respondents. This, coupled with our expectations of completing a certain minimum number of interviews per day, seemed to have generated an undesirable pressure on the investigators to complete their task quickly. In such a situation, it was possible that some investigators might not have spent the necessary time to establish an adequate rappòrt with the interviewees or to probe in detail their responses to open-end questions. The field supervisors became aware of such problems in the beginning itself and constantly tried to guide the investigators so as to strike a proper balance between the scheduled plan of work and demands of the local field situations. Although a good number of the investigators were from the scheduled tribes, variation in tribal languages/dialects created some problems, especially in Dangs. The investigators tried to tackle such problems with the help of local informants. It is difficult to estimate the impact of such circumstances on the quality of the data collected.

Coding, computerization and analysis of data

The data obtained in the houselisting forms and the interview schedules were numerically coded. We have followed the usual procedure for coding these data. A draft code-book for each set of data was prepared. The investigators were given appropriate training in coding the data. Once the investigators were familiar with the draft code-book, a part of the data-set was randomly selected and pre-tested. In the light of these experiences the code-book was revised and finalized.

While it was relatively easy to develop adequate numerical codes for responses to close-end questions, we had to pass through several trial-and-error procedures for developing numerical codes for responses to open-end questions. In the beginning, a broad classificatory scheme was developed on the basis of past experiences and a random examination of data-sets from different sample villages. Later on, new categories were added as we came across responses that did not fit into the coded categories. After the data were computerized, the categories of such variables were finally recoded into appropriate categories on the basis of a detailed examination of their distribution.

The house-listing data were coded into one card per household. The interview data were first coded into three cards per respondent, but on an examination of the frequency distribution of selected certain variables, it was deemed necessary to code afresh certain aggregate data for each household ; hence one more card per interview was added.

A very closely supervised procedure for the coding work was followed. In the beginning, the coding work of each coder was completely checked by the research officer. Once the efficiency level of the coders was established, checking was limited to about 20 per cent of the households. All coders were given sufficient time to familiarize themselves with the coding scheme. The data were coded, card by card, so as to keep the need for remembering at a time, the codes of various items to the minimum. All coders sat around a table and were asked to bring to the notice of one another all such items that might require fresh consideration. All decisions made in this regard were noted by all the coders so as to maintain consistency in coding.

The data were punched on IBM cards. All cards were verified by machine. Then, several consistency checks were carried out, and efforts were made to remove the inconsistencies whenever encountered. This required a considerable amount of checking and rechecking with the original data. The data were then transferred to magnetic tapes. Several frequency counts (by villages, talukas, districts, castes/tribes and occupation) of selected variables were obtained. After debugging the data and recoding of certain variables, the data were transformed into a continuous record. The details regarding the definitions of key variables and the procedures followed for developing weighted measures are given in the respective chapters.

The facilities provided by the Government of Gujarat Computer Center (ICL 1901), the Gujarat University Computer Center (IBM 1620), and the Physical Research Laboratory Computer Center (IBM 360-44) were used for computerisation and analysis of the data.

3

EDUCATIONAL DEVELOPMENT IN THE TRIBAL SUB-PLAN AREA

IN THE first chapter, we have examined the literacy patterns among the tribals in the sub-plan area. Although we attempted to collate the scattered data to obtain a broad picture of education among the tribals in general, there is need, especially from the point of view of developing suitable programmes, to obtain a more detailed picture of education in the rural areas of the tribal sub-plan.

In this chapter, we shall first examine different indicators of the educational development of people in the sample villages. Since caste/community is related to education, the educational development of people belonging to different castes/communities will be examined separately. This will focus on the educational development of the tribals in the context of the educational development of the other castes/communities residing in the same area. Next, the educational development of different tribal groups will be examined. In view of the fact that occupation is related to caste/community/tribe on the one hand and to educational development on the other, the inter-relationships among caste/community/tribe, occupation and education will be examined. It must be noted that the picture of the educational development of people that emerges from this study pertains only to the rural areas of the tribal sub-plan in which certain minimum facilities for education, generally for high school education, are available. The analysis presented in this chapter is based on the data obtained for preparing house-lists of the sample villages. A brief description of the categories of different variables used in this chapter is given below.

Description of variables

Educational development

The following indicators of educational development have been used in this study :

(1) the highest level of education attained by any member among (a) males and (b) females in the household ;
(2) the percentage of illiterate (a) boys and (b) girls in the age-group 5—17 years ;
(3) the percentage of (a) boys and (b) girls in the age-group 5—17 years who are attending primary/middle/high schools.

The variable highest level of education attained by any male/female member in the family was first coded into 17 categories, and later on grouped into 10 categories. For the purpose of cross-tabular analysis, these categories are collapsed (so as to allow for a certain minimum frequency in each cell) into six categories, namely, (i) Nil, (ii) 1—4 standards (iii) 5—7 standards, (iv) 8—10 standards, S.S.C. failed, P.T.C., (v) S.S.C., College education, and (vi) Graduate. While examining inter-tribe variation in educational development, these categories are further collapsed into four categories, namely (i) Nil, (ii) 1—4, standards, (iii) 5—10 standards, S.S.C. failed, P.T.C. and (iv) S.S.C., College education. S.S.C./College education has been defined as indicating a high level of education.

Caste/community

The households in the sample villages were first classified into six broad categories of caste/community, namely, (1) Scheduled tribes, (2) Scheduled castes, (3) Muslim, (4) Christian, (5) Parsi, and (6) Hindu. In view of the differential social status of sub-castes, especially within Hindus, it was felt necessary to classify the Hindu sub-castes into an adequate number of categories. No ready-made list of the Hindu sub-castes, arranged in a hierarchical order, is available. Therefore, a frequency distribution of Hindu households, by sub-caste, was obtained. Then, three sociologists (the researchers and the additional field supervisor) independently arranged these sub-castes into a hierarchical order. It was not possible to arrange about 100 sub-castes, found in the study, into the same number of ordered categories. So, it was decided to group the Hindu sub-castes into only a limited number of ordered categories. With this view, the sub-castes were first grouped into several categories, and then after a series of sequential regrouping of sub-castes into wider groups, the Hindu sub-castes were finally classified into four broad categories. For convenience, the sub-categories of Hindus have been labelled, in an ascending order of social status, as (1) Hindus : Low, (2) Hindus : Middle, (3) Hindus : High I, and (4) Hindus : High II. One difficulty was that the investigators had noted, in some cases, surnames as sub-castes. In such cases, occupation, of the heads of the family was used as a guide for classifying them in appropriate categories. Thus, the variable caste/community, in this monograph, is composed of nine categories. A simple frequency distribution of all Hindu households in the sample villages, by sub-caste, is given in Appendix 3.

Occupation

Information regarding the main occupation of the heads of households was first coded as per the 3-digit codes of the National Classification of Occupations. A simple frequency distribution of heads of households in the sample villages is given, according to the detailed classification of occupations, in Appendix 4. Later on, about 130 categories of occupations encountered in the house-listing forms were grouped into 11 categories, namely, (1) Occupation not reported, (2) Retired, (3) Other labourers, (4) Agricultural labourers, (5) Artisans, skilled workers, etc. (lower level), (6) Artisans, skilled workers, etc. (upper level), (7) Clerks, etc. (lower level), (8) Clerks (upper level), technicians, etc. (9) Farm owners and Livestock farmers, (10) Officers and Small businessmen, (11) Professionals and Big businessmen. In the cross-tabular analysis, these occupational categories are further regrouped into seven categories. These regrouped categories are (i) Retired and Occupation not reported (1+2), (ii) Agricultural labourers (4), (iii) Other labourers (3), (iv) Artisans (5+6), (v) Farm owners and Livestock farmers (9), (vi) Clerks (7+8), (vii) Professionals, Officers and Businessmen (10+11). While examining the inter-tribe variation in the occupations of the heads of households, these categories are further collapsed into four categories, namely, (i) Others (1+2+3+4+5 +6), (ii) Agricultural labourers (4), (iii) Farm owners (9), and (iv) White-collar workers (7+8+10+11).

Tribes/tribal groups

All the ten categories of major tribes/tribal groups, whose population is more than a lakh, are retained in the analysis. Two categories of Koli/Kolcha and Kotwalia are also added. Since the number of households in the other tribes/tribal groups was relatively small, they were grouped in a residual categary marked 'Others'.

Educational development of different castes/communities

One major factor associated with educational achievement is the educational environment of the family/community. It is a very broad concept that includes the value that the members attach to education, the educational attainment of the members, the interest that the members take in the education of the younger generation, and so on. It is a known fact that the value of education opérates in a cumulative manner. Individuals who have been able to attain a certain level of education usually aspire for their children at least as much as or higher than their own level of educational achievement. The educational environment of the family plays an important role in motivating the younger generation to obtain education. Many a time, the parents' education is used as an indicator of the educational environment of the family. But, in a situation where the tradition of education is not very widely prevalent, the level of parents' education is likely to be relatively low. Further, while measuring the educational environment, we must also take into account the differential value-orientation toward education of males and females prevalent in our society. It was, therefore, felt that the highest level of education obtained by any member among (a) males and (b) females will serve as good indicators of the educational development as well as the educational environment of the family. Theoretically, it is possible to combine these two variables into a single variable indicating the highest level of education attained by any male or female member in the household. However, in view of the generally prevailing situation of males having attained a higher level of education than females in the same household, it was felt that a separate examination of these two indicators of education will provide a more detailed picture of the differential levels of education attained by males and females than when these two categories are combined into a single indicator. The number of illiterate boys and girls in the age-group 5—17 years indicates the lack of a proper environment for education of the younger generation in the family. And finally, the number of boys and girls attending primary/middle/high schools will indicate the prevalent or changing educational environment of the family. Thus, an examination of these indicators presents a detailed picture of education among people in the rural areas of the tribal sub-plan. This will also present a comparative picture of education among the tribals vis-a-vis other communities. The relevant data are given in Tables 3.1 to 3.3.

The percentage distributions of the households, showing the highest level of education attained by any member among males and females, are given, by caste/community, in Table 3.1. Three observations should be made from this table.

First, the educational development of the people in the tribal sub-plan area is generally very low. The educational development of the females is much lower than that of the males. In 62.7 per cent of the households, women have not obtained any formal education as against 33.2 per cent of the households wherein men have not obtained any formal education. Regarding the highest level of education attained by any member among the males, the percentages of households vary from 20.7 per cent for primary education to 3.9 per cent for graduation. Regarding the highest level of education attained by any member among the females, the percentages of households vary from 15.7 per cent for primary education to 0.8 per cent for graduation.

Secondly, when caste/cummunity is controlled, it is found that the tribals are at the lowest, and the high caste Hindus II are at the highest level of educational development. The scheduled castes are above the tribals but much below the low caste Hindus. The educational development of the Muslim males falls above

TABLE 3.1 : Percentage distribution of households, showing the highest level of education attained by any member among males and females, by caste/community*

Caste/Community			Highest level of education attained						Total	
			Nil	1-4 std.	5-7 std.	8-10 std.	S.S.C.	Graduate		
1.	S.T.	M	44.5	23.4	15.3	9.8	5.9	1.1	100.0	(9975)
		F	75.7	13.7	5.3	3.2	2.0	0.2	100.0	(9975)
2.	S.C.	M	28.8	23.0	21.7	12.6	11.5	2.4	100.0	(673)
		F	64.3	19.6	8.9	4.4	2.4	0.2	100.0	(673)
3.	Mulsim	M	13.2	22.6	30.8	15.3	15.0	3.0	100.0	(889)
		F	46.3	24.8	15.5	8.4	4.7	0.2	100.0	(889)
4.	Christian	M	—	[4]	[6]	[6]	[10]	[2]		(28)
		F	[5]	[8]	[4]	[7]	[4]	[0]		(28)
5.	Parsi	M	[5]	[2]	[5]	[8]	[9]	[5]		(34)
		F	[11]	[6]	[4]	[6]	[5]	[2]		(34)
6.	Hindu : Low	M	19.6	22.0	23.7	15.2	15.4	4.1	100.0	(942)
		F	48.8	19.3	15.4	10.1	6.0	0.4	100.0	(942)
7.	Hindu : Middle	M	16.0	17.9	30.0	17.7	13.9	4.5	100.0	(657)
		F	42.0	19.0	19.8	11.4	7.0	0.8	100.0	(657)
8.	Hindu : High I	M	10.8	13.2	23.7	22.5	22.8	7.0	100.0	(1202)
		F	40.5	20.5	18.9	13.0	6.4	0.5	100.0	(1202)
9.	Hindu : High II	M	6.4	5.9	15.6	22.1	29.8	20.2	100.0	(1461)
		F	21.4	14.3	18.6	22.3	17.8	5.6	100.0	(1461)
	Total	M	33.2	20.7	18.3	13.0	11.0	3.9	100.0	(15861)
		F	62.7	15.7	9.5	6.9	4.5	0.8	100.0	(15861)

*Figures within brackets indicate frequencies.

the middle caste Hindu males, but that of the Muslim females falls below the middle caste Hindu females. The total number of the Christian and the Parsi households is very small in this sample. However, it seems that the educational development of Christians and Parsis in the sample villages compares favourably with that of the high caste Hindus II. Further, in all categories of caste/community, the educational development of women is lower than that of men.

Thirdly, examining the percentages of households with at least one member among males/females having attained the various levels of education, we find that the same pattern continues, that is, the tribals are at the bottom and the high caste Hindus II are at the top. More specifically, the ascending rank-order of caste/community categories is (1) Scheduled tribes, (2) Scheduled castes, (3) Muslims, (4) Low caste Hindus, (5) Middle caste Hindus, (6) High-caste Hindus I (7) Parsis and Christians, and (8) High-caste Hindus II.

It is found from Table 3.2 that in about one-fifth of the households at least one boy is illiterate, and in about one-fourth of the households at least one girl is illiterate. The percentage of such households is the highest among the tribals and the lowest among the high-caste Hindus II. The pattern of relationship between caste/community and number of illiterate boys/girls is the same as that between caste/community and the highest level of education attained by any member among males/females. In fact, in about 30 per cent of the tribal households, at least one boy/girl is illiterate. The percentage of such households among the scheduled castes is also very high. In view of the fact that there is already some facility available for primary/middle/high school education in the sample villages and that there are several programmes of assistance to the scheduled caste/tribe students, it is needless to add that such a high proportion of households with illiterate boys/girls is an evidence of a lack of value for education among them. While the distribution of households given in this table provides a picture of a lack of a proper educational environment, it is still necessary, in view of the likely differential number of boys/girls in the age-group 5-17 years among different categories of caste/community, to obtain an adequate estimate of illiterate boys and girls among them. This

TABLE 3.2 : **Percentage disribution of households, showing the number of illiterate boys/girls, by caste/community***

Caste/Community			Nil/Not applicable	No. of illiterates in the age-group 5-17 years.				Total	
				One	Two	Three	Four or more		
1.	S.T.	B	71.1	18.4	7.8	2.1	0.7	100.0	(9975)
		G	68.0	20.0	8.6	2.0	0.5	100.0	(9975)
2.	S.C.	B	85.1	11.6	2.4	0.7	0.1	100.0	(673)
		G	75.3	16.9	6.4	1.0	0.3	100.0	(673)
3.	Muslim	B	90.0	7.2	2.2	0.4	0.1	100.0	(889)
		G	86.5	9.2	3.7	0.3	0.2	100.0	(889)
4.	Christian	B	100.0	0.0	0.0	0.0	0.0	100.0	(28)
		G	100.0	0,0	0.0	0.0	0.0	100.0	(28)
5.	Parsi	B	[31]	[3]	—	—	—		(34)
		G	[32]	—	—	—	[2]		(34)
6.	Hindu : Low	B	89.7	6.5	2.7	0.8	0.3	100.0	(942)
		G	84.4	11.1	3.7	0.6	0.2	100.0	(942)
7.	Hindu : Middle	B	89.3	7.3	2.6	0.3	0.5	100.0	(657)
		G	88.4	7.6	3.0	0.6	0.3	100.0	(657)
8.	Hindu : High I	B	91.6	5.9	1.9	0.5	0.1	100.0	(1202)
		G	89.7	6.2	3.2	0.7	0.2	100.0	(1202)
9.	Hindu : High II	B	98.0	1.8	0.2	0.0	0.0	100.0	(1461)
		G	96.7	3.0	0.2	0.1	0.0	100.0	(1461)
	Total	B	78.7	13.8	5.5	1.5	0.5	100.0	(15861)
		G	75.6	16.1	6.5	1.4	0.4	100.0	(15861)

*Figures within brackets indicate frequencies.

is found in Table 3.3.

It is a sad commentary on the utilization of available facilities for education that as much as about one-third of the boys and about one-half of the girls are illiterate. This indicates a generally low esteem that the people in this area have for education. The proportion of illiterate girls is considerably higher than that of illiterate boys. The proportion of illiterate boys/girls is the highest among the tribals and the lowest among the high-caste Hindus II. Usually, the proportion of illiterate boys/girls decreases as we move up the ladder of caste/community. It must be particularly noted that the percentages of illiterate boys and girls among the tribals and the scheduled castes are considerably greater than those among the low-caste Hindus.

Examining the enrolment of boys and girls in the primary/middle/high schools, it is found that the percentages of those enrolled decrease with an increase in the level of education, and that the percentages for boys are greater than those for girls. This is true of all categories of caste/community. In absence of data regarding the age-distribution of these boys and girls, it is not possible to strictly compare between-caste/community differences in their enrolment at the various levels of education. If one were to assume a more or less equitable age-distribution of boys and girls in the various castes/communities, it becomes apparent that the enrolment in the various levels of education is very closely associated with the level of social status of caste/community.

In sum, the data presented in Tables 3.1 to 3.3 indicate very clearly that the educational development of the people in the tribal sub-plan area is generally low. Examining these data separately for various castes/communities, it is found that their educational progress is positively related to their level of social status. The tribals are at the lowest level of the education pyramid.

Inter-tribe variation in educational development

We have noticed a considerable variation in the literacy rates of the major tribal groups in Gujarat. All studies attempting to examine the extent of education among the tribals in different states as well as at the national level have found that their educational development has not been uniform. It is, therefore,

TABLE 3.3 : **Percentages showing education among boys/girls attending school, by caste/community***

Caste/Community			No information	Illiterate	Attending school			Total	
					Primary	Middle	High		
1.	S.T.	B	4.6	44.5	34.0	14.7	2.2	100.0	(9623)
		G	2.4	63.3	24.2	9.0	1.1	100.0	(7269)
2.	S.C.	B	2.2	19.0	49.1	25.6	4.1	100.0	(679)
		G	0.4	43.4	41.5	13.8	0.9	100.0	(528)
3.	Muslim	B	2.7	13.2	56.2	25.1	2.8	100.0	(914)
		G	3.4	23.0	47.9	25.0	0.7	100.0	(727)
4.	Christian	B	[0]	[0]	[9]	[14]	[2]		[25]
		G	[2]	[0]	[11]	[10]	[0]		[23]
5.	Parsi	B	[0]	[3]	[6]	[2]	[1]		[12]
		G	[0]	[8]	[1]	[2]	[1]		[12]
6.	Hindu : Low	B	3.9	14.9	47.6	27.8	5.8	100.0	(966)
		G	2.2	27.5	42.9	25.7	1.7	100.0	(743)
7.	Hindu : Middle	B	0.9	15.5	45.0	32.7	5.9	100.0	(646)
		G	0.0	23.0	41.1	31.5	4.4	100.0	(479)
8.	Hindu : High I	B	0.0	11.7	45.7	35.2	7.4	100.0	(1191)
		G	0.0	20.1	45.6	30.0	4.3	100.0	(934)
9.	Hindu : High II	B	0.0	2.3	42.2	40.3	15.2	100.0	(1384)
		G	0.0	4.6	44.0	41.0	10.4	100.0	(1143)
	Total	B	3.4	32.1	38.9	21.3	4.3	100.0	(15440)
		G	1.9	46.9	31.9	16.9	2.4	100.0	(11858)

*Figures within brackets indicate frequencies.

necessary to examine whether and to what extent there is inter-tribe variation in the educational development of the tribals in the rural areas of the tribal sub-plan.

Inter-tribe variation in educational development must be viewed in the context that the educational development of the tribals is the lowest among the various sections of the population. At one end, there is not a single male member, with any formal education in 44.5 per cent of the tribal households, and there is not a single female member with any formal education in 75.6 per cent of the tribal households. At the other end, only 7 per cent of the tribal households have at least one male member having attained S.S.C./College education and only 2.2 per cent of the tribal households have at least one female member having attained that level of education. It is for this reason that some categories of education have been further collapsed while examining the highest level of education attained by any member among males/females. The relevant data regarding the educational development of various tribal groups are given in Tables 3.4 and 3.5. The following observations should be made in this regard.

First, the percentage of households in which no male member has obtained any formal education varies from 30.4 per cent for Dhodias to 89.6 per cent for Kotwalias. Similarly, the percentage of households in which no female member has obtained any formal education varies from 54.9 per cent for Dhodias 99.1 per cent for Kotwalias. The percentage of illiterate boys among the different tribes varies from 28.1 per cent for Dhodias to 90.5 per cent for Kotwalias, and the percentage of illiterate girls varies from 36.2 per cent for Dhodias to 98.5 per cent for Kotwalias. The percentage of households with no male member having any formal education is lower among Dhodias, Dhankas, Koli/Kolchas and Chaudharis than the average for the total group, that among Bhils and Rathwas is just about the average, and that among the rest of the tribal groups is far greater than the average. The percentage of households with no female member having any formal education is lower among Dhodias, Chaudharis, Koli/Kolchas and Dhankas than the average for the total group, that among Koknas is just about the average, and that among the rest of the tribal groups is far greater than the

TABLE 3.4 : Percentage distribution of households, showing the highest level of education attained by any member among males/females, separately for each tribe/tribal group

Tribe/tribal group			Highest level of education attained				Total	
			Nil	1-4 std.	5-10 std.	S.S.C. & above		
			1	2	3	4	5	
1.	Bhil, etc.	M	44.6	24.2	24.9	6.3	100.0	(3788)
		F	80.2	11.2	6.8	1.8	100.0	(3788)
2.	Dubla, etc.	M	54.1	25.3	17.6	3.0	100.0	(922)
		F	81.9	14.2	3.3	0.7	100.0	(922)
3.	Dhodia	M	30.4	21.9	34.4	13.3	100.0	(1096)
		F	54.9	20.5	19.3	5.3	100.0	(1096)
4.	Gamit, etc.	M	54.9	19.2	19 5	6.3	100.0	(870)
		F	79.3	12.4	6.1	2.2	100.0	(870)
5.	Nayaka, etc.	M	57.2	24.5	17.0	1.3	100.0	(318)
		F	80.8	12.3	6.9	0.0	100.0	(318)
6.	Chaudhri, etc.	M	37.9	17.9	32.2	12.0	100.0	(884)
		F	60.5	16.0	17.5	6.0	100.0	(884)
7.	Dhanka, etc.	M	31.9	32.6	29.7	5.9	100.0	(866)
		F	73.4	19.5	6.0	1.0	100.0	(866)
8.	Kokna, etc.	M	48.6	20.6	25.5	5.2	100.0	(325)
		F	75.1	14.2	10.2	0.6	100.0	(325)
9.	Rathwa, etc.	M	44.3	27.6	22.4	5.7	100.0	(366)
		F	86.3	11.2	2.5	0.0	100.0	(366)
10.	Koli/Kolcha	M	37.7	32.5	24.7	5.2	100.0	(77)
		F	71.4	11.7	15.6	1.3	100.0	(77)
11.	Varli	M	76.7	13.4	8.1	1.7	100.0	(172)
		F	95.9	2.9	1.2	0.0	100.0	(172)

TABLE 3.4 : (*Contd.*)

			1	2	3	4	5	
12.	Kotwalia	M	89.6	10.4	0.0	0.0	100.0	(106)
		F	99.1	0.9	0.0	0.0	100.0	(106)
13.	Others	M	34.6	22.2	36.2	7.0	100.0	(185)
		F	80.0	13.0	5.9	1.1	100.0	(185)
	Total	M	44.5	23.4	25.1	7.0	100.0	(9975)
		F	75.6	13.7	8.5	2.2	100.0	(9975)

Note : Figures in brackets indicate frequencies.

average. The percentage of illiterate boys is lower among Dhodias, Dhankas, Koli/Kolchas and Chaudharis than the average for the total group, that among Bhils and Nayakas is just about the average, and that among the rest of the tribal groups is far greater than the average. The percentage of illiterate girls is lower among Dhodias, Chaudharis and Dhankas than the average for the total group, that among Nayakas is just about the average, and that among the remaining tribal groups is far greater than the average.

Secondly, 13.3 per cent of the Dhodia and 12.0 per cent of the Chaudhari households have at least one male member having attained S.S.C./College education. The percentage of households with at least one female member having attained S.S.C./College education is 6 per cent for Chaudhris, 5.3 per cent for Dhodias, and 2.2 per cent for Gamits. Similar percentages for the remaining tribal groups are below the average of the total group.

Thirdly, only 2.2 per cent of the boys and 1.1 per cent of the girls in the age-group 5—17 years are attending high school. The percentage of boys/girls attending high school is greater among Dhodias, Chaudharis and Koli/Kolchas than the average for the total group, while that among Bhils and Koknas is about the same as the average. In the absence of data regarding age-distribution of boys/girls in different tribal groups, it is not possible to compare their enrolment data in detail. In the case of several tribal groups, the cells for boys/girls attending middle and high school are blank or contain a very small percentage ; this indicates the lack of even middle or high school level education in the younger generation and the possibility of a serious problem of wastage and stagnation among them.

Fourthly, on the basis of these indicators of educational development, it is seen that the educational development of Dhodias, Chaudharis. Dhankas and Koli/Kolchas is above the average level of educational development of the tribals in general. The rank of Dhodias on all indicators is consistently at the top. The educational development of Bhils, Koknas and Nayakas is at the average level of educational development of the tribals in general. The educational development of Gamits, Rathwas, Dublas, Varlis and Kotwalias is far below the average level of educational development of the tribals in general. In fact, the

TABLE 3.5 : **Percentages showing education among boys/girls attending school, separately for each tribe/tribal group**

Tribe/tribal group		No information	Illiterate	Attending school			Total	
				Primary	Middle	High		
		1	2	3	4	5	6	
1. Bhil, etc.	B	3.2	45.9	34.7	14.0	2.2	100.0	(3695)
	G	1.7	68.7	21.5	7.0	1.1	100.0	(2580)
2. Dubla, etc.	B	—	59.1	30.8	9.2	0.9	100.0	(779)
	G	0.9	77.6	17.7	3.4	0.4	100.0	(678)
3. Dhodia	B	2.2	28.1	38.4	26.6	4.7	100.0	(992)
	G	2.0	36.2	36.4	23.3	2.1	100.0	(889)
4. Gamit, etc.	B	2.7	52.0	30.7	13.5	1.1	100.0	(733)
	G	1.7	69.2	21.7	6.7	0.7	100.0	(540)
5. Nayaka, etc.	B	6.0	45.8	34.1	13.4	0.7	100.0	(299)
	G	3.7	63.0	26.0	7.3	—	100.0	(246)
6. Chaudhri, etc.	B	0.1	39.1	37.1	20.7	3.0	100.0	(696)
	G	—	47.5	31.4	17.9	3.2	100.0	(630)
7. Dhanka, etc.	B	11.0	34.5	42.3	10.5	1.7	100.0	(951)
	G	6.0	57.8	31.8	4.3	0.1	100.0	(680)
8. Kokna, etc.	B	9.7	50.0	17.3	20.6	2.4	100.0	(340)
	G	1.4	67.4	21.0	9.2	1.0	100.0	(295)
9. Rathwa, etc.	B	13.6	50.0	27.2	8.5	0.7	100.0	(574)
	G	3.3	79.8	16.1	0.8	—	100.0	(361)
10. Koli/Kolcha	B	—	36.3	47.8	9.7	6.2	100.0	(113)
	G	—	66.7	11.8	17.6	3 9	100.0	(51)
11. Varli	B	1.2	72.0	23.6	3.2	—	100.0	(157)
	G	0.7	93.4	5.2	0.7	—	100.0	(134)

TABLE 3.5 : (*Contd.*)

		1	2	3	4	5	6	
12. Kotwalia	B	2.4	90.5	7.1	—	—	100.0	(84)
	G	—	98.5	1.5	—	—	100.0	(65)
13. Others	B	20.0	20.5	35.2	21.4	2.9	100.0	(210)
	G	25.8	41.7	25.8	6.7	—	100.0	(120)
Total	B	4.6	44.5	34.0	14.7	2.2	100.0	(9623)
	G	2.4	63.3	24.2	9.0	1.1	100.0	(7269)

Note : Figures in brackets indicate frequencies.

educational development of Dublas, Varlis and Kotwalis is almost negligible.

Finally, the educational development of the most progressive group among the tribals is comparable only with that of the scheduled castes. While the performance of the Dhodia males seems to be almost at par with that of the scheduled caste males, the performance of the Dhodia and Chaudhari females is above that of the scheduled caste females.

Such a pattern of educational development of the tribals points out the need for examining the factors related to the differential educational development of various castes/communities/tribes. Since occupation is usually found related to caste/community/tribe and education, we shall examine next the interrelationship between caste/community/tribe, occupation and education.

Caste/community and occupation

The percentage distribution of households, showing occupation of the heads of the households is given, separately for each category of caste/community, in Table 3.6. It is found from this table that a majority of the heads are involved in agricultural activities ; 47.4 per cent of the heads are farm owners and 19.1 per cent of them are agricultural labourers. Only about 18 per cent of the heads are white-collar workers (clerks, technicians, businessmen, professionals, etc.).

When caste/community is controlled, it is seen that the percentage of those employed in agriculture is fairly high in all categories of caste/community. Over one-half of the heads of the tribal households and about one-third of the heads of the scheduled caste households are farm owners. Similarly, about one-third of the heads of the tribal households and about one-fourth of the heads of the scheduled caste households are labourers ; most of them are agricultural labourers. It should be noted that 30 out of 34 heads of the Parsi households are farm owners. About 45 per cent of the heads in the two categories of the high-caste Hindus are farm owners. In the absence of data on the land-holdings of the various castes/communities, it is not possible to indicate their social status based on such a broad occupational category. There is a fairly high proportion of artisans among the low and middle

TABLE 3.6 : **Percentage distribution of households, showing occupation of heads of households by caste/community**

Caste/Community	Retired, not reported	Agricultural labourers	Other labourers	Artisans	Farm owners/ livestock farmers	Clerks	Prof./Officers/ businessmen	Total	
1. S.T.	.0.3	28.2	7.0	2.8	54.4	5.8	1.5	100.0	(9975)
2. S.C	0.7	18.4	9.4	24.1	33.0	11.6	2.8	100.0	(673)
3. Muslim	1.9	2.7	6.6	18.9	24.6	15.4	29.8	100.0	(889)
4. Christian	—	—	[1]	[2]	[8]	[11]	[6]	—	[28]
5. Parsi	—	—	[1]	—	[30]	[2]	[1]	—	[34]
6. Hindu : Low	0.3	1.2	5.2	47.0	30.8	8.0	7.5	100.0	(942)
7. Hindu : Middle	0.9	3.3	5.2	37.6	16.6	17.1	18.2	100.0	(657)
8. Hindu : High I	0.9	2.4	5.4	4.7	47.2	23.8	15.6	100.0	(1202)
9. Hindu : High II	1.5	0.2	0.3	4.3	44.2	14.9	34.6	100.0	(1461)
Total	0.5	19.1	6.2	8.9	47.4	9.5	8.4	100.0	(15861)

*Figures within brackets indicate frequencies.

caste Hindus, scheduled castes and Muslims. (The high proportion of artisans in the low and middle caste Hindus may partly be an antifact of the assignment of artisan castes to these two categories.)

The percentage of those employed in white-collar occupations increases as we move up the social ladder. While only 7.3 per cent of the tribal heads are employed in white-collar occupations, about one-half of the heads among the high-caste Hindus II are employed in white-collar jobs. Since most white-collar occupations are dependent on educational qualifications, such a pattern of white-collar occupations of the heads from different castes/communities indicates a relatively high level of educational development of the higher castes.

Inter-tribe variation in occupation

The percentage distribution of the tribal households, showing occupation of the heads of households, is given, separately for each tribal group, in Table 3.7. Since most of the tribals are farm owners or agricultural labourers, the occupational categories of clerks, etc. and businessmen/officers/professionals have been collapsed into a single category of white-collar occupations, and the remaining occupational categories have been grouped into a residual category. It is found that the percentage of heads employed in white-collar occupations is relatively greater among Koli/Kolchas, Dhodias, Koknas and Chaudharis than the average for the total group. None of the Kotwalia heads is employed in white-collar occupations, and only a small percentage of the heads among Varlis, Rathwas and Nayakas is employed in white-collar occupations. Almost all of the Kotwalia heads (94.3%), who are in the residual category of occupation, are labourers. While three-fourths of the Dubla heads are agricultural labourers, 86.1 per cent of the Rathwa heads are farm owners. About one-half to two-thirds of heads among Varlis, Dhodias, Bhils, Chaudharis and Dhankas are farm owners. Such a pattern of occupations in the different tribal groups seems to suggest, in the context of their educational development as examined earlier in this chapter, that white-collar occupations and farm ownership are probably linked with their relatively high level of educational development. It is, therefore, necessary to examine the relationship between occupation of the heads of households and educational development of the members in their households.

TABLE 3.7 : **Percentage distribution of households, showing occupation of heads of households, separately for each tribe/tribal group**

Tribe/tribal group	Retired, not reported, other labourers, artisans	Agricultural labourers	Farm owners/ livestock farmers	White-collar workers	Total	
1. Bhil, etc.	7.9	23.3	61.1	7.7	100.0	(3788)
2. Dubla, etc.	10.1	82.2	2.8	4.9	100.0	(922)
3. Dhodia	12.2	21.2	55.0	11.6	100.0	(1096)
4. Gamit, etc.	8.5	37.5	48.4	5.6	100.0	(870)
5. Nayaka, etc.	23.6	28.3	45.0	3.1	100.0	(318)
6. Chaudhri, etc.	7.2	21.8	61.7	9.3	100.0	(884)
7. Dhanka, etc.	4.7	21.2	67.1	6.9	100.0	(866)
8. Kokna, etc.	15.4	14.5	60.0	10.2	100.0	(325)
9. Rathwa, etc.	2.7	8.2	86.1	3.0	100.0	(366)
10. Koli/Kolcha	23.4	22.1	39.0	15.6	100.0	(77)
11. Varli	20.9	26.7	51.2	1.2	100.0	(172)
12. Kotwalia	94.3	5.7	0.0	0.0	100.0	(106)
13. Others	8.1	1.1	88.6	2.2	100.0	(185)
Total	10.1	28.2	54.4	7.3	100.0	(9975)

Note : Figures in brackets indicate frequencies.

Occupation and educational development

The percentage distribution of the households, showing the highest level of education attained by any member among males/ females, is given, by occupation of the heads of households, in Table 3.8.

It is found from this table that in the labour (agricultural as well as other) households, the males in about 55 per cent of the households and the females in about 80 per cent of the households have not obtained any formal education. The respective proportions in the households of the farm owners are one-third for the males and two-thirds for the females. As one moves up

TABLE 3.8 : **Percentage distribution of households, showing the highest level of education attained by any member among males/females, by occupation of heads of households**

Occupation of heads of households		Highest level of education attained							
		Nil	1-4 std.	5-7 std.	8-10 std.	S.S.C.	Graduate	Total	
1. Retired, not	M	22.7	9.1	22.7	19.3	19.3	6.9	100.0	(88)
reported	F	48.9	18.2	9.1	11.4	10.2	2.2	100.0	(88)
2. Agricultural	M	55.5	25.3	12.2	4.8	1.9	0.2	100.0	(3027)
labourers	F	83.9	11.9	2.7	1.1	0.4	—	100.0	(3027)
3. Other labourers	M	54.8	23.1	14.8	5.5	1.8	0.1	100.0	(989)
	F	80.1	13.5	4.4	1.3	0.6	—	100.0	(989)
4. Artisans	M	24.1	23.6	29.6	12.5	9.1	1.0	100.0	(1413)
	F	52.7	21.5	13.4	8.9	3.3	0.2	100.0	(1413)
5. Farm owners/Live-	M	33.7	22.1	18.0	14.4	9.3	2.5	100.0	(7515)
stock farmers	F	66.7	15.2	8.0	6.2	3.5	0.4	100.0	(7515)
6. Clerks, etc.	M	5.8	11.1	21.9	22.9	33.3	5.0	100.0	(1507)
	F	32.2	20.9	21.9	13.4	9.8	1.8	100.0	(1507)
7. Professionals/Officers/	M	4.4	8.1	19.8	18.8	25.2	23.7	100.0	(1322)
Businessmen	F	25.0	16.5	19.1	18.2	16.8	4.4	100.0	(1322)
Total	M	33.2	20.6	18.3	13.0	11.1	3.8	100.0	(15861)
	F	62.7	15.7	9.5	6.9	4.4	0.8	100.0	(15861)

Note : Figures in brackets indicate frequencies.

the occupational hierarchy, the proportion of such households decreases considerably. It is rather surprising to note that even in the households where the heads are employed in white-collar jobs, the males in 5 per cent of the households and the females in 25 per cent to 30 per cent of the households have not obtained any formal education. This is perhaps due to the fact that businessmen are included in this category. Examining the percentages in the other categories of education, it is found that the higher the level of occupation of the head of the household, the greater the percentage of households with at least one male/female member who has obtained a high level of education. Thus, there is a monotonic relationship between occupation of the heads of the households and the highest level of education obtained by any member among males/females.

Examining the percentages showing education among boys and girls, by occupation of the heads of the households (Table 3.9), it is found that the percentages of illiterate boys and girls are the highest among the agricultural labourers and the lowest among the white-collar workers. About three-fifths of the boys and three-fourths of the girls in the agricultural labourers' households are illiterate. Although the respective percentages decrease in the case of the other labourers' households, they are quite high ; about one-half of the boys and two-thirds of the girls in such households are illiterate. Then come the households of farm owners wherein about one-third of the boys and about one-half of the girls are illiterate. The percentages of illiterate boys and girls decrease as one moves up the occupational hierarchy. Further, in each category of occupation, the percentage of illiterate girls is greater than that of illiterate boys.

A similar pattern is also found with regard to the enrolment of boys and girls. While only about 40 per cent of the boys and 23 per cent of the girls from the agricultural labourers' households are attending school, about 95 per cent of the boys and 92 per cent of the girls from the top category of occupation are attending school. That is, the percentages of the boys and the girls attending school increase as one moves up the occupational hierarchy. Further, in each category of occupation, the percentage of those attending school decreases as one moves from the primary to the high school enrolment. This is true of boys as

TABLE 3.9 : **Percentages showing education among boys/girls, by occupation of households**

Occupation of heads of households		No information	Illiterates	Attending school			Total	
				Primary	Middle	High		
1. Retired, not reported	B	67.5	2.5	17.0	10.0	3.0	100.0	(200)
	G	41.9	8.1	31.1	16.3	2.3	100.0	(86)
2. Agricultural labourers	B	1.2	59.2	29.4	9.3	0.9	100.0	(2750)
	G	1.4	75.7	18.4	4.3	0.2	100.0	(2128)
3. Other labourers	B	2.3	52.3	31.2	13.4	0.8	100.0	(872)
	G	2.7	64.7	26.0	6.4	0.1	100.0	(692)
4. Artisans	B	1.7	18.2	47.6	28.6	3.9	100.0	(1307)
	G	1.6	30.4	42.9	23.5	1.6	100.0	(1065)
5. Farm owners/live-stock	B	4.0	32.1	38.5	21.0	4.4	100.0	(7618)
farmers	G	1.7	51.5	30.3	14.2	2.3	100.0	(5692)
6. Clerks, etc.	B	0.3	8.8	52.0	32.9	6.0	100.0	(1375)
	G	1.9	13.4	48.1	32.7	3.9	100.0	(1120)
7. Professionals/Officers/	B	0.5	4.4	47.7	36.3	11.1	100.0	(1318)
Businessmen	G	0.2	8.3	42.8	40.7	8.0	100.0	(1075)
Total	B	3.4	32.0	39.0	21.3	4.3	100.0	(15440)
	G	1.9	46.9	31.9	16.9	2.4	100.0	(11858)

Note : Figures in brackets indicate frequencies

well as girls. In brief, the occupation of the heads of households is very strongly and monotonically related to the educational attainment of the 5—17 years old boys/girls.

Since a majority of the tribal heads are farm owners or agricultural labourers, it will be instructive to examine separately the relationship between the occupation of the heads of households and educational development of the tribals. The relevant data are given in Tables 3.10 and 3.11.

It may be noted that in all categories of occupation the percentages of households with no male/female member having any formal education are somewhat greater for the tribals (Table 3.10) than those in the respective categories of the total population in the study area (Table 3.8). Similarly, the percentages of the tribal households with at least one male/female member having obtained certain levels of formal education are smaller than those for the total population. As in the case of the total population, there is among the tribals also a monotonic relationship between occupation of the heads of the households and the highest level of education attained by any member among males as well as females. Comparing the percentages of illiterate boys/girls and the percentages of boys/girls attending school, given in Tables 3.11 and 3.9, a similar pattern of relationship is also observed.

Thus, the data regarding the highest level of education attained by any member among males/females in the households, the proportions of illiterates, and the proportions of those attending school among the 5—17 years old boys/girls clearly indicate that the educational development of the people residing in the rural areas of the tribal sub-plan is generally low. Caste/community is closely associated with education of the members in the household. The higher the social status of caste/community, the greater the educational attainment of its members. The tribes are at the bottom and the high-caste Hindu II are at the top of the pyramid of educational development. A greater proportion of the males than that of the females have attained a high level of education ; sex differences in educational achievement are found in all categories of caste/community, but they tend to decrease as one moves up the social hierarchy of castes/communities. The occupation of the heads of households is also strongly related to caste/community on the one hand and to educational

TABLE 3.10 : **Percentage distribution of tribal households, showing the highest level of education attained by any member among males/females, by occupation of heads of households**

Occupation of heads of households		Highest level of education attained				Total	
		Nil	1-4 std.	5-10 std.	S.S.C. and above		
1. Retired, not reported,	M	56.6	21.4	19.9	2.1	100.0	(1010)
other labourers	F	80.6	13.0	5.9	0.5	100.0	(1010)
2. Agricultural labourers	M	57.2	24.8	16.1	1.8	100.0	(2814)
	F	84.9	11.2	3.5	0.4	100.0	(2814)
3. Farm owners/live-stock	M	40.5	24.5	28.3	6.7	100.0	(5424)
farmers	F	75.1	14.1	8.8	2.0	100.0	(5424)
4. White-collar workers	M	7.3	13.5	44.3	34.9	100.0	(727)
	F	37.3	21.0	29.2	12.5	100.0	(727)
Total	M	44.4	23.5	25.2	6.9	100.0	(9975)
	F	75.6	13.7	8.5	2.2	100.0	(9975)

Note : Figures in brackets indicates frequencies.

TABLE 3.11 : Percentages showing education among tribal boys/girls, by occupation of heads of households

Occupation of heads of households		No information	Illiterate	Attending school			Total	
				Primary	Middle	High		
1. Retired, not reported,	B	9.7	52.1	26.2	11.5	0.5	100.0	(910)
other labourers, artisans	G	7.3	63.9	23.4	5.1	0.3	100.0	(757)
2. Agricultural labourers	B	2.6	60.3	28.3	8.1	0.7	100.0	(2583)
	G	1.2	77.3	17.2	4.0	0.3	100.0	(1992)
3. Farm owners/live-	B	5.0	39.6	36.1	19.6	2.7	100.0	(5458)
stock farmers	G	2.1	61.9	25.1	9.5	1.4	100.0	(3979)
4. White-collar workers	B	2.2	12.9	50.0	29.5	5.4	100.0	(672)
	G	2.2	22.2	44.2	28.5	2.9	100.0	(541)
Total	B	4.6	44.5	34.0	14.7	2.2	100.0	(9623)
	G	2.4	63.4	24.2	8.9	1.1	100.0	(7269)

Note : Figures in brackets indicate frequencies.

development on the other hand. A similar relationship between occupation of the heads of the households and the educational development of the tribals is also found. Sex differences in the various indicators of educational development are found in all categories of occupation. Such a pattern of inter-relationships between caste/community, occupation and indicators of educational development suggests the need for controlling occupation while examining the relationship between caste/community and educational development. However, in view of the primary interest of the study in examining the educational development of the tribals, we shall examine next the relationship between occupation of the heads of households and educational development of the different tribal groups.

Inter-tribe variation in educational development, controlling for occupation

In the light of a differential educational development and a fair amount of variation in the occupation of the heads of the households in the various tribal groups, it is necessary to examine the extent to which the differential educational development of the tribal groups is related to differences in their occupation. This is shown in Tables 3.12 and 3.13. It may be noted that these data are presented for only three occupational categories (agricultural labourers, farm owners and white-collar workers) in which about 90 per cent of the heads are employed. Further, since there are, among Kotwalias, only six households in the category of agricultural labourers and none at all in the categories of white-collar workers and farm owners, the category of Kotwalias is omitted in these two tables. The following observations should be made regarding the general pattern of relationship between occupation of the heads of households and educational development of the different tribal groups.

First, with regard to the highest level of education attained by any member among the males/females as well as education among the 5-17 years old boys/girls, it is found that there is a positive relationship between occupation of the heads of the households and educational development of all tribal groups. The educational development of the agricultural labourers is of the lowest order, that of the white-collar workers is of the highest

TABLE 3.12 : Cumulative percentage distributions of households, showing the highest level of education attained by any member among males/females by occupation of heads of households, separately for each tribe/tribal group*

Highest level of education attained	White-collar occupations		Farm-owners		Agricultural labourers	
	Males	Females	Males	Females	Males	Females
	1	2	3	4	5	6
Dhodia						
1. S.S.C. and above	38.6	16.5	13.8	5.0	4.3	2.6
2. 5—10 std., S.S.C. fail	84.3	45.6	50.6	27.1	33.2	15.5
3. 1—4 std.,	95.3	67.6	73.7	47.8	54.8	34.0
4. Nil	100.0	100.0	100.0	100.0	100.0	100.0
	(127)	(127)	(603)	(603)	(232)	(232)
Chaudhri, etc.						
1. S.S.C. and above	58.5	23.2	9.2	5.9	3.6	1.0
2. 5—10 std., S.S.C. fail	91.4	68.3	44.6	23.0	26.4	9.8
3. 1—4 std.	95.1	76.8	62.8	40.8	49.2	24.8
4. Nil	100.0	100.0	100.0	100.0	100.0	100.0
	(82)	(82)	(545)	(545)	(193)	(193)
Dhanka, etc.						
1. S.S.C. and above	26.7	6.7	5.7	0.9	0.0	0.0
2. 5—10 std., S.S.C. fail	83.4	25.0	36.0	7.3	19.0	1.1
3. 1—4 std.	98.4	68.3	70.8	27.6	51.6	9.8
4. Nil	100.0	100.0	100.0	100.0	100.0	100.0
	(60)	(60)	(581)	(581)	(184)	(184)
Bhil. etc,						
1. S.S.C. and above	31.2	10.3	5.8	1.4	1.2	0.1
2. 5—10 std., S.S.C. fail	79.5	39.4	31.6	6.9	16.0	3.0
3. 1—4 std.	92.9	61.0	55.5	16.9	44.3	13.8
4. Nil	100.0	100.0	100.0	100.0	100.0	100.0
	(292)	(292)	(2313)	(2313)	(883)	(883)
Konka, etc						
1. S.S.C. and above	9.1	3.0	5.6	0.5	2.1	0.0

TABLE 3.12 : (*Contd.*)

	1	2	3	4	5	6
2. 5—10 std., S.S.C. fail	39.4	30.3	37.4	11.3	12.7	2.1
3. 1—4 std.	72.7	45.5	60.0	28.7	23.3	6.4
4. Nil	100.0	100.0	100.0	100.0	100.0	100.0
	(33)	(33)	(195)	(195)	(47)	(47)
Gamit, etc.						
1. S.S.C. and above	53.1	24.5	5.0	1.4	2.5	0.3
2. 5—10 std., S.S.C. fail	85.8	51.0	30.4	8.5	11.7	1.8
3. 1—4 std.	98.0	65.3	52.5	26.8	27.7	7.3
4. Nil	100.0	100.0	100.0	100.0	100.0	100.0
	(49)	(49)	(421)	(421)	(326)	(326)
Dubla, etc.						
1. S.S C. and above	24.4	6.7	[3]	[0]	1.5	0 3
2. 5—10 std., S.S.C. fail	60.0	31.1	[10]	[2]	17.2	2.1
3. 1—4 std.	84.4	55.5	[20]	[9]	42.1	14.8
4. Nil	100.0	100.0	100.0	100.0	100.0	100.0
	(45)	(45)	(26)	(26)	(758)	(758)
Rathwa, etc.						
1. S.S.C. and above	[4]	[0]	4.4	0.0	6.7	0.0
2. 5—10 std., S.S.C. fail	[11]	[1]	26.3	2.5	20.0	0.0
3. 1—4 std.	[11]	[2]	55.8	13.9	33.9	6.7
4. Nil	[11]	[11]	100.0	100.0	100.0	100.0
	(11)	(11)	(315)	(315)	(30)	(30)
Koli/Kolcha						
1. S.S.C. and above	[3]	[1]	3.3	0.0	[0]	[0]
2. 5—10 std., S.S.C. fail	[10]	[5]	33.3	20.0	[1]	[0]
3. 1—4 std.	[10]	[8]	93.3	40.0	[7]	[0]
4. Nil	[12]	[12]	100.0	100.0	[17]	[17]
	(12)	(12)	(30)	(30)	(17)	(17)
Nayaka, etc.						
1. S.S.C. and above	[1]	[0]	0.7	0.0	0.0	0.0
2. 5—10 std., S.S.C. fail	[6]	[2]	16.8	6.3	12.2	4.4
3. 1—4 std.	[9]	[4]	34.3	12.6	43.3	17.7

TABLE 3.12 (*Contd.*)

	1	2	3	4	5	6
4. Nil	[10]	[10]	100.0	100.0	100.0	100.0
	(10)	(10)	(143)	(143)	(90)	(90)
Varli						
1. S.S.C. and above	[1]	[0]	1.1	0.0	2.2	0.0
2. 5—10 std., S.S.C. fail	[1]	[1]	9.1	0.0	17.4	0.0
3. 1—4 std.	[1]	[1]	27.3	3.4	30.4	2.2
4. Nil	[2]	[2]	100.0	100.0	100.0	100.0
	(2)	(2)	(88)	(88)	(46)	(46)
Others						
1. S.S.C. and above	[1]	[0]	6.1	1.2	[1]	[0]
2. 5—10 std., S.S.C. fail	[2]	[1]	44.5	7.3	[1]	[0]
3. 1—4 std.	[4]	[1]	67.7	20.7	[1]	[0]
4. Nil	[4]	[4]	100.0	100.0	[2]	[2]
	(4)	(4)	(164)	(164)	(2)	(2)

*Figures within brackets indicate frequencies.

order, and that of the farm owners falls in-between these two groups. There are, however, a few reversals ; almost all of them involve a difference of about one or two per cent ; even this difference may be partly due to the small size of Ns. Only in the case of Nayakas, the educational development of the agricultural labourers is somewhat higher than that of the farm owners.

Secondly, within each category of tribe and occupation, the educational development of the males is higher than that of the females. There are considerable sex differences in the educational development of all tribal groups. They are the largest among the white-collar workers, but they generally decrease as one moves to the categories of the farm owners and the agricultural labourers.

Thirdly, the range in the percentage of households with any male member having attained a high level of education is from 58.5 per cent (Chaudharis) to 9.1 per cent (Koknas) among the white-collar workers, from 13.8 per cent (Dhodias) to 0.7 per cent (Nayakas) among the farm owners, and from 6.7 per cent (Rathwas) to 1.2 per cent (Bhils) among the agricultural labourers. Similarly,

TABLE 3.13 : **Cumulative percentages showing education among boys/girls, by occupation of heads of households, separately for each tribe/tribal group***

Education	White-collar Occupations		Farm-owners		Agricultural labourers	
	Boys	Girls	Boys	Girls	Boys	Girls
	1	2	3	4	5	6
1. *Dhodia*						
Attending—						
(a) High school	5.4	8.6	6.2	2.2	3.1	0.0
(b) Middle School	51.8	39.8	34.6	27.9	17.9	19.9
(c) Primary school	96.4	81.7	72.8	63.8	58.2	53.2
Illiterate	97.3	95.7	99.1	97.9	98.0	97.8
N.A.	100.0	100.0	100.0	100.0	100.0	100.0
	(112)	(93)	(563)	(498)	(196)	(186)
2. *Chaudhri, etc.*						
Attending—						
(a) High school	3.6	0.0	4.3	4.6	0.0	0.7
(b) Middle school	30.9	49.0	26.4	21.5	13.0	10.0
(c) Primary school	94.5	92.1	61.5	52.9	45.1	36.4
Illiterate	100.0	100.0	100.0	100.0	97.6	100.0
N.A.	100.0	100.0	100.0	100.0	100.0	100.0
	(55)	(51)	(447)	(414)	(162)	(140)
3. *Dhanka, etc.*						
Attending—						
(a) High school	3.2	0.0	2.2	0.2	0.0	0.0
(b) Middle school	17.5	13.8	13.8	4.2	7.2	0.8
(c) Primary school	85.8	81.0	57.4	36.3	39.0	14.5
Illiterate	92.1	91.3	87.0	93.3	95.9	97.6
N.A.	100.0	100.0	100.0	100.0	100.0	100.0
	(63)	(58)	(646)	(470)	(195)	(124)
4. *Bhil, etc.*						
Attending—						
(a) High school	6.9	2.3	2.6	1.3	0.2	0.2
(b) Middle school	34.7	31.3	17.7	7.5	7.1	2.4
(c) Primary school	83.8	73.8	53.8	27.7	34.2	18.2
Illiterate	99.6	100.0	96.5	98.2	96.6	98.4

TABLE 3.13 : (*Contd.*)

	1	2	3	4	5	6
N.A.	100.0	100.0	100.0	100.0	100.0	100.0
	(291)	(221)	(2298)	(1537)	(867)	(632)
5. *Kokna, etc.*						
Attending—						
(a) High school	[0]	0.0	2.6	1.6	4.4	0.0
(b) Middle school	[7]	25.0	27.4	10.0	11.1	3.2
(c) Primary school	[17]	61.1	54.4	29.9	26.7	9.7
Illiterate	[18]	91.7	100.0	99.5	97.8	100.0
N.A.	[25]	100.0	100.0	100.0	100·0	100.0
	(25)	(36)	(230)	(191)	(45)	(31)
6. *Gamit, etc.*						
Attending—						
(a) High school	8.5	[2]	0.3	0.4	1.0	0.5
(b) Middle school	51.0	[11]	16.8	10.9	6.0	1.0
(c) Primary school	95.7	[24]	56.6	43.1	25.8	10.2
Illiterate	100.0	[28]	95.4	96.7	98.3	99.5
N.A.	100.0	[28]	100.0	100.0	100.0	100.0
	(47)	(28)	(322)	(239)	(298)	(216)
7. *Dubla, etc.*						
Attending—						
(a) High school	2.4	2.9	[0]	0.0	0.5	0.4
(b) Middle school	21.9	23.3	[2]	0.0	8.6	2.2
(c) Primary school	65.8	58.8	[16]	21.2	37.3	17.6
Illiterate	97.5	100.0	[25]	100.0	98.9	98.9
N.A.	100.0	100.0	[28]	100.0	100.0	100.0
	(41)	(34)	(28)	(33)	(644)	(550)
8. *Rathwa, etc.*						
Attending—						
(a) High school	[0]	[0]	0.6	0.0	2.5	[0]
(b) Middle school	[0]	[0]	9.2	0.9	12.5	[0]
(c) Primary school	[7]	[3]	35.3	16.7	42.5	[2]
Illiterate	[13]	[4]	85.2	96.8	100.0	[23]
N.A.	[16]	[4]	100.0	100.0	100.0	[23]
	(16)	(4)	(509)	(316)	(40)	(23)
9. *Koli/Kolcha*						
Attending—						
(a) High school	[0]	[0]	21.2	[2]	[0]	[0]
(b) Middle school	[3]	[2]	45.4	[9]	[0]	[0]
(c) Primary school	[8]	[4]	96.9	[13]	[2]	[0]

TABLE 3.13 : (*Contd.*)

	1	2	3	4	5	6
Illiterate	[8]	[5]	100.0	[20]	[25]	[9]
N.A.	[9]	[5]	100.0	[20]	[25]	[9]
	(9)	(5)	(33)	(20)	(25)	(9)
10. *Nayaka, etc.*						
Attending—						
(a) High school	[0]	[0]	0.7	0.0	0.0	0.0
(b) Middle school	[2]	[1]	12.2	5.8	14.7	7.5
(c) Primary school	[5]	[3]	37.2	18.3	55.7	47.5
Illiterate	[11]	[10]	96.0	95.8	85.2	100.0
N.A.	[13]	[11]	100.0	100.0	100.0	100.0
	(13)	(11)	(148)	(120)	(61)	(40)
11. *Varli*						
Attending—						
(a) High school	—	[0]	0.0	0.0	0.0	0.0
(b) Middle school	—	[0]	3.6	0.0	5.0	0.0
(c) Primary school	—	[0]	33.4	7.5	35.0	2.7
Illiterate	—	[1]	97.7	100.0	100.0	100.0
N.A.	—	[1]	100.0	100.0	100.0	100.0
	—	(1)	(84)	(67)	(40)	(37)
12. *Others*						
Attending—						
(a) High school	[1]	[0]	2.6	0.0	[1]	[0]
(b) Middle school	[2]	[0]	28.7	9.0	[2]	[0]
(c) Primary school	[3]	[0]	74.5	45.7	[2]	[0]
Illiterate	[3]	[0]	97.4	97.5	[2]	[2]
N.A.	[4]	[2]	100.0	100.0	[2]	[2]
	(4)	(2)	(153)	(83)	(2)	(2)

*Figures within brackets indicate frequencies
N.A.=Information not available.

the range in the percentage of households with any female member having attained a high level of education is from 24.5 per cent (Gamits) to 3.0 per cent (Koknas) among the white-collar workers, from 5.9 per cent (Chaudharis) to zero per cent (Koli/Kolchas, Nayakas and Rathwas) among the farm owners, and from 2.6 per cent (Dhodias) to 0.1 per cent (Bhils) among the agricultural labourers. Thus, there is a considerable amount of inter-tribe variation in the percentage of households with any male/female member having attained S.S.C./College education. A similar pattern of inter-tribe variation is found in the percentages of households with any male/female member having attained the post-primary or primary level of education.

Fourthly, the range in the percentage of boys attending primary/middle/high schools is from 96.4 per cent (Dhodias) to 65.8 per cent (Dublas) among the white-collar workers, 96.9 per cent (Koli/Kolchas) to 33.4 per cent (Varlis) among the farm owners, and from 58.2 per cent (Dhodias) to 26.7 per cent (Koknas) among the agricultural labourers. Similarly, the range in the percentages of girls attending primary/middle/high schools is from 92.1 per cent (Chaudharis) to 58.8 per cent (Dublas) among the white-collar workers, from 63.8 per cent (Dhodias) to 7.5 per cent (Varlis) among the farm owners, and from 53.2 per cent (Dhodias) to 2.7 per cent (Varlis) among the agricultural labourers.

Finally, it should be noted that the inter-tribe differences in the percentages of households with any male/female member having attained a high level of education as well as in the percentages of boys/girls attending primary/middle/high schools are relatively larger among the white-collar workers than those among the farm owners and the agricultural labourers. Such a pattern seems to be due to a generally low level of educational development of all tribal groups but a growing trend towards attending education among the children of those in the higher levels of occupation.

It may be useful to examine the relationship between occupation of the heads of households and educational development within each tribal group. With this view, brief descriptive statements regarding educational development of different occupational groups within each tribal group are made in the following paragraphs.

Among Dhodias, 55 per cent of the household heads are farm owners, 21.2 per cent are agricultural labourers, and 11.6 per cent are white-collar workers. The percentages of households with any member among males and females having attained a high level of education are, respectively, 38.6 per cent and 16.5 per cent among the white-collar workers, 13.8 per cent and 5 per cent among the farm owners, and 4.3 per cent and 2.6 per cent among the agricultural labourers. The percentages of boys and girls attending school are, respectively, 96.4 per cent and 81.7 per cent among the white-collar workers, 72.8 per cent and 63.8 per cent among the farm owners, and 58.2 per cent and 53.2 per cent among the agricultural labourers. Such high percentages indicate that the overall educational development of Dhodias is very high. More than one-half of the boys and the girls of the agricultural labourers are attending school. This is indeed indicative of the educational progress among them.

Among Chaudharis, 61.7 per cent of the household heads are farm owners, 21.8 per cent are agricultural labourers, and 9.3 per cent are white-collar workers. The educational development of the Chaudhari white-collar workers is somewhat higher than that of the Dhodia white-collar workers, but the educational development of the Chaudhari farm owners and agricultural labourers is lower than that of Dhodias in the respective occupational categories.

Among Dhankas, 67.1 per cent of the household heads are farm owners, 21.2 per cent are agricultural labourers, and 6.9 per cent are white-collar workers. The educational development of Dhankas is markedly lower than that of Dhodias and Chaudharis in all categories of occupation. It should be noted that the distribution of households in the three categories of occupation is very similar among Chaudharis and Dhankas; and yet, there are considerable differences in the percentages of various indicators of their educational development.

Among Bhils, 61.1 per cent of the household heads are farm owners, 23.3 per cent are agricultural labourers, and 7.7 per cent are white-collar workers. It should be noted that the distribution of households in the three occupational categories is almost similar among Dhankas and Bhils; and educational progress in terms of the highest level of education attained by any member among males/females is higher among Bhils than among Dhankas but the percentages of boys/girls attending school are generally lower among Bhils than those among Dhankas in the three occupational categories.

Among Koknas, 60 per cent of the household heads are farm owners, 14.5 per cent are agricultural labourers, and 10.2 per cent are white-collar workers. Although the percentage of the white-collar households among Koknas is slightly lower than that of Dhodias, the educational development of even the Kokna white-collar households is way behind that of the other tribal groups considered so far. The same is true of the Kokna farm owners, who form 60 per cent of all Kokna households in this study.

Among Gamits, 48.4 per cent of the household heads are farm owners, 37.5 per cent are agricultural labourers and 5.6 per cent are white-collar workers. The educational development of the Gamit white-collar workers, in terms of the highest level of education attained by any member among males/females, is quite impressive; it is comparable to the Chaudhari white-collar workers. Similarly, the percentages of the Gamit boys and girls attending school among the farm owners are comparable to those of Dhankas, but Gamits seem to lag behind the other tribal groups with regard to their educational development in other respects.

Among Dublas, 82.2 per cent of the household heads are agricultural labourers while only 45 heads are white-collar workers and 26 heads are farm owners. The educational development of the Dubla agricultural labourers is comparable to that of the Dhanka agricultural labourers.

Among Rathwas, 86.1 per cent of the household are farm owners while only 11 heads are white-collar workers and 30 heads are agricultural labourers. Only 4.4 per cent of the households of farm owners have at least one member among males having attained a high level of education. The percentages of boys and girls attending school among the farm owners are, respectively, 35.3 per cent and 16.7 per cent. The educational development of the Rathwa farm owners is thus very low.

There are only 77 households of Koli/Kolchas in the sample; out of them, the heads of 30 households are farm owners, 17 heads are agricultural labourers, and 12 heads are white-collar workers. The number of boys and girls in the various categories of occupation is also very small. It is not possible to compare the percentages based on such small Ns in the various categories with similar percentages of the other tribal groups. However, an examination of the frequencies in various categories indicates that a fairly large number of boys/girls from the households of the white-collar workers and farm owners attend school, but a majority of those from the agricultural labourers' households do not attend school.

Among Nayakas, 45 per cent of the household heads are farm owners and 28.3 per cent are agricultural labourers; there are only ten households of white-collar workers. Only one male member each among the white-collar workers and the farm owners has attained a high level of education. The percentages of boys and girls attending school are respectively, 37.2 per cent and 18.3 per cent among the farm owners, and 55.7 per cent and 47.5 per cent among the agricultural labourers. Such higher percentages of boys and girls attending school among the agricultural labourers than those among the farm owners may be attributable partly to random behaviour of a relatively small number of agricultural labourers. This pattern, no doubt, puts the educational development of the Nayaka agricultural labourers almost at par with that of the Dhodia agricultural labourers.

Among Varlis, 51.2 per cent of the household heads are farm owners and 26.7 per cent are agricultural labourers; there are only 2 households of white-collar workers. Only one household each among the farm owners and the agricultural labourers has at least one member among males having attained a high level of education. The percentages of boys and girls attending school are, respectively, 33.4 per cent and 7.5 per cent among the farm owners and 35 per cent and 2.7 per cent among the agricultural labourers.

In brief, the data presented in this chapter show that the educational development of the tribals is very low. There are considerable differences, by sex and tribe, in their educational development. As in the case of the general population, among the tribals also there is a strong relationship between occupation of the heads of households and educational development of their members.

4

COMMUNITY CONTEXTS AND EDUCATIONAL DEVELOPMENT OF THE TRIBALS

INTRODUCTION

SOCIAL scientists have suggested the importance of community-contextual variables, besides that of individual and familial variables, in explaining variation in educational aspirations/achievement of the people. At the aggregate level, region, state, district, taluka, rural-urban areas and such other geographical units have been used as contextual variables while examining their relationship to educational aspirations/achievement of the people. At the micro level, some attempts have been made, especially in the Western countries, to develop some measure of socio-economic status of community or neighbourhood, and then to examine its relationship to educational aspirations/achievement of the students residing in it. In such studies, some individual or composite measures of households or residents in a community/neighbourhood in terms of their caste, race, education, occupation, income, etc. are used as indicators of its socio-economic status or social contexts in general. The logic behind using such individual or composite measures to define the contexts of a community/neighbourhood is very simple. Such variables have been found closely related to the educational aspirations/achievement, and it is, therefore, argued that the composition of a community/neighbourhood in terms of these variables is indicative of the general climate for education in the community/neighbourhood.

We have noted, in Chapter 1, considerable differences in the literacy rates and levels of education among people residing in different districts/talukas and rural-urban areas. Although no specific efforts are generally made to point out differences in such geographical units that might be related to differences in the literacy rates and levels of education among their residents, one implicit suggestion is that they differ in terms of developmental infrastructures, including the facilities for education. All of the sample villages in this study have certain minimum facilities for education. The data collected in the houselisting forms provide a good opportunity to examine the relationship of other contextual variables to the educational development of the tribals.

Defining village as a community, an attempt is made in this chapter to examine the relationship of certain community contextual variables to the educational development of the tribals. For this purpose, caste/community, occupation of the heads of households and various indicators of the educational development of the village have been suggested as measures of community contexts. More specifically, (i) distributions of households in a given village according to (a) caste/community, (b) occupation of heads of households, and (c) the highest level of education attained by any member among males/females in the households, and (ii) the percentages of 5—17 years old boys/girls, in the village (a) who are illiterate and (b) who are attending primary/middle/high schools have been suggested as measures of community contexts of the village.

Two broad methodological approaches are generally used for examining the relationship of the community contextual variables to the educational development of the tribals, namely, to examine separately the relationship between each of them and educational development of the tribals, or to develop a composite measure of all of them and examine its relationship to educational development of the tribals. We have chosen here a different but simple approach, namely, the sample villages are grouped into four broad categories on the basis of the proportion of the non-tribal households and development score of each village. There were certain considerations in choosing this approach. A composite measures will not reveal the relationship of each community contextual variable to educational development of the tribals separately. Further, after using a sophisticated statistical procedure for determining adequate weights for different components of the composite measure, it would be necessary, for the purpose of a cross-tabular analysis, to group the 64 sample villages into a limited number of categories. In view of the interrelationship between caste/community, occupation and educational development observed in the previous chapter, it is very likely that the composition of villages into broad categories based on a composite measure may not be much different from that obtained by a simple procedure.

Village category

The community context of the tribals is defined in this study in terms of the proportion of the non-tribals and development score of the village. For this purpose, the sample villages were first ordered according to the proportion of the tribal population in the villages, and then divided into four categories so that each one of them would consist of an almost equal number of villages. These categories are as under :

Village category	*Tribal population*	*No. of villages*	*Mean development score*
I	25—50 %	16	14.13
II	50—80 %	17	8.30
III	80—96 %	16	5.13
IV	96—100%	15	3.47

Since the proportion of the tribal population and the development score of the villages are highly correlated, such an ordered set of village categories corresponds fairly well to an ordered set of village categories based on their development score. It should be mentioned that all villages in category I have a relatively high development score (that is, greater than 8) and all villages in category IV have a relatively low development score (that is, lower than 8) ; but the two middle categories contain a mix of villages with high and low development scores. More specifically, 7 villages in category II and 3 villages in category III have a high development score (that is, greater than 8) and the remaining villages in these two categories have a low development score (that is, lower than 8). In view of such a mix of villages (with low and high development scores) in the two middle categories, they are sub-divided, later on in this chapter, on the basis of their development scores, as under :

Village category	*Tribal population*	*No. of villages*	*Mean development score*
II(a)	50—80%	7	12.29
II(b)	50—80%	10	4.80
III(a)	80—96%	3	9.30
III(b)	80—96%	13	4.15

Before examining the relationship between the village categories and educational development of the tribals, it is necessary to demonstrate that the village categories based on the proportion of the non-tribal population and development score are also indicative of their corresponding composition in terms of caste/community, occupation and educational development.

Social composition of village categories

Caste/community

The caste/community-wise percentage distribution of the households in each village category is given in Table 4.1. The overall distribution of households in the sample villages seems to be fairly representative of the households in a tribal area. About

TABLE 4.1 : **Percentage distribution households, by caste/ community, separately for each village category**

Caste/community	Village category I	II	III	IV	Total
1. S.T.	40.8	60.8	88.3	97.5	62.9
2. S.C.	7.2	3.5	1.7	0.3	4.2
3. Muslim	9.4	5.4	1.8	0.1	5.6
4. Parsi/Christian	0.5	0.2	0.3	0.5	0.4
5. Hindu : low	9.2	5.9	3.5	0.4	5.9
6. Hindu : middle	6.3	5.5	0.3	0.2	4.1
7. Hindu : high I	11.2	9.5	2.2	0.5	7.6
8. Hindu : high II	15.5	9.3	1.8	0.5	9.2
Total	100.0 (6463)	100.0 (4327)	100.0 (2575)	100.0 (2496)	100.0 (15861)

*Since the total number of Parsi and Christian households in the sample villages is very small, and since their educational development is comparably high, these two categories have been grouped in this table.

63 per cent of the households in the sample villages belong to the scheduled tribes. Additional one-fourth of the households are of Hindus ; a majority of them are of the high-caste Hindus. Harijans, Muslims and the low-caste Hindus constitute about 5 per cent each. Only a very small proportion of Parsi and Christian households is found in the sample villages.

The caste/community-wise distribution of the households in different village categories brings out their differential composition. The percentage of the tribal households in village category I is only 40.8 per cent and it increases to 60.8 per cent in category II, to 88.3 per cent in category III and to 97.5 per cent in category IV. It should be noted that the percentages of households belonging to the other castes/communities decrease as one moves from category I to category IV. The percentage of the high-caste Hindus is about 26 per cent in category I, but it is reduced to only 1 per cent in category IV. Similarly, the percentages of the low-caste Hindus, the middle-caste Hindus and Muslims are reduced as one moves from category I to IV. Such a caste/community-wise distribution of the households in these village categories indicates rather a distinct social composition of villages in the tribal area. At one end of the village categories, that is in category I, the villages are evidently non-tribal and are composed of a relatively high proportion (about one-fourth) of high-caste Hindu households. At the other end of the village categories, that is in category IV, the villages are composed almost entirely of the tribal households. Although the villages in the middle two categories are composed of a fairly high proportion of the tribal households, they indicate a good mix of the non-tribal households between the two extremes. Such a differential mix of households belonging to different castes/communities in the four village categories provides an adequate opportunity to examine the relationship of community contexts to educational development of the tribals in the tribal sub-plan area.

Occupation

The percentage distribution of households, showing occupation of the heads of households in each village category, is given in Table 4.2. It is found that the percentage of the household heads employed in each of the two white-collar categories is the highest

TABLE 4 2 : **Percentage distribution of households, showing occupation of heads of households, separately for each village category**

Occupation of heads of households		Village category				Total
		I	II	III	IV	
1.	Retired, N.A.	1.1	0.3	0.2	0.1	0.6
2.	Agricultural labourers	21.7	21.0	17.4	10.7	19.1
3.	Other labourers	6.6	8.2	4.3	4.0	6.2
4.	Artisans	14.6	7.9	3.3	1.7	8.9
5.	Farm owners/ Livestock farmers	29.5	45.6	66.3	77.2	47.4
6.	Clerks, etc.	13.1	10.0	4.7	4.4	9.5
7	Officers/Professionals	13.4	7.1	3.9	2.0	8.3
	Total	100.0 (6463)	100.0 (4327)	100.0 (2575)	100.0 (2496)	100.0 (15861)

in village category I ; it decreases as one moves from category I to category IV. A similar pattern is found with regard to the percentage of the household heads employed as agricultural labourers, artisans and other labourers ; there is only a slight reversal in the percentage of other labourers in category II. Only with regard to the percentage of the household heads who are farm owners, it is found that the percentage increases as one moves from category I to category IV. In view of the differential socio-economic status of various categories of occupation, it is evident from the table that the four village categories correspond to the proportion of the heads of households who are employed in the two categories of white-collar occupations.

Educational development

The data regarding the various indicators of educational development in different village categories are given in Tables 4.3 and 4.4. It is found from Table 4.3 that the percentage of households with no member among males/females having attained any formal education is the lowest in category I, and that it systematically increases as one moves from category I to category IV. Similarly, the percentages of the households having at least one member among males/females in the four categories of post-primary education are the highest in category I ; they generally decrease as

TABLE 4.3 : **Percentage distribution of households, showing the highest level of education attained by any male/famale member of the household, separately for each village category**

Highest level of education attained		Village category I	II	III	IV	Total
				MALES		
1.	Nil	26.8	35.0	36.3	43.2	33.2
2.	1—4 Std.	18.9	20.2	26.0	20.4	20.6
3.	5—7 Std.	19.9	18.5	16.9	14.9	18.3
4.	8—10 Std.	14.3	12.5	11.6	12.2	13.0
5.	S.S.C., Some còllege	14.3	10.5	7.6	7.2	11.1
6.	Graduate	5.8	3.2	1.6	2.1	3.8
	Total	100.0 (6463)	100.0 (4327)	100.0 (2575)	100.0 (2496)	100.0 (15861)
				FEMALES		
1.	Nil	54.6	65.9	68.1	72.6	62.7
2.	1—4 Std.	17.0	14.6	17.2	12.7	15.7
3.	5—7 Std.	11.9	9.2	6.8	6.5	9.5
4.	8—10 Std.	9.3	5.8	4.7	4.8	6.9
5.	S.S.C., Some college	5.9	4.0	2.9	3.0	4.4
6.	Graduate	1.3	0.4	0.4	0.4	0.8
	Total	100.0 (6463)	100.0 (4327)	100.0 (2575)	100.0 (2496)	100.0 (15861)

one moves from category I to category IV, but only in category III a slight reversal in this pattern is seen. With regard to the percentage of the households with at least one member in the 1-4 standard category, there is no clear pattern in the four village categories. There is, however, an overall correspondence in the proportion of the non-tribals in the village categories and the percentage of households with at least one member among males/females in the various categories of education. The higher proportion of the non-tribals in a village category, the greater percentage of households with at least one member having attained a high level of education.

It is found from Table 4.4 that the percentage of the 5-17 years old illiterate boys/girls is the lowest in category I; it

TABLE 4.4 : **Percentages showing education among boys/girls in the age-group 5-17 years, separately for each village category**

	Education	Village category				Total
		I	II	III	IV	
				BOYS		
1.	No information (presumably literate)	0.8	4.6	4.3	1.6	2.6
2.	Illiterate	23.3	37.1	38.2	41.0	32.3
3.	Attending primary school	44.9	33.2	39.1	36.2	39.3
4.	Attending middle school	25.1	21.1	15.9	18.7	21.5
5.	Attending high school	5.9	4.0	2.5	2.5	4.3
	Total	100.0 (6135)	100.0 (4475)	100.0 (2441)	100.0 (2256)	100.0 (15307)
				GIRLS		
1.	No information (presumably literate)	1 2	2.2	3.0	0.1	1.6
2.	Illiterate	36.0	51.8	56.8	57.4	47.0
3.	Attending primary school	37.7	29.0	28.4	25.9	32.0
4.	Attending middle school	21.6	15.2	10.8	14.6	17.0
5.	Attending high school	3.5	1.8	1.0	2.0	2.4
	Total	100.0 (4817)	100.0 (3370)	100.0 (1951)	100.0 (1688)	100.0 (11825)

systematically increases as one moves from category I to category IV. Similarly, the percentage of boys/girls attending primary/middle/high schools are the highest in category I and the lowest in category IV. Although there are certain small reversals in the two middle categories in this regard, there is an overall correspondence in the proportion of the non-tribals in a village category and the percentages of boys/girls who are attending primary/middle/high schools. It should also be noted that the boys and girls about whom we do not have any information have presumably attended school sometimes, but were drop-outs at the time of the study. We do not know when they dropped out of school.

There are usual sex differences in the various indicators of educational development in the four village categories. There is a positive and strong relationship between the proportion of the non-tribals in a village and the educational progress of males and females in general, and of boys and girls in particular. Thus, the data presented in Tables 4.3 and 4.4 clearly indicate that the proportion of the non-tribals in a village is positively related to its educational development.

In sum, caste/community, occupation of the heads of households and educational development are positively related to the proportion of the non-tribals in the village. These data demonstrate that an ordered classification of villages based on the proportion of the non-tribals provides a simple measure of their socio-economic status in terms of caste/community, occupation and educational development.

Our analysis of the data presented so far has been geared to the purpose of establishing the differential social composition of the sample villages. We shall now examine whether and to what extent the community context of the villages is related to the educational development of the tribals.

Community contexts and educational development of tribals

The tribal households are more or less equitably distributed in the four village categories : 26.4 per cent in category I, 26.4 per cent in category II, 22.8 per cent in category III, and 24.4 per cent in category IV. The community contexts of the tribals in different village categories are markedly different. The tribals in category I live amidst preponderent non-tribals, including a fairly high proportion of the high-caste Hindus. They live in a community where many household heads hold white-collar jobs. The educational development of their community as a whole is impressive—about three-fourths of the boys and two-thirds of the girls attend school. In such community contexts, we would expect a conducive community environment for education and, therefore, a relatively high level of educational development of the tribals. At the other end, almost all households in village category IV are tribal, only a very small proportion of the household heads is employed in white-collar occupations, and their educational development is very low. In such community contexts, we would expect a relatively low level of educational development of the tribals.

Village category and educational development

The cumulative percentage distribution of the tribal households, showing the highest level of education attained by any member among males/females, is given in Table 4.5. It is found that the proportion of the non-tribal households in the village category and the percentage of the tribal households with at least one member among males/females are inversely related. For example, while in category I, only 0.8 per cent of the tribal households have at least one male member who is a graduate, it is twice as much in category IV. The cumulative percentage in the other categories of education, for males as well as females, generally

TABLE 4.5 : **Cumulative percentage distribution of tribal households, showing the highest level of education attained by any member among males/females, separately for each village category**

Highest level of education		Village category				Total
		I	II	III	IV	
		MALES				
1.	Graduate	0.8	1.2	0.7	1.6	1.1
2.	S.S.C., Some college	5 8	6.4	6.9	8.5	7.0
3.	8—10 Std.	13.1	16.3	17.2	20.6	16.8
4.	5—7 Std.	28.1	31.5	33.8	35.3	32.1
5.	1—4 Std.	52.9	53.2	60.8	56.0	55.5
6.	Nil	100.0	100.0	100.0	100.0	100.0
		(2636)	(2630)	(2275)	(2434)	(9975)
		FEMALES				
1.	Graduate	0.0	0.2	0.3	0.3	0.2
2.	S.S.C., Some college	1.5	2.1	2.1	3.1	2.2
3.	8—10 Std.	3.9	4.6	5.6	7.7	5.4
4.	5—7 Std.	8.3	9.3	11.2	14.1	10.7
5.	1—4 Std.	21.4	21.8	28.3	26.5	24.4
6.	Nil	100.0	100.0	100.0	100.0	100.0
		(2636)	(2630)	(2275)	(2434)	(9975)

indicate a similar pattern. It is observed that the greater the proportion of the tribal households in a village category, the higher the proportion of the tribal households with at least one member among males/females having a relatively high level of education. It should be noted that the development of education among the tribals in general is very low and, therefore, the smaller percentages in the categories of high levels of education are likely to be the results of random fluctuations.

The cumulative percentages, showing education among the tribal boys/girls, are given in Table 4.6. There is an inverse relationship between the proportion of the non-tribals in a village category and the level of education among boys/girls. For example, while 49.7 per cent of the boys and 30.6 per cent of the girls in category I are attending primary/middle/high schools, 56.1 per cent of the boys and 41.4 per cent of the girls in category IV are attending schools. On the other hand, while 46.1 per cent of the boys and 67.2 per cent of the girls

TABLE 4.6 : **Cumulative percentages showing education among tribal boys/girls in the age-group 5-17, separately for each village category**

Education of boys/girls	Village category I	II	III	IV	Total
			BOYS		
1. *Attending*					
(a) High school	1.5	2.6	2.0	2.5	2.2
(b) Middle school	13.7	16.9	16.9	20.4	16.9
(3) Primary school	49.7	45.3	54.5	56.1	50.9
2. *Illiterate*	95.8	93.8	95.1	97.4	95.4
3. *No informatian*	100.0	100.0	100.0	100.0	100.0
	(2362)	(2875)	(2172)	(2214)	(9623)
			GIRLS		
1. *Attending*					
(a) High school	0.8	1.0	0.7	1.9	1.1
(b) Middle school	7.1	8.6	9.2	16.1	10.1
(c) Primary school	30.6	30.1	36.3	41.4	34.3
2. *Illiterate*	97.8	97.1	96.9	98.9	97.6
3. *No information*	100.0	100.0	100.0	100.0	100.0
	(1776)	(2079)	(1748)	(1666)	(7269)

in village category I are illiterate, 41.3 per cent of the boys and 57.4 per cent of the girls in village category IV are illiterate. The percentages of illiterate boys/girls and the percentages of boys/girls attending schools in the two middle categories fall within the range of the two extreme categories. Although there are some reversals in the pattern, there is a fair correspondence in the percentages showing the various indicators of educational development of the tribals and the proportion of the tribal households in the four village categories. Thus, the hypothesis of a positive relationship between the proportion of the non-tribals and the educational development of the tribals in a village community does not have any supporting evidence in this study. It is still necessary to probe this matter further so as to rule out the possibility of any confounding influence of other variables. There are two important points to be considered in this regard. One, the observed relationship might have been somewhat influenced by the mix of villages with high and low development scores in the two middle categories. Second, there is a possibility that the differential educational development of the tribals in the four village categories might be due to the differential distribution of tribals engaged in white-collar workers, farm owners and agricultural labourers in the village categories.

Village category and educational development, controlling for development score

Although there is a fair correspondence in the proportion of the non-tribals and the development score of the villages in the four village categories, separating the two middle categories that contain a mix of villages with high and low development scores would provide a distinct classification of the villages so as to examine whether the development score is related to the educational development of the tribals. We should then examine how the proportion of the non-tribals in a village community is related to the educational development of the tribals even when we control for development scores. The relevant data are given in Tables 4.7 and 4.8. It may be noted that the two middle village categories are sub-divided into two categories each, the category (a) containing the villages with a high development score, and the category (b) containing the villages with a low

TABLE 4.7 : **Cumulative percentage distribution of tribal households showing the highest level of education attained by any member among males/females, by development scores and village category**

Highest level of education attained		High development scores				Low development scores			
		Village category				Village category			
		I	II(a)	III(a)	Total	II(b)	III(b)	IV	Total
					MALES				
1.	Graduate	0.8	1.2	0.8	0.9	1.1	0.7	1.6	1.2
2.	S.S.C., Some college	5.8	6.2	7.9	6.2	6.6	6.7	8.5	7.5
3.	8–10 Std.	13.1	16.4	18.8	14.8	16.2	16.8	20.6	18 3
4.	5—7 Std.	28.1	29.8	30.4	28.9	33.2	34.9	35.3	34.7
5.	1—4 Std.	52.9	50.4	42.6	50.9	56.1	66.4	56.0	59.4
6.	Nil	100.0	100.0	100.0	100.0	100.0	100.0	100.0	100.0
		(2636)	(1363)	(533)	(4532)	(1267)	(1742)	(2434)	(5443)
					FEMALES				
1.	Graduate	0.0	0.1	0.4	0.1	0.2	0.3	0.3	0.3
2.	S.S.C., Some college	1.5	1.7	4.1	1.9	2.5	1.4	3.1	2.4
3.	8—10 Std.	3.9	3.9	10.1	4.7	5.3	4.2	7.7	6.0
4.	5—7 Std.	8.3	9.3	16.9	9.7	9.3	9.5	14.1	11.5
5.	1—4 Std.	21.4	21.5	27.6	22.2	22.1	28.5	26.5	26.1
6.	Nil	100.0	100.0	100.0	100.0	100.0	100.0	100.0	100.0
		(2636)	(1363)	(533)	(4532)	(1267)	(1742)	(2434)	(5443)

development score. The data in these two tables have been arranged in a cumulative manner. It will facilitate alternative examinations of the data in the event that one desires to use different cutting points for defining a relatively high level of educational development of the tribals.

It is found from these two tables that there is a negative relationship between the development score of villages and the educational development of the tribals residing in them. In other words, the percentages of households in the various categories of education, showing that at least one member among males/females has attained education up to that level (see total columns), are greater for the villages with a low development score than those for the villages with a high development score. Similarly, the percentages of boys/girls attending schools are greater for the villages with a low development score than those for the villages with a high development score. Further, within each category of development score, it is found that the general pattern of a negative relationship between the village category (proportion of the non-tribals) and the educational development of the tribals continues. No doubt, there are some reversals in this relationship ; still, the overall direction of the relationship is clearly not supportive of the hypothesis of a positive relationship between the socio-economic status of community (as measured in terms of the proportion of the non-tribals) and the educational development of the tribals. Thus, even when we control for development scores, there is a somewhat positive relationship between the proportion of the tribals in a village and their educational development.

Village category and occupational distribution

In view of a positive relationship between occupation of the heads of households and educational development, it is necessary to examine whether there is a differential distribution of occupation of the heads of the tribal households in the village categories and whether it can explain the differential educational development of the tribals in them.

The percentage distribution of the tribal households, showing occupation of the heads of the households, is given separately for each village category, in Table 4.9. It is found that the per-

TABLE 4.8 : **Cumulative percentages showing education among tribal boys/girls in the age-group 5-17, by development scores and village category**

Education of boys/girls	High development scores				Low development scores			
	Village category				Village category			
	I	II(a)	III(a)	Total	II(b)	III(b)	IV	Total
BOYS								
1. *Attending*								
(a) High school	1.5	2.8	3.6	2.1	2.5	1.6	2.5	2.2
(b) Middle school	13.7	18.0	20.1	15.7	15.9	16.1	20.4	17.8
(c) Primary school	49.7	46.7	43.2	48.1	44.0	56.9	56.1	53.0
2. *Illiterate*	96.8	93.6	99.5	95.4	94.0	94.1	97.4	95.4
3. *No information*	100.0	100.0	100.0	100.0	100.0	100.0	100.0	100.0
	(2362)	(1340)	(389)	(4091)	(1535)	(1783)	(2214)	(5532)
GIRLS								
1. *Attending*								
(a) High school	0.8	0.7	2.0	0.9	1.4	0.3	1.9	1.2
(b) Middle school	7.1	10.3	12.4	8.8	7.0	8.2	16.1	11.1
(c) Primary school	30.6	32.8	30.9	31.4	27.3	37.9	41.4	36.6
2. *Illiterate*	97.8	97.7	98.8	97.9	96.4	96.3	98.8	97.3
3. *No information*	100.0	100.0	100.0	100.0	100.0	100.0	100.0	100.0
	(1776)	(1042)	(405)	(3223)	(1037)	(1343)	(1666)	(4046)

TABLE 4.9 : **Percentage distribution of tribal households showing occupation of heads of households, controlling for development scores and village category**

Occupation of heads of households	High development scores				Low development scores				
	Village category				Village category				Grand Total
	I	II(a)	III(a)	Total	II(b)	III(b)	IV	Total	
1. Retired, N.A.	0.6	0.2	0.0	0.4	0.0	0.2	0.1	0.1	10.2
2. Agricultural labourers	49.4	22.7	8.8	36.6	39.8	22.0	10.9	21.3	28.2
3. Other labourers	9.9	14.7	16.1	12.1	3.9	4.1	3.0	3.0	7.1
4. Artisans	3.3	6.5	1.9	4.1	0.9	2.0	1.8	1.6	2.7
5. Farm owners/ Livestock farmers	27.4	43.3	66.3	36.7	50.3	70.4	77.8	69.1	54.5
6. Clerks, etc.	7.5	11.4	5.6	8.5	3.8	2.7	4.2	3.6	5.8
7 Professionals/Officers/ Businessmen	1.9	1.2	1.3	1.6	1.3	1.7	1.1	1.3	1.5
Total	100.0 (2636)	100.0 (1363)	100.0 (533)	100.0 (4532)	100.0 (1267)	100.0 (1742)	100.0 (2434)	100.0 (5443)	100.0 (9975)

centages of the tribal household heads employed in the two white-collar occupations are higher in the villages with a high development score than those in the villages with a low development score ; they are also higher in the villages in category I than those in the villages in category IV. Thus, we cannot expect that the white-collar occupation of the household heads provides a clue to the differential educational development of the tribals in the four village categories. Nonetheless, there is a positive relationship between the proportion of the non-tribals and the percentage of the tribal household heads employed as agricultural labourers in different village categories. There is also an inverse relationship between the proportion of the non-tribals and the percentage of the tribal farm owners in the village categories. While about one-half of the tribal household heads are agricultural labourers in category I, this proportion generally decreases as one moves from category I to category IV. Only one-tenth of the tribal household heads in category IV are agricultural labourers. But, while about one-fourth of the tribal household heads are farm owners in category I, this proportion increases as one moves from category I to category IV. Almost three-fourths of the tribal household heads in category IV are farm owners. Such a distribution of occupation of the tribal household heads in the village categories indicates the need for controlling this variable while examining the educational development of the tribals in different village categories.

Village category and educational development, controlling for development score and occupation

We notice from Table 4.9 that the heads of 54.5 per cent of the tribal households in the sample villages are farm owners and the heads of 28.2 per cent of them are agricultural labourers. It will, therefore, be possible to examine the relationship of the village category to educational development within each of these two occupational categories. But, in view of a smaller percentage of households in the two categories of white-collar occupations, they have been collapsed. Accordingly, the relevant data for examining the relationship between the proportion of the non-tribals (village category) and educational development of the tribals, controlling for development score, are given separately for (a) white-collar workers, (b) farm owners, and (c) agricultural labourers in Tables 4.10 and 4.11. Several observations should be made from these tables.

First, the positive relationship between occupation of the household heads and the various indicators of educational development, found earlier in chapter 3 for all households in the sample villages, also holds true for the tribal households. The higher the level of occupation of the household head, the higher the level of education attained by any member among males/females ; similarly, the higher the level of occupation of the household head, the greater the percentages of boys/girls attending high/middle/primary schools. This holds true even when we control for development score.

It is necessary to examine in detail the relationship between the occupation of the household heads and the percentages of boys and girls who are attending school. Among white-collar households, the percentages of the boys attending school range from 74 per cent in village category II (b) to 99.1 per cent in village category IV, and the percentages of the girls attending school range from 70 per cent in village category III (a) to 84.6 per cent in village category IV. Such a range of the percentages of boys/girls attending school indicates an increasing trend towards schooling in the younger generation. But, unfortunately this trend is very strongly related to the socio-economic status of the family as indicated by the type of occupation of the head. While the household heads, who are employed in white-collar occupations, seem to be concerned about enrolling their children in school, the same does not hold good for the farm owners and the agricultural labourers. Among the farm owners, the range of the percentage of boys attending school is from 49.2 per cent to 63 per cent, and that of girls attending schools is from 26.1 per cent to 41.4 per cent. Similar percentages in the case of the agricultural labourers are disappointingly low ; the range of the percentage of boys attending school is from 22.7 per cent to 49.8 per cent and that of girls attending school is from 5.2 per cent to 35.3 per cent. Such a situation calls for special efforts to boost enrolment of the school-age children from the apparently poor sections of the tribals.

Secondly, the negative relationship between the development

TABLE 4.10 : **Cumulative percentage distribution of tribal households, showing the highest level of education attained by any member among males/females, by development scores, village category, and occupation of heads of households**

Highest level of education attained	High development scores				Low development scores			
	Village category				Village category			
	I	II(a)	III(a)	Total	II(b)	III(b)	IV	Total
	1	2	3	4	5	6	7	8
(a) White-collar occupations								
MALES								
1. S.S.C. & above	29.8	25.0	43.2	29.1	40.6	43.4	47.7	44.8
2. 5—10 std., S.S.C. fail	77.8	68.6	78.3	74.4	86.0	90.8	86.2	87.4
3. 1—4 std.	95.9	87.8	86.4	92.1	89.1	96.4	93.9	93.7
4. Nil	100.0	100.0	100.0	100.0	100.0	100.0	100.0	100.0
	(248)	(172)	(37)	(457)	(64)	(76)	(130)	(270)
FEMALES								
1. S.S.C. & above	10.5	8.1	29.7	11.2	15.7	17.1	13.1	14.8
2. 5—10 std.; S.S.C. fail	39.1	30.8	54.0	37.2	43.8	48.7	52.3	49.2
3. 1—4 std.	59.3	54.6	62.1	57.8	71.9	77.6	66.9	71.1
4. Nil	100.0	100.0	100.0	100.0	100.0	100.0	100.0	100.0
	(248)	(172)	(37)	(457)	(64)	(76)	(130)	(270)

TABLE 4.10 : (*Contd.*)

		1	2	3	4	5	6	7	8
		(b) Farm-owners/Live-stock farmers							
		MALES							
1.	S.S.C. & above	6.9	5.1	6.2	6.2	8.3	6.2	6.9	6.9
2.	5—10 std., S.S.C. fail	32.1	31·3	30.6	31.6	42.8	35.2	35.2	36.5
3.	1—4 std.	55.5	53.8	42.8	52.3	72.4	67.3	56.4	62.7
4.	Nil	100.0	100.0	100.0	100.0	100.0	100.0	100.0	100.0
		(723)	(590)	(353)	(1666)	(638)	(1226)	(1894)	(3758)
		FEMALES							
1.	S.S.C. & above	1.1	1.0	3.1	1.5	3.1	1.0	2.7	2.2
2.	5—10 std., S.S.C. fail	7.5	7.1	17.5	9.5	11.7	8.9	12.8	11.3
3.	1—4 std.	19.4	17.6	29.4	20.9	27.2	28.5	25.3	26.6
4.	Nil	100.0	100.0	100.0	100.0	100.0	100.0	100.0	100.0
		(723)	(590)	(353)	(1666)	(638)	(1226)	(1894)	(3758)

TABLE 4.10 : (*Contd.*)

		1	2	3	4	5	6	7	8
		(c) Agricultural Labourers							
		MALES							
1.	S.S.C. & above	1.6	1.9	8.5	1.9	1.0	1.8	3.4	1.8
2.	5—10 std., S.S.C. fail	16.5	17.2	25.5	16.9	15.3	24.9	19.9	19.5
3.	1—4 std.	42.5	37.9	31.9	41.4	32.3	60.3	46.2	44.8
4.	Nil	100.0	100.0	100.0	100.0	100.0	100.0	100.0	100.0
		(1303)	(309)	(47)	(1659)	(505)	(384)	(266)	(1155)
		FEMALES							
1.	S.S.C. & above	0.3	0.9	—	0.5	0.2	—	1.5	0.4
2.	5—10 std., S.S.C. fail	3.0	5.1	4.2	3.7	1.6	4.1	9.8	4.3
3.	1—4 std.	14.6	14.8	6.3	14.4	8.3	20.0	25.2	16.1
4.	Nil	100.0	100.0	100.0	100.0	100.0	100.0	100.0	100.0
		(1303)	(309)	(47)	(1659)	(505)	(384)	(266)	(1155)

TABLE 4.11 : **Cumulative percentages showing education among tribal 5-17 years old boys/girls, by development scores, village category and occupation of heads of households**

Education	High development scores				Low development scores			
	Village category				Village category			
	I	II (a)	III (a)	Total	II (b)	III (b)	IV	Total
	1	2	3	4	5	6	7	8
(a) White-collar occupations								
BOYS								
1. *Attending—*								
(a) High school	2.8	6.0	5.6	4.2	13.0	2.5	6.8	7.3
(b) Middle school	28.3	32.7	38.9	30.5	45.4	37.9	44.4	42.8
(c) Primary school	82.9	88.7	83.3	85.2	74.0	88.5	99.1	89.0
2. *Illiterate*	100.0	100.0	100.0	100.0	100.0	100.0	100.0	100.0
	(216)	(150)	(18)	(384)	(77)	(79)	(117)	(273)
GIRLS								
1. *Attending—*								
(a) High school	4.2	0.9	3.3	2.9	6.3	1.5	2.9	3.2
(b) Middle school	28.2	31.3	30.0	29.5	39.6	23.0	42.3	35.9
(c) Primary school	70.1	81.7	70.0	74.4	77.1	79.9	84.6	81.5
2. *Illiterate*	100.0	100.0	100.0	100.0	100.0	100.0	100.0	100.0
	(167)	(115)	(30)	(312)	(48)	(65)	(104)	(217)

TABLE 4.11 : (*Contd.*)

	1	2	3	4	5	6	7	8
				(b) Farm Owners/Livestock Farmers				
				BOYS				
1. *Attending—*								
(a) High school	3.0	3.9	4.0	3.5	3.2	2.0	2.7	2.6
(b) Middle school	18.2	21.5	24.2	20.4	20.7	17.6	21.9	20.3
(c) Primary school	58.5	50.2	49.2	53.7	58.7	63.0	58.9	60.2
2. *Illiterate*	100.0	100.0	100.0	100.0	100.0	100.0	100.0	100.0
	(693)	(586)	(248)	(1527)	(816)	(1169)	(1674)	(3659)
				GIRLS				
1. *Attending—*								
(a) High school	0.6	1.3	2.3	1.2	2.0	0.3	2.3	1.6
(b) Middle school	6.6	8.7	14.3	9.0	8.5	8.8	16.2	12.2
(c) Primary school	32.2	26.1	34.1	30.1	35.3	40.1	41.4	39.8
2. *Illiterate*	100.0	100.0	100.0	100.0	100.0	100.0	100.0	100.0
	(468)	(476)	(258)	(1202)	(537)	(924)	(1231)	(2692)

TABLE 4.11 : (*Contd.*)

	1	2	3	4	5	6	7	8
(c) Agricultural Labourers								
BOYS								
1. *Attending*—								
(a) High school	0.5	1.4	6.8	0.9	0.4	0.8	0.4	0.5
(b) Middle school	8.6	10.9	9.1	9.1	7.4	12.7	6.5	9.0
(c) Primary school	40.3	38.5	22.7	39.4	24.7	49.8	39.0	36.5
2. *Illiterate*	100.0	100.0	100.0	100.0	100.0	100.0	100.0	100.0
	(1070)	(283)	(44)	(1397)	(486)	(388)	(246)	(1120)
GIRLS								
1. *Attending*—								
(a) High school	0.3	—	2.6	0.4	—	—	0.5	0.1
(b) Middle school	3.3	7.8	—	4.2	1.1	4.6	10.0	4.5
(c) Primary school	19.7	28.5	5.2	21.0	11.2	27.9	35.3	22.7
2. *Illiterate*	100.0	100.0	100.0	100.0	100.0	100.0	100.0	100.0
	(873)	(217)	(38)	(1128)	(357)	(262)	(221)	(841)

score of the villages and the educational development of the tribals generally continues even when occupation of the household heads is controlled. In each of the three occupational categories, the percentages of the households with at least one member among males/females having attained a high level of education as well as the percentages of boys/girls attending school are generally greater for villages with a low development score than those for the villages with a high development score. There are only a few reversals, involving small percentage differences, in this pattern.

Thirdly, in each of the three occupational categories, the percentages of the households with at least one member among males/females having attained a high level of education as well as the percentages of boys/girls attending school are generally greater for the village category IV than those for the village category I. Since all the sample villages in category I are preponderently non-tribal with a high development score and all the sample villages in category IV are preponderantly tribal with a low development score, it seems clear that the hypothesis of a positive relationship between the community contexts of the villages (as measured in terms of the proportion of the non-tribal population) and the educational development of the tribals does not get any support from these data ; there is instead a negative relationship between them.

Fourthly, there is no clear relationship between the village category and the various indicators of the educational development of the tribals within each category of development score and occupation of the heads of households. However, if we were to compare the percentages in the two extreme village categories within each set of high/low development score and occupational category (that is, the percentages in category I with those in category III (a) among the villages with a high development score, and the percentages in category II (b) with those in category IV among the villages with a low development score), it is found that in about three-fourths of the comparisons the percentages indicating a higher level of educational development of the tribals are greater for those residing in the villages with a greater proportion of the tribal population than for those residing in the villages with a smaller proportion of the tribal population. That is, the percentages are greater in village category III (a) than those in village category I, and they are greater in village category IV than those in village category II (b).

Fifthly, it must also be noted that the usual sex differences in the various indicators of educational development of the tribals are found even when we control for development score of the villages, occupation of the household heads, and village category.

Finally, the impact of differences in development score, village category and occupation of the household heads is generally additive. The cumulative percentages given in these tables allow the readers to use any cutting point for defining a high/low level of education. Suppose, if one were to define high level of educational development as at least one member among males having attained S.S.C. or a higher level of education, it is found that the highest percentage (47.7%) is in the category of those employed in white-collar occupations and residing in the villages with a low development score and almost one hundred per cent tribal population. As against this, only about 1.6 per cent of the households in the category of those employed as agricultural labourers and residing in villages with a high development score and preponderantly non-tribal population have at least one member among males who has attained that level of education. One can similarly examine these data from several angles and would notice such a general pattern.

In brief, the cross-tabular analysis presented in this chapter clearly indicates that the educational development of the tribals in the sample villages is negatively related to the proportion of the non-tribals residing in the villages. Such a relationship generally continues, even when we control for development score of the villages and occupation of the household heads.

5

SOCIAL CLASS AND EDUCATIONAL DEVELOPMENT

A REVIEW of the available data regarding literacy, enrolment and educational attainment of the tribals in Gujarat (Chapter 1) indicates very clearly that they are at the lowest level of the educational pyramid. There is a considerable variation, in terms of sex, rural-urban residence and district, in their literacy rates. An analysis of the house-listing data of 64 villages (two villages from each taluka) in the tribal sub-plan area of Gujarat, supports the hypothesis that the educational attainment of various castes/communities is positively related to their level of social status (Chapter 3). An examination of the inter-tribe variation in educational attainment also shows that the educational attainment of the most progressive group among the tribals is comparable with only that of the scheduled castes. It is also found that occupation of the heads of the households is strongly related to caste/community on one hand and to educational attainment on the other hand. Such a general pattern of relationship between occupation of the heads of the households and educational attainment is also observed among different tribal groups. The educational attainment of the agricultural labourers is the lowest, that of the white-collar workers is the highest, and the educational attainment of the farm owners falls in-between these two categories. In Chapter 4, it was first demonstrated that the village categories, based on the proportion of the non-tribal population and development score of the villages, are also indicative of their corresponding composition in terms of caste/community, occupation and educational development. Examining the hypothesis regarding the relationship of community contexts to the educational attainment of the tribals, it was found that the educational attainment of the tribals in the sample villages is negatively related to the proportion of the non-tribals residing in the villages ; such a relationship generally continues, even when development score of the village and occupation of the heads of the households are controlled. Thus, our efforts has so far been to bring together a variety of macro-level and community contextual data that focused on the educational development of the tribals vis-a-vis the other castes/communities.

One important and consistent finding in the literature on sociology of education is that social class background of individuals is positively and strongly related to their educational and occupational aspirations and achievement. Even in the case of the weaker sections, such as the scheduled castes and the scheduled tribes, it has been often mentioned that the benefits of the government programmes of financial and other assistance for education accrue most to the children of the privileged among them. This is not surprizing since several factors associated with a high level of educational aspirations/achievement are positively correlated to socio-economic characteristics. It has been also found that home environment, normative climate, informational channels and motivational factors that are conducive to a high level of educational aspirations/achievement are positively correlated to high levels of socio-economic characteristics (Shah and Patel, 1977 : 90).

We shall now examine the relationship of educational development of the tribals to their social contexts, defined in terms of certain individual and familial characteristics. More specifically, the relationship between social class, awareness (that is, knowledge of facilities and progrommes of assistance, exposure to mass media and urban influences, and perceived importance of education) and educational development of the tribals will be examined in this and the next chapters. For this purpose, we shall analyze the interview data collected from 884 heads of the tribal households in the study area. In this chapter, we shall first describe certain background characteristics of the respondents and their family members. Then, a more detailed examination of the educational attainment of the tribals in the younger (5—17 years) as well as the older (18+ years) age-groups will be made.

We shall also examine (i) reasons for (a) no schooling and (b) dropping out during primary/secondary/college education, and (ii) educational/occupational expectations of the household heads of the school-going children. Later, the relationship between social class and educational attainment of the tribals will be examined. Finally, after an examination of the inter-tribe variation in their educational attainment, we shall attempt to find whether and to what extent the relationship between social class and educational attainment holds true for different tribal groups.

Background characteristics

The details regarding selected background characteristics of the sample households are given in Table 5.1. It can be seen from this table that the sample consists of a fair representation of different tribal groups. The tribewise percentage distribution of the sample households corresponds fairly well with that of the population of various tribal groups in the rural areas of Gujarat.

Only about one-third of the households are joint families. A

TABLE 5.1 : **Percentage distribution of respondents, by selected background characteristics**

A. Tribe and sub-tribe	
1. Bhil, etc. (Vasava, Dungri, Garasia, Dugri Bhil, Tadvi Bhil, Rawal Bhil, Garasia, other Bhils)	33.4
2. Dubla/Halpati, Talavia	6.7
3. Dhodia	8.6
4. Gamit, Padvi, Mavchi	6.2
5. Chaudhari, etc.	6.6
6. Rathwa	4.4
7. Dhanka, Tadvi, Valvi	11.0
8. Kokna, Kukni, Kokni	4.8
9. Nayaka	5.5
10. Patelia	2.8
11. Varli	3.1
12. Koli, Kolcha, Kunbi	3.7
13. Kotwalia, Vitolia	2,7
14. Pardhi, Borpi	0.5
	100.0
	(884)

TABLE 5.1 : (*Contd.*)

B. Type of family			
Individual			63.7
Joint			33.5
N.A.			2.8
			100.0
			(884)
C. Size of family			
1—5			41.3
6—10			51.6
11—15			6.7
16—21			0.4
			100.0
			(884)
D. Age and sex of members			
Age	*Males*	*Females*	*Total*
0—4	11.9	14.3	13.0
5—17	36.0	33.3	34.7
18+	52.1	52.4	52.3
Total	100.0	100.0	100.0
	(2977)	(2733)	(5710)

large majority of the tribal households are individual families. Their size is also small. About two-fifths of the households have upto five members, about one-half of them have six to ten members, and only about 7 per cent of the households have more than 10 members. The distribution of household members, by age and sex, indicates that the proportions of the males and the females in the age-groups 5—17 years and 18+ years are almost equal. The interview data contain information for about two thousand children of school-going age and about three thousand adults.

Highest level of education attained by any member among males/females in the households

A bivariate percentage distribution of the sample households showing the highest level of education attained by any member among males/females is given in Table 5.2. It is found that about one-fourth of the sample households are totally illiterate, that is.

TABLE 5.2 : **Bivariate percentage distribution of sample households showing the highest level of education attained by any male/female member**

Highest level of education attained by any female member	Highest level of education attained by any male member							
	Nil	1-4 std.	5-7 std.	8-10 std.	S.S.C.	Some college	Gradu- ate	Total
1. Nil	26.7	16.8	12.5	5.7	1.9	1.2	0.1	64.9
2. 1—4 std.	2.0	5.0	4.8	4.2	1.3	0.5	0.0	17.8
3. 5—7 std.	0.8	1.2	1.8	3.1	1.1	0.9	0.3	9.2
4. 8—10 std.	0.2	0.3	1.0	1.6	1.3	0.8	0.3	5.5
5. S.S.C.	0.1	0.1	0.1	0.3	0.0	0.3	0.2	1.1
6. Some college	0.0	0.1	0.0	0.6	0.0	0.2	0.2	1.1
7. Graduate	0.0	0.0	0.0	0.1	0.0	0.0	0.2	0.3
Total	29.8	23.5	20.2	15.6	5.6	3.9	1.3	99.9 (884)

none of the male or the female members in these households has obtained any education. About one-fourth of the households have at least one male or female member who has obtained education upto the fourth standard only. About one-fifth of the households have at least one male or female member who has obtained a middle level of education (5—7 standard). The percentage of the households having at least one male or female member, who has obtained secondary or higher level of education, decreases rapidly as one moves upward in the ladder of education. There are only about 6 per cent of the households having at least one male or female member who has obtained some post-matric education.

The marginals in this table give a comparative picture of the highest level of education obtained by any member among males and females in the sample households. There is the usual pattern of relatively very low percentage of households with at least one female member having obtained some formal education. It is hardly necessary to point out that such a situation is indicative of a lack of importance attached to female education among the tribals.

It should be noted that the educational attainment of the tribals, as found in the interview data, is more impressive than that observed from the house-listing data (Table 3.4). At one end, the percentage of households having no male member with any formal education is 29.8 per cent in the interview data against 44.5 per cent in the house-listing data. At the other end, the percentage of households with at least one male member having attained S.S.C. and above level of education is 11.0 per cent in the interview data as against 7.0 per cent in the house-listing data. A similar pattern is also found when we compare the data regarding the highest level of education attained by any female member. This obviously suggests that the estimate of the educational attainment of the tribals, based on the interview data, will be somewhat higher than that based on the house-listing data. This, in turn, means that the handicaps to an appropriate development of education among the tribals, that we might find from the interview data, may be somewhat less estimated than those existing in reality.

Education among household members

A detailed examination of education among the members in the sample households can be made from Table 5.3. This table shows

TABLE 5.3 : **Education by age and sex**

	5—17 years			18 years		
Education	Boys	Girls	Total	Males	Females	Total
1. Did not go to school at all	36.3	59.6	46.9	54.0	89.6	71.2
2. Dropped out during primary school (1—7 std.)	10.4	6.2	8.5	26.0	5.5	16.2
3. Dropped out during secondary school (8—11 std.)	2.4	1.1	1.8	12.4	3.1	7.9
4. Going to school	50.9	33.1	42.8	2.8	0.8	1.8
5. Dropped out during college or after completing S.S.C.	—	—	—	4.0	0.8	2.4
6. Obtained a college degree	—	—	—	0.8	0.2	0.5
Total	100.0 (1073)	100.0 (910)	100.0 (1983)	100.0 (1552)	100.0 (1434)	100.0 (2986)

education among 5+ years old members of the sample households, by age and sex. This table provides a comparative picture of education among males and females in the younger and the older generations. As would be expected, the educational attainment of the males is higher than that of the females ; similarly, the educational attainment of the younger generation (5—17 years) is higher than that of the older generation (18+ years). The percentages of boys and girls with no formal schooling and the percentages of those who dropped out during the primary and secondary stages of education are substantially lower in the younger generation than the respective percentages in the older generation.

It should be noted that 36.3 per cent of the boys and 59.8 per cent of the girls in the age-group 5—17 years did not go to school at all while 54 per cent of the adult males and 89.6 per cent of the adult females did not go to school at all. Such high percentages of those who did not go to school at all suggests a need to examine the possibility that almost all members in certain tribal households did not go to school at all. An examination of the percentages of household members without any schooling revealed that about one-half of the households had more than three-fourths of their adult males without any schooling, and about five-sixths of the households had more than three-fourths of their adult females without any schooling. The percentages of households having almost all the 5—17 years old boys and girls without any schooling were 27.9 per cent and 52.9 per cent, respectively. This is indicative of the changing picture of education among the tribals. And yet, it is a sad commentary on the variety of programmes of educational assistance to the tribals during the last three decades that about one-third of the boys and three-fifths of the girls in the 5—17 years age-group never went to school.

Educational background of the family and literacy among children

Not all of these 5—17 years old children are illiterate. However, some of them have managed to pick up little bit of reading/writing. It may be mentioned that 56.7 per cent of the sample households did not have any illiterate child in the age-group 5—17 years, about one-third of the households had one or two illiterate children, and the remaining about 10 per cent of the households had three or more illiterate children. An examination of the background of the illiterate children (280 boys and 407 girls) reveals that most of them come from families with no or little education among the adults in the family (Table 5.4). The most disturbing fact is that about 44 per cent of the illiterate boys and 18 per cent of the illiterate girls come from the households that have their counterpart members with some education. The case of these 120 illiterate boys and 72 illiterate girls dampens the usual expectation that once a member in the family obtains some education (that is once the norm or value of education is imbibed in a family), motivation for educating younger children, at least of the same sex, will be self-generating. It seems that there is an urgent-need for developing imaginative programmes for providing continuous motivation to parents and children who have not imbibed, through generations, the norm of education.

TABLE 5.4 : **Percentages of 5—17 years old illiterate boys and girls, by the highest level of education attained by any male/female member in the household**

Highest level of education attained by any male member	Illiterate Boys	Illiterate Girls	Highest level of education attained by any female member	Illiterate Boys	Illiterate Girls
1. Nil	56.1	34.6	1. Nil	88.5	82.3
2. 1—4 std.	20.7	24.6	2. 1—4 std.	6.1	12.8
3. 5—7 std.	10.0	22.4	3. 5—7 std.	2.5	2.9
4. 8—10 std.	6.8	10.3	4. 1—10 std.	1.8	1.5
5. S.S.C.	2.1	3.2	5. S.S.C.	0.7	0.5
6. Some college	4.3	4.2	6. Some college	0.4	—
7. Graduate	—	0.7	7. Graduate	—	—
Total	100.0 (280)	100.0 (407)	Total	100.0 (280)	100.0 (407)

Reasons for no schooling

As indicated in Table 5.3, about one-half of the adult males and about 90 per cent of the adult females had no schooling. When asked about the reasons in this regard, the household heads of about two-thirds of these males as well as females did not give any reason (Table 5.5). Presumably, there was no specific reason;

TABLE 5.5 : **Percentages showing reasons for no schooling, by age and sex**

Reasons	5—17 years		18+ years	
	Boys	Girls	Boys	Girls
1. Not mentioned	28.8	19.2	70.4	66.0
2. Lack of facilities for education in the village or around it	2.1	2.9	0.8	0.9
3. To help in the occupational/household activities of the family	30.3	33.1	13.3	13.4
4. Could not afford expenses for education	25.2	19.9	8.8	8.7
5. Not customary to study	0.5	16.8	0.1	7.7
6. Physical/mental handicaps	1.8	1.3	0.6	0.9
7. Others	11.3	6.8	6.0	2.4
Total	100.0 (389)	100.0 (543)	100.0 (839)	100.0 (1285)

may be, the norm of education had hardly trickled in their family and community when they were growing up. The usual reasons were mentioned for no schooling of about one fifth of the males and the females in this age-group—the children in the tribal society are required to help their family in its occupational and household activities or that the economic condition of their family is too poor to afford even the meagre expenses of primary education. In addition, no doubt, the tradition of not sending girls to school acts as a formidable factor in this regard

About one-third of the boys and four-fifth of the girls in the age-groups 5-17 years did not go to school at all (see Table 5.3). The need for or the practice of requiring young children to help the family in its occupational and household activities continues to be a major reason for no schooling of about one-third of the children. It is note-worthy that a lack of educational facilities in the village was mentioned as a reason by only a very small proportion of the respondents. About one-fourth of the boys and one-fifth of the girls could not go to school because of their poor economic condition; their parents could not afford the necessary expenses for studies. While we did not attempt to probe this aspect in detail, it seems that such a situation calls for examining the need for providing necessary schooling aids to the tribal students who attend school in their own village. The custom of not sending girls to school was mentioned as a deterant factor in the case of about one-sixth of the girls in the younger age-group. It is not enough to establish primary and secondary schools in villages; it is also necessary to strengthen extension work to persuade parents to send their children to school.

Reasons for dropping out from school

As noted earlier (Table 5.3), the percentages of dropouts during the primary and secondary stages of schooling are lower for the younger generation than those for the older generation. But this is true for boys rather than for girls. The percentage of the girls dropping out during the primary stage of schooling in the older generation is almost the same as that in the younger generation; this indicates, given a low enrolment percentage of the girls, the continuation of a dismal situation of female education among the tribals. Examining the reason for droping out (Table 5.6), it is found that the two major factors that are associated with no schooling operate also for dropping out from school. The demand on children to help their family in its occupational and household activities and inability of their parents to afford expenses for continuing schooling dominate the scene. It may be noted that 14 per cent of the parents (N=392) whose sons were attending school and 15.6 per cent of the parents (N=231) whose daughters were attending school reported that their children do not attend school daily. In addition, the parents of 15.3 per cent of the boys and 19.1 per cent of the girls reported that their children did not attend school punctually. Thus, a lack of regular and punctual attendance in school by the children seems to be a result of the demands made on them by their family in its household and occupational activities.

The third major reason for dropping out from school is a failure in examination. Although we do not have any quantitative data, the general impression gathered during the field data collection is that irregular attendance leads to failure in examination and that results almost immediately into dropping out. Also, inability of the parents to help their children in homework and their indifferent attitudes toward schooling in general seem to be responsible for rather an almost immediate decision to drop out. Such a situation calls for strengthening several of the one-teacher

TABLE 5.6 : **Reasons for dropping out during primary/secondary/college education, by age and sex**

Reasons	5-- 17 years				18+ years					
	Primary		Secondary		Primary		Secondary		College	
	Boys	Girls	Boys	Girls	Boys	Girls	Boys	Girls	Boys	Girls*
1. Not mentioned	5.4	13.1	[6]	[2]	6.9	12.5	11.5	4.5	22.6	[3]
2. Lack of facilities for education in the village or around it	4.5	8.2	[1]	—	7.7	2.5	5.7	9.1	8.1	—
3. To help in the occupational/household activities of the family	34.7	31.2	[6]	[1]	47.6	42.4	25.5	29.5	14.5	—
4. Got a job	2.7	1.6	[1]	—	4.2	—	15.6	2.3	30.6	[4]
5. Failed, inability to study	19.6	13.1	[7]	[2]	8.2	10 0	18.8	13.6	6.5	[1]
6. Did not feel necessary to study further	2.7	4.9	—	[2]	2.5	3.8	4.7	9.1	3.2	[2]
7. Could not afford expenses for education	25.0	9.8	[4]	[1]	19.9	7.5	13.5	—	12.9	—
8. Not customary to study further	—	9.8	—	[2]	1.5	17.5	—	11.4	—	—
9. Physical/Mental handicaps	1.8	1.6	[1]	—	—	—	—	—	—	—
10. Married ; others	3.6	6.7	—	—	1.5	3.8	4.7	20.5	1.6	[1]
Total	100.0 (112)	100.0 (56)	(26)	(10)	100.0 (403)	100.0 (80)	100.0 (192)	100.0 (44)	100.0 (62)	(11)

*Frequencies are given in these columns.

primary schools in villages and revamping the system of schooling so as to eliminate the need for parents to help their children in their school work. Parents' desire regarding education and occupation of their children may be a major factor associated with dropping out of school or early completion of the educational career of school-going children. We shall, therefore, examine the desire of the household heads regarding education and occupation o the school-going children.

Desire regarding education and occupation of school-going children

The percentages showing the desire of the household heads regarding the level of education their children should attain are given, separately for boys and girls who are currently studying at different levels of education, in Table 5.7. This table indicates that most household heads desire their school-going children to attain as much education as they can or would like to attain. Such a generalized response is perhaps indicative of their indifference in the matter. The household heads of about one-fourth of the boys and about one eighth of the girls desire their children to be graduates. In addition, the household heads of about one-fifth of the boys and one-fourth of the girls desire their children to complete high school education. Although their educational expectations are lower for the girls than those for the boys, the table clearly shows that an increasing proportion of the tribal parents desire their children, once they continue to move upward in schooling, to complete secondary or college education. The household heads of about one-fourth of the girls desire that their daughters complete only primary or some post-primary education. This is indicative of a generally low level of felt need for girls' education in the traditional tribal society.

The desire of parents regarding education of their children should generally be positively related to their occupational expectations. However, it is found from Table 5.8 that the household heads of about one-third of the boys and about one-half of the girls have not indicated their occupational expectations. This probably indicates that these tribal parents do not associate the need for education of their children with their occcupational expectations. Even in the case of those household heads who indicated specific occupational expectations, it is found that their

TABLE 5.7 : **Percentages showing parents' desire Regarding the level of education their children should attain, separately for boys and girls currently studying**

Level of education desired by parents	Boys				Girls			
	in primary school	in secondary school	in post S.S.C. Class	Total	in primary school	in secondary school	in post S.S.C. Class*	Total
1. Primary (1—7 std.)	3.1	—	—	2.5	16.4	—	—	14.1
2. Secondary (8—10 std.)	7.7	1.4	—	6.5	10.8	3.0	—	9.6
3. S.S.C	20.3	26.4	—	19.7	26.3	27.3	[3]	26.5
4. Graduation	18.8	34.7	55.3	23.1	8.9	30.3	[6]	12.7
5. Technical education	0.6	1.4	—	0.7	—	—	—	—
6. Very high education	0.6	4.2	7.9	1.5	0.4	—	—	0.3
7. As much as they can/ would like to study	38.3	30.5	34.2	37.0	26.0	36.4	[1]	26.5
8. Not thought about it	5.4	1.4	2.6	4.8	4.5	3.0	[1]	4.5
9. Not mentioned	5.2	—	—	4.2	6.7	—	—	5.8
Total	100.0 (479)	100.0 (72)	100.0 (38)	100.0 (589)	100.0 (269)	100.0 (33)	(11)	100·0 (313)

*Frequencies are given in this column.

TABLE 5.8 : **Percentages showing parents' desire regarding occupation of their children, separately for boys and girls currently studying**

Occupation desired by parents	Boys				Girls			
	in primary school	in secondary school	in post S.S.C. class	Total	in primary school	in secondary school	in post S.S.C. class*	Total
1. Not mentioned	37.3	29.2	26.3	35.7	56.9	24.2	[3]	52.5
2. Cultivation	2.7	1.4	—	2.4	2.6	—	—	2.2
3. Artisan, skilled work	1.3	—	—	1.0	0.7	—	—	0.6
4. Retail shop	0.8	—	—	0.7	0.4	—	—	0.3
5. Class IV jobs	1.3	1.4	—	1.2	0.4	—	—	0.3
6. Service (details not given)	25.9	26.4	23.7	25.8	13.8	15.2	—	13.4
7. Police, conductor, etc.	3.3	4.2	—	3.2	—	—	—	—
8. Teacher, nurse, clerk, VLW, etc.	14.0	20.8	5.2	14.3	19.7	42.4	[2]	22.0
9. Clerical (higher level)	9.4	11.1	39.5	11.5	4.8	18.2	[5]	7.7
10. Govt. officials, professionals	4.0	5.5	5.3	4.2	0.7	3.0	[1]	1.0
Total	100.0 (479)	100.0 (72)	100.0 (38)	100.0 (589)	100.0 (269)	100.0 (33)	(11)	100.0 (313)

*Frequencies are given in this column.

world-view is rather limited. The household heads of about one-fourth of the boys and one-eighth of the girls have simply indicated that they would expect their children to be involved in some job. Most of the others expect their children to obtain clerical, teaching and other middle-level white-collar jobs. The household heads of only 4.2 per cent of the boys and 1 per cent of the girls desire their children to be in higher levels of jobs and professions. Thus, the occupational expectations of most tribal parents are at most and probably focused on lower-level salaried jobs in the government and other organizations that offer them reserved positions.

Measurement of social class

Caste, education, occupation, income and many other objective as well as subjective measures have been used as indicators of social class. For parsimony, quantitatively sophisticated techniques were used in this study to obtain a composite measure of social class. It is a weighted combination of education and occupation of the head of household, total income, area of land under cultivation and of land owned, ownership of vehicles, animals (oxen, cows/buffaloes, calves, sheep/goats) and poultry, type of residence, type of utensils in daily use, and possession of certain selected items (cot with pati or kathi, watch, cycle, stove and radio).

It may be mentioned that the respondents were asked questions concerning occupation of each family member, monthly income of salaried persons and those working as labourers in agricultural or other sector, the type and quantum of agricultural produce, etc. On the basis of their response to these items, income from different sources (agricultural produce, agricultural/other labour, salaried/professional/business activities, and seasonal occupations) was separately calculated and then summed up so as to obtain total income of the household. While there was no other source to check the reliability of the income data, it is felt that such a detailed procedure to obtain the income data provide a fair estimate of their income. It is needless to mention that the other items do not present any specific or serious problem of reliability of data.

Information on education was coded into eight categories

(illiterate, can read and write, primary education up to 7th standard, vernacular final or P.T.C., 8th to 11th standard, S.S.C. pass, some post-S.S.C. diploma or college education, and graduation from college). Occupation was coded into nine categories (other labourers, agricultural labourers, craftsmen, artisans, cultivators, class IV servants, conductors/drivers and white-collar workers). Ownerships of vehicles were coded into three categories (handcart, bullock/animal-driven cart, tractor), and type of residence was coded into three categories (hut, kachcha house and pucca house). Information regarding utensils used for domestic purposes was coded into four categories (earthen, alluminium, copper/brass, and stainless steel). The categories of education, occupation, ownership of vehicles, type of residence and utensils in daily use were coded in a consecutive ascending order starting with 1. The actual number of different types of animals and poultry was used. With regard to possession of other items (cot with pati, cot with kathi, watch, cycle, stove and radio), a binary coding (0,1) was used. The Ns, means and standard deviations of these variables are given in Table 5.9.

In order to develop a composite measure of social class, two different procedures were followed to weight the items. A factoring method was used to obtain weights for the thirteen items which are measured on at least an ordinal scale. The weight of the six binary-coded items were decided somewhat arbitrarily; however, the criterion for assigning weights equal to the proportion of the respondents who did not possess the respective items was used.

The thirteen scaled items were factor-analyzed using the principal factoring method. For this, the PA2 option of the SPSS programme package was used. This option automatically replaces the main diagonal elements of the correlation matrix with communality estimates, and employs an iteration procedure for improving the estimation of communality. This produced a four-factor structure. The factor matrix was orthogonally rotated according to varimax criterion. In order to build composite scales of variables, the SPSS programme package provides for an option which produces the best set of coefficients for the variables in such a way that the correlation between the composite variable and the hypothetical factor is maximum. Using the option, the weights of the items on the four factors were obtained. These

TABLE 5.9 : **Variables included in the composite SES scores (means, standard deviations and weights)**

Variables	N	Mean	Std. dev.	Weights based on factor analysis			
				Factor 1	Factor 2	Factor 3	Factor 4
1	2	3	4	5	6	7	8
A. *Variables in the factor analysis*							
1. Education of head	882	1.95	1.26	—.08969	—.01345	.31954	.01368
2. Occupation of head	842	5.33	2.44	—.04241	.02892	.22426	—.03150
3. Total income (in hundred)	876	30.72	25.54	—.04809	.06266	.21989	—.01713
4. Total land under cultivation (vighas)	569	9.33	9.29	.37251	—.10899	·00850	.08412
5. Total land under cultivation (vighas)	539	9.02	9.28	.72292	.03305	—.02639	—.40407
6. Type of vehicles	145	2.01	0.35	—.13176	—.31609	.03261	1.05648
7. Oxen	464	2.25	1.09	.01242	.05989	—.05522	.06149
8. Cows/buffaloes	445	2.03	1.43	—.04368	.65624	—.07741	.02761
9. Calves	346	1.77	1.20	—.03570	.18470	—.02512	.02272
10. Sheep/goats	224	4.04	4.82	—.07372	.18114	.00288	.05785
11. Chicken	399	5.20	4.65	—.04249	.09580	.02471	.03118
12. Type of residence	883	1.93	0.43	—.04497	—.04031	.25092	—.01531
13. Type of utensils used	872	2.91	1.15	—.02686	—.11955	.23996	.01825

TABLE 5.9 : (*Contd.*)

B. *Other Variables (Binary)*		*Weight assigned**
14. Cot with pati/palang	84	.905
15. Cot with kathi	766	.133
16. Watch	206	.767
17. Cycle	136	.846
18. Stove	111	.874
19. Radio	123	.861

*Weight assigned = $\frac{\text{N — no. Possessing the item}}{\text{N}}$

weights are given in Table 5.9. Next, the score on each item was multiplied by the respective weight on each factor. Then, sums of factor-weighted scores of all items on the four factors were obtained, standardized, and added so as to obtain a sum of factor-weighted standerdized scores of all items.

Then, binary-coded items were assigned weights obtained by using the formula

$$W_1=\frac{N-n_1}{N}$$, where N=total sample size, and

n_1=the no. of respondents possessing the item.

Then, a sum of the weighted scores on the six binary-coded items was obtained and standardized.

Finally, the sum of the standardized factor-weighted scores and the standardized weighted scores of the binary-coded items was obtained. The range of sum of scores of all the SES items, thus weighted and standardized, was from —7.7426 to 19.3175. The composite scores were then relocated by adding 7.7426 to each score so as to obtain positive SES scores.

In sum, the composite measure of social class (referred to as SES scores hereafter) used in this study is obtained by a combination of factor-weighted 13 variables and somewhat arbitrarily weighted 6 binary-coded items.

The intercorrelations of the social class variables and the SES scores are given in Table 5.10. The correlation coefficients of the SES scores vary from a minimum of r=.30 for X_{15} (cot with kathi) to r=.66 for X_4 (land cultivated) and X_5 (land owned). With a view to obtaining a limited number of social class variables that can account for the maximum variance in the SES scores, a linear stepwise multiple regression analysis was performed. This provides a means of choosing independent variables which will provide the best prediction possible with the fewest independent variables. The procedure recursively constructs prediction equations, starting with a single independent variable which is the best predictor and then adding one independent variable at a time to the regression equation such that it provides the best prediction in conjuction with the independent variables in the preceding equation. The selection of the additional independent variable is based on its tolerance value.

TABLE 5.10 : **Inter-correlation of social class variables and SES scores**

	Variables	X_1	X_2	X_3	X_4	X_5	X_6	X_7	X_8	X_9	X_{10}
X_1	Education	—	.27	.33	.15	.13	.09	.05	.21	.23	.13
X_2	Occupation		—	.22	.15	.13	.08	.10	.17	.14	.12
X_3	Income			—	.24	.24	.09	.23	.28	.26	.22
X_4	Land cultivated				—	.95	.36	.52	.37	.35	.08
X_5	Land owned					—	.38	.49	.35	.34	.10
X_6	Vehicle						—	.23	.44	.23	—.26
X_7	Oxen							—	.48	.35	.16
X_8	Cows/buffaloes								—	.40	.37
X_9	Calves									—	.28
X_{10}	Sheet/goats										—

TABLE 5.10 : (*Contd.*)

Variables	X_{11}	X_{12}	X_{13}	X_{14}	X_{15}	X_{16}	X_{17}	X_{18}	X_{19}	X_{20}
X_{11} Education	.11	.24	.24	.26	.21	.35	.30	.33	.32	.39
X_{12} Occupation	.20	.28	.09	.16	.26	.21	.17	.12	.18	.46
X_{13} Income	.23	.25	.21	.21	.14	.42	.33	.42	.35	.50
X_{14} Land cultivated	.24	.35	.20	.22	.08	.22	.20	.18	.21	.66
X_{15} Land owned	.26	.38	.20	.22	.09	.24	.25	.19	.22	.66
X_{16} Vehicle	—.12	.18	.04	.12	.13	.08	.09	.15	.14	.53
X_{17} Oxen	.21	.19	.09	.13	.05	.16	.16	.09	.16	.49
X_{18} Cows/Buffaloes	.35	.23	.05	.10	.09	.15	.11	.06	.15	.47
X_{19} Calves	.27	.16	—.04	.16	.04	.17	.09	.11	.17	.40
X_{20} Sheep/Goats	.32	.13	—.05	.18	.10	.07	.01	.01	.15	.31
X_{21} Chicken	—	.13	.03	.10	.11	.14	.13	.05	.15	.35
X_{22} Residence		—	.27	.20	.42	.33	.28	.28	.28	.48
X_{23} Utensils			—	.18	.23	.33	.29	.31	.31	.37
X_{24} Cot with Pati				—	.04	.29	.23	.24	.29	.39
X_{25} Cot with Kathi					—	.17	.14	.13	.15	.30
X_{26} Watch						—	.52	.51	.56.	.55
X_{27} Cycle							—	.53	.45	.52
X_{28} Stove								—	.48	.48
X_{29} Radio									—	.51
X_{30} SES										—

A summary of the stepwise multiple regression analysis is given in Table 5.11. It is found from this table that X_5 (total land-owned) explains 43.3 per cent of the variance in the SES scores. With the addition of X_{16} (watch), 59.8 per cent of the variance in the SES scores is explained. It is instructive to note that ten social class variables together can explain the total variance in the SES scores. A perusal of these ten variance indicate that it is not necessary to include income data to construct SES scale for the tribals. In other words, it is possible to capture the income component of the SES scale by bringing in other income-related variables which are relatively easy to measure.

TABLE 5.11 : **Summary of stepwise multiple regression analysis**

	Dependent Variable=SES Scores Independent-variables in the stepwise Regression equations	Multiple R	Multiple R^2
X_5	Total land owned (vighas)	0.658	0.433
X_{16}	Watch	0.773	0.598
X_6	Vehicle	0.834	0.695
X_{10}	Sheep/Goats	0.902	0.813
X_2	Occupation of head	0.934	0.875
X_{17}	Cycle	0.955	0.912
X_{13}	Type of utensils	0.967	0.935
X_4	Total land under cultivation (Vighas)	0.976	0.953
X_8	Cows/buffaloes	0.983	0.967
X_{11}	Chicken	0.998	0.997

For the purposes of cross-tabular analysis presented in this report, the respondents in the sample were first rank-ordered according to their SES score, and then the sample was divided into almost equal thirds, labelled as low, middle and high categories of social class. A summary of the characteristics (items included in the composite SES variable) of the respondents in the three social class categories is given in Table 5.12.

It is found from this table that almost three-fourths of the respondents in the low social class category are agricultural or other labourers. None of them has obtained education beyond the primary level ; only 14.7 per cent of them have obtained primary education. The mean land cultivated/owned by them is less than one vigha and the mean yearly income of their family is

Rs. 2,022. All of them live in kachcha houses, and only 13.4 per cent of them use copper/brass utensils. The means of animals/ poultry owned by them are meagre ; less than one per cent of them possess items like a wrist watch or a radio.

TABLE 5.12 : **Characteristics of respondents, by social class**

Characteristics		Social class			
		Low	Middle	High	Total
1		2	3	4	5
1. *Education of head*					
(a) S.S.C. and above	%	—	0.7	5.3	1.9
(b) 8—10 std., P.T.C.	%	—	4.6	10.9	5.0
(c) Upto 7th std.	%	14.7	35.3	41.1	30.2
2. *Occupation of head*					
(a) White-collar workers, shop owners, professionals	%	—	2.7	9.8	4.1
(b) Cultivators, owners	%	15.7	65.7	68.4	49.7
(c) Agricultural and other labour	%	73.5	13.4	4.2	30.8
3. *Yearly Income of the Family*					
(a) Total (Rs.)	$\bar{X}$	2022	2539	4649	3044
(b) Per Capita (Rs.)	$\bar{X}$	383	400	645	473
4. *Land (Vighas)*					
(a) Under cultivation	$\bar{X}$	0.87	5.45	11.97	6.01
(b) Owned	$\bar{X}$	0.71	4.82	11.24	5.50
5. *Animals and Poultry*					
(a) Oxen	$\bar{X}$	0.21	1.26	2.13	1.18
(b) Cows/Buffaloes	$\bar{X}$	0.15	0.95	2.01	1.02
(c) Calves	$\bar{X}$	0.11	0.66	1.33	0.69
(d) Sheep/Goats	$\bar{X}$	0.37	1.11	1.63	1.02
(e) Chicken	$\bar{X}$	1.39	2.64	3.04	2.35
6. *Type of Residence*					
Pakka House	%	—	2.0	16.8	6.1
7. *Utensils in daily use*					
(a) Stainless steel	%	—	—	2.1	0.7
(b) Copper/Brass	%	13.4	28.7	66.0	35.5

TABLE 5.12 : (*Contd.*)

1		2	3	4	5
8. *Possession of selected items*					
(a) Cot with pati/palang	%	0.7	4.0	24.6	9.5
(b) Cot with kathi	%	67.2	95.7	97.5	86.7
(c) Wrist watch	%	0.7	15.7	55.1	23.3
(d) Cycle	%	—	7.7	39.6	15.4
(e) Stove	%	—	3.3	35.4	12.6
(f) Radio	%	0.3	6.0	36.5	13.9
(g) Bullock/animal driven cart	%	—	—	49.8	16.1
N		299	300	285	884

About two-thirds of the respondents in the middle social class category are cultivator-owners, but the mean land cultivated/owned by them is about five vighas. About one-third of them have obtained primary education, and a small proportion of them have obtained some education beyond the primary level. The mean yearly income of their family is Rs. 2,539, but the mean per capita income of their family is only slightly higher than that of those in the low social class category. The mean number of animals/poultry owned by them is higher than that for the low social class category. Only 2 per cent of them reside in pacca houses and a little over one-fourth of them use copper/brass utensils. About one-sixth of them possess a wrist watch, but only about 6 to 7 per cent of them possess items like a cycle and a radio.

About one-tenth of the respondents in the high social class category are white-collar workers ; about two-thirds of them are cultivator-owners, and the mean land cultivated/owned by them is about 12 vighas. The mean yearly income of their family is more than double that of those in the low social class category. Almost all those who have obtained S.S.C. and above level of education are in the high social class category. About one-sixth of them live in pacca houses and about two-thirds of them use copper/brass utensils. The mean number of oxen and cows/buffaloes owned by them is slightly over two. About one-third to one-half of them possess items like a wrist watch, a cycle, a stove, and a radio. All those who own a bullock/animal-driven cart are included in the high social class category. In brief, there is a positive and monotonic relationship between the various social class variables and the levels of social class used in the cross-tabular analysis.

Social class and educational attainment

The relationship between social class and educational attainment of the tribals can be examined from Tables 5.13 and 5.14. The data regarding various indicators of educational attainment of the tribals are given in these two tables. It is found that none of the male members in a little over one-half of the households in the low social class category has obtained any formal education ; similarly, none of the female members in 86.6 per cent of the households in the low social class category has obtained any formal education. The percentage of households with no male/female member having obtained any formal education decreases as we move up the ladder of social class ; there are, in the high social class category, only 10.2 per cent of the households with no male member having obtained any formal education and 38.2 per cent of the households with no female member having obtained any formal education. With regard to the highest level of education

TABLE 5.13 : **Percentage distributions of households showing the highest level of education attained by any male/female member, by socio-economic status**

Social Class	Highest level of education					
	Nil	1—4 std.	5—10 std.	S.S.C. & above	Total	
		(a) *Attained by any male member*				
Low	53.8	25.4	19.4	1.4	100.0	(299)
Middle	24.3	27.7	42.6	5.4	100.0	(300)
High	10.2	16.8	45.9	27.0	100.0	(285)
Total	29.8	23.4	35.8	11.0	100.0	(884)
		(b) *Attained by any female member*				
Low	86.6	10.7	2.0	0.7	100.0	(299)
Middle	68.7	18.7	11.3	1.3	100.0	(300)
High	38.2	24.2	31.2	6.4	100.0	(285)
Total	64.9	17.8	14.6	2.6	100.0	(884)

attained by any male/female member in the household, there is a positive and monotonic relationship between social class and the percentage of households in the various categories of education ;

TABLE 5.14 : **Education by social class, age and sex**

Socio-economic Status	Did not go to school at all	Dropped out during primary school	Dropped out during secondary school	Going to school		Total	
			(a) 5—17 years old Males				
Low	55.5	10.6	1.7	32.2		100.0	(301)
Middle	36.3	10.8	1.9	51.0		100.0	(369)
High	21.8	9.9	3.5	64.8		100.0	(403)
Total	36.3	10.4	2.4	50.9		100.0	(1073)
			(b) 5—17 years old Females				
Low	80.2	3.3	0.8	15.7		100.0	(242)
Middle	65.3	5.6	0.9	28.2		100.0	(320)
High	40.2	8.6	1.4	49.8		100.0	(348)
Total	59.6	6.1	1.1	33.1		100.0	(910)
			(c) 18 years old Males				
Low	78.6	17.5	2.9	0.5	0.5	100.0	(435)
Middle	56.2	29.7	10.1	1.6	2.4	100.0	(505)
High	34.8	28.9	20.9	5.6	9.8	100.0	(612)
Total	54.0	26.0	12.4	2.8	4.8	100.0	(1552)
			(d) 18 years old Females				
Low	98.6	1.2	—	—	0.2	100.0	(415)
Middle	93.2	4.8	1.1	0.7	0.2	100.0	(457)
High	80.2	9.4	6.9	1.4	2.1	100.0	(562)
Total	89.6	5.5	3.1	0.8	1.0	100.0	(1434)

that is, the percentage of households with at least one male/female member having attained a certain level of education increases with an increase in the level of social class. Thus, there are, in the high class category, 27 per cent of the households with at least one male member having obtained S.S.C. or above level of education (as against only 1.4 per cent of the households in the low social class category) and 6.4 per cent of the households with at least one female member having obtained S.S.C. or above level of education (as against only 0.7 per cent of the households in the low social class category).

Examining the level of education attained by all members of the households in the interview study, there is again a positive and monotonic relationship between social class and education among the tribals in each category of age and sex. It should be noted that a little over three-fourths of the adult males and almost all of the adult females in the low social class category never went to school. Although the percentages of those having no schooling are somewhat reduced in the case of the younger generation, one-half of the boys and over three-fourths of the girls in the low social class category never went to school. As against this, about four-fifths of the boys and three-fifths of the girls in the high social class category have been able to obtain some formal education. This speaks about the failure of our even primary school programmes to reach to the poor among the tribals.

The percentages of those dropping out during the primary and the secondary stages of education need to be examined in the context of those who have ever been able to join school. The ratios of the percentage of those dropping out during primary education to the percentage of those ever attending school show that in each category of sex and age, the drop-out rate is inversely related to social class. This is also generally true in the case of the percentage of those dropping out during the secondary stage of education.

Examining the percentages of the 5—17 years old boys and girls going to school, it is found that there is a strong positive relationship between social class and the percentage of those going to school. The percentage of the school-going boys in the high social class category is twice that in the low social class category. Similarly, the percentage of the school-going girls in the high social class category is thrice that in the low social class category. This shows that there is a greater impact of social class on the education of girls than that on the education of boys.

Only 2.8 per cent of the adult males and 0.8 per cent of the adult females go to school. Even if it is assumed that all of them are enrolled in classes for some post-matric education, this indicates that a very low percentages of the tribals go for higher education. The percentages of those going to school and the percentages of those having passed the S.S.C. examination indicate that social class and higher education among the tribals are also positively related.

In brief, the data presented in Tables 5.13 and 5.14 clearly show that there is a positive and strong relationship between social class and educational attainment of the tribals.

Social class and desire regarding education and occupation of school-going children.

The percentages showing the educational and occupational expectations of the household heads of the school-going children are given in Tables 5.15 and 5.16. The percentages of the school-going children whose household heads have not mentioned any specific level of education or any specific type of occupation they

TABLE 5.15 : **Percentages of school-going children showing their parents' desire regarding the level of education they should attain, by socio-economic status**

Socio-economic Status	Desired Level of Education						
	Not thought about it: As much as they can	Primary	Second-ary	S.S.C.	College Gradu-ation	Total	
Low	41.5	10.9	12.5	27.3	7.8	100.0	(128)
Middle	40.0	7.6	9.0	26.1	17.3	100.0	(278)
High	41.9	5.2	5.9	21.2	25.8	100.0	(458)
Total	41.2	6.8	7.9	23.7	20.4	100.0	(864)*

*38 School-going children for whom relevant data were not available have been omitted from this table.

TABLE 5.16 : **Percentages of school-going children showing the type of occupation their parents desire them to follow, by socio-economic status**

Socio-economic status	Desired type of occupation						
	Not mentioned	Cultivation, Artisan, etc.	Service (details not given)	White-collar occupations (lower level)	White-collar occupations (higher level)	Total	
Low	41.4	3.1	32.8	17.2	5.5	100.0	(128)
Middle	34.5	5.8	22.7	24.5	12.5	100.0	(278)
High	39.7	4.8	19.7	17.9	17.9	100.0	(458)
Total	38.2	4.9	22.6	19.9	14.4	100.0	(864)*

*38 School-going children for whom relevant data were not available have been omitted from this table.

would desire them to obtain are almost equal in all categories of social class. This indicates that the household heads of about two-fifths of the school-going children, irrespective of their social class, have perhaps indifferent attitudes regarding education and occupation of their school-going children. Further, the pattern of their educational expectations is positively related to social class; that is, the higher the level of social class the greater the percentage of the school-going children whose household heads desire them to obtain a higher level of education. In the high social class category, the household heads of about one-fourth of the school-going children desire them to obtain a college degree, as against the household heads of only 7.8 per cent of the school-going children from the low social class category. A similar relationship is also found between social class and occupational expectations of the household heads. In the high social class category, the household heads of about one-fifth of the school-going children desire them to obtain an upper-level white-collar occupation as against the household heads of only one-twentieth of the school-going children from the low social class category.

In sum, there is a strong and positive relationship between social class and educational/occupational expectations of the household heads of the school-going children.

Inter-tribe variation in educational attainment

One consistent finding regarding education of the tribals is that there is an uneven development of education among different tribes. The inter-tribe variation in the educational attainment of the sample households can be examined from Tables 5.17 and 5.18.

It is found from Table 5.17 that there is a considerable inter-tribe variation in the highest level of education attained by any male/female member in the household. About one-fifth of the Dhodia households have at least one male member having attained a high (S.S.C. and above) level of education. In the case of five other tribal groups (Bhil, Gamit, Chaudhari, Rathwa and Kokna), this percentage decreases to about 12 per cent. Similar percentages of Dublas, Dhankas and Patelias are somewhat lower (about 8% to 9%) than that for the total sample. The percentages of households with at least one male member having attained a high level of education in the remaining tribal groups are quite low or nil. Similarly, about 7 per cent to 8 per cent of the Dhodia and Gamit households have at least one female member having attained a high level of education. This percentage decreases to about 5 per cent in the case of the Chaudhari households, and to about 2 per cent in the case of the Bhil, Dhanka, Kokna, Koli and Dubia groups. In brief, in terms of the percentage of households having at least one male/female member with a high level of education, Dhodias top the list. The next come Gamits and Chaudharis. Bhils, Rathwas and Koknas, who have a higher percentage of households with at least one male member having attained a high level of education than the average for the total group, lag quite behind in the matter of female education.

We find from Table 5.18 that the educational attainment of the males is higher than that of the females in all tribal groups; similarly, the educational attainment of the younger generation is higher than that of the older generation. Such a pattern is observed with regard to the percentages of those who did not go to school at all, and the percentages of those who dropped out during the primary and the secondary stages of schooling.

There is a considerable inter-tribe variation in the pattern. The percentages of those who did not go to school at all vary

TABLE 5.17 : **Percentage distribution of households, showing the highest level of education attained by any male/female member, by tribe****

Tribe*	Highest level of education: Nil	1—4 std.	5—10 std.	S.S.C. & above	Total	
	(a) Attained by any male member					
1. Dhodia	13.3	19.7	44.7	22.3	100.0	(76)
2. Gamit	32.7	14.5	40.2	12.6	100.0	(55)
3. Chaudhari	22.4	33.0	32.6	12.0	100.0	(58)
4. Bhil	28.3	21.0	38.2	12.5	100.0	(295)
5. Dhanka	19.4	35.7	35.8	9.1	100.0	(98)
6. Kokna	21.5	23.9	42.7	11.9	100.0	(42)
7. Patelia	28.0	20.0	44.0	8.0	100.0	(25)
8. Dubla	30.3	34.0	27.5	8.5	100.0	(59)
9. Rathwa	28.1	28.3	30.8	12.8	100.0	(39)
10. Nayaka	45.0	18.4	36.6	—	100.0	(49)
11. Varli	48.2	7.4	40.7	3.7	100.0	(27)
12. Koli	57.5	15.2	21.3	6.0	100.0	(33)
13. Kotwalia	83.4	16.6	—	—	100.0	(24)
14. Pardhi	[1]	[2]	[1]	—	—	(4)
Total	29.8	23.4	35.8	11.0	100.0	(884)
	(b) Attained by any female member					
1. Dhodia	36.9	14.5	40.7	7.9	100.0	(76)
2. Gamit	49.2	29.1	14.5	7.2	100.0	(55)
3. Chaudhari	65.6	15.7	13.6	5.1	100.0	(58)
4. Bhil	64.9	17.9	14.8	2.4	100.0	(295)
5. Dhanka	57.2	28.6	12.2	2.0	100.0	(98)
6. Kokna	66.5	21.5	9.6	2.4	100.0	(42)
7. Patelia	72.0	20.0	8.0	—	100.0	(25)
8. Dubla	74.5	11.9	11 9	1.7	100.0	(59)
9. Rathwa	71.9	23.0	5.1	—	100.0	(39)
10. Nayaka	81.8	8.1	10.1	—	100.0	(49)
11. Varli	81.5	3.7	14.8	—	100.0	(27)
12. Koli	81.9	12.1	6.0	—	100.0	(33)
13. Kotwalia	100.0	—	—	—	100.0	(24)
14. Pardhi	[3]	[1]	—	—	—	(4)
Total	65.0	17.8	14.6	2.6	100.0	(884)

* Only the broad categories of the tribal groups are indicated in this and subsequent table. For details regarding composition of different tribal groups, see Table 5.1.

** Figures within brackets indicate frequencies.

TABLE 5.18 : Education by tribe, age and sex

Tribe	Did not go to school at all	Dropped out during primary school	Dropped out during secondary school	Going to school	Total	
1	2	3	4	5	6	7
		(a) *5—17 years old males*				
1. Dhodia	22.5	11.2	5.6	60.7	100.0	(89)
2. Gamit	37.1	5.7	2.9	54.3	100.0	(70)
3. Chaudhari	32.8	15.5	6.9	44.8	100.0	(58)
4. Bhil	35.3	6.8	1.8	56.1	100.0	(380)
5. Dhanka	31.1	9.8	1.5	57.6	100.0	(132)
6. Kokna	34.0	3.8	1.9	60.3	100.0	(53)
7. Patelia	28.0	8.0	4.0	60.0	100.0	(25)
8. Dubla	36.7	28.3	—	35.0	100.0	(60)
9. Rathwa	35.8	17.0	1.9	45.3	100.0	(53)
10. Nayaka	50.9	16.9	1.7	30.5	100.0	(59)
11. Varli	55.0	7.5	2.5	35.0	100.0	(40)
12. Koli	62.5	12.5	3.1	21.9	100.0	(32)
13. Kotwalia	[10]	[2]	—	[5]	—	(17)
14. Pardhi	[1]	[1]	[—]	[3]	—	(5)
Total	36.3	10.4	2.4	50.9	100.0	(1073)
		(b) *5—17 years old females*				
1. Dhodia	33.3	8.6	3.2	54.9	100.0	(93)
2. Gamit	35.2	13.0	1.8	50.0	100.0	(54)
3. Chaudhari	57.4	6.4	—	36.2	100.0	(47)
4. Bhil	59.7	6.3	1.3	32.7	100 0	(303)
5. Dhanka	49.1	9.4	—	41.5	100.0	(106)
6. Kokna	63.3	2.0	—	34.7	100.0	(49)
7. Patelia	74.1	3.7	3.7	18.5	100.0	(27)
8. Dubla	83.6	—	—	16.4	100.0	(61)
9. Rathwa	75.4	3.5	—	21.2	100.0	(57)
10. Nayaka	72.5	5.0	—	22.5	100.0	(40)
11. Varli	79.2	4.2	—	16.6	100.0	(24)
12. Koli	82.1	3.6	3.6	10.7	100.0	(28)
13. Kotwalia	[16]	—	—	[3]	—	(19)
14. Pardhi	[1]	[1]	—	—	—	(2)
Total	59.6	6.2	1.1	33.1	100.0	(910)

TABLE 5.18 : (*Contd.*)

Tribe	Did not go to school at all	Dropped out during primary school	Dropped out during secondary school	Going to school	Passed S.S.C.	Total	
			(c) *18 years old males*				
1. Dhodia	39.0	29.5	15.4	6.7	9.4	100.0	(149)
2. Gamit	42.6	35.1	13.8	2.1	6.4	100.0	(94)
3. Chaudhari	51.1	27.1	13.5	3.1	5.2	100.0	(96)
4. Bhil	51.9	24.5	15.9	3.6	4.1	10.00	(534)
5. Dhanka	53.5	32.6	9.6	1.1	3.2	100.0	(187)
6. Kokna	52.1	21.1	14.1	2.8	9.9	100.0	(71)
7. Patelia	62.0	20.0	12.0	—	6.0	100.0	(50)
8. Dubla	53.5	32.0	6.2	2.1	6.2	100.0	(97)
9. Rathwa	61.9	22.4	9.2	3.9	2.6	100.0	(76)
10. Nayaka	70.7	21.3	8.0	—	—	100.0	(75)
11. Varli	71.1	18.4	7.9	—	2.6	100.0	(38)
12. Koli	69.6	19.6	4.3	2.2	4.3	100.0	(46)
13. Kotwalia	96.8	3.2	—	—	—	100.0	(31)
14. Pardhi	[6]	[2]	—	—	—	100.0	(8)
Total	54.0	26.0	12.4	2.8	4.8	100.0	(1552)
			(d) *18 years old females*				
1. Dhodia	78.1	8.9	8.9	2.7	1.4	100.0	(146)
2. Gamit	82.1	11.2	2.2	1.1	3.4	100.0	(89)
3. Chaudhari	85.1	8.0	2.3	1.1	3.5	100.0	(87)
4. Bhil	89.6	5.5	3.7	0.6	0.6	100.0	(509)
5. Dhanka	92.1	6.1	—	0.6	1.2	100.0	(164)
6. Kokna	96.6	3.4	—	—	—	100.0	(59)
7. Patelia	92.5	2.5	—	2.5	2.5	100.0	(40)
8. Dubla	91.2	2.2	6.6	—	—	100.0	(91)
9. Rathwa	98.2	1.8	—	—	—	100.0	(57)
10. Nayaka	95.4	4.6	—	—	—	100.0	(65)
11. Varli	95.2	2.4	2.4	—	—	100.0	(42)
12. Koli	95.4	2.3	2.3	—	—	100.0	(43)
13. Kotwalia	100.0	—	—	—	—	100.0	(34)
14. Pardhi	[7]	[1]	—	—	—	—	(8)
Total	89.6	5.5	3.1	0.8	1.0	100.0	(1434)

from 22.5 per cent (Dhodia) to 62.5 per cent (Koli) for boys and from 33.3 per cent (Dhodia) to 83.6 per cent (Dubla) for girls in the younger generation and from 39.0 per cent (Dhodia) to 96.8 per cent (Koli) for males, and from 78.1 per cent (Dhodia) to 100.0 per cent (Kotwalia) for females in the older generation. The percentages of those who dropped out during the primary and seconary stages of schooling also vary considerably from one tribal group to another. However, the percentages of drop-outs from primary school are substantially high among the Dubla, Rathwa, Nayaka and Chaudhri boys.

The percentages of those going to school vary from about 60 per cent (Dhodia and Kokna) to about 20 per cent (Koli) for boys, and from 54.9 per cent (Dhodia) to 16.4 per cent (Dubla) for girls in the younger generation. Among adults, only 2.8 per cent of the males and 0.8 per cent of the females are going to school. The percentages of those going to school is the highest among Dhodias.

The percentages shown in the last colum of Tables 5.18 (c) and 5.18 (d) indicate the extent to which the tribals have been able to attain a high level (S.S.C. or above) of education. It is found that about 10 per cent of the Dhodia and Kokna males have attained a high level of education. This is reduced to about 5 per cent to 6 per cent among Dublas, Gamits, Patelias and Chaudharies. While no adult male among Nayakas, Kotwalias and Pardhis has passed even the S.S.C. examination, the percentages of those having obtained such a high level of education among the remaining tribal groups are only about 2 per cent to 4 per cent. It should be noted that there is no adult female, among several tribal groups, who has attained even the S.S.C. level of education. Only about 2 per cent to 3 per cent of the females among Gamits, Chaudharis and Patelias have attained S.S.C. or above level of education. These data clearly indicate that even the tribal groups like Dhodias and Koknas, among whom about 10 per cent of the adult males have obtained S.S.C. or above level of education, do not seem to encourage their women folks to obtain a high level of education.

Considering the various indicators of educational attainment, it can be said that the overall educational attainment of Dhodias is of the highest order ; that is, their percentages in the categories of the various indicators of a high level of educational attainment are considerably higher than those for the total sample. They are followed by Gamits and Chaudharies who too have, with regard to several indicators, higher percentages than those for the total sample. At the next level are Bhils, Dhankas and Koknas, the percentages for whom are about the same as, or only silghtly higher than, those for the total sample. The educational attainment of the rest of the tribal groups is considerably lower than that of the total sample. It should, however, be noted that the 5—17 years old Dubla and Patelia children seem to be slowly advancing, but the picture of the educational attainment of Nayakas, Varlis, Kolis and Kotwalias is very dismal.

When inquired about the level of education the household heads desire their school-going children to obtain, it was found (Table 5.19) that the household heads of about one-fourth to one-third of the school-going children among Dhodias and Chaudharies desire them to obtain a college degree. They are followed by Gamits (22.7%), Bhils (20.3%) and Koknas (16.7%). Examining the percentages of the school-going children whose household heads desire them to obtain S.S.C. level of education, a similar pattern is found among these tribal groups. It should also be noted that about two-fifths of the Dubla household heads desire their children to obtain S.S.C. level of education.

As regards the type of occupation the household heads desire their school-going children to obtain, it was found (Table 5.20) that most of them do not desire their daughters to take up any economic activity outside the family. This is reflected in the relatively high percentage of school-going children whose household heads have not answered this query. Further, the household heads of about one-fourth of the school-going children desire them to obtain some job, but they do not have any specific idea regarding the type of jobs they desire. The household heads of about one-third of the school-going children desire them to be engaged in some white-collar occupations ; most of them desire their children to be teachers and clerks presumably in the government and semi-government organizations that have reserved positions for the tribals. Examining the percentages in the last two columns of this table, it is found that the household heads of a little over one-fifth of Chaudhari and Gamit school-going children

TABLE 5.19 : **Percentage of school-going children showing their parents' desire regarding the level of education they should attain by tribe***

Tribe	Desired level of education						
	Not thought about it, as much as they can	Primary	Secondary	S.S.C	College Graduate	Total	
1. Dhodia	21.7	1.7	5.8	37.5	33.3	100.0	(120)
2. Gamit	31.8	10.6	15.2	19.7	22.7	100.0	(66)
3. Chaudhari	24.4	13.3	15.6	17.8	28.9	100.0	(45)
4. Bhil	44.5	7.2	6.7	21.3	20.3	100.0	(320)
5. Dhanka	71.2	2.7	3.6	12.6	9.9	100.0	(111)
6. Kokna	37.4	10.4	16.7	18.8	16.7	100.0	(48)
7. Patelia	38.1	9.5	—	23.8	28.6	100.0	(21)
8. Dubla	37·5	12.5	3.1	40.6	6.3	100.0	(32)
9. Rathwa	64.0	11.1	8.3	8.3	8.3	100.0	(36)
10. Nayaka	35.7	3.6	—	32.1	28.6	100.0	(28)
11. Varli	—	[1]	[5]	[12]	—	—	(18)
12. Koli	[2]	—	[2]	[5]	[2]	—	(11)
13. Kotwalia	[3]	[1]	—	[1]	—	—	(5)
14. Pardhi	—	—	—	—	[3]	—	[3]
Total	41.2	6.8	7.9	23.7	20.4	100.0	(864)**

*Figures within brackets indicate frequencies
**33 School-going Children for whom relevant data were not available have been omitted from this table.

desire them to be engaged in upper-level white-collar occupations. They are followed by Bhils, Dhodias and Dhankas. The percentages in the remaining categories are very small. These data show that very few tribal parents have a high level of occupational expectations for their school-going children

Our analysis of the data so far has clearly indicated that the educational attainment of the tribals is strongly and positively related to their social class. There is a considerable amount of variation in the educational attainment of different tribal groups. It is, therefore, necessary to examine whether and to what extent there is a differential social class composition among the tribal groups. This can be examined from Table 5.21.

It can be seen from this table that the social class composi-

TABLE 5.20 : **Percentages of school-going children showing the type of occupation their parents desire them to follow, by tribe***

Tribe	Desired type of occupation						
	Not mentioned	Cultivation—Artisans, etc.	Service-details not given	White-collar occupation (lower level)	White-collar occupation (upper level)	Total	
1. Dhodia	40.9	5.8	23.3	15.8	14.2	100.0	(120)
2. Gamit	33.3	9.1	15.2	21.2	21.2	100.0	(66)
3. Chaudhari	28.9	4.4	24.4	17.8	24.5	100.0	(45)
4. Bhil	39.7	4.1	17.8	22.8	15.6	100.0	(320)
5. Dhanka	40.6	1.8	28.8	16.2	12.6	100.0	(111)
6. Kokna	16.7	6.3	41.7	29.1	6.2	100.0	(48)
7. Patelia	47.6	—	14.3	23.8	14.3	100.0	(21)
8. Dubla	62.5	—	28.1	9.4	—	100.0	(32)
9. Rathwa	58.3	2.8	25.0	11.1	2.8	100.0	(36)
10. Nayaka	28.6	7.1	7.1	42.9	14.3	100.0	(28)
11. Varli	[7]	—	[10]	[1]	—	—	(18)
12. Koli	[2]	[3]	[1]	[1]	[4]	—	(11)
13. Kotwalia	[1]	[1]	[3]	—	—	—	(5)
14. Pardhi	—	—	—	—	[3]	—	(3)
Total	38.2	4.9	22.6	19.9	14.4	100.0	(864)**

*Figures within brackets indicate frequencies.

**38 School-going children for whom relevent data were not available have been cmitted from this table.

tion of different tribal groups is quite varied. On one hand, almost two-thirds of Dhodias are in the high social class category while all of Kotwalias, on the other hand, are in the low social class category. In fact, there is a fair correspondence between the percentage of households belonging to high social class among different tribal groups and their rank order in terms of their overall educational attainment. The only glaring exception in this regard is of Rathwas. Although a little over one-half of the Rathwa households are in the high social class category, and consequently rank just behind Dhodias, they lag quite behind several other tribal groups in terms of their educational attain-

TABLE 5.21 : **Percentage distribution of tribal households, by social class***

Tribe	Social class				
	Low	Middle	High	Total	
1. Dhodia	19.7	17.1	63.2	100.0	(76)
2. Gamit	30.9	21.8	47.3	100.0	(55)
3. Chaudhari	29.3	32.8	37.9	100.0	(58)
4. Bhil	25.8	42.0	32.2	100.0	(295)
5. Dhanka	28.6	37.8	33.6	100.0	(98)
6. Kokna	42.9	32.0	26.1	100.0	(42)
7. Patelia	4.0	72.0	24.0	100.0	(25)
8. Dubla	59.4	22.0	18.6	100.0	(59)
9. Rathwa	2.6	41.0	56.4	100.0	(39)
10. Nayaka	51.0	36.7	12.3	100.0	(49)
11. Koli	69.7	24.2	6.1	100.0	(33)
12. Varli	70.4	25.9	3.7	100.0	(27)
13. Kotwalia	100.0	—	—	100.0	(24)
14. Pardhi	—	[2]	[2]		(4)
Total	33.8	33.9	32.3	100.0	(884)

*Figures within brackets indicate frequencies.

ment. The educational attainment of Rathwas is even below that of Dublas.

Social class and educational attainment of different tribal groups

We have so far demonstrated that there are considerable social class and inter-tribe differences in the educational attainment of the tribals. Since there is also a considerable amount of variation in the social class composition of different tribal groups in this study, it is necessary to examine whether and to what extent the positive relationship between social class and educational attainment holds true for different tribal groups. We, no doubt, need to control for age-group and sex while examining the social class differences in the educational attainment of the different tribal groups. When we attempt such a four-level cross-classification of the data, we face the usual problem of adequate frequencies in the categories of social class. Nonetheless, the percentages showing certain selected indicators of educational attainment are given in Tables 5.22 (a) and 5.22 (b) for each

TABLE 5.22 (a) : **Percentages showing those who did not go to school at all and those who are going to school among 5—17 years old children, by Sex, Social Class and Tribe***

Tribe	Social Class	Boys: Did not go to school	Boys: Going to school	Boys: N	Girls: Did not go to school	Girls: Going to school	Girls: N
1	2	3	4	5	6	7	8
1. Dhodia	L	(10)	(3)	15	(13)	(1)	16
	M	(3)	(13)	17	(3)	(8)	12
	H	12.3	66.7	57	23.1	64.6	65
2. Gamit	L	59.1	31.9	22	(7)	(3)	11
	M	(5)	(4)	10	(4)	(11)	16
	H	21.1	71.0	38	29.6	48.2	27
3. Chaudhari	L	(4)	(5)	10	(8)	(2)	11
	M	39.1	43.6	23	(9)	(5)	16
	H	24.0	44.0	25	50.0	50.0	20
4. Bhil	L	51.3	38.7	80	78.0	18.6	59
	M	37.0	55.2	154	71.8	22.8	131
	H	24.7	66.4	146	36.3	51.3	113
5. Dhanka	L	41.9	45.2	31	74.1	22.2	27
	M	39.1	50.0	46	44.2	41.8	43
	H	18.2	70.9	55	36.1	55.6	36
6. Kokna	L	(10)	(8)	19	(12)	(3)	15
	M	30.0	60.0	20	(10)	(5)	16
	H	(2)	(12)	14	(9)	(9)	18
7. Patelia	L	—	—	—	(2)	—	2
	M	(4)	(10)	17	(11)	(2)	14
	H	(3)	(5)	8	(7)	(3)	11
8. Dubla	L	41.7	30.6	36	90.6	9.4	32
	M	(4)	(6)	15	76.2	23.8	21
	H	(3)	(4)	9	(6)	(2)	8
9. Rathwa	L	—	—	—	—	—	—
	M	(10)	(5)	17	90.0	10.0	20
	H	25.0	52.8	36	67.6	27.0	37
10. Nayaka	L	70.4	18.5	27	(10)	(3)	14
	M	34.8	34.8	23	(14)	(2)	17
	H	(3)	(5)	9	(5)	(4)	9
11. Koli	L	(16)	—	18	(18)	—	19
	M	(4)	(6)	13	(5)	(1)	7
	H	—	(1)	1	—	(2)	2
12. Varli	L	61.5	30.8	26	(13)	(3)	17
	M	(6)	(6)	14	(5)	(1)	6
	H	—	—	—	(1)	—	1

TABLE 5.72 (a) (*Contd.*)

1	2	3	4	5	6	7	8
13. Kotwalia	L	(10)	(5)	17	(16)	(3)	19
	M	—	—	—	—	—	—
	H	—	—	—	—	—	—
14. Pardhi	L	—	—	—	—	—	—
	M	—	—	—	(1)	—	1
	H	(1)	(3)	5	—	—	1
Total	L	55.5	32.2	301	80.2	15.7	242
	M	36.3	51.0	369	65.3	28.2	320
	H	21.8	64.8	403	40.2	49.8	348

* 1. Figures within parentheses indicate frequencies.
2. Percentages/frequencies for those who dropped out during primary/secondary school are not shown in the table.

category of social class by tribe, age-group and sex. It may be noted that the frequencies have been indicated within parenthesis in the cases where the total number in a social class category is less than 20. For the sake of convenience, we have not presented the requisite percentages/frequencies of those who dropped out during primary/secondary school.

We have adequate Ns in each category of social class for Bhils and Dhankas only. It can be observed that there is a positive and monotonic relationship between social class and the educational attainment of both these tribal groups even when age-group and sex are controlled. With regard to several other tribal groups, for whom it is possible to compare the percentages of two social class categories, we also find that there is a positive and monotonic relationship between their level of social class and educational attainment. If we examine the relative frequencies in each social class category for the remaining tribal groups, the trend is clearly supportive of our hypothesis regarding a strong and positive relationship between social class and educational attainment. We also find that there are considerable differences in the educational attainment of the males and the females in each category of social class, age-group and tribe. Similarly, the differences by age-group continue within each category of social class, sex and tribe.

Given the limitation of adequate Ns in several categories of social class, tribe, sex and age-group in the data presented in Tables 5.22 (a) and 5.22 (b), an attempt is made in Table 5.23 to

TABLE 5.22 (b) : **Percentages showing those who did not go to school at all, those who are going to school and those who have passed S.S.C. among adults (18 years), by sex, social class and Tribe***

Tribe	Social Class	Males: Did not go to school	Males: Going to school	Males: Passed S.S.C.	Males: N	Famales: Did not go to school	Famales: Going to school	Famales: Passed S.S.C.	Famales: N
1	2	3	4	5	6	7	8	9	10
1. Dhodia	L	65.0	—	—	20	100.0	—	—	20
	M	52.4	—	—	21	(16)	—	—	19
	H	31.5	9.3	12.9	108	72.9	3.7	2.0	107
2. Gamit	L	66.7	—	4.2	24	91.7	—	—	24
	M	(6)	(1)	(1)	18	(14)	—	(1)	17
	H	34.6	1.9	7.7	52	77.0	2.1	4.2	48
3. Chaudhari	L	76.9	—	—	26	96.0	—	4.0	25
	M	67.9	3.5	—	28	95.4	—	—	24
	H	23.8	4.8	11.8	42	71.0	2.6	5.3	38
4. Bhil	L	78.4	1.8	—	116	100.0	—	—	107
	M	56.0	1.9	3.0	207	93.6	0.9	—	202
	H	33.2	6.2	7.5	211	80.0	0.5	1.5	200
5. Dhanka	L	76.0	—	—	46	97.4	—	—	39
	M	54.1	—	2.6	74	95.2	—	—	63
	H	37.3	3.0	6.0	67	85.5	1.6	3.2	62
6. Kokna	L	74.0	—	—	27	100.0	—	—	21
	M	60.0	—	—	20	(17)	—	—	18
	H	20.8	8.3	29.2	24	95.0	—	—	20
7. Patelia	L	(1)	—	—	1	(2)	—	—	2
	M	62.5	—	3.1	32	96.0	4.0	—	25
	H	(10)	—	(2)	17	(11)	—	(1)	13

TABLE 5.22 (b) : (*Contd.*)

1	2	3	4	5	6	7	8	9	10
8. Dubla	L	68.6	—	—	51	98.1	—	—	52
	M	43.5	4.4	4.4	23	(19)	—	—	19
	H	30.5	4.3	21.7	23	65.0	—	—	20
9. Rathwa	L	(1)	—	—	1	(1)	—	—	1
	M	72.0	—	—	25	(17)	—	—	17
	H	56.0	6.0	4.0	50	97.4	—	—	39
10. Nayaka	L	88.9	—	—	36	100.0	—	—	33
	M	61.3	—	—	31	88.0	—	—	25
	H	(2)	—	—	8	(7)	—	—	7
11 Koli	L	87.5	—	—	32	100.0	—	—	29
	M	(4)	(1)	(1)	13	(9)	—	—	11
	H	—	—	(1)	3	(3)	—	—	3
12. Varli	L	83.3	—	4.2	24	96.4	—	—	28
	M	(5)	—	—	8	(11)	—	—	12
	H	(2)	—	—	4	(2)	—	—	2
13. Kotwalia	L	96.8	—	—	31	100.0	—	—	34
	M	—	—	—	—	—	—	—	—
	H	—	—	—	—	—	—	—	—
14. Pardhi	L	—	—	—	—	—	—	—	—
	M	(4)	—	—	5	(5)	—	—	5
	H	(2)	—	—	3	(2)	—	—	3
Total	L	78.6	0.5	0.5	435	98.6	—	0.2	415
	M	56.2	1.6	2.4	505	93.2	0.7	0.2	457
	H	34.8	5.6	9.8	612	80.2	1.4	2.1	562

*1. Figures within parentheses indicate frequencies.
2. Percentages/frequencies for those who dropped out during primary/secondary school are not shown in the table.

examine inter-tribe and social class differences in the educational attainment of the tribals, controlling for age-group only. When the data are thus collapsed for both the sexes, we find that there are sharp social class differences in the educational attainment of the tribals. Even in the case of Dhodias whose educational attainment is at the top, about three-fourths of the 5—17 years old children from the low social class category did not go to school at all as against only one-fifth of those from the high social class category. Similar social class differences are also found among other tribal groups. Although there are considerable inter-tribe differences in the percentages of the 5—17 years old children who did not go to school at all, it should be noted that social class differences are much more pronounced than the inter-tribe differences. It should also be noted that the social class differences in the percentages of those who did not go to school at all are generally more pronounced in the younger generation than in the older generation. Further, although there is a reduction, from the older to the younger generation, in the percentages of those who did not go to school at all among all tribal groups, such a reduction is generally greater for those in the higher social class than that for those in the lower social class. This suggests that the tribals belonging to the higher social class have probably benefited more than those belonging to the lower social class from the expanding facilities for education and presumably also due to the special programmes of government assistance for the educational development of the tribals.

In sum, there is clearly a positive relationship between social class and educational attainment among the different tribal groups. This is true for the older as well as the younger generation and for the males as well as the females from different tribal groups. The differences in the educational attainment by sex and age-group continue for the tribals in each category of social class, however. While the available data do not give any direct evidence regarding the utilization of government assistance for education by the different tribal groups, the differential educational attainment of the tribals belonging to different social class suggests that those belonging to higher social class have presumably taken a greater advantage of such assistance than their counterparts from the lower social class.

TABLE 5.23 : **Educational attainment of different tribal groups by social class and age-group**

Tribe	Social Class	5—17 years			18+ years			
		Did not go to school	Going to school	N	Did not go to school	Going to school	Passed S.S.C.	N
1	2	3	4	5	6	7	8	9
1. Dhodia	L	74.3	12.9	31	82.5	—	—	40
	M	20.7	72.4	29	67.5	—	—	40
	H	18.0	65.6	122	52.1	6.5	7.5	215
2. Gamit	L	60.6	30.3	33	79.1	—	2.1	48
	M	34.6	57.7	26	57.1	2.9	5.7	35
	H	24.6	61.5	65	55.0	2.0	6.0	100
3. Chaudhari	L	57.1	33.4	21	86.2	—	2.0	51
	M	46.2	38.4	39	80.8	1.9	—	52
	H	35.6	46.6	45	46.2	3.8	8.8	80
4. Bhil	L	62.6	30.2	139	88.8	0.9	—	223
	M	53.0	40.3	285	74.5	1.5	1.5	409
	H	29.7	59.9	259	56.0	3.4	4.6	411
5. Dhanka	L	56.9	34.5	58	85.9	—	—	85
	M	41.6	46.1	89	73.0	—	1.5	137
	H	25.3	64.8	91	60.5	2.3	4.6	129
6. Kokna	L	64.7	32.4	34	85.4	—	—	48
	M	44.4	47.2	36	76.3	—	—	38
	H	34.4	65.6	32	54.6	4.5	15.9	44
7. Patelia	L	(2)	—	2	(3)	—	—	3
	M	48.3	38.7	31	77.1	1.8	1.8	57
	H	(10)	(8)	19	70.0	—	10.0	30

TABLE 5.23 : (*Contd.*)

1	2	3	4	5	6	7	8	9
8. Dubla	L	64.7	20.6	68	83.5	—	—	103
	M	55.6	30.5	36	69.1	2.4	2.4	42
	H	(9)	(6)	17	46.6	2.3	11.6	43
9. Rathwa	L	—	—	—	(2)	—	—	2
	M	75.7	18.9	37	83.3	—	—	42
	H	46.6	39.7	73	74.2	3.4	2.2	89
10. Nayaka	L	70.8	19.5	41	94.3	—	—	69
	M	55.0	25.0	40	73.2	—	—	56
	H	(8)	(9)	18	(9)	—	—	15
11. Koli	L	91.9	—	37	93.5	—	—	61
	M	45.0	35.0	20	54.1	4.2	4.2	24
	H	—	(3)	3	(3)	—	(1)	6
12. Varli	L	67.4	25.6	43	90.4	—	1.9	52
	M	55.0	35.0	20	80.0	—	—	20
	H	(1)	—	1	(4)	—	—	6
13. Kotwalia	L	72.2	22.2	36	98.5	—	—	65
	M	—	—	—	—	—	—	—
	H	—	—	—	—	—	—	—
14. Pardhi	L	—	—	—	—	—	—	—
	M	[1]	—	1	(9)	—	—	10
	H	[1]	[3]	6	(4)	—	—	5
Total	L	66.5	24.8	543	88.4	0.2	0.4	850
	M	49.8	40.3	689	73.9	1.1	1.3	962
	H	30.4	57.8	751	56.6	3.6	6.1	1173

*1. Figures within parentheses indicate frequencies.

2. Percentages/frequencies for thoes who dropped out during primary/secondary school are not shown in the table.

6

SOCIAL CLASS AWARENESS AND EDUCATIONAL DEVELOPMENT

THE ANALYSIS of the house-listing and interview data shows that the educational attainment of the tribals is of the lowest order. Although there is a considerable amount of inter-tribe variation in their educational attainment, it needs to be noted that the educational attainment of the most progressive group among the tribals is comparable with only that of the scheduled castes. Further, we do not find any support for the hypothesis that educational attainment of the tribals residing in the villages with a greater proportion of the non-tribals is likely to be higher than that of the tribals residing in the villages with a lower proportion of the non-tribals. In other words, the community contexts or the educational climate as captured by the proportion of the non-tribals residing in the village do not seem to be positively related to the educational attainment of the tribals. As in the general population, there is a positive and strong relationship between social class and educational attainment of the tribals also. This relationship is stronger for the girls than for the boys. There is also a strong and positive relationship between social class and educational/occupational expectations of the household heads of the school-going children. While it is true that the educational attainment of some of the tribal groups (Dhodias, for example) is considerably higher than the other tribal groups (Kotwalias, for example), it needs to be emphasized that there is a considerable amount of variation in the social class composition of different tribal groups. An examination of the relationship between social class and different indicators of educational attainment, controlling for age-group, sex and tribe, shows that the social class differences in educational attainment are much more pronounced than the inter-tribe differences in educational attainment. Given the special programmes of assistance to the tribals, it is most disturbing to find that social class differences, with regard to the percentages of those who never attended school, are generally more pronounced in the younger generation than in the older generation. A detailed examination of the data suggests that the tribals belonging to the higher social class have probably benefitted more than those belonging to the lower social class from the expanding facilities for education and presumably also due to the special programmes of government assistance for the educational development of the tribals.

Such a situation raises a crucial question for the planning and administration of special programmes of assistance to the tribals, namely, whether, and to what extent, information concerning educational facilities and special programmes of assistance reaches to the tribals. Two important antecedent conditions for utilizing available facilities and assistance for education by an individual are that he is aware of available facilities and assistance for education and also that he perceives the importance of acquiring education. We shall, therefore, examine in this chapter the extent to which the tribals are aware of available facilities and special programmes of governmental assistance for education, and the extent to which they perceive importance of acquiring education and are exposed to mass media and urban influences. Our approach will, no doubt, be to examine inter-tribe and social class variations in their awareness and the extent to which their awareness is related to their educational attainment.

Measurement of 'Awareness'

The interview schedule contained 18 questions/items designed to find out (a) whether the respondent is aware of the facilities and special programmes of assistance to the tribals for education/jobs, (b) the extent to which the respondent is exposed to mass media and has urban contacts and (c) their perception of the importance of acquiring education. These items can be grouped into four sub-categories as under :

(a) Respondent's awareness of general facilities for

education (that is, whether the respondent knows about available facilities for education—adult education classes, primary schools, secondary schools, ITIs, colleges and hostels) ;

(b) Respondent's awareness of special programmes of assistance to the tribals for education/jobs (that is, whether the respondent knows about *ashramsholas*, preference given to the tribals for admission to educational institutions, scholarships, reservation of seats for the tribals in medical and engineering colleges, and reservation of jobs for the tribals in the government and semi-government organizations) ;

(c) Respondent's exposure to mass media and urban contacts (that is, whether the respondent sees films, reads newspapers and visits the district head-quarters) ; and

(d) Respondent's perception of the importance of acquiring education based on his agreement/disagreement to the following statements :

(1) Do you believe that the children of your family can progress only if they are educated ?
(2) Would you educate your children even if you have to endure hardships ?
(3) Do you believe that it would be of great advantage to the members of your community if any one from your community becomes a doctor ?
(4) Do you believe that it would be of great advantage to the members of your community if any one from your community becomes a government official ?

The above-mentioned items were designed on the assumption that if the head of a household is aware of available facilities for education and special programmes of assistance to the tribals for education/jobs, he is more likely to motivate the members of his household to acquire education. Further, if he is frequently exposed to mass media and has urban contacts, his world-view is likely to be broad-based and this, in turn, is likely to act as a positive factor for motivating the other members to obtain education. The four statements regarding his per ception of importance of education are designed on the assumption that if the head of a household perceives some direct benefits of education likely to accrue to his family and the community and is willing to endure hardships to educate his children, he is likely to motivate the members of his household to acquire education. It should, however, be pointed out that there is no assumption regarding any sequential linkage between the categories of items included in this study.

For reasons of parsimony and convenience, it was felt necessary to combine the responses to all of these items into a single score. For this purpose, the responses to each item were first grouped into dichotomies (yes/no, high/low, or agree/disagree). A positive or a high-level response was coded as 1, and a negative or a low-level response was coded as 0. Then, the score on each item was assigned a weight equal to the proportion of the respondents in the low level category of the respective item, that is,

$$W_1 = \frac{N - n_1}{N}$$, where N=total sample size, and

n_1=the no. of respondents in the positive or high-level category.

Next, the sum of the weighted scores on all the items was obtained. The sum of the weighted scores indicates the overall level of "awareness" of the prepondents. For the purposes of cross-tabular analysis, the respondents obtaining a total score equal to or greater than one-half (4.28) of the maximum possible sum (8.555) of weighted scores are categorized as indicating a high level of awareness and those obtaining a total score less than one-half of the maximum possible sum of weighted scores are categorized as indicating a low level of awareness.

The analysis, discussion and presentation of data regarding the items on awareness are organized in the following manner. First, the percentages showing positive or high-level responses to these items in the total sample are examined. Next, the inter-tribe and social-class variations in their responses are examined. It is felt that this would indicate the likely gaps in diffusion of information and extension work that the government administration would need to bridge so as to maximize utilization of various programmes. Second, in view of the diflerences by social class and tribe in the educational attainment of the tribals, we shall examine the mean ($\bar{x}$) and coefficient of relative variation (CRV) of the awareness scores of the respondents in each category of social class and tribe simultaneously. Third, we shall examine, in a cross-tabular analysis, the relationship between awareness and educational attainment among the tribals, controlling for tribe, sex and age-group. And finally, we shall similarly examine the relationship between awareness and educational attainment among the tribals, controlling for social class, sex and age-group.

The percentages showing the respondents' awareness of various items are shown, by tribe, in Table 6.1 ; similarly, the percentages showing the respondents' awareness of various items are shown, by social class, in Table 6.2. Let us examine these data according to the above-mentioned four categories of items.

Knowledge regarding general facilities for education

It is found that most of the tribals are generally aware of adult education classes, primary schools and secondary schools, but a sizeable section of the tribals is still unaware of facilities for specialized and higher education. It seems that they know about facilities for education that are generally located in their own or nearby villages, but they remain unaware of the educational facilities located in cities and other distant places. Only about one-fourth of the respondents know of Industrial Training Institutes (ITIs) and about one-half of them know about colleges and hostel facilities. It should also be noted that a large proportion of the Kotwalia, Varli, Koli and Dubla respondents are unaware of such facilities. Further, the relationship of social class to the proportion of the respondents who know about such general facilities for education is positive and monotonic. Such a relationship suggests the need for devising mechanisms to inform the tribals (especially those belonging to lower social classes) about the available facilities for specialized and higher education that are generally located in larger towns and cities in their own as well as adjoining districts.

TABLE 6.1 : **Percentages showing awareness among respondents, by tribe**

Awareness	Tribe							
	Dhodia	Gamit	Chaudhari	Bhil	Dhanka	Kokna	Patelia	Dubla
1	2	3	4	5	6	7	8	9
(*a*) *Knows about general facilities for education*								
1. Adult Education class	81.6	94.5	84.5	78.4	87.8	90.5	92.0	72.9
2. Primary school	100.0	100.0	96.6	95.9	96.9	100.0	100.0	96.6
3. Secondary school	94.8	98.2	93.1	86.8	87.8	78.5	100.0	81.4
4. I.T.I.	32.9	41.8	36.2	29.2	29.6	16.7	56.0	22.0
5. College	61.8	65.5	50.0	51.2	42.8	.35.8	96.0	45.8
6. Hostel	64.5	63.6	55.2	63.1	61.3	66.7	76.0	40.7
(*b*) *Knows about programmes of assistance to tribals for education/jobs*								
7. Ashramshala	89.5	96.4	96.6	87.8	91.8	97.6	80.0	72.9
8. Preference in admission	40.8	41.8	44.8	45.8	40.8	31.0	52.0	32.2
9. Scholarships	90.8	69.1	69.0	72.9	76.5	71.4	84.0	76.3
10. Reservation in medical/engineering colleges	22.4	36.4	31.0	33.6	34.7	19.0	48.0	18.6
11. Reservation of jobs in govt. etc.	52.6	45.5	39.7	47.8	39.8	23.8	64.0	23.7
(*c*) *Exposure to mass media, etc.*								
12. Has seen films many times	23.7	27.3	8.6	10.2	11.2	—	—	11.9
13. Reads newspapers often/daily	19.7	29.1	15.5	14.2	11.2	16.7	16.0	10.2
14. Visits district head-quarters often/daily	40.8	60.0	25.8	30.2	30.6	16.7	72.0	49.2

TABLE 6.1 : (*Contd.*)

1	2	3	4	5	6	7	8	9
(*d*) *Perceived importance of education*								
15. Children can progress only if they are educated	88.2	70.9	74.1	80.3	84.7	92.9	76.0	78.0
16. Will endure hardships to educate children	68.4	65.5	70.7	67.1	79.6	88.1	60.0	42.4
17. A doctor from the community will be of great advantage	85.5	81.8	87.9	81.7	92.9	97.6	88.0	81.4
18. A govt. official from the community will be of great advantage	92.1	89.1	94.8	83.4	91.8	95.2	84.0	98.4
N	76	55	58	295	98	42	25	59

TABLE 6.1 : (*Contd.*)

Awareness	Tribe						
	Rathwa	Nayaka	Koli	Varli	Kotwalia	Pardhi*	Total
1	2	3	4	5	6	7	8
(*a*) *Knows about general facilities for education*							
1. Adult Education class	82.1	77.6	66.7	88.9	66.7	[3]	81.3
2. Primary school	92.3	87.8	100.0	96.3	100.0	[4]	96.7
3. Secondary school	81.2	77.6	75.8	77.8	41.7	[4]	86.0
4. I.T.I.	30.8	28.6	15.2	3.7	—	[0]	28.3
5. College	74.4	49.0	36.3	7.4	4.2	[3]	50.0
6. Hostel	66.7	59.2	69.7	14.8	37.5	[3]	59.6
(*b*) *Knows about programmes of assistance to tribals for education/jobs*							
7. Ashramshala	79.5	83.7	93.9	92.6	8.3	[2]	88.6
8. Preference in admission	43.6	24.5	24.2	14.8	4.2	[3]	38.7
9. Scholarships	76.9	69.4	48.5	59.3	4.2	[2]	71.3
10. Reservation in medical/engineering colleges	38.5	20.0	21.2	3.7	0.0	[0]	28.5
11. Reservation of jobs in govt., etc.	61.5	22.4	21.2	11.1	0.0	[1]	40.0
(*c*) *Exposure to mass media, etc.*							
12. Has seen films many times	5.1	8.2	—	—	4.2	[1]	10.6
13. Reads newspapers often/daily	5.1	6.1	9.1	7.4	—	[1]	13.7
14. Visits district head-quarters often/daily	33.4	34.7	15.2	18.5	8.3	[2]	33.5

TABLE 6.1 : (*Contd.*)

1	2	3	4	5	6	7	8
(*d*) *Perceived importance of education*							
15. Children can progress only if they are educated	59.0	57.1	97.0	96.3	95.8	[2]	80.0
16. Will endure hardships to educate children	48.7	42.9	78.8	48.1	62.5	[2]	65.4
17. A doctor from the community will be of great advantage	64.1	65.3	100.0	96.3	100.0	[4]	84.6
18. A govt. official from the community will be of great advantage	66.7	61.2	100.0	96.3	100.0	[4]	86.4
N	39	49	33	27	24	4	884

*Figures within brackets indicate frequencies.

Knowledge regarding special programmes of assistance to the tribals for education/jobs.

About ninety per cent of the respondents are aware of ashram-shalas and about seventy per cent of the respondents are aware of scholarships available to the tribals. But only about one-fourth to two-fifths of the respondents know that preferences are given to the tribals for admission to educational institutions, reservation of seats in medical and engineering colleges and reservation of jobs in the government and semi-government organizations. It may be noted that the percentages of the respondents who are aware of such special programmes of assistance to the tribals are smaller than the percentages of those who are aware of college and hostel facilities. Most of the Varli, Kotwalia and Pardhi respondents are unaware of important programmes for reservation in educational institutions and jobs in the government. Although there is a considerable amount of inter-tribe variation in the respondents' knowledge regarding such special programmes, the social class differences in this regard are quite pronounced. The relationship of social class to the proportion of the respondents who know about such special programmes of assistance to the tribals is positive and monotonic. Only about 10 per cent to 20 per cent of the respondents in the low social class category, as against 46 per cent to 66 per cent of the respondents in the high social class category, are aware of such programmes. Such a situation is again a pointer to the need for mobilizing appropriate information channels to inform the tribals about such matters.

Exposure to mass media and urban contacts

In view of a very low literacy rate, remoteness of the tribal villages, and generally poor economic condition of the tribals, we would not expect a large proportion of the respondents to have had opportunity to see films, read newspapers or visit the district head quarters very often. It is, therefore, not surprising that only about 10 per cent of the respondents often see films, and about 14 per cent of the respondents frequently or daily read newspapers. It is, however, very striking that about one-third of the respondents visit the district head-quarters very often. No inquiry was made regarding the purpose of their visits to the district head-

TABLE 6.2 : **Percentages showing awareness among respondents, by social class**

Awareness	Social class			Total
	Low	Middle	High	
(a) Knows about general facilities for education				
1. Adult Education class	74.3	80.7	89.4	81.3
2. Primary school	97.0	94.3	99.0	96.7
3. Secondary school	74.6	87.3	96.5	86.0
4. I.T.I.	16.7	26.0	42.8	28.3
5. College	28.4	53.0	69.5	50.0
6. Hostel	44.5	59.0	76.2	59.6
(b) Knows about programmes of assistance to tribals for education/jobs				
7. Ashramshala	87.3	88.0	90.5	88.6
8. Preference in admission	20.7	38.0	58.2	38.7
9. Scholarships	52.5	72.7	89.5	71.3
10. Reservation in medical/ engineering colleges	13.4	27.0	46.0	28.5
11. Reservation of jobs in govt., etc.	19.1	36.7	65.6	40.0
(c) Exposure to mass media, etc.				
12. Has seen films many times	4.3	7.7	20.4	10.6
13. Reads newspapers often/daily	2.6	11.0	28.1	13.7
14. Visits district head-quarters often/daily	19.7	33.3	48.1	33.5
(d) Perceived importance of education				
15. Children can progress only if they are educated	79.3	75.7	85.3	80.0
16. Will endure hardships to educate children	54.8	64.7	77.2	65.4
17. A doctor from the community will be of great advantage	86.3	81.3	86.3	84.6
18, A govt. official from the community will be of great advantage	87.0	81.7	90.9	86.4
N	299	300	285	884

quarters. The pattern of inter-tribe and social class differences, observed earlier, also continues with regard to the three items of exposure to mass media and urban contacts.

Perceived importance of education

More than four-fifths of the respondents have responded positively to three of the four items regarding their perception of importance of education ; most of the tribals believe that their children can progress only if they are educated ; they also believe that if any one member from their community becomes a government official or a doctor, it will be advantageous to their community. The inter-tribe and social class differences, although present to some extent, are dampened in this regard. Only the Rathwa and Nayaka respondents lag behind the respondents from the other tribal groups in this matter. However, when inquired whether they will endure hardships to educate their children, only two-thirds of the respondents indicated that they would do so. In this regard, there is a positive and monotonic relationship between social class and the proportion of the respondents willing to endure hardships to educate their children. This suggests a possibility that most of the low social class respondents who indicated their unwillingness to endure hardships to educate their children may be unable to do so. In other words, it may be a question of inability rather than unwillingness of the respondents in the low social class category. It should also be noted that a large proportion of the Dubla, Rathwa, Nayaka and Varli respondents did not indicate their willingness to endure hardships to educate their children.

In sum, these data indicate that a fairly large number of the tribals are still unaware of the facilities and programmes for specialized and higher education. In spite of a lack of knowledge regarding facilities for education and special programmes of assitance to the tribals, it seems that a fairly large proportion of the tribals perceive importance of educating their children. Although there is a considerable amount of inter-tribe variation in the proportions of the tribals indicating positive or high-level responses to the various items of awareness, the social class differences in this regard are more pronounced than the inter-tribe differences. We shall, therefore examine these data, controlling for tribe and social class simultaneously. This is shown in Tables 6.3 (a) and 6.3 (b).

TABLE 6.3(a) : **Arithmetic means and coefficients of relative variation (CRV) of awareness, by tribe**

Tribe	$\overline{X}$	CRV	N
1. Dhodia	3.54	0.54	76
2. Gamit	3.84	0.56	55
3. Chaudhari	3.14	0.66	58
4. Bhil	3.18	0.63	295
5. Dhanka	3.16	0.62	98
6. Kokna	2.69	0.64	42
7. Patelia	4.14	0.38	25
8. Dubla	2.67	0.57	59
9. Rathwa	3.18	0.57	39
10. Nayaka	2.50	0.76	49
11. Koli	2.44	0.70	33
12. Varli	1.72	0.68	27
13. Kotwalia	1.33	0.35	24
14. Pardhi	2.68	0.54	4
Total	3.05	0.64	884

Awareness

As mentioned earlier, the measure of awareness used in this study is a sum of weighted scores of the respondent's responses to 18 items. It should be noted that the mean awareness score for the total group (3.05) is less than even one-half of the possible maximum score of the measure. The coefficient of variation in the scores of the respondents is also relatively large. We find that the Patelia respondents have the highest mean score (4.14), and the Kotwalia respondents have the lowest mean score (1.33). Both of these tribal groups show the lowest variation in their awareness scores. All of the tribal groups that have been found to have a higher level of educational attainment have a mean score of 3.05 and above (that is, higher than the mean score for the total sample). Those tribal groups that have a lower level of educational attainment have a lower score than that for the total sample. It may be noted that the mean score of awareness increases with the level of social class, from 2.10 for the low

TABLE 6.3(b) : **Arithmetic means and coefficients of relative variation (CRV) of awareness, by social class**

Tribe	Low Social Class			Middle Social Class			High Social Class		
	$\overline{X}$	CRV	N	X	CRV	N	X	CRV	N
1. Dhodia	2.12	0.47	15	3.77	0.50	13	3.91	0.50	48
2. Gamit	2.75	0.56	17	3.60	0.62	12	4.66	0.46	26
3. Chaudhari	2.48	0.75	17	2.53	0.68	19	4.17	0.51	22
4. Bhil	2.11	0.80	76	3.04	0.63	124	4.23	0.43	95
5. Dhanka	2.38	0.69	28	2.66	0.61	37	4.38	0.46	33
6. Kokna	2.02	0.60	18	2.51	0.49	13	3.99	0.56	11
7. Patelia	5.46	—	1	3.65	0.42	18	5.39	0.20	6
8. Dubla	2.23	0.65	35	2.89	0.41	13	3.82	0.42	11
9. Rathwa	0.00	—	1	2.84	0.60	16	3.57	0.50	22
10. Nayaka	2.51	0.73	25	1.92	0.91	18	4.17	0.46	6
11. Koli	1.53	0.28	23	4.16	0.41	8	5.60	0.13	2
12. Varli	1.54	0.42	19	2.32	0:86	7	0.84	—	1
13. Kotwalia	1.33	0.35	24	—	—	—	—	—	—
14. Pardhi	—	—	—	1.55	0.11	2	3.80	0.28	2
Total	2.10	0.70	299	2.94	0.62	300	4.17	0.46	285

social class category to 4.17 for the high social class category. Thus, the mean awareness score for the high social class category is twice that for the low social class category. The coefficient of variation in the awareness scores decreases as one moves from the low social class category to the high social class category. While examining the awareness scores, controlling simultaneously for tribe and social class, it should be noted that Ns in some of the cells in the table are very small ; consequently, the mean scores in such cells are likely to be unstable. Nevertheless, it can be seen that the inter-tribe variation within each category of social class is considerably reduced. On the other hand, the social class differences in the awareness scores within each category of tribe are generally striking. Except for a few cells with a very low N, we find that the relationship between social class and awareness scores is positive and monotonic in each tribal category. Excluding the cells with N less than 10, we find that Kotwalias in the low social class category have the lowest mean score of awareness (1.33) and Gamits in the high social class category have the highest mean score of awareness (4.66). This shows the range of gap that is needed to be reduced in the level of awareness among the tribals regarding available facilities and special programmes of assistance to the tribals for education/jobs. We shall now examine the relationship between awareness and educational attainment.

Awareness and educational attainment, controlling for tribe

Since there are significant differences, by sex and age-group, in the educational attainment of the tribals, it is necessary to control for these two variables while examining the relationship between awareness and educational attainment of the tribals. This is so done in Tables 6.4 (a) and 6.4 (b). It may be noted that we are examining two indicators of educational attainment of the boys and the girls in the age-group 5—17, namely, the percentages of those who never went to school and the percentages of those who are currently in school. For the adults, we are examining one additional indicator of educational attainment, namely, the percentage of those who have passed the S.S.C. Examination. The following observations should be made from these tables.

TABLE 6.4(a) : Percentages showing those who did not go to school at all and those who are going to school among 5—17 years old children, by sex, tribe and awareness*

	Tribe	Awareness	Boys			Girls		
			Did not go to school	Going to school	N	Did not go to school	Going to school	N
1.	Dhodia	Low	29.8	52.6	57	47.4	42.1	57
		High	9.7	77.4	31	11.1	75.0	36
2.	Gamit	Low	50.0	38.1	42	43.2	43.2	37
		High	18.5	81.5	27	[3]	[11]	17
3.	Chaudhari	Low	38.1	45.2	42	70.0	20.0	30
		High	[3]	[7]	16	[6]	[11]	17
4.	Bhil	Low	44.2	46.3	240	71.6	23.7	194
		High	20.3	73.9	138	38.5	48.6	109
5.	Dhanka	Low	36.1	51.5	97	52.4	39.3	84
		High	17.6	76.5	34	38.1	52.4	21
6.	Kokna	Low	42.5	50.0	40	72.5	25.0	40
		High	[1]	[12]	13	[2]	[7]	9
7.	Patelia	Low	[3]	[5]	11	[10]	[1]	12
		High	[4]	[10]	14	[10]	[4]	15
8.	Dubla	Low	40.0	30.0	50	83.7	16.3	49
		High	[2]	[6]	10	[10]	[2]	12
9.	Rathwa	Low	43.3	36.7	30	73.5	26.5	34
		High	26.1	56.5	23	78.3	13.0	23
10.	Nayaka	Low	55.3	29.8	47	83.3	16.6	30
		High	[4]	[6]	8	[4]	[4]	10
11.	Koli	Low	77.3	13.6	22	95.8	—	24
		High	[3]	[4]	10	—	[3]	4
12.	Varli	Low	53.8	35.9	39	79.2	16.7	24
		High	[1]	—	1	—	—	—
13.	Kotwalia	Low	[10]	[5]	17	[16]	[3]	19
		High	—	—	—	—	—	—
14.	Pardhi	Low	—	[2]	3	[1]	—	2
		High	[1]	[1]	2	—	—	—
	Total	Low	43.7	42.7	737	68.6	25.9	636
		High	20.5	70.6	327	39.2	49.8	273
		Total	36.6	51.3	1064	59.7	33.1	909

* 1. Figures within brackets indicate frequencies.
2. Percentages/frequencies for those who droppedout during Primary/Secondary school are not shown in the table.

TABLE 6.4(b) : **Percentages showing those who did not go to school at all, those who are going to school, and those who have passed S.S.C. among adults, by sex, tribe and awareness***

Tribe	Awareness	Males				Females			
		Did not go to school	Going to school	Passed S.S.C	N	Did not go to school	Going to school	Passed S.S.C	N
1. Dhodia	Low	48.4	6.3	4.2	95	86.5	—	—	89
	High	22.2	7.4	18.5	54	64.9	7.0	3.5	57
2. Gamit	Low	52.8	—	1.9	53	89.8	—	2·0	49
	High	29.3	4.9	12.2	41	50.0	2.5	5.0	40
3. Chaudhari	Low	61.5	1.5	3.1	65	94.7	—	3.5	57
	High	29.0	6.5	9.7	31	66.7	3.3	3.3	30
4. Bhil	Low	68.2	0.6	1.5	336	94.4	0.3	—	319
	High	24.5	8.7	8.7	196	81.6	1.1	1.6	190
5. Dhanka	Low	59.5	0.7	1.3	153	95.4	—	—	130
	High	26.5	2.0	11.8	34	79.4	2.9	5.9	34
6. Kokna	Low	64.2	—	3.8	53	95.7	—	—	46
	High	[3]	[2]	[5]	17	[13]	—	—	13
7. Patelia	Low	86.4	—	4.5	22	100.0	—	—	18
	High	50.0	—	8.3	24	86.4	4.5	4.5	22
8. Dubla	Low	60.5	1.3	3.9	76	96.1	—	—	76
	High	28.6	4.8	14.3	21	[10]	—	—	15
9. Rathwa	Low	76.9	—	—	39	96.9	—	—	32
	High	45.9	8.1	5.4	37	100.0	—	—	25
10. Nayaka	Low	78.6	—	—	56	95.9	—	—	49
	High	[9]	—	—	18	[15]	—	—	16
11. Koli	Low	83.3	—	—	36	100.0	—	—	34
	High	[2]	[1]	[2]	10	[7]	—	—	9

(*Contd.* TABLE 6.4 b)

12. Varli	Low	75.0	—	2.8	36	97.6	—	—	41
	High	—	—	—	1	—	—	—	1
13. Kotwalia	Low	96.8	—	—	31	100.0	—	—	34
	High	—	—	—	—	—	—	—	—
14. Pardhi	Low	[6]	—	—	7	[6]	—	—	7
	High	—	—	—	1	[1]	—	—	1
Total	Low	64.5	1.0	1.9	1085	94.5	0.1	0.3	981
	High	28.7	6.8	10.9	485	79.0	2.2	2.4	453
	Total	54.4	2.9	4.8	1543	89.6	0.8	1.0	1434

• 1. Figures within brackets indicate frequencies.
2. Percentages/frequencies for those who dropped out during Primary/Secondary school are not shown in the table.

First, there is a positive relationship between the level of awareness of the heads of households and educational attainment of the members. This is true for all the categories of age-group and sex. Within each category of age-group and sex, the percentage of those who did not go to school is considerably lower for those in the high awareness category than that for those in the low awareness category. However, the differences by age-group and sex continue. In fact, the impact of age-group, sex and the level of awareness on educational attainment is additive. For example, 95 per sent of the adult females from the low awareness category never went to school as against only 21 per cent of the 5—17 years old boys from the high awareness category. Similar differences in the other indicators of educational attainment are also found in the cross-pressured cells.

Second, when the above data are further classified by tribe, we face the problem of adequate cell frequencies in some of the categories. Nonetheless, it seems very obvious that within each category of tribe, the level of awareness is positively related to educational attainment. Here again, the differences by age-group and sex continue. For example, among Dhodias only 9.7 per cent of the 5--17 years old boys from the high awareness category never went to school as against 86.5 per cent of the adult females from the low awareness category. Similarly, among Rathwas, 26.1 per cent of the 5—17 years old boys from the high awareness category did not go to school as against 96.9 per cent of adult females from the low awareness category. Thus, age-group, sex, awareness and tribe seem to have an additive impact on the educational attainment of the tribals.

Third, a full comparison of percentages in the various categories of age-group, sex, and awareness within each tribal group is not possible on account of the limitation of adequate cell frequencies; wherever such a comparison is possible, it is found that the percentage of girls going to school in the high awareness category is almost equal to, or sometime even higher than, the percentage of boys going to school in the low awareness category. For example, among Dhodias 52.6 per cent of the 5—17 years old boys from the low awareness category go to school as against 75 per cent of the 5—17 years old girls from the high awareness category. Similarly, among Dhankas 52.4

per cent of the 5—17 years old girls from the high awareness category go to school as against 51.5 per cent of the 5—17 years old boys from the low awareness category. Thus, in the younger generation, with regard to the percentage of those going to school, a high level of awareness seems to be a more powerful factor than sex.

Finally, only 4.8 per cent of the adult males have passed the S.S.C. Examination. But here again, within each tribal group the percentage for those in the high awareness category is considerably higher than that for those in the low awareness category. It may be noted that the between-tribe differences in the percentages of those having passed the S.S.C. examination are somewhat smaller for those in the low awareness category than similar differences for those in the high awareness category.

Awareness and educational attainment, controlling for social class

Given positive and strong relationships between social class and educational attainment, between social class and awareness, and between awareness and educational attainment, it is necessary to examine the extent to which the relationship between social class and educational attainment of the tribals is mediated by the level of awareness. This can be examined from Tables 6.5 (a) and 6.5 (b). The following observations should be made from these data.

First, the pattern of a positive and strong relationship between social class and educational attainment of the tribals continues even when we control simultaneously for sex, age-group and the level of awareness. That is, within each category of sex, age-group and level of awareness, we find a positive and strong relationship between social class and educational attainment. This is true for all the three indicators of educational attainment.

Second, within each category of social class the differences in educational attainment by sex, age-group and level of awareness also continue. In fact, the impact of sex, age-group, level of awareness and social class seems to be additive. Thus, only 17.2 per cent of the 5—17 years old boys from the high social class and high awareness category never went to school as against almost all of the adult females from the low social class

TABLE 6.5(a) : Percentages showing those who did not go to school at all and those who are going to school among 5—17 years old children, by sex, social class and awareness*

Social Class	Aware-ness	Boys			Girls		
		Did not go to school	Going to school	N	Did not go to school	Going to school	N
Low	Low	56.9	30.7	267	81.4	15.2	210
	High	45.5	45.5	333	74.2	19.4	31
Middle	Low	43.0	44.9	272	70.5	24.4	254
	High	18.7	72.5	91	45.5	42.4	66
High	Low	26.8	56.1	198	50.0	41.3	172
	High	17.2	73.9	203	30.7	60.0	176
Total	Low	43.7	42.7	737	68.6	25.9	636
	High	20.5	70.6	327	39.2	49.8	273
	Total	36.6	51.3	1064	59.7	33.1	909

* Percentages for those who dropped out during primary/secondary school are not shown in the table.

and low awareness category. Similarly, in the younger generation, only 15.2 per cent of the girls from the low social class and low awareness category go to school as against almost three-fourths of the boys from the high social class and high awareness category. Even among the adults, only 0.3 per cent of the females from the low social class and low awareness category passed the S.S.C. Examination as against 14.5 per cent of the males from the high social class and high awareness category.

Finally, it should be noted that among the younger boys and the adult males, a higher level of awareness seems to be successful in considerably reducing, or even completely eliminating, the social class differences in the adjoining categories. This will be obvious if we compare the percentages of all the indicators of educational attainment in the low social class but high awareness category with those for the middle social class but low awareness category. The same pattern is found while comparing the percentages of those in the middle social class but high awareness category with the percentages of those in the high social class but low awareness category. This, however, does

TABLE 6.5(b) : **Percentages showing those who did not go to school at all, those who are going to school and those who have passed S.S.C. among adults, by sex, social class and awareness***

Social class	Awareness	Males				Females			
		Did not go to school	Going to school	Passed S.S.C.	N	Did not go to school	Going to school	Passed S.S.C.	N
Low	Low	82.1	—	0.3	374	98.6	—	0.3	361
	High	58.3	3.3	1.7	60	98.1	—	—	54
Middle	Low	65.3	0.5	1.1	377	95.9	—	0.3	341
	High	31.1	4.9	6.6	122	85.3	2.6	—	116
High	Low	47.9	2.9	5.2	307	87.5	0.4	0.4	279
	High	21.8	8.3	14.5	303	72.8	2.5	3.9	283
Total	Low	66.2	1.0	2.0	1058	94.5	0.1	0.3	981
	High	28.7	6.8	10.9	485	79.0	2.2	2.4	453
	Total	54.4	2.9	4.8	1543	89.6	0.8	1.0	1434

* Percentages for those who dropped out during Primary/Secondary school are not shown in the table.

not hold true for the girls and the adult females. It is interesting to note that there is practically no difference in the educational attainment of the 5—17 years old boys in the middle social class but high awareness category and the high social class but low awareness category. Such a pattern of relationships of social class and awareness to educational attainment of boys and adult males shows that it would be possible for the society to dampen, to a certain extent, the influence of social class if it could increase the level of awareness in the target group, especially when the society extends financial and other assistance for education.

Given the differences in the educational attainment of the tribals by age-group, sex, tribe, social class and level of awareness, it would be necessary to control for all these variables while examining the educational attainment of the tribals. However, the data presented in Tables 6.4 (a) and 6.4 (b) show that an additional control for social class will render the problem of adequate cell frequencies almost unsurmountable. The limitations of the available data, therefore, do not allow us to examine the intricacies of relationships between these variables any further.

In sum, the analysis of the data presented in this chapter clearly show that strong social class differences in the educational attainment of the tribals do persist. What is generally observed in the wider society is also found among the tribals. Although the goal of the society should be to continue its struggle for eliminating, or at least drastically reducing, social class differences in such basic development programmes, which are designed on the basis of accepted tenets of a policy of protective discrimination, the reality of the situation suggests that considerable efforts are necessary to mobilize information channels and extension work to make the tribals aware of the available facilities and special programmes of assistance for their educational development. Necessary inputs in this direction are not only likely to raise the level of their educational development but also to reduce, to a certain extent, social class differences in the utilization of the facilities and programmes of assistance.

7

SUMMARY

INTRODUCTION

FOR THE past three decades, the goverment has been following a policy of protective discrimination so as to promote the educational and economic interests of the weaker sections including the scheduled tribes. The government has launched several programmes to motivate and assist the scheduled tribes to obtain education. Since the tribal population is concentrated in certain areas, the government formulates a special sub-plan for accelerating, with intensive inputs, the development of the tribals in such areas.

The present study examines, in detail, the educational development of the tribals residing in the rural areas of the tribal sub-plan in Gujarat. A review of the available data regarding literacy, enrolment and educational attainment of the tribals in Gujarat is a starting point for the present study. This review indicates that the tribals are at the lowest level of the educational pyramid. The increase in the literacy rates of the tribals, during 1961-1971, was also the lowest. There is also a considerable variation, by sex, rural-urban residence and district, in their literacy rates. An examination of the literacy rates in the rural areas of the tribal sub-plan brings out a more dismal picture of literacy among the tribals. There are considerable inter-taluka and inter-tribe variations in the male and the female literacy rates of the tribals in this area. It is found that the lowest male literacy rate (22) is among Bhils residing in Jhagadia taluka and the highest male literacy rate (516) is among Dhodias residing in Mahuva taluka. Similarly, the lowest female literacy rate (2) is among Rathwas residing in Devgadhbaria taluka and the highest female literacy rate (273) is among Dhodias residing in Mahuva taluka. The lowest level of education among the tribals is indicated by the fact (according to the 1961 Census), that only 27 per 1,000 rural females and 119 per 1,000 rural males had obtained the primary or junior basic education. Further, the tribals are a way behind the others in regard to enrolment at all levels of education. It is alarming that the tribals in Gujarat registered a sharp fall in the coefficient of equality for enrolment at all levels of education, from 56.9 in 1960-61 to 46.7 in 1965-66. Although the 1973-74 enrolment data indicate an impressive increase in their enrolment in primary schools, they still lag behind the general population, especially with regard to their enrolment at the higher levels of education. The drop-out rate among the tribals is higher than that in the total population. In other words, inquality in educational attainment increases sharply as one moves to higher levels of education.

In view of the low-level, uneven educational development of the tribals, this study examines the social contexts of their educational development. The social contexts of tribal education examined in this study are divided into four categories. First, the argument of this study is that the educational development of the tribals must be examined in the context of the educational development of the other castes/communities residing in the same area. Secondly, in view of the relatively high level of educational development of the non-tribals, it is hypothesized that the tribals residing in a village community with a relatively high proportion of the non-tribals are more likely to show a higher level of educational development than those residing in a village community with a relatively low proportion of the non-tribals. Thirdly, there is a need to examine the oft-mentioned observation that the benefits of the government programmes of financial and other assistance for education accrue most to the children of the privileged among them. And finally, two important antecedent conditions for utilizing available facilities and assistance for education by an individual are that he is aware of available facilities and special programmes of assistance for education and that he perceives the importance of acquiring education. The present study attempts to examine the educational development of the tribals in relation to these four broad categories of social contexts.

This study is conducted in 32 talukas which constitute the tribal sub-plan area of Gujarat. About 72 per cent of the total tribal population of the state resides in the tribal sub-plan area. In view of the fact that a little over 90 per cent of the tribal population in the sub-plan area resides in the rural areas, the setting of the study is restricted to only the rural part of tribal sub-plan area.

Sample

A two-stage sampling design was used in this study. In the first stage, two villages from each of the 32 talukas in the tribal sub-plan area were selected. The villages were selected on the basis of a systematic examination of the available data so as to obtain two villages from each taluka that have rather contrasting characteristics of (a) a modest proportion of the tribal population and a high development score and (b) a high proportion of the tribal population and a low development score. Then, complete lists of all households in the selected villages were prepared. Certain information regarding education of the household members was also collected in the house-listing form. In the second stage, at least 10 households from each village were selected by a stratified random procedure. The criteria used for stratification were (1) villages/talukas and (2) tribal groups. The tribal groups from different talukas were selected on the basis of the distribution of their population in different talukas as well as the consideration for including the smaller tribal groups which were not found in the previous study (Shah and Patel, 1977) but which appeared in the house-lists. While the households belonging to smaller tribal groups not found in the previous study were selected with certainty, the probability of selection of other households differed for different tribal groups in the 32 talukas of the tribal sub-plan area. The criterion of selecting, as far as possible, a minimum of 5 households from each tribal group in each village was applied. In all, the interview data were collected from 884 heads of the households.

The data

Two sources of data have been used in this study, namely, house-listing data interview data. While preparing the house-lists, information was collected, from each household in the selected villages, regarding scheduled tribe/sub-tribe, scheduled caste/sub-caste, other caste/community, major occupation of the head of the household, the highest level of education attained by any male/female member in the household, the number of boys/girls currently studying in primary/middle/high school, and the number of illiterate/total boys/girls in the age-group 5—17 years. The houselisting data were collected from 15,861 households. The interview schedule was designed to collect information regarding (1) tribe, sub-tribe, religion, (2) sex, marital status, education and occupation of all members, (3) educational/occupational expectations for those going to school and reasons for those who dropped out of school, (4) annual income, land-holding, cattle, type of housing, utensils and other household possessions, (5) knowledge and use of various facilities/assistance for education ; willingness and ability for providing education to children without government assistance, and sacrifice the family was willing to make for educating children, (6) opinions regarding statements concerning education, and (7) information regarding exposure to mass media and urban contacts. After pretesting and necessary revision, the interview schedule was administered to the heads of the selected households. The house-listing information was collected during February-March, 1977 and the interview data were collected during March-June, 1977. The data were collected by trained field investigators. The field work was supervised by the researcher with the assistance of another faculty member of the Department of Sociology.

The data collected in the house-listing forms and the interview schedules were numerically coded, punched on IBM cards, and then transferred to magnetic tapes. Necessary checks and cross-checks of the data were carried out during all these operations. The facilities provided by the Government of Gujarat Computer Center (ICL 1901), the Gujarat University Computer Center (IBM 1620), and the Physical Research Laboratory Computer Center (IBM 360-44) were used for computerization and analysis of the data. In order to easily identify the differential characteristics of several sub-groups at every possible stage, we have preferred to use simple and multiple cross-tabular analysis. Only for the purposes of developing weighted measures of social class and awareness, complicated statistical procedures have been used. The relevant methodological details are given in the main body of the report and appendices.

Educational development in the tribal sub-plan area

The Educational development of the tribals must be examined in the context of the educational development of the other castes/communities residing in the same area. Three indicators of educational development of a caste/community/tribe are examined from the house-listing data: (a) the highest level of education attained by any member among males/females in the household, (b) the number of illiterate boys/girls in the age-group 5-17 years, and (c) the number of boys/girls attending primary/middle/high school. It is found that the educational development of people in the tribal sub-plan area is generally very low. Examining the various indicators of educational development, separately for various castes/communities, the house-listing data indicate (Chapter 3) that educational development is positively related to the social status of the castes/communities. The educational development of the tribals is the lowest, and that of the high-caste Hindus II is the highest. The educational development of the scheduled castes is above that of the scheduled tribes, but much below that of even the low-caste Hindus. The educational development of the Muslim males falls above that of the middle-caste Hindus, but the educational development of the Muslim females falls below that of the middle-caste Hindus. The educational development of Christians and Parsis generally compares favourably with that of the high-caste Hindus II. It may be noted that in about 30 per cent of the tribal households, at least one boy/girl is illiterate ; further, the percentages of illiterate boys and girls among the scheduled tribes as well as the scheduled castes are considerably greater than those among even the low-caste Hindus. Also, in 44.5 per cent of the tribal house-holds, there is not a single male member with any formal education ; in 75.6 per cent of the tribal households, there is not a single female member with any formal education. Only 7.0 per cent of the tribal households have at least one male member having attained S.S.C./College education and only 2.2 per cent of the tribal households have at least one female member having attained that high level of education.

There is a considerable inter-tribe variation in the educational development of the tribals. An examination of the various indicators of educational development shows that Dhodias and Chaudharis are far above the average level, Dhankas, Bhils and Koknas are at the average level and Rathwas, Dublas, Varlis and Kotwalias are far below the average level of educational development of the tribals in general. In fact, the educational development of Dublas, Varlis and Kotwalias is almost negligible. With regard to the educational development of Gamits, Koli/Kolchas and Nayakas, there are some differences in their rankings based on the house-listing and the interview data. More specifically, Gamits indicate a very low level of education in the house-listing data but a very high level of education in the interview data. Similarly, we find that Koli/Kolchas and Nayakas, who indicate an average level of educational development in the houselisting data, indicate a much lower educational development in the interview data. This suggests that the random sample of these three tribal groups in the interview study has not resulted into their appropriate representation in the interview study. It may also be noted that the educational development of the most progressive group among the tribals is comparable to that of only the scheduled castes. While the performance of the Dhodia males seems to be almost at par with that of the scheduled caste males, the performance of the Dhodia and Chaudhari females is above that of the scheduled caste females.

There are considerable differences, by occupation, between castes/communities as well as between different tribal groups. There is a monotonic relationship between the occupational status of the household head and the educational attainment of its members. This is true of all castes/communities as well as the tribal groups. Even when occupation is controlled, considerable differences, by sex and tribe, are found in the educational development of the tribals. A detailed description of the educational development of the major tribal groups is given, separately for each category of sex and occupation, in Chapter 3.

Community contexts and educational development of tribals

In Chapter 4, the relationship between community contexts and educational development of the tribals is examined. For this purpose, the sample villages are divided into four categories on the basis of the proportion of the non-tribals. Since the proportion of the non-tribal population and the development score of a village are highly correlated, it is argued that an ordered set of village categories, based on the proportion of the non-tribals, corresponds fairly well to an ordered set of categories of the villages, based on their development scores. Then, it is demonstrated that caste/community, occupation of the household heads and educational development are positively related to the proportion of the non-tribals in a village.

The tribal households are more or less equitably distributed in the four village categories ; however, the community contexts of the tribals in these village categories are markedly different. At one end, the tribals in category I live amidst preponderent non-tribals, including a fairly high proportion of high-caste Hindus. They live in a community in which many household heads are white-collar workers. The educational development of their community as a whole is impressive—about three-fourths of the boys and two-thirds of the girls attend school. In such community contexts, we would expect a conducive community environment for education and, therefore, a relatively high level of educational development of the tribals. At the other end, almost all the households in village category IV are tribal, only a very small proportion of the household heads are employed in white-collar occupations, and their educational progress is very low. In such community contexts, we would expect a relatively low level of educational development of the tribals. However, no supporting evidence is found in this study for this hypothesis of a positive relationship between the proportion of the non-tribals and the educational development of the tribals in a village community. We find instead a negative relationship between the proportion of the non-tribals and the educational development of the tribals ; such a relationship generally continues, even when development score and occupation of the household heads are controlled.

Social class and educational development

There are two major considerations for examining the relationship between social class and educational development of the tribals. First, an important and consistent finding in the literature on sociology of education is that the social class background of individuals is positively and strongly related to their educational and occupational aspirations/achievement. Secondly, it is often mentioned that the benefits of the government programmes of assistance to the tribals accrue most to the children of the privileged among them. Indeed, the educational development of some of the tribal groups is found to be substantially higher than that of the others. Such a situation raises one important question, namely, is the differential educational development of the tribal groups a consequence of their probably differential social class composition, or is it likely to be a consequence of certain other characteristics specific to different tribal groups? An attempt is made, in chapter 5, to answer this question on the basis of the interview data.

Since the interview data constitute a different set of data, we first examine the educational development of the respondent households in the interview study. The educational development of the tribals, as found in the interview study, is somewhat more impressive than that observed from the house-listing data. This obviously suggests that the estimate of the educational development of the tribals, based on the interview data, will be somewhat higher than that based on the house-listing data. This, in turn, means that the handicaps, to an appropriate development of education among the tribals, that we might find from the interview data may be somewhat underestimated as compared to those existing in reality.

It may be noted that differences, by sex and age-group, are also observed in the interview data. It is found that 36.3 per cent of the boys and 59.8 per cent of the girls in the younger generation, and 54.0 per cent of the males and 89.6 per cent of the females in the older generation never went to school. Most of those without any schooling belong to certain families. What is most disturbing is the fact that about 44 per cent of the illiterate boys and 18 per cent of the illiterate girls come from the households that have their counterpart members with some education.

The reasons for no schooling are the same as those often mentioned in this regard—the children in the tribal society are required to help their family in its occupational and household activities or that the economic condition of their family is too poor to afford even the meagre expenses of primary education. In addition, the tradition of not sending girls to school acts as a formidable factor. Similar reasons are also given for dropping out from school. A lack of regular and punctual attendance and a failure in examination were also mentioned as reasons for dropping out. Although the educational expectations of the household heads of those who go to school are lower for the girls than those for the boys, it is found that an increasing proportion of the tribal parents desire their children, once they continue to move upward in schooling, to complete secondary or college education. However, the occupational expectations of most tribal parents are very modest and probably focused on lower level salaried jobs in the government and other organizations that offer them reserved positions.

In the absence of any readily available simple measure of social class of the tribals, we have developed a composite measure of social class in this study. It is a combination of weighted scores of 19 items. The regression analysis presented in the study indicates that ten out of nineteen social class variables can explain the total variance in the composite measure. A perusal of these ten items further indicate that it is not necessary to include income data to construct a composite measure of social class of the tribals. In other words, it is possible to capture the income component of the SES scale by bringing in other income-related variables which are relatively easy to measure.

There is a positive and strong relationship between social class and educational attainment of the tribals. Such a relationship is consistently found when different indicators of their educational attainment are used. There is also a considerable amount of variation in educational attainment as well as social class composition of the different tribal groups. This leads us to examine the relationship between social class and educational attainment among different tribal groups. When we control for sex and age-group we face the problem of adequate Ns in some of the categories. Nonetheless, on an examination of the percentages and relative frequencies in the various categories of social class, one notices a clear trend in support of the hypothesis regarding a strong and positive relationship between social class and educational attainment. When the data are collapsed for both the sexes, we find that there are sharp social class differences in the educational attainment of different tribal groups. Even in the case of Dhodias, whose educational attainment is at the top, about three-fourths of the 5-17 years old children from the low social class category did not go to school at all as against only one-fifth of those from the high social class category. It is also found that social class differences are much more pronounced than the inter-tribe differences. Further, the social class differences in the percentages of those who did not go to school at all are generally more pronounced in the younger generation than those in the older generation. Although there is a reduction among all tribal groups, from the older to the younger generation, in the percentages of those who did not go to school, such a reduction is generally greater for the higher social class than that for the lower social class. While the available data do not provide any direct evidence regarding the utilization of government assistance for education by different tribal groups, the differential educational attainment of the tribals belonging to different social classes suggests that those belonging to higher social classes have presumably taken a greater advantage of such assistance than their counterparts from the lower social classes.

Social class, awareness and educational development

Two important antecedent conditions for utilizing available facilities and assistance for education by an individual are his awareness of available facilities and assistance for education and his perception of the importance of acquiring education. In Chapter 6, we analyze data regarding 18 items in this regard. For convenience, these items are grouped into four broad categories, namely, (a) knowledge of general facilities for education, (b) knowledge of special programmes of assistance to the tribals for education/jobs (c) exposure to mass media and urban contacts, and (d) perceived importance of education. It is .found that a fairly large number of tribals are still unaware of the facilities and programmes for specialized and higher education. For example, only about one-fourth of the respondents know about Industrial Training Institutes, and about one-half of them know about colleges and hostels. Similarly, only about one-fourth to two-fifths of the respondents know about preferences given to the tribals for admission to educational institutions, reservation of seats in medical and engineering colleges, and reservation of jobs in the government and semi-government organizations. While it is not surprizing to find that only about 10 per cent of the respondents had often seen films and about 14 per cent of the respondents almost regularly read newspapers, it is very striking that about one-third of the respondents visit the district head-quarters very often. More than four-fifths of the respondents believe that their children can progress only if they are educated ; they also believe that if an individual from their own community becomes a government official or a doctor, it will be advantageous to their community. Thus, most of them perceive importance of education. But only two-thirds of the respondents indicate that they would endure hardships to educate their children. It should be noted that there are considerable differences by social class and tribe in all these matters. However, the social class differences are more pronounced than the inter-tribe differences. When the responses to these items are combined into a composite weighted measure of awareness, the mean awareness score for the total group (3.05) is found to be less than even one-half of the possible maximum score of the measure. The differences by social class and tribe are also observed. The mean score of awareness increases with the level of social class, from 2.10 for the low social class category to 4.17 for the high social class category. When social class and tribe are controlled simultaneously, the inter-tribe differences within each category of social class are reduced, but the social class differences in the awareness scores within each category of tribe remain generally striking.

There is a positive relationship between the level of awareness of the househould heads and the educational attainment of the members. Further, within each category of tribe, the level of awareness is positively related to educational attainment. The differences by sex and age-group also continue. However, in the younger generation, with regard to the percentage of those going to school, a high level of awareness seems to be a more powerful factor than sex.

The pattern of a positive and strong relationship between social class and educational attainment of the tribals continues even when we control simultaneously for sex, age-group and level of awareness. Further, within each category of social class, the differences in educational attainment by sex, age-group and level of awareness also continue. In fact, the impact of sex, age-group, level of awareness and social class seems to be additive. Among younger boys and adult males, a higher level of awareness seems to be successful in considerably reducing, or even completely eliminating, the social class differences in the adjoining categories. This shows that it would be possible for the society to dampen, to a certain extent, the influence of social class if it could increase the level of awareness in the target group, especially when the society extends financial and other assistance for education.

Importance and implications of the study

This study is taken up to assist the planners and administrators in the design and execution of programmes for the educational development of the tribals. Given the need and emphasis for concentrating efforts in the tribal sub-plan area, the study provides a detailed picture of the educational development of the tribals in the rural areas of the tribal sub-plan. It provides, on the one hand, empirical evidences for several generalizations that are based largely on impressions and rather unsystematic observations. It examines, on the other hand, certain theoretically and practically important hypotheses concerning the educational development of the tribals.

The study documents that the educational development of the people residing in the rural areas of the tribal sub-plan is very low, and further that the educational development of the tribals is the lowest among all sections of the population. In view of the fact that the study is conducted in the rural areas, it is possible that some of those tribals, who have attained a high level of education, have moved to urban areas and, therefore, the overall picture of tribal education may be a little better than the one found in this study. On the other hand, the study is conducted in the villages with some facilities for post-primary education. It is, therefore, possible that the picture of educational development of the tribals residing in the villages, where facilities for post-primary education are not available, is much worse than the one found in this study. As in the general population, there are considerable differences, by sex, age-group, and social class, in the educational attainment of the tribals in the study area.

There are indeed considerable inter-tribe differences in their educational attainment. The study also documents that the educational development of the most progressive tribal group is comparable to that of only the scheduled castes. This finding should dampen the argument of those who are apparently impatient with the continuation, from one decade to another, of the special programmes of financial and other assistance for enhancing the educational development of the tribals. A detailed documentation of the various indicators of the educational development of different tribal groups points out the need for additional programmes of assistance and extension work to motivate different tribal groups that have not benefited so far from the expanding facilities for education. In this regard, the specification of such tribal groups in the study should be helpful to the planners and administrators.

The study also documents the extent to which the tribals are unaware of the available facilities and special programmes of assistance. The observed positive relationship of awareness to educational development, even when social class, sex and age-group are controlled, points out a major lacuna in our efforts to enhance the educational attainment of the tribals. Considerable efforts are necessary to mobilize information channels and extension work in this regard. In fact, it is this variable which seems to have potential not only for raising the level of their educational attainment but also for reducing, to a certain extent, social class differences in their educational development.

From the theoretical view-points, the study examines four broad categories of social contexts of the educational development of the tribals. It is not surprizing to find a positive relationship between the level of social status of castes/communities and their educational development or between occupation of the household heads and educational development of different castes/

communities as well as of the tribals. But, it is important to note that there are considerable inter-tribe differences in the educational attainment of the tribals within each category of occupation.

Next, we examine the relationship of the social composition and the level of development of the village community to their educational development. Our finding, which is contrary to the hypothesis of a positive relationship between the proportion of the non-tribals and educational development of the tribals in a village community, suggests that the theory of diffusion of norms of education is perhaps not applicable across the non-tribal/tribal axis but is relevant within the broad spectrum of cultural homogeneity of the tribals.

We find that there are considerable social class and inter-tribe differences in their educational attainment. To a certain extent, the social class differences are more pronounced than the inter-tribe differences. This is not surprizing; what is true of the general population is also true of the tribal society that there are considerable social class differences in their educational attainment. The study indicates presumably an emergent stratification system, based on class criteria, among different tribal groups. This also suggests a need for combining the class as well as the caste criteria to understand the stratification system among the tribals. Further studies are necessary to understand the nature of status hierarchy, if there is one, among different tribal groups and to examine how the class criteria cut across such a status hierarchy among them. Our examination of the fourth category of social contexts brings out an important link of 'awareness' between the relationship of social class to educational development of the tribals.

We should like to point out an important methodological offshoot of this study. It uses a sophisticated statistical procedure to construct a composite SES scale for the tribals, but it demonstrates that it is possible to capture the income component of the SES scale by bringing in other income-related variables which are relatively easy to measure.

We should add a parenthetic note here. In our previous study of the scheduled caste/tribe post-matric scholars (Shah and Patel, 1977:195), it was observed that on the basis of an examination of the occupational background of their parents, the post-matric study did not support the hypothesis that the benefits of government assistance for higher education accrue mostly to children of the privileged families among them. A composite measure of social class used in this study, however, documents considerable social class differences in the educational attainment of the tribals. The readers of both these studies should keep in mind the differences in the nature of data of the two studies. The previous study, based on an examination of the data available from the scholarship application forms, examined the background characteristics of the users of post-matric scholarships. The present study examines several indicators of educational attainment, right from the primary to higher levels of education, of the tribals on the basis of interview data collected from the rural areas of the tribal sub-plan. We would like to reiterate that while the present study does not give any direct evidence regarding the utilization of government assistance for education by different tribal groups, the differential educational attainment of the tribals belonging to different social classes suggests that those belonging to the higher social class have presumably taken a greater advantage of such assistance than their counterparts from the lower social class.

REFERENCES

Ahmed, Karuna 1979, "Towards a Study of Education and Social Change," *Economic and Political Weekly*, Vol. XIV, No. 4 (January 27), 157-164.

Bose, A.B. 1969, "Problems of Educational Development of Scheduled Tribes," in *Report of the Commissioner for Scheduled Castes and Scheduled Tribes*, 1968-69, New Delhi : 134-149.

Bureau of Economics and Statistics, Government of Gujarat 1974 (Details were obtained from a draft report).

Chitnis, Suma 1978, "Education of the Scheduled Castes and Scheduled Tribes in Maharashtra," in Shah, A.B. (ed.), *The Social Context of Education*. New Delhi : Allied Publishers Pvt. Ltd.

Desai, B.M., Ranjit Gupta, T.K. Moulik and V.S. Vyays 1976, *Rural Development for Rural Poor : Dharampur Project*. Vol. II. Ahmedabad : Center for Management in Agriculture, Indian Institute of Management. (Mimeographed)

Director of Census Operations, Gujarat 1972 *District Census Handbook* (for all districts in Gujarat). Ahmedabad : Director, Government Printing and Stationery, Gujarat State.

Naik, J.P. 1971 (a) *Education of the Scheduled Castes* (1965-66). New Delhi : Indian Council of Social Science Research, Occasional Monographs no. 5.

1971 (b) *Education of the Scheduled Tribe* (1965-66). New Delhi : Indian Council of Social Science Research, Occasional Monographs no. 5.

Nie, Norman H., Dale H. Bent and C. Hadlai Hull 1970 *SPSS : Statistical Package for the Social Sciences*. New York : McGraw-Hill Book Company.

Registrar General and Census Commissioner, India 1975 *Census of India 1971, Series I, Scheduled Castes and Scheduled Tribes* (*Table C-VIII Parts A and B*). New Delhi : Registrar General and Census Commissioner of India.

Shah, Vimal P. 1975 *The Educational Problems of Scheduled Caste and Scheduled Tribe School and College Students in India (A Statistical Profile)*. Parts I and II. Surat : Center for Regional Development Studies (now Center for Social Studies) (in print).

Shah, Vimal P. and Tara Patel 1977 *Who Goes to College? Scheduled Caste/Tribe Post-matric Scholars in Gujarat.* Ahmedabad : Rachana Prakashan.

Superintendent of Census Operations, Gujarat 1964 *Census of India 1961, Volume V : Gujarat, Part V-A, Tables on Scheduled Castes and Scheduled Tribes*. Delhi : Manager of Publications.

APPENDICES

APPENDIX—I

Selected Characteristics of the Sample Villages*

District/Taluka/Village	Total population	No. of occupied households	% S.T. population	% literate	Development score
1	2	3	4	5	6
1. *Dist. : Vadodara*					
(1) *Ta. : Chhota-Udepur*					
1. Tejgadh	3508	520	43.4	28.3	18
2. Khatiyavant	1154	160	62.7	15.4	4
(2) *Ta. : Tilakwada*					
1. Savli	1508	275	47.3	41.5	10
2. Katkoi	490	77	96.3	35.3	6
(3) *Ta. : Nasavadi*					
1. Wagach	1667	277	64.0	30.9	7
2. Dughdha	420	52	96.4	28.8	—
2. *Dist. : Bharuch*					
(1) *Ta. : Sagbara*					
1. Sagbara	1494	342	58.0	32.1	13
2. Pat	1128	153	80.1	40.8	—
(2) *Ta. : Dediapada*					
1. Dediapada	3059	579	48.1	42.6	14
2. Ghantoli	953	121	95.9	25.4	3
(3) *Ta. : Valia*					
1. Valia	2871	469	44.7	46.4	17
2. Bhamadia	893	138	87.9	24.2	7
(4) *Ta. : Jhagadia*					
1. Umalla	2554	475	45.6	37.4	18
2. Vadkhunta	570	89	95.6	26.3	1

APPENDIX—I (*Contd.*)

1	2	3	4	5	6
(5) *Ta.* : *Nandod*					
1. Kevadia	1626	356	52.3	45.0	12
2. Khadgada	1502	169	84.4	24.7	6
3. *Dist.* : *Valsad*					
(1) *Ta.* : *Dharampur*					
1. Nana Pondha	1494	249	81.8	14.7	9
2. Virval	844	115	99.2	44.0	5
(2) *Ta.* : *Bansda*					
1. Pratapnagar	1212	164	71.0	45.5	9
2. Raibor	1100	177	99.9	16.1	3
(3) *Ta.* : *Chikhli*					
1. Tankal	2124	379	60.5	42.5	14
2. Agasi	1086	178	84.2	29.7	3
(4) *Ta.* : *Pardi*					
1. Rentlav	1973	294	29.4	55.6	17
2. Nanawaghchhipa	1242	182	93.9	38.1	7
(5) *Ta.* : *Umbergaon*					
1. Valwada	2555	375	49.0	31.5	14
2. Manekpur	1442	228	81.4	25.4	3
4. *Dist.* : *Panchmahals*					
(1) *Ta.* : *Jhalod*					
1. Sanjali	2767	432	25.7	41.5	13
2. Hadmatkhunta	713	103	100.0	18.7	2
(2) *Ta.* : *Dohad*					
1. Gangardi	1270	223	46.9	41.3	10
2. Panchwada	1012	150	98.7	22.2	7
(3) *Ta.* : *Santrampur*					
1. Gothib	2042	350	61.5	26.4	14
2. Limdi	2652	300	96.6	17.3	6
(4) *Ta.* : *Limkheda*					
1. Dudhia	1496	249	26.5	39.6	11
2. Kanzar	426	62	99.8	2.8	—

APPENDIX—I (*Contd.*)

1	2	3	4	5	6
(5) *Ta.* : *Devgadhbaria*					
1. Ranjitnagar	3202	453	58.4	21.2	11
2. Sagtala	611	113	94.9	11.1	9
5. *Dist.* : *Sabarkantha*					
(1) *Ta.* : *Vijaynagar*					
1. Vijaynagar	3110	561	24.5	38.2	15
2. Biladia	714	126	98.5	46.2	4
(2) *Ta.* : *Khedbrahma*					
1. Demti	2245	365	99.2	6.7	3
2. Ambamahuda	524	91	97.0	14.9	2
(3) *Ta.* : *Bhiloda*					
1. Bhavanpur	612	111	56.9	27.0	7
2. Lusadia	825	336	80.4	47.5	6
(4) *Ta.* : *Meghraj*					
1. Vank	482	76	52.7	16.6	2
2. Ghorvada	718	109	77.0	14.3	2
6. *Dist.* : *Surat*					
(1) *Ta.* : *Uchhal*					
1. Karod	1836	264	92.8	19.9	7
2. Khabda	989	131	93.0	17.6	5
(2) *Ta.* : *Vyara*					
1. Panchol	1468	238	89.4	33.7	10
2. Lakhali	1008	161	97.6	25.8	3
(3) *Ta.* : *Valod*					
1. Kamalchhod	3513	578	50.1	41.9	15
2. Kanjod	760	102	96.6	47.5	1
(4) *Ta.* : *Songadh*					
1· Vadi Bhensrot	1395	184	97.5	17.4	—
2. Bodisavar	362	45	96.1	46.7	3
(5) *Ta.* : *Nijar*					
1. Kevelda	4308	538	51.9	28.1	7
2. Khodde	2199	275	95.6	20.0	3

APPENDIX—I (*Contd.*)

1	2	3	4	5	6
(6) *Ta.* : *Mahuva*					
1. Mahuva	3033	558	39.3	55.0	16
2. Samba	1358	218	97.3	41.0	2
(7) *Ta.* : *Mandvi*					
1. Baudhan	5136	972	33.5	47.5	12
2. Gantoli	2489	382	97.5	24.3	7
(8) *Ta.* : *Mangrol*					
1. Tarsadi	3186	595	32.0	50.1	12
2. Kevdi (Sarda)	1131	174	70.6	49.3	7
(9) *Ta.* : *Bardoli*					
1. Astan	1174	170	46.6	48.6	14
2. Bhuvasan	523	107	63.7	32.1	6
7. *Dist.* : *Dangs*					
(1) *Ta.* : *Ahwa*					
1. Waghai	3127	649	58.3	36.7	20
2. Shingana	453	60	99.6	28.5	7

Source : 1971 District Census Handbook.

APPENDIX—II

Distribution of Total and Sample Tribal Households by Tribe, Separately for Each Village

Village		Households	
	Tribe	Total	Sample
	1. Dist. : Baroda -1. Ta. : Chhota Udepur		
1. Tejgadh	Rathwa	101	10
	Natyaka	74	5
	Tadvi Bhil	23	6
	Others	2	—
	Total	200	21
2. Khantiyavant	Rathwa koli	64	11
	Rathwa	38	6
	Tadvi	43	6
	Others	7	—
	Total	152	23
	Dist. : Baroda—2. Ta. : Naswadi		
1. Waghach	Tadvi	32	5
	Bhil, etc.	127	5
	Rathwa	—	1
	Total	159	11
2. Dughdha	Nayaka	1	1
	Dungri Bhil	34	10
	Others	4	—
	Total	39	11
	1. Dist. : Baroda—3. Ta. : Tilakwada		
1. Savli	Tadvi	27	6
	Dungri Bhil	88	10
	Others	1	—
	Total	116	16

APPENDIX—II (*Contd.*)

2.	Katkoi	Tadvi	58	10
		Others	5	—
		Total	63	10
		2. Dist. : Bharuch—1. Ta. : Sagbara		
1.	Sagbara	Dhanka	28	11
		Nayaka	1	1
		Padvi	1	1
		Tadvi	5	3
		Vasava	73	—
		Koli	7	—
		Chaudhari	5	—
		Total	120	16
2.	Pat	Tadvi	2	2
		Vasava	111	11
		Others	1	—
		Total	114	13
		2. Dist. : Bharuch—2. Ta. : Dediapada		
1.	Dediapada	Tadvi	35	5
		Vasava	211	5
		Talavia	1	1
		Others	7	—
		Total	254	11
2.	Ghantoli	Tadvi	2	2
		Vasava	115	10
		Kotwalia	2	1
		Others	2	—
		Total	121	13
		2. Dist. : Bharuch—3. Ta. : Valia		
1.	Valia	Tadvi	4	2
		Vasava	185	6
		Gamit	3	3
		Others	3	—
		Total	195	11

APPENDIX– II (*Contd.*)

2.	Bhamadia	Vasava	131	11
		Gamit	3	3
		Total	134	14
		2. Dist. : Bharuch—4. Ta. : Jhagadia		
1.	Umalla	Tadvi	22	5
		Vasava	153	5
		Total	175	10
2.	Vadkhunta	Vasava	82	11
		Total	82	11
		2. Dist. : Bharuch—5. Ta. : Nandod		
1.	Kevadia	Tadvi	124	10
		Vasava	12	
		Nayaka	2	
		Halpati	1	
		Total	139	10
2.	Khadgada	Tadvi	168	10
		Others	3	
		Total	171	10
		3. Dist. : Valsad—1. Ta. : Dharampur		
1.	Nanapondha	Dhodia	80	5
		Kukna	99	6
		Kolcha	8	6
		Varli	12	9
		Nayaka	5	—
		Dubla	19	—
		Total	223	26
2.	Virval	Dhodia	93	6
		Borpi	2	2
		Others	3	—
		Total	98	8

APPENDIX—II (*Contd.*)

		3. Dist. : Valsad—2. Ta. : Bansda		
1.	Pratapnagar	Dhodia	98	5
		Kukna	5	5
		Dubla	26	—
		Total	129	10
2.	Raibor	Kolcha	9	9
		Kukna	76	5
		Vitolia	6	4
		Varli	30	—
		Kokni	4	—
		Dhodia	3	—
		Total	128	18
		3. Dist. : Valsad—3. Ta. : Chikhli		
1.	Tankal	Dhodia	133	6
		Dubla	28	5
		Nayaka	26	5
		Koli	23	—
		Total	210	16
2.	Agasi	Dhodia	61	5
		Kukna	29	10
		Kolcha	18	6
		Others	3	—
		Total	111	21
		3. Dist. : Valsad—4. Ta. : Pardi		
1.	Rentlav	Dhodia	38	6
		Halpati	18	6
		Varli	1	1
		Kukna	1	1
		Others	4	—
		Total	62	14
2.	Nana Wagh Chhipa	Dhodia	167	11
		Total	167	11

APPENDIX—II (*Contd.*)

3. Dist. : Valsad—5. Ta. : Umbergaon

1.	Valwada	Dhodia	41	5
		Halpati	104	5
		Varli	8	5
		Total	153	15
2.	Manekpur	Dhodia	20	5
		Halpati	18	5
		Varli	119	10
		Valvi	2	1
		Total	159	21

4. Dist. : Panchmahals—1. Ta. : Jhalod

1.	Sanjeli	Bhil etc.	112	13
		Total	112	13
2.	Hadmatkhuta	Bhil etc.	100	10
		Total	100	10

4. Dist. : Panchmahals—2. Ta. : Dohad

1.	Gangardi	Patelia	68	10
		Bhil etc.	26	—
		Total	94	10
2.	Panchwada	Patelia	73	5
		Rawal Bhil	8	8
		Bhil etc.	47	.
		Total	128	13

4. Dist. : Panchmahals—3. Ta. : Santrampur

1.	Gothib	Bhil etc.	200	5
		Patelia	5	5
		Others	1	—
		Total	206	10
2.	Limdi	Bhil etc.	279	8
		Patelia	14	5
		Tadvi	7	6
		Others	1	
		Total	301	19

APPENDIX—II (*Contd.*)

		4. Dist. : Panchmahals—4. Ta. : Limkheda		
1.	Dudhia	Bhil etc.	63	10
		Total	63	10
2.	Kanzar	Bhil etc.	38	5
		Tadvi Bhil	27	5
		Others	3	
		Total	68	10
		4. Dist. : Panchmahals—5. Ta. : Devgadhbaria		
1.	Ranjitnagar	Vasava	18	6
		Rathwa	159	11
		Nayaka	28	—
		Tadvi	1	—
		Mota Nayaka	1	—
		Total	207	17
2.	Sagtala	Nayaka	84	10
		Others	1	
		Total	85	10
		5. Dist. : Sabarkantha—1. Ta. : Vijayanagar		
1.	Vijaynagar	Dungri Garasia	40	10
		Others	3	—
		Total	43	10
2.	Biladia	Dungri Garasia	93	11
		Others	5	
		Total	98	11
		5. Dist. : Sabarkantha—2. Khedbrahma		
1.	Demti	Dungri Bhil	323	10
		Total	323	10
2.	Ambamahuda	Dungri Bhil, Garasia	78	11
		Total	78	11

APPENDIX—II (*Contd.*)

		5. Dist. : Sabarkantha—3. Ta. : Bhiloda		
1.	Bhavanpur	Dungri Bhil Garasia	60	10
		Total	60	10
2.	Lusadia	Dungri Bhil Garasia	106	10
		Total	106	10
		5. Dist. : Sabarkantha—4. Ta. : Meghraj		
1.	Vank	Dungri Garasia	44	10
		Total	44	10
2	Ghorvada	Dungri Garasia	79	10
		Total	79	10
		6. Dist. : Surat—1. Ta. : Uchhal		
1.	Karod	Vasava	103	5
		Valvi	146	5
		Gamit	21	5
		Others	8	—
		Total	278	15
2.	Khabda	Vasava	68	5
		Valvi	32	5
		Gamit	23	5
		Padvi	8	5
		Dubla	4	—
		Halpati	2	—
		Mavchi	1	—
		Kathad Bhil	3	—
		Total	141	20
		6. Dist. : Surat—2. Ta. : Vyara		
1.	Panchol	Pavagadhi Chaudhri	112	6
		Kukna	11	5
		Mota Nayaka	1	1
		Dhodia	14	5
		Gamit	85	—
		Dungri Bhil	1	—
		Halpati	2	—
		Total	225	17

APPENDIX—II (*Contd.*)

2.	Lakhali	Gamit	125	6
		Dungri Bhil	28	5
		Others	5	—
		Total	158	11
		6. Dist. : Surat—3. Ta. : Valod		
1.	Kamalchhod	Chaudhari	175	11
		Halpati	148	5
		Others	7	—
		Total	330	16
2.	Kanjod	Chaudhari	102	10
		Dhodia	2	2
		Others	3	—
		Total	107	12
		6. Dist. : Surat—Ta. : Songadh		
1.	Vadi Bhensrot	Gamit	146	6
		Chaudhari	48	5
		Kotwalia	20	5
		Others	2	
		Total	216	16
2.	Bodisavar	Mota Chaudhari	30	6
		Kotwalia	14	5
		Gamit	11	—
		Dhodia	1	—
		Pavagadhi Chaudhari	3	—
		Total	59	11
		6. Dist. : Surat—5. Ta. : Nizar		
1.	K—Velde	Vasava	18	5
		Valvi	55	5
		Padvi	299	6
		Nayaka	11	5
		Koli	—	5
		Koli Gamit	3	—
		Chaudhari	3	—
		Total	381	26

APPENDIX—II (*Contd.*)

2.	Khodde	Valvi	116	5
		Padvi	83	6
		Nayaka	9	5
		Others	9	
		Total	217	11
		6. Dist. : Surat—Ta. : Mahuva		
1.	Mahuva	Mota Nayaka	14	5
		Halpati	102	5
		Pardhi	5	2
		Dhodia	97	5
		Others	6	—
		Total	224	17
2.	Samba	Mota Nayaka	44	6
		Dhodia	13	5
		Total	177	11
		6. Dist. : Surat—7. Ta. : Mandvi		
1.	Gaudhan	Halpati	204	5
		Vasava	127	5
		Gamit	4	3
		Others	4	—
		Total	339	13
2.	Ghantoli	Chaudhari	332	5
		Vasava	54	5
		Kotwalia	3	1
		Others	5	—
		Total	394	11
		6. Dist. : Surat—8. Ta. : Mangrol		
1.	Tarsadi	Dubla Halpati	100	5
		Vasava	93	5
		Others	7	—
		Total	200	10

APPENDIX—II (*Contd.*)

2.	Kevdi	Chaudhari	11	5
		Vasava	85	5
		Kotwalia	6	2
		Others	4	—
		Total	106	12
		6. Dist. : Surat—9. Ta. : Bardoli		
1.	Astan	Mota Chaudhari	9	5
		Halpati	67	6
		Total	76	11
2.	Bhuvasan	Mota Nayaka	1	1
		Halpati	63	11
		Total	64	12
		7. Dist. : Dangs—1. Ta. : Ahwa		
1.	Waghai	Kunbi	7	7
		Mavchi	1	1
		Varli	2	2
		Kukna	4	4
		Kokni	83	6
		Mota Chaudhari	18	3
		Pavagadhi Chaudhari	2	2
		Nayaka	12	5
		Kotwalia	61	6
		Dhodia	109	5
		Vasava	22	—
		Gamit	18	—
		Halpati	6	—
		Padvi	3	—
		Dubla	2	—
		Chaudhari	2	—
		Total	352	41
2.	Shingana	Gamit	29	5
		Vasava	23	6
		Others	9	—
		Total	61	11

APPENDIX—III

Frequency Distribution of Households in the Broad Categories of Hindus, by Sub-caste

Hindus : High Castes I		*Hindus : High Castes II*	
1. Bariya Patel	3	1. Brahmin	275
2. Patidar-Patel	222	2. Vania	454
3. Kadva Patel	51	3. Leva Patel	612
4. Koli Patel	211	4. Parekh	5
5. Kanbi Patel	3	5. Kale	1
6. Bhavsar	18	6. Desai	101
7 Rajput	476	7. Diwan	1
8. Pancholi	1	8. More	2
9. Thakore	5	9. Kulkarni	1
10. Meghani	1	10. Sharma	3
11. Patil	4	11. Nayak	1
12. Rathod	3	12. Bhatiya	3
13. Patni Patel	1	13. Mehta	2
14. Khant Thakore	22		
15. Gayakwad	1	Total	1461
16. Anjana Patel	62		
17. Luhana	1		
18. Modh Patel	18		
19. Gurjar Patel	19		
20. Kanami	1		
21. Sumara	1		
Total	1124		

APPENDIX—III (*Contd.*)

Hindus : Middle Castes		*Hindus : Low Castes*	
1. Marwadi	13	1. Kumbhar	282
2. Mysooriya	8	2. Luhar	157
3. Rajasthani	1	3. Chaudhari Patel	3
4. Bhaiya	20	4. Valand	61
5. Maratha	134	5. Lakhara	1
6. Sindhi	20	6. Dhobi	15
7. Naidu	1	7. Kadiya	7
8. Punjabi	13	8. Bhoi	26
9. Khandesi	3	9. Kachhi	1
10. Jaiswal-Madrasi	5	10. Raval	31
11. Kathiawadi	2	11. Gorvala	3
12. Suthar	96	12. Chauhan	10
13. Darji	86	13. Maru	1
14. Sadhu	16	14. Bangadivara	1
15. Soni	60	15. Gohil	1
16. Neravara	1	16. Hutadwara	2
17. Ghanchi	64	17. Ahir	9
18. Barot	4	18. Manan	2
19. Choksi	1	19. Bharwad	20
20. Dehniya	1	20. Saparia	1
21. Mangana	2	21. Salat	5
22. Modi	6	22. Rabari	19
23. Mali	7	23. Kalal	2
24. Contractor	1	24. Khatri	5
25. Kandoi	1	25. Gurkha	2
26. Rana	4	26. Sathwara	2
27. Kachhiya Patel	2	27. Rao	1
28. Kansara	1	28. Thakarda	88
29. Goswami	4	29. Bhandari Patel	9
30. Baria-Solanki	73	30. Dabgar	11
31. Gadhvi	1	31. Vanjhara	52
32. Tamboli	1	32. Vaghri	29
33. Gosai	5	33. Machhi	69
		34. Odd	14
Total	657	Total	942

APPENDIX—IV

Frequency Distribution of Households in the Sample Villages, by Occupation of the Head of the Household

N.C.O. Code	Occupations	
	1. *Professionals and Big Businessmen*	
020	Architects and Town Planners	10
070	Physicians and Surgeons Allopathic	22
071	Physicians and Surgeons Ayurvedic	12
074	Dental Surgeons	1
075	Veterinarians	4
120	Accountants and Auditors	8
134	Librarians, Archievists and Curators	3
140	Lawyers	1
211	Administrative and executive officials, State Government	16
213	Administrative and executive officials, Local Bodies	1
219	Administrative and executive officials, Govt. and Local Bodies	11
230	Directors and Managers	1
241	Working Proprietors, Directors and Managers, Construction	30
250	Working Proprietors, Directors and Managers and Related Executives, Transport	11
299	Administrative Executive and Managerial Workers, N.E.C.	12
400	Merchants and Shopkeepers, Wholesale Trade	11
		154
	2. *Officers and Small Businessmen*	
053	Agronomists and Agricultural Scientists	6
139	Social Scientists and Related Workers, N.E.C.	3
151	Teachers, Higher Secondary and High Secondary School	148
159	Teachers (Not Specified)	99
190	Ordained Religious Workers	50
269	Managers, Hostel	12

APPENDIX—IV (*Contd.*)

300	Clerical Supervisors (Office Superintendents, Head Clerks & Section Heads)	5
301	Other Supervisors (Inspectors, etc.)	29
309	Clerical and other Supervisors N.E.C.	2
320	Stenographers and Stenotypists	1
330	Book Keepers and Accounts Clerks	32
331	Cashiers	5
341	Automatic Data Processing Machine Operators	2
357	Ticket Collectors, Checkers Examiners	6
360	Station Masters and Station Superintendents, Transport	1
361	Post Master, Telegraph, Masters and other Supervisors	5
369	Yard Foremen Railway, Tronsport and Communication Supervisors, N.E.C. Loco Foremen	
370	Guards and Brakesmen Railway	1
401	Merchants and Shopkeepers Retail Trade	708
409	Merchants and Shopkeepers, Wholesale and Retail Trade N.E.C.	13
411	Purchasing Agent	1
440	Agents and Salesmen, Insurance	3
441	Agents, Brokers, and Salesmen Real Estate	1
442	Agents and Brokers, Securities & Shares	1
443	Agents Brokers and Salesmen Advertising and other Business services, Propagandist	9
450	Money lenders (including indigeneous bankers)	3
499	Sales Workers, N.E.C.	2
600	Farm Managers and Supervisors Crop Production	28
983	Drivers-Railways	1
		1177
	3. *Farm-owners and Live-stock Farmers*	
610	Cultivators (owners)	7488
621	Live-stock farmers	28
		7516
	4. *Clerks, technicians, etc. (upper level)*	
010	Laboratory Assistants	—
028	Surveyors	1
031	Civil Engineering Overseers and Technicians	4
030	Engineering Technicians N.E.O.	3
076	Pharmacist, Dispenser, Compounder Vaccinators,	
080	Inoculators and Medical Assistants	9
085	Midwives and Health Visitors	14

APPENDIX—IV (*Contd.*)

089	Nursing, Sanitary and other Medical and Health Technicians	15
090	Scientific, Medical and other Technical Persons	3
104	Statistical Investigators and Related Workers	5
137	Village level workers	32
153	Primary Teachers	253
154	Pre-Primary Teachers	2
310	Village Officials	54
321	Typists	1
350	Clerks, General	191
351	Stock Verifier	4
390	Telephone Operators	6
391	Telegraphist and Signallers	2
		615
	5. *Clerks, etc. (lower level)*	
358	Office Attendants (Peons, Daftaries, etc.)	220
359	Clerical and Related Workers (including Proof-readers & Copy-holders) N.E.C.	2
371	Conductors, Transport	16
380	Postmen	24
439	Salesmen, Shop Assistants and Related Workers N.E.C.	26
500	Hotel and Restaurant Keepers	45
571	Policemen and Detectives	147
574	Watchmen, Chowkidars and gate-keepers	43
599	Service Workers N.E.C.	133
660	Foresters and Related Workers	60
720	Supervisors and foremen, metal smelting, converting and Reginning	1
771	Grain Millers, Parchers and Related Workers	23
841	Watch, Clock and Precision Instrument, makers (except electrical)	4
851	Electricians, Electrical fitters and related workers	5
854	Radio and Television mechanics and Repairmen	1
855	Electrical Wiremen	9
986	Drivers-motor vehicles	133
		892
	6. *Artisans, Skilled Workers (upper level)*	
520	Cooks and Cook-Bearers	20
652	Gardners and Nursery Workers	6
772	Crushers and pressers-oil seeds	5

APPENDI—IV (*Contd.*)

777	Bakers, Confectioners, Candy and Sweetmeat makers and other food processors	4
791	Tailors and Dress Makers	235
811	Carpenters	146
835	Machine Tool Operators	5
842	Machinery Fitters and machine Assemblers	5
843	Motor Vehicle Mechanics	7
845	Mechanics, Repairmen, other	33
872	Welders and Flame Cutters	1
881	Jewellers, Goldsmiths and Silversmiths	93
961	Stationary Engines and Related Equipment Operators	4
969	Stationary Engines and Related Equipment Operators N.E.C	3
985	Pointsmen, Signalsmen, and Shunters-Railway	21
		592
	7. *Artisans, Skilled Workers, etc.* (*lower level*)	
431	Street Vendors, Canvessers and News Vendors	104
550	Laundrymen, Washermen and Related Workers	17
560	Hair-Dressers, Barbers, Beautician and Related Workers	90
681	Fishermen, Inland and Coastal Waters	41
728	Metal Platers and Coaters	5
732	Sawyers, Plywood Makers and Related Wood Processing Workers	1
751	Fiber-Preparers	11
755	Weavers and Related Workers	6
756	Carpet Makers and Finishers Coir Weavers	1
774	Butchers and Meat Preparers	11
784	Bidi Makers	11
801	Shoe-makers and shoe repairers	30
809	Leather Cutters, Lasters and Sewers and Related Workers	8
821	Stone Cutters and Carvers	5
831	Blacksmiths, Hammersmiths and Forging Press Operators	102
873	Sheet Metal Workers	1
892	Potters and Related Clay and Abrasive Framers	112
911	Paper and Paper Board Product Makers	1
939	Painters N.E.C.	1
941	Musical Instrument Makers and Tuners	3
942	Basketry Weavers and Brush makers	216
951	Bricklayers, Stone Masons and Tile Setters	34
957	Glaziers, Photo Framer	1

APPENDIX—IV (*Contd.*)

981	Ships Deck Ratings, Barge Crews and Boatmen	6
987	Drivers-Animal and Animal drawn Vehicles	3
		821
	8. *Agricultural Labourers*	
630	Agricultural Labours	3027
	9. *Other Labourers*	
002	Beggary	11
191	Non-Ordained Religious Workers	1
521	Butlers, Bearers and Waiters	13
530	Ayahs, Nurse, Maids	1
531	Domestic Servants	12
541	Sweepers, Cleaners and Related Workers	34
642	Watermen	1
651	Farmworkers, Animals, Birds and Insect Rearing	16
661	Harvesters & Gatherers of Forest Products including Lac (Except Logs)	1
663	Charcoal Burners and Forest Product Processors	9
669	Loggers and Other Forestry Workers N.E.C.	126
712	Qarrymen	1
999	Labourers, N.E.C.	763
		989
	10. *Retired*	
001	Retired	53
000	Not mentioned	25
		78
	Grand Total :	15861

INDEX

Citizen Participation and Democratic Governance: In Our Hands

Edited by

RAJESH TANDON
MOHINI KAK

25 Years PRIA

Published for
PRIA, NEW DELHI
by
CONCEPT PUBLISHING COMPANY, NEW DELHI-110059

ISBN:
81-8069-431-3 (PB)

First Published 2007

Published and Printed by
Ashok Kumar Mittal
Concept Publishing Company,
A/15-16, Commercial Block, Mohan Garden,
New Delhi-110059 (INDIA)

Phones : 25351460, 25351794
Fax : 091-11-25357103
Email : publishing@conceptpub.com

Preface

As we began to take stock of our experiences in PRIA over the past 25 years, it became clear that PRIA's journey has been focused on participation and empowerment. Through a series of issues, PRIA has attempted to create capacities among the poor and the marginalized to participate effectively in their own development. Various methods and processes were designed to contribute towards this mission, keeping in view the differing contexts in which people live and operate.

This book contains a series of articles which have been derived from the practical experiences of PRIA, specially drawing on the past five years. The collection identifies the parameters of democratic governance from local to national and global levels; it concludes that the principles of governance remain the same, whether they apply to local or global level institutions.

At the core of the discourse on democratic governance is the issue of active citizenship—how people learn to be and act like citizens. This is where the articles in this volume describe the places where such possibilities of active citizenship emerge, and conditions which facilitate the same. Issues of solid waste management and education of girl child became rallying points for expression of active citizenship.

As we share PRIA's past experiences and lessons from its journey so far, we dedicate this volume to the spirit of partnership that many citizens have shared with us. Their commitment, generosity and perseverance have given us energy and hope. We hope that the discussions on this set of experiences will indicate possible directions for the future work of PRIA.

I want to take this opportunity to thank my colleagues who worked on this volume. Special thanks are due to our donors and supporters—Sida, SDC, Ministry of Panchayati Raj (GOI), Cordaid, IDS (under DRC programme)—whose contributions have supported the work reported here and the publication of this volume.

May the Silver Jubilee reflections enrich our work collectively.

New Delhi
February 7, 2007

Rajesh Tandon
President, PRIA

Contents

The Contributors

Bandyopadhyay, Kaustuv Kanti, Ph.D. in Physical Anthropology, University of Ranchi, with 17years of work experience with specific interest in urban governance.

Dwivedi, Anju, M.A. Anthropology, Lucknow University 14 years of experience on training and participatory research.

Dwivedi, Shailendra, Ph.D. Sociology, Department of Humanities and Social Sciences, IIT Kanpur, 11 years of experience on civil society building and local self governance.

Farrell, Martha, M.A. (Social Work), Delhi School of Social Work, Delhi University with 25 years of experience in the field of gender and education.

Ghose, Nilanjan, M.A. (Social Work), Visva Bharati (Central University) Shantiniketan, West Bengal, 5 years of experience on environmental and urban governance issues.

Jaitli, Namrata, M.A. (Social Work), Delhi School of Social Work, New Delhi with 12 years of work experience in the development sector.

Kak, Mohini, M.A. (Social Work), Tata Institute of Social Sciences, Mumbai, 4 years of experience on civil society building and local self-governance.

Mohanty, Ranjita, Ph.D. Environmental Sociology, Centre for the Study of Social Systems, Jawahar Lal University, Delhi with 10 years of experience in the field of research.

Pant, Mandakini, Ph.D. in Sociology, University of Rajasthan, Jaipur with16 years of academic and research experience.

Rai, Manoj Kr., M.Sc. Statistics, Banaras Hindu University with 21years of work experience on local self-governance.

All contributors have worked with PRIA in different capacities on issues of strengthening civil society and local self-governance. They have been engaged in facilitating research and advocacy initiatives, capacity building and networking initiatives, forwarding PRIA's efforts at strengthening citizen participation in governance.

1

Participation, Civil Society, Democratic Governance and Citizenship

A Journey of Ideas and Practices

Rajesh Tandon and ***Mohini Kak***

History of Participation

Participation emerged from the margins of development discourse in the 1970s with the assertion of the Basic Needs Approach by the ILO. "Donor Governments passed legislations and defined goals that put 'popular participation' on their agendas" (Cornwall, 2000). Included in the programme of action of the World Employment Conference in 1976, reinforced by the World Conference on Agrarian Reform and Rural Development (1979), participation became the buzzword in all debates on development.

The World Conference on Agrarian Reform and Rural Development stated:

> "Participation by the people in the institutions and systems which govern their lives is a basic human right and also essential for realignment of political power in favour of disadvantaged groups for social and economic development" (cited in Oakley 1995:3).

Although pushed through in various declarations, legislations, policy guidelines and agendas, participation was understood differently by both those who advocated it and those who implemented or practiced it.

Cornwall (2000) outlines the arguments made for participation in the 1960s and 1970s into three distinct tributaries—participation done 'for' the people, 'by' the people and 'with' the people. The 'for' the people argument centred on the necessity of participation in increasing or improving efficiency and affectivity of development projects-an argument which has survived over time and is still at the centre stage of the participation debate. It led to the inclusion of participation as an inalienable component of all development schemes.

The 'by' the people stream of thought looked at participation from the standpoint of a struggle for "right, recognition and more equitable distribution of resources" (Cornwall, 2000). This broader vision of participation was embraced by the United Nations Research Institute for Social Development (UNRISD), which defined participation as "the organised efforts to increase control over resources and regulative institutions in given social situations on the part of groups and movements hitherto excluded from such control" (Pearse and Stiefel, 1979 cited in Cornwall, 2000: 21).

Such a perspective saw participation not only as a token form of involvement and opinion-seeking for formulation and implementation of development projects and planning, but as participation where people have the right to make decisions that matter. This rights-based approach involved a vision of participation, which talked about "social changes that are needed for self-determination and self-governance" (Cornwall, 2000).

The third argument or perception of Participation was grounded in the belief that "people cannot be developed; they can only develop themselves" (Nyerere 1978, cited in Hall et al., 1982: 13). Such a perspective not only valued people's knowledge and capacities but placed responsibility on those who were facilitating participation to enable the process itself to bring about empowerment.

This alternative vision to participation and development brought together the work of a confluence of proponents and practitioners of adult education in the late 1970s and early 1980s. Inspired by the work of Paolo Friere, Myles Horton, Roby Kidd and Julius Nyerere, the International Council for Adult Education became the node for supporting and promoting Participatory Research in a number of countries across the world (Hall, 1984).

"The 1980s saw the rise of popular organisations for whom participation implied an entirely different set of understandings and practices. The distinction between 'participatory development' and 'peoples' self-development' (Rahman, 1995), came to capture the tension between mainstream and alternative approaches to development. Within the mainstream, participation was largely seen as a means to involve people in activities initiated by development agencies or the State. In contrast, people's self-development involved a process of collective action and mobilisation that could lead to self-reliant development and the capacity to negotiate on new terms with those with power, including the State" (Stiefel and Wolfe, 1994; cited in Cornwall, 2000: 24).

In India, the seeds of this inspiratory perspective bore fruit with the establishment of the Society for Participatory Research in Asia (PRIA) in 1982. With a strong belief in participation through people's self-development, it was an attempt by a small group of persons to promote, advocate and practice principles of *participatory research* to bring about change in the 'mainstream' understanding of participation that existed in the country.

The Community Development Programmes run by the Government in the 1950s represented the prevalent understanding of participation in the country. Participation was seen as a form of involvement where planning was centralized and implementation made participatory through involvement of people, mainly as implementers or monitory contributors for these programmes. This understanding generally ignored people's views, needs and involvement in the planning of programmes, resulting in their failure to reduce poverty and reach out to the poor and the marginalised sections of society.

PRIA's efforts at introducing an 'alternative vision of participation' in the region began with participatory research, evaluation and training initiatives that pushed the agenda of participation through self-development and respect of local knowledge. Studies on the 'Role of Adult Education in Community Involvement in Primary Health Care' and the 'Impact of the Forest Policy on Forest Dwellers in Himachal Pradesh' in 1982 were pioneering efforts that both represented as well as advocated this alternative perspective.

Participation and Participatory Research

Participatory Research not only introduced a new understanding of participation, its principles led to the emergence of a new methodology of participatory development which focused on empowerment through knowledge generation and capacity building.

Participatory Research demystified research and knowledge generation by moving it from the exclusive purview of academics and experts to the public domain. It advocated that the purpose of research was not only to generate knowledge but also to ensure the utilization of knowledge in initiating the process of social change. The relevance of research, thus, was not in its validation by academic peers but in its acceptance by the larger social system and its effectiveness in bringing about change. Without this social research was irrelevant. Over the years, Participatory Research received support from the Latin American tradition of Action Research and there emerged a stream of work round the concept of Participatory Action Research (Fals-Borda and Rahman, 1991).

Participatory Research was based on the belief that "people cannot be liberated by a consciousness and knowledge other than their own" (Rahman, 1982). Empowering the 'have-nots' involved their participation in valuing their existing knowledge and in producing and using new knowledge. In other words, Participatory Research was about valuing and believing in people's knowledge and capacities. It was a "process of liberation which begins with faith in people and in their capacity to take their own decisions" (Fernandes and Tandon, 1981).

Participatory Research, thus, believes that through the process of knowledge sharing and elaboration, people become owners of the knowledge they generate, and develop the ability to value and analyze their own knowledge. This process of knowledge generation is, therefore, a step towards awareness building and consciencetisation leading to social transformation and action.

This belief in the power of knowledge, knowledge owned and generated by ordinary people, became visible during PRIA's initial encounters with oppressive, conservative and centralist power structures. Participatory studies on occupational health and environment issues contributed to popular movements against unfair laws and practices. Studies on 'Workers Awareness and

Occupational Health' in 1984, followed by extensive efforts at workers' education helped facilitate a more aware and informed workers' movement on workplace health and safety issues. PRIA's involvement in the Studies on the Impact of Large Development Projects in Bihar along with a number of groups and individuals emphasised the role of PRIA as a support organisation aimed at providing informational and capacity building support through participatory methods that both informed and strengthened popular movements. These initiatives not only firmly established PRIA's philosophy of 'Knowledge is Power' but also helped it gain credence as a method of social action and change.

With a clear objective of bringing about social change participatory research does not claim to be a value-neutral process but a process committed to the poor and the marginalised sections of society. It has "a necessary relationship with social transformation and action" (Fernandes and Tandon, 1981). To ensure this social action and change, the methods followed during the process of participatory research become important. Increased understanding among the marginalised about their social setting becomes essential for them to attain the confidence and capacity to inquire into and undertake social action for social transformation. This necessarily entails the process of organisation building.

Knowledge drawn from the people collectively, when shared back with them collectively, generates a shared understanding and a thread that often binds them as a collective. It is through the creation of such a collective or organisation, and not through a single individual, that social change is visualised. It is through this belief in collective strength that "Participatory research attempts to remove the established dichotomy of knowing and using that knowledge. Knowledge for the sake of knowing is de-emphasised; knowing is linked to a concrete action. This enhances the quality of knowledge as well as informs the basis for action" (Tandon, 2002).

At the global level this approach of participation gained roots in the 80s; it soon found allies in the institutions of international development assistance and slowly emerged as a front-runner in the development debates of the 90s. Methods and tools of Participatory Rural Appraisal (PRA) became readily utilised in the planning and monitoring of development projects around the world (Chambers, 1997).

Participation and Civil Society

With the fall of the Berlin Wall and the Soviet Union at the turn of the 1990s, new democracies emerged in Eastern and Central Europe. Many authoritarian regimes in Latin America and Asia became new democracies. In this political landscape re-emerged the notion of *civil society*.

Like participation, civil society was an idea that had undergone many conceptual transformations over history. It not only meant different things to different people but played different roles at different times.

"Depending on whose version one follows, civil society is either a specific product of Nation-State and Capitalism, or a universal expression of collective life of individuals, at work in all countries and stages of development but expressed in different ways according to history and context" (Edward, 2004).

Classical and late medieval thinkers like Aristotle, Plato and Hobbes saw both civil society and the state as political associations governing social conflict through the imposition of rules and therefore, as being indistinguishable from each other. "The state represented the 'civil' form of society and 'civility' described the requirements of good citizenship" (Edward, 2004).

The period of enlightenment marked by the French and American Revolutions, saw civil society gain prominence as an entity independent of the State. It was seen as a "defense against unwarranted intrusions by the State on newly realised individual rights and freedoms" (Edward, 2004). A 'self-regulating universe of associations' committed to a set of ideals that needed to be protected from the State, civil society's role lay in resisting despotism.

Thinkers like Alexis de Tocquevelle's, built on this theme and highlighted the value of voluntary associations in curbing the power of centralised institutions and in nurturing pluralism. A highly articulate civil society was seen as a "protector of individuals from the tyrannical state" (Oomen, 2004) and as the "foundation of a stable democratic polity, a defense against domination by one group and a barrier to anti-democratic forces" (Edward, 2004).

However, this view did not take into account the conflicts and inequalities that existed within society and between different economic and political interests within civil society, without which the understanding of civil society was incomplete. Gramsci and Habermas developed their notions of civil society around the concept of 'public sphere'—an arena where shared meanings were constructed democratically through communication and engagement (both from above and below) aimed at dismantling inequality and differences between groups.

Therefore, broadly speaking, ideas about civil society revolved around the perception of civil society as 'part' of society (as an associational life); as a 'kind' of society (normative with social goals); and as a 'public sphere'. Never did a single perception gain prominence over the other, and the understanding of civil society today incorporates aspects of all three themes (Edward, 2004).

Civil society, today, can be defined as "the sum of individual and collective initiatives directed towards the pursuit of common public good" (Tandon and Mohanty, 2002). This definition recognizes both individual and collective initiatives, as well as appreciates the existence of conflicts of interests between various sections of society while talking of 'public good'. Public good too means different things to different people and by emphasizing the word 'common' it signifies the value of civil society in bringing about and working towards a common understanding in society.

Understood in this way, civil society has passed through many phases. It occupied a unique position of being both at the fringes and at the centre-stage during the mid 19th century when there were rallying cries for freedom from the colonised states. These calls for freedom advocated for nation-states...for governments of the people, by the people and for the people...for democracy. Despite this emphasis on 'people' in these liberation movements, the State was still acknowledged as supreme and civil society as subsidiary to the State. Civil society had the primary role of supporting state structures and dictates and helping the state fulfil its responsibilities. It was only in the late 1980s that cracks in state supremacy appeared, giving way to the emergence of a market-driven society.

Questions on the State's roles and capacity for economic development led to the emergence of solutions which demanded liberation of economic activity from the clutches of the State. As the economic liberalization agenda gained strength, the role of the State in governing society diminished, while the space for civil society increased.

This widening space for civil society mediation in the 1990s not only affected the roles and relevance of civil society but also affected the discourse on development. As opposed to the traditional perspective of participation in development, this new perspective to development saw participation as a means to self-reliance. 'Self-help' and 'do-it-yourself' became the key ingredients of the participation in development paradigm. In this period the perspective of 'users as choosers' gained momentum (Cornwall and Gaventa, 2000). Participation was linked to 'ownership' where citizens and ultimate users 'bought into' development to ensure a stake and thus ensure sustainability of initiatives.

This also heralded the emergence of the empowerment approach to development. With its focus on individual self-reliance and individual rights of participation and decision-making, it found support from both the capitalist and the neo-liberal approaches of entrepreneurship and individual freedom of choice. This largely individual-focused understanding of empowerment, missed the collective nature of empowerment necessary for challenging power structures (Narayan, 2002). With the growing strength of the women's movement, the definition of empowerment became more broad based and sought to address different aspects of 'power' within the term empowerment i.e. power over, power to, power with and power within (Oxaal and Baden, 1997).

International development discourse began to link civil society with a perspective of empowerment as a process that "requires the full participation of people in the formulation, implementation and evaluation of decisions determining the functioning and well being of societies" (Copenhagen Declaration of the World Summit on Social Development, 1995). Call to civil society to promote participation and empowerment of the poor followed.

This perspective on empowerment demanded new capacities and roles from citizens. It required them to re-orient themselves from receivers of welfare and benefits to actors in the development process whose capacity to participate determined the receipt of benefit or service. This transformation of citizens from passive recipients to active agents was not easy to incorporate. Although it looked good in policy agenda, its transformation in reality not only required an attitudinal change but also an orientation of citizens on processes of participation in governance and in decision-making. Further more, such an effort not only required pushing for attitudinal changes in citizens but more so in the attitudes and structures of the government and their functionaries.

"Participation is not simply achieved from above with new policy statements, but requires multiple strategies of institutional change, capacity building and behavioural change" (Gaventa, 2006).

As government mechanisms were believed to be too rigid, people unfriendly and centralised, the task of bringing about change in the perspectives of citizens and governance was left to 'civil society'. In this backdrop, the role of civil society organisations gained ground and they carved out a space, which was the backbone of renewed efforts at self-development and self-reliance through knowledge and capacity building—a perspective advocated by proponents of *participatory research* in late 1970s.

The transformation from an environment where it had to push for space, to one where there was ample space that needed to be ably filled, meant a stronger focus on strengthening civil society organisations to enable them to deliver capacity building initiatives throughout the country. Thus, the 1990s for PRIA was a period of strengthening *Support Organisations* and creating networks of civil society organisations, from the grassroot to the national level, in an attempt to consolidate and secure the space created for civil society.

This period saw a series of capacity building initiatives aimed at organisation building, management, accounting, documentation, leadership, community organisation etc. to enable civil society organisations and community based organisations to utilise the spaces so created. PRIA strengthened its mandate as a support organisation which focused on knowledge and awareness generation about rights and provided capacity building support; it resisted becoming a service delivery organisation, even when opportunities for economic empowerment were emerging.

Soon it became clear that organisation and capacity building for creating 'ownership' in the development process was not a solution to the widening poverty gap and increasing marginalisation. The neo-liberal perspective failed to recognize that the existing inequalities in society might act as barriers to the ownership process. Only those with the socio-economic capacity and position to 'own' and maintain resources in the village would be able to partake in this development process, leaving out those with no resources to own. Hindering economic and social structures and hierarchies barred any sense of ownership, responsibility and decision-making from the hands of the marginalised (Tandon and Mohanty, 2006).

Although participation through ownership and self-help provided citizens and civil society a greater role in the development process, its effectiveness remained questionable due to existing social and political structures, which limited people's choices within an 'acceptable' narrow framework.

"The participatory rhetoric asserted that local people knew best, emphasizing the importance of engaging them in making and shaping development initiatives. Yet, the strikingly similar form that 'participatory' projects of this era took, serves as an indication that despite rumours of its demise, the blueprint approach to development was far from dead. The very nature of the choices available to local people were so circumscribed by the processes used to determine avenues for action, that it was barely possible to imagine, let alone articulate alternatives (Craig and Porter, 1997, cited in Cornwall, 2000: 29).

The failure of this economically viable planned approach to participation and development gave way to the long advocated demand of re-structuring the government, moving away from centralised structures of power to decentralization. Civil society alone could not be the panacea unless overarching government structures were made more conducive to people's participation and bottom-up planning. By the mid-1990s, increasing demands for democratic decentralization as a strategy for sustainable development echoed in the development corridors in the form of the debate on 'good governance'.

Participation, Civil Society and Good Governance

Recognition of the structural constraints to the development process came in the late 80s and early 90s with the World Bank report in 1989 on Sub-Saharan Africa, which claimed that the Bank's programmes had been rendered ineffective by a 'crisis of governance'.

This report was a culmination of a long ongoing debate, which demonstrated how the capacity of the State to respond to diverse interests and expectations was declining. The growing alienation of the poor and marginalised from the elite-dominated institutions of government was leading to a growing disenchantment of people with State institutions. The primary reason for this alienation was seen as the increasing gap in policies and their practical application attributed to issues of corruption, administrative inefficiency, lack of transparency, etc. in the governing mechanisms.

The concept of 'good governance' with its basis on 'sound development management' was advocated as a solution to the development dilemma. "The World Bank (1992: 3) defined it as 'the manner in which power is exercised in the management of a country's economic and social resources for development'. Its four key dimensions were specified as public sector management (capacity and efficiency); accountability; the legal framework for development; and information and transparency" (Jayal and Pai, 2001).

According to the UNDP, "Good Governance addresses the allocation and management of resources to respond to collective problems. It is among other things, participatory, transparent and accountable. It is also effective and equitable. And it promotes the rule of law" (Commonwealth Foundation, 2002).

In its policy papers OECD clearly states, "governments increasingly realize that they will not be able to conduct and effectively implement policies, as good as they may be, if their citizens do not understand and support them" (Commonwealth Foundation, 2002).

The emphasis on reforming government institutions acted as a catalyst for efforts towards decentralization, which till now had often been used in rhetoric by politicians but had never found its roots on the ground. Decentralization through strengthening local self-governance meant 'giving away' of power. For example, in India through the introduction of the 73rd and 74th Constitutional Amendment Acts in 1992, the three Fs (functions, finances and functionaries), which had always been in the hands of Central and State Governments had to be shared through devolution with elected representatives at the local level. This meant not only setting up institutions of *local self-governance* but also providing them with the functions, finances, and functionaries to fulfil their mandate. In terms of deepening democracy, this was a historic period as it meant that a largely representative democracy came close to becoming a *participatory democracy* where people not only voted for their representatives but also had continued access to them. For the first time, people had a say over the development decisions in their localities. The concepts of 'ownership' and 'participation' had an altogether new meaning in this context. It meant ownership and participation in decisions and their outcomes.

Drawing on its experiences and reflections of engaging with various stakeholders, from community based groups to State institutions, PRIA looked at the introduction of *democratic decentralization* as an opportunity and a challenge to ensure that these institutions of planning and decision-making were made truly participatory and empowering. It applied the principles of participatory research in its efforts at strengthening institutions of local self-governance. From structured capacity building workshops for elected representatives of these new bodies to massive awareness campaigns involving community based organisations (Gram Sabha Mobilisation and Voters Awareness), to participatory research studies and analysis—all efforts were aimed at strengthening both the 'demand' and 'supply' sides of these local institutions. This meant developing voices from below as well as advocating for strengthening the institutional capacity of these local bodies and representatives to deliver the goods.

This deepening of democracy had obvious implications for citizens and civil society. It meant an increased role for civil society and its emergence and recognition as the 'Third Sector'. Civil society carved a space between the State and the Market, distinctive yet in cooperation with both other sectors. It acted as a buffer to ensure the rights of the poor and marginalised who were facing increased exclusion with the ever-widening gap, between the 'haves' and the 'have-nots'. As a mediator between the two forces it aimed at counteracting the declining power of the State and the increasing power of the market by advocating for a space for the 'voices of the marginalised'.

Civil society thus became both a vehicle as well as an outcome of promoting good governance, whereby the development priorities could be pursued. Governance was defined as "the joint responsibility of the state, market, and citizens to mobilise public resources and promote public decision-making towards the advancement of common public good" (Tandon and Mohanty, 2002).

In its expanded existence in the 1990s, all three roles of civil society—economic, social and political—came to the fore. On the economic front civil society not only found itself 'humanising capitalism' by promoting progressive social policies and accountability but also in securing livelihoods and providing services where states and markets were weak. In its social role, civil society gained prominence as a reservoir of intellectual and cultural innovation and in 'caring'. In its political role, civil society was seen as a crucial counterweight to state and market power by promoting transparency, accountability and good governance.

In this context, the key issues and challenges facing civil society were educating citizens on civil rights and responsibilities, motivating new leadership from the marginalised sections specially women, *dalits* and tribals (in recognition of hindering social structures), and sensitizing government officials and institutions to citizen participation making them accountable.

"Whether it is the political processes of democracy or the socio-economic processes of development, citizen participation is considered as the key. This represents a shift in the way the people are seen *vis-à-vis* governance. From the state-centric governance where people were considered as beneficiaries of state policies and programmes, and from the market driven affairs where people are treated as mere consumers, we have arrived at a juncture where finally people are recognised as 'citizens' with rights to engage and participate in the processes and institutions of development and governance" (Tandon and Mohanty, 2006).

For citizens, good governance and democratic decentralization meant a whole new outlook towards *citizenship*. Citizenship meant, not only citizens by right of franchise but also citizens by rights and responsibilities. It meant an exploration of the questions 'Who is a citizen and what does a good citizen do?'

Such questions tend to yield two types of responses—one focusing on legal status with an accompanying package of rights and responsibilities and another focusing on citizenship as practice, i.e., active participation in the affairs of the community and the state for the betterment of the community and society. Combining the two perspectives one may say that citizenship is not simply "a legal status, a passive bundle of rights and responsibilities but also an active practice" (Tandon and Mohanty, 2006).

Citizen participation in governance specially in the local spheres, thus, becomes a crucial determinant of effectiveness of local governments. Failures of service delivery to the marginalised and the poor, as well as inefficiencies in performing local governments mandates, are partly due to ineffective citizens engagement with governance.

Deliberating over the need to mobilise citizen participation for making democratic decentralization and good governance possible, PRIA organised a large gathering of civil society activists, development workers, trade unionists, members of local government, citizen leaders and administrators in Bhopal (1999). The deliberations reflected on the learning and experiences of civil society organisations working on the issues of Citizenship, Participation and Democracy over the past decade and discussed ways forward, aiming to give better shape, energy and direction to future endeavours.

Citizen participation was the challenge, and the key to its realization was believed to be a sense of ownership and belonging. The deliberations reflected that ownership and belonging could only be realised when individuals and groups felt that their contributions to the governance process were valuable and that they were responsible and accountable to themselves and to their community. For this, it was not only essential to have a participatory environment with a space for individuals to express their thoughts but also a change in value systems of society and polity which believed in democratic ways of functioning—at home, in the community, at the workplace and in society.

Participation and Citizenship in the New Millennium

With rights come responsibilities; with greater rights come greater responsibilities. Thus, the rights-based approach to citizenship and participation in governance not only places greater responsibility on citizens but also depends on greater participation by citizens for its success. In the new millennium, we stand at a point where structures of democratic decentralization are in place, citizenship and rights have acquired a depth they never had before, participation is recognised as an inalienable component to ensure sustainable development and yet participatory development and decentralised decision making are a far cry from reality. At this juncture, a time for reflection, looking back at successes, failures, learning and experiences is necessary to move forward.

It is important to understand that active participation requires both structural change in the patterns of power as well as attitudinal changes in the beliefs and expectations of citizens, in short, the political culture (Blackburn, 2000: cited in Commonwealth Foundation, 2002). For this it is important to socialize people into participation not only through capacity building on participatory exercises but also by ensuring the enhancement of knowledge, ability and dispositions; the knowledge of rights, existing power equations and their functioning; the ability to deliberate, negotiate with and influence others to develop opinions; the ability to work together to affect decisions; and the ability and disposition to question. Gaventa (1999) argues that development of critical consciousness is essential for full citizenship—a critical questioning stance, skepticism towards authority, a sense of efficacy and self-confidence.

These attitudinal changes require reinforcement from supportive structures. Although institutions of local self-governance have been put in place in most countries, their functionality in terms of independent planning, decision-making, and financing remains a distant dream. "In many developing countries, decentralization refers to downloading of responsibility to local levels, without requisite funding and with increasingly centralised decision making at all levels" (Commonwealth Foundation, 2002).

Another aspect that needs to be recognised in all efforts at ensuring *participatory citizenship* is the existence of deep-seated social inequalities. "In social settings marked by deep and persistent inequalities based on caste, class and gender, which govern peoples relationships with the state, and with each other, citizenship, in reality, comes to privilege the better-off" (Tandon and Mohanty, 2006). The more privileged are more easily able to access rights and resources as citizens, as opposed to the underprivileged whose demands for rights often lead to conflicts—as they are seen as threatening to unbalance the power equation.

In this emerging context of citizenship in a participatory, decentralised democracy, civil society needs to re-look at its role in facilitating the construction of new relationships between the citizens and the state. It is essential to emphasize that good governance does not mean offloading of responsibilities and withdrawal by the state but a transformation from a provider to a facilitator. The role of civil society then is not to devalue the state but to make it more responsive, accountable and responsible. "Good governance does not necessarily mean less but sometimes more appropriate government" (Weiss, 2000).

Appropriate government means appropriate devolution of functions with powers to do them justice. PRIA's engagements with Central and State Government institutions to make this 'appropriate government' possible saw attempts at pushing for activity mapping and clearer devolution through a series of Round-Table Conferences on Devolutions in 2004 and more recently through endeavours at engaging with State Finance Commissions in 2005-06.

It is also important to realize that if people today are not participating in the processes of governance, then there is a need to re-think the citizenship that we are advocating. Perhaps, the meaning of this new citizenship has been imposed on them just like other policy reforms, which are defined from above. Maybe there is a need to go back to the roots of participatory research where knowledge was generated by the people themselves and therefore resulted in sustainable change. Perhaps it is time to go back to the roots and have people define citizenship and its manifestations themselves.

This book is a compilation of a practitioner's perspective, both theoretical and practical, from years of grappling with the issues of participation, governance and citizenship. Highlighting emerging challenges, each paper attempts to inform practice as well as provoke deliberations on the key concern of 'how to take citizenship forward in an era of disappearing boundaries and an emerging notion of global governance'.

Tracing the conceptual growth of the concept of Governance, Dr. Tandon in his paper talks about the dilemmas and issues facing governance in a global world. He argues that governance today needs to be understood in the light of public goods. Good governance is about efficiency in delivery of public services and accountability to citizens. It is no longer the sole responsibility of the State but involves participation and partnership of civil society and the market sector. He contends that while the State by virtue of its nature is accountable to citizens, the question facing us is 'how to make the market and civil society accountable?' In the context of a globalised era, this question has broader implications, especially in the light of accountability to citizens: local and global.

While local governments are responsible and accountable for delivery of local public goods, who determines the accountability of global institutions for delivery of global public goods; or the accountability of national governments for delivery of international commitments?

Looking at accountability from a local dimension, Dr. Ranjita Mohanty raises the issue of Tribal Rights and State Accountability in the backdrop of an industrial era. Basing her analysis on case studies of industrial sites of big industrial houses like the Tatas (in Orissa) and the Jindals (in Chhattisgarh) to small mining enterprises (in Jharkhand), she questions the accountability and commitment of the State in an era where the role of the State is declining while that of the Market is increasing. Since rights and citizenship are derived from the State, the State's collusion with the markets results in the defender becoming the violator. For the marginalised, for whom rights are the sole basis of citizenship and inclusion, this means further powerlessness and exclusion.

In his paper Manoj Rai draws from experiences of democratic decentralization, theory and practice, to embark on a critical journey of challenges, successes and failures in advocacy efforts towards ensuring effective democratic decentralization in India. Focusing on the trinity of institutions, i.e. the State Election Commission, the State Finance Commission and the District Planning Committee, as institutional mechanisms that need to be strengthened for a vibrant and strong local government, he talks about a growing understanding, yet resistance among politicians and bureaucrats on the need to take local government seriously. Drawing from the series of Round-Table Conferences on Devolution organised by the Ministry of Panchayati Raj he clearly outlines the lacunae in the system, giving a lucid report of the State-wise status of devolution of powers to Local Governments in the country.

The role of civil society in enhancing citizen participation and in ensuring democratic performance is the theme of Dr. Shailendra Dwivedi's paper. Using empirical examples of educational and mobilisation campaigns by civil society organisations, he highlights the processes that facilitate change and help in inclusion of the marginalised into mainstream political participation. He argues that overcoming barriers of social exclusion, economic dependency and illiteracy to enhance effective participation in the political and social arena, requires not only knowledge and capacity enhancement but methods of communication which bring about an attitudinal change; an attitudinal change that incorporates democratic norms and values such that participation is experienced as normative and not as an anomaly by citizens. In the context of increasing apathy of ordinary citizens towards institutions of governance, Dr. Dwivedi expresses the need for civil society organisations to facilitate citizen participation, ensuring deepening of democracy and equitable distribution of power in society.

Mandakini Pant and Martha Farrell's paper gives a gender based analysis of governance and empowerment. It maps the evolution of the concept of gender in development from being an end in itself to a rights-based approach where gender is seen as a means to holistic development. Drawing from an empirical study on Gender in Governance, Pant and Farrell highlight the institutional and social constructions of gender, which act as barriers for effective participation of women in governance. Critiquing the simplistic 'add women' agenda they recommend engendering strategies to address the history of exclusion, marginalization and invisibility of women's voices which prevent them from exercising their agency. At the practical level, capacity building and collective support from community-based groups is seen as a confidence enabler, while gender mainstreaming in governance and civil society organisations is seen as the larger agenda necessary for taking gender equality forward.

Nilanjan Ghose's paper addresses the emerging issue of citizen participation in Urban Governance. He argues that sustainable urbanization is the greatest challenge for the future and the key to economic growth and environmental sustainability of cities lies with urban local bodies. Comparing two models of citizen engagement in the management of solid waste, being undertaken in two municipalities in India (Pithoragarh, in Uttaranchal and Mudhubani, in Bihar), he states that when citizens are involved in planning and monitoring they develop a sense of ownership and responsibility. The sustainability of involvement however, depends on the formal spaces created by urban local bodies for citizen engagement. In this process civil society can, and should, simply play a facilitator's role. Citizen participation ensures community monitoring of municipal services, serving as an accountability and pressure mechanism that ensures efficient and effective service delivery. Concluding, he states that inclusive governance is the only means of deepening democracy and promoting active citizenship in urban locales.

In his paper Dr. Kaustuv Kanti Bandyopadhyay explores the expanded meaning of citizenship in an era where citizenship has gone much beyond simple legal and political rights to a 'right to participate'. This new understanding of citizenship emerges from efforts at deepening democracy through decentralization of powers to local bodies. He asserts that the space created for participation and assertion of citizenship rights requires the development of a new 'active' citizen, who is aware about reality, willing to work towards change and strives for public good through collective efforts. This 'citizen leader' provides a channel for inarticulated marginalised voices and is at the core of effective democracy. Suggesting that serious thought be given for the capacity building, institutional and civil society support of this new emerging citizen leadership, Dr. Bandyopadhyay stresses upo the centrality of their roles in preventing alienation of the State and making citizenship real.

Reflecting on the theoretical roots and trends that the concept of participation has traveled through, Anju Dwivedi and Namrata Jaitli in their paper look at where participation stands today. Despite an evolutionary journey in the development paradigm, 'participation in development' is still marred by continued poverty, discrimination, social exclusion and marginalisation. Outlining empirical participatory methodologies of community monitoring (report card and social audit) and multi-stakeholder dialogues, Dwivedi and Jaitli state that despite the success of these methodologies in empowering people to participate, there still exists a danger that the instrumental role of participation overrides the social transformational one. The challenge is to demystify participatory processes and build the capacities of both practitioners and citizens to participate in processes of governance. Without this, democracy and citizenship, as we visualize it, will remain a far cry from reality.

This collection represents the evolution, in thoughts and ideas, of 25 years of PRIA's experiential journey of engagement with the concepts of participation, civil society, governance and citizenship. The debate it generates will be the start of a long journey of enabling an active citizenry for whom democratic participation is no longer just a 'right' but a way of life.

REFERENCES

Blackburn, James, (2000), *Popular Participation in a Prebendal Society: A Case Study of Participatory Municipal Planning in Sucre*, Bolivia, Ph.D. Thesis, University of Sussex.

Chambers Robert, (1997), *Whose Reality Counts: Putting the First Last*, Intermediate Technology Publication.

Citizenship, Participation and Democracy, Sammelan, Nov 19-21, 1999, Bhopal.

Commonwealth Foundation (1999), *Citizens and Governance: Civil Society in the New Millennium*, London.

Commonwealth Foundation, (2002), *The Citizens and Governance Programme: Issues for Debate* (Volume 1)—Occasional Papers #1-3 of the Citizens and Governance Programme.

Cornwall, Andrea and Gaventa, John, (2000), 'From Users and Choosers to Makers and Shapers: Repositioning Participation in Social Policy', *IDS Bulletin*, 31 (4): 50-62.

Cornwall, Andrea, (2000), *Beneficiary, Consumer, Citizen: Perspectives on Participation for Poverty Reduction*, Sida Studies No. 2.

De-regulating the Mind: Democratising Society: Report of the Seminar of PRIA's 10th Anniversary Programme, Feb. 5-6, 1992, New Delhi.

Edward, Michael, (2004), *Civil Society*, Polity Press and Blackwell Publishing Ltd., UK.

Hall, Budd, (1984), *Participatory Research: Popular Knowledge and Power*, Participatory Research Group, Toronto.

Hall, Budd, Arthur Gillette and Rajesh Tandon (Ed.), 1982, Creating Knowledge: A Monopoly? Participatory Reseach Network Series No. 1, PRIA, New Delhi.

Jayal, Niraja Gopal and Sudha Pai, (ed), (2001), *Democratic Governance in India: Challenges of Poverty, Development and Identity*, Sage Publications.

Mahajan, Gurpreet (ed.), (2003), *The Public and the Private: Issues of Democratic Citizenship*, Sage Publications.

Narayan, Deepa (ed.), (2002), *Empowerment and Poverty Reduction: A Sourcebook*, The World Bank, Washington DC.

Oakley, P., (1995), 'Peoples participation in development projects', INTRAC Occasional Papers Series, 7, Oxford: INTRAC.

Oomen, T.K., (2004), *Nation, Civil Society and Social Movements: Essays in Political Sociology*; Sage Publications, New Delhi.

Orlando, Fals-Borda and Rahman, M.A., (1991), *Action and Knowledge: Breaking the monopoly with Participatory Action Research*, New York: Apex Press.

Oxaal, Zoe and Sally Baden, (1997), Gender and Empowerment: Definitions, Approaches and Implications for Policy (Briefing prepared for the Swedish International Development Office (SIDA), October; BRIDGE (development gender) Institute of Development Studies, University of Sussex, Brighton, UK.

Rahman, Muhammad Anisur, (1982), The Theory and Practice of Participatory Action Research; Paper prepared for Plenery Session on "Contradictions, Conflicts and Strategies of Societal Change", at the Tenth World Congress of Sociology to be held in Mexico in August, 1982; Rural Employment Policies Branch, Employment and Development Department, ILO Geneva.

Tandon, Rajesh and Ranjita Mohanty, (2002), *Civil Society and Governance*, Samskriti.

Tandon, Rajesh and Ranjita Mohanty, (ed.), (2006), *Participatory Citizenship: Identity, Exclusion and Inclusion*, Sage Publications.

Tandon, Rajesh, (ed.), (2002), *Participatory Research: Revisiting the Roots*, Mosaic Books New Delhi.

Walter, Fernandes, and Rajesh Tandon, (ed.) (1981), Participatory Research and Evaluation: Experiments in Research as a Process of Liberation, Indian Social Institute, New Delhi.

Weiss, Thomas G., (2000), Governance, good governance and global governance: Conceptual and actual challenges, *Third World Quarterly*, Vol. 21, No. 5, 795-914.

2

Governance of Public Goods
Local and Global

Rajesh Tandon

In the past five years or so, the vocabulary of 'governance' has become common usage. In our own practice aimed at empowerment of the poor and the marginalized, we have begun to define our programmatic focus on 'governance where people matter'. In presenting our work to many others, we use the phrase 'promotion of democratic governance'.

Till recently, it was reasonably clear to us, and the constituencies we worked with, that government is an important actor; in reality, in our context the most important actor in promoting just and sustainable development. Understanding how government functions, analysing its multiple roles (as regulator, policy-maker, service provider, resource-giver, etc.) and strategising how to influence it and access its support, resources and programmes in the interest of the poor and the marginalized, used to be an important set of competencies in our practice.

'Governance' began to make sense to us in our practical efforts to mainstream people's (particularly the poor and the excluded) engagement and participation with the affairs of the government at different levels, in particular at local level. But, we began to ask ourselves; is 'governance' the 'thing' that governments do? Or is it more than that? And, is there something like 'good' governance, a universal standard for all governments everywhere? Again, our practice seemed to throw up issues which suggested that a more historical and conceptual exploration of the concept of governance may deepen our own practice in future. This paper, therefore, is an attempt to examine the historical roots, theoretical interpretations and practical ambiguities in the concept of 'governance'.

Roots

There are two basic questions in defining the meaning of government. As Jreisat (2004) puts, these are "Who governs? And, How well?" How a government is formed? And, how it performs?

The government governs its territory; simply stated, this is what has been taught in political science theories. By extension, it governs all the inhabitants of that territory.

"A nation state is a type of politico-military rule that has a distinct geographically defined territory over which it exercises jurisdiction; has sovereignty over its territory; has a government made up of public offices and roles that control and administer the territory and population subject to the state's jurisdiction; its population manifests, to a greater or lesser degree, a sense of national identity; and it can rely to a greater or lesser degree on the obedience and loyalty of its inhabitants" (Opello and Roscow, 2005).

Democracy implies that government governs with the consent of the governed. The governed can withdraw their consent, and change those in government. "In theoretic terms, democracy is a form of governance in which citizens control public policy and public action, by electing persons of their choice to represent them" (Kamal, 2000).

Some governments, in some periods, govern efficiently to the satisfaction of the governed. In case of some other governments and in other periods, the governed may become dissatisfied with the way government functions. "Good governance is characterized by among other things, collaboration, transparency, inclusiveness, responsiveness, equity and accountability—all interrelated and reinforcing" (Commonwealth Foundation, 2002).

It has been usually accepted in popular thinking that democratic forms of governments generally govern to the satisfaction of the governed; specially when democratic form is compared with monarchy, autocracy or dictatorship. This received wisdom did not hold true for the rapidly growing economies of such 'Asian tigers' as Taiwan, Singapore and South Korea in the

1970s and 1980s which were then governed as autocracies; the economic miracle of China today is being led by a government which cannot be readily called democratic. "Statistical studies find that neither authoritarianism nor democracy is a factor in determining either the rate of economic growth or how it is distributed" (HDR, 2004).

Yet Sen (1999) argues that "The economic policies and circumstances that led to the economic success of East Asian economies are by now acknowledged as a list of helpful policies. There is nothing whatsoever to indicate that any of these policies are inconsistent with greater democracy."

The original dictionary meaning of 'govern' is 'to regulate by authority' or 'administer by laws'. Thus government is a political authority mandated by laws to regulate and administer a territory or peoples. In this original sense, there was no word called 'governance'. Thus, by extension, governance was what the governments did. This indeed was the generally accepted meaning till very recently. It was only in the 1990s that reference to 'governance' began to appear in the language of development discourse. It seems that the World Bank began to talk about governance as accumulated evidence on its development projects around the world began to show that the manner in which the government functioned in the recipient country had a lot to do with the impact of their projects. UNDP (1997) described it as an exercise of economic, political and administrative authority to manage the affairs of a country. It further argued for 'good' governance to imply rule of law, equity, transparency, accountability and participation in the conduct of governments. Around this period, OECD, World Bank and other international institutions also echoed similar interpretations to governance. (Wyman, 2001) In my view the conceptualisation of good governance should not only include democratisation of the State but also democratisation of the social sphere. Tandon (2002) defined it as "the joint responsibility of the State, market and citizens to mobilise public resources and promote public decision-making towards the advancement of common public good". Good governance, therefore, not only entails reform of public services, efficiency and cost effectiveness of public agencies but also ensures participation of the poor, the marginalized and the under represented.

Aid and Governance

The driving force for such formulations was a growing concern that international development assistance was not having the desired impact in addressing the problems faced by the people of the developing countries. Even in those countries where formal institutions of democracy were in place, they were not functioning effectively to reduce poverty and marginalisation. It was then argued that the manner of functioning of the governments needed to be radically transformed for the delivery of desired outcomes to the people.

"Advancing human development requires governance that is democratic in both form and substance—for the people and by the people. When institutions function badly, poor and vulnerable people tend to suffer the most. It is not only about whether judges are trained, but whether they observe due process and are blind to differences of race and class. It is not only about whether schools are built, but whether students in poor districts are as well equipped as students in affluent areas. It argues that countries can promote human development for all only when they have governance systems that are fully accountable to all people—and when all people can participate in the debates and discussions that shape their lives" (HDR, 2002).

Likewise the World Bank stated, "The challenge is formidable, because making services work for poor people involves changing not only service delivery arrangements but also public sector institutions" (WDR, 2004).

One strand of improvements that were attempted by some governments came under the label of 'new public management'. In this approach, it was decided to modernize the system of public administration as it had become inefficient, corrupt and aloof. Therefore, the systems of administration were reformed; civil service was given better training; corporate management principles and systems of target-setting, budgeting, performance appraisal etc. were introduced; more consultations with people (beneficiaries of welfare and consumers of services) were held. As a result of this 'corporatist' influence, the 'old public administration' became the 'new public management'. This approach was based on the assumption that the public bureaucracies had become inefficient because their administrative philosophy and procedures were out-of-date (Farnham and Horton, 1996).

The second strand attempted to invite private businesses in economic decision-making; it was felt that the expertise and resources of the business sector could contribute to improved policies for economic development and infrastructure building. It was also realized that the scale of investment needed for the development in many countries required resources beyond the means of the government. Thus began the strand of public-private partnerships (PPP). It was assumed that such partnerships implied involvement of business sector in some aspects of the 'governance' of the country (Nelson, 1996).

While this may well be so in some developing countries which adopted a soviet-style planned economy model of economic development after independence, it was not so for some rapidly growing economies. Beeson (2001) has argued that the political authority and market institutions in countries of East Asia have been part of the same organizing principle, and that there has been no contrasting framework of business organizing or independent policy dialogue outside the governments there.

An extension of this strand later included civil society. Its entry came from the need for greater participation of people and communities in the design, implementation, monitoring and maintenance of development projects. Community participation and participatory development strategies had begun to get mainstreamed in international institutions by the early 1990s (the World Bank formulated a Participation Policy in 1994 to be applied to all its projects). Participation of stakeholders in making decisions around the use of developmental resources had been acknowledged. This became one essential argument for its inclusion in the meaning of 'governance'. "Good governance sees and includes citizens as active participants in the process of governance" (Commonwealth Foundation, 2004).

"It was a shift from state centric governance where people were considered as beneficiaries of state policies and programmes, and from market driven affairs to a juncture where people were finally recognized as 'citizens' with rights to engage and participate in the processes and institutions of development and governance"(Tandon and Mohanty, 2006).

Another argument in this regard was provided by the

experiences of countries of Eastern/Central Europe in early 1990s. Citizens' movements to overthrow former totalitarian communist regimes had gained much visibility. This was hailed as the rise of civil society. By mid 1990s, therefore, a new model of development and democracy had become part of the then 'Washington Consensus'. It projected and argued for a tri-sectoral model comprising of government, business and civil society. Thus the trinity became the architecture of 'governance', specially its qualified version 'good governance'.

Good governance "is the joint responsibility of players in the public sector, the corporate private sector and civil society at the national, international, multi-national and multi-lateral levels" (Commonwealth Foundation, 2002). The UNDP Administrators report to the Executive Board in 1994 acknowledges that "relationships between government and the private sector and between the private sector and civil society are essential to creating a strong enabling environment for sustainable human development" (UNDP, 1997).

Thus began a new phase of theoretical argumentation and practical elaboration of the concept of 'governance' in the late 1990s.

Main Theoretical Approaches

There seems to be considerable agreement in the literature on defining governance as an exercise of authority, mostly political authority in relation to a territory. A somewhat more expansive definition has called it 'steering' of society or an organisation (Jreisat, 2004).

In the discourse on governance, two main strands can be delineated. The first can be called Institutionalist and the other Processual (some call it behavioural). The proponents of the former essentially look at governance in the form of institutional architecture; those who argue for the latter, focus on modes and ways of working together, irrespective of institutional arrangements.

Institutionalist

The Institutionalist argument is about recognition that exercise of governance is the responsibility of some institutions. Institutions are essential in governance of modern societies. Institutions of the government (specially in democracies) have withstood their relevance over generations (Nye and Donahue, 2000). There is a need to pay attention to how these institutions are designed and operated, particularly in including the inputs, ideas and feedbacks from civil society and business sectors. This thinking can also be identified with the theorisation of 'The Third Way' (Giddens, 1998). Such approaches were argued for and practiced in UK, Canada, New Zealand in the mid to late 1990s.

Giddens (1998) argued that the "Reform of the State and Government should be a basic orienting principle of Third way politics—a process of the deepening and widening of democracy". Government at all levels was mistrusted partly because it was cumbersome and ineffective. Restructuring the government should follow the ecological principle of 'getting more from less', understood not as downsizing but as improving delivered value. *"The new democratic state should promote devolution, double democratisation, renewal of the public-sphere transparency, administrative efficiency, mechanisms of direct democracy and the government as a risk manager"* in response to globalisation.

There is another strand in Institutionalist thinking which goes beyond the institutional arrangements of the public sector. Young (1997) takes an institutionalist approach to governance without any reference to political authority; he calls for 'social institutions that mediate governance'. His emphasis is on regimes (meaning principles and rules) as the basis of such mediation. Such a strand argues for creating new formal institutional mechanisms which mediate interdependent obligations of different actors from the government, civil society and business. Public-Private Partnerships provide one form of government-business institutional arrangements. Such institutional arrangements are bi-polar, between government and business. It typically entails joint ventures with equity participation and investment around some type of public infrastructure (common ones are roads, power, ports/airports, telecommunications etc.).

"Private sector involvement in management, financing or ownership will in most cases be needed to ensure a commercial orientation in infrastructure"(World Bank, 1994).

There has also been some skepticism towards these PPPs. The most dominant critique has questioned this approach as a strategy in disguise to promote 'privatisation of public institutions'. It further argues that by adopting this approach the government reduces its obligations to society by off-loading responsibility to the business sector. "One of the key differences between public-private partnerships and privatisation is 'responsibility'. Under privatisation the responsibility for delivery and funding a particular service rests with the private sector. Public-private partnership on the other hand involves full retention of responsibility by the government for providing service" (Planning Commission, 2004).

The second critique of this approach points out the missing P in this arrangement—the P of people; where are the people? The civil society does not find much space in such new institutional arrangements. In developing such partnerships, the critiques argue, that citizens need to be given a central, not peripheral, role. The Kampala Vision on Multi-Sectoral Partnerships for Democracy and Development (2003) states that "People have an inherent right and concomitant duty to be involved in and actively participate in governance; and that governments have a responsibility to meaningfully and constructively engage citizens, civil society and other non-state actors in the affairs of their countries."

One common mode of new forms of institutional arrangements which include clear roles for civil society are discussed under the broad rubric of 'public service contracting'. In this approach, governments develop new forms of institutional mechanisms which include contractual arrangements for civil society to deliver some welfare and care services. The planning and monitoring of activities in such service-delivery arrangements are typically supervised by the appropriate government agency, and actual delivery is carried out by the civil society organisations. Such arrangements have made it possible for the basic public services to be delivered to the distant, remote, poor, marginalized and invisible individuals and families in many countries. Such institutional innovations have also made it possible for more appropriate and better quality services to be rendered, without wastage of public funds (as is typically the case when government bureaucracies operate on their own). Cohen (2001) notes that governments have a history of delegating responsibility to other non-state institutions to perform some of its roles; "the state's essential role is that of establishing boundaries around those activities and persons over which it claims authority".

Such a view allows for the possibility of changing (over time and contexts) roles and obligations (and how they are met) of the government. Thus some governments may shift some functions to private sector from the public responsibility after an improved economic situation (the domestic aviation sector in India, for example). The possibility of such a transfer of functions "depends on the strength of the private sector, the administrative capacity of the government to regulate private suppliers, the performance of public sector providers and the political consensus for private provision" (World Bank, 1994).

Criticisms to such institutional arrangements have essentially looked at two issues. First, it is argued that such arrangements may be a strategy to 'privatise' public services such that the government bears no responsibility (in the long run) to deliver them to society. This may particularly hurt the poor and the vulnerable families most severely, as they may not be able to pay for 'private' provisions of such services. The second argument suggests that civil society is deviating from its core functions if it enters into institutional arrangements with governments to deliver services. Thus contractual basis of public service delivery takes civil society away from its other tasks, particularly those associated with monitoring the government institutions and holding them accountable.

"Civil society is seen in a diametrical relation with the state, existing as a legitimate arena of defense against the state and as a natural condition of freedom against the institutional despotism of the State, or as a product of historical product of multi-dimensional relations arising from the emergence of the market seeking the freeing up of the economy from the arena of politics and extra economic relations." (Abugre, 1999)

The most recurring theoretical questioning of an institutionalist approach to 'governance' is based on the concept of political authority. It is argued that a singular political authority is essential for the task of administering and regulating a particular territory, including the business and civil society. Thus, new institutional arrangements creates the risk of 'fragmentation of singular political authority' (Krahmann, 2003); it may also expand the domain of agents exercising political authority through 'inclusion of legitimacy'. Thus, regulating the territory or administering the laws may become compromised when multiple institutions (including non-state institutions) try to exercise political authority. There are fears raised in relation to conflicting jurisdictions for multiple political authorities as well as possible inefficiencies arising out of the splitting of tasks and responsibilities. It is also argued that multiple institutions exercising some form of political authority in 'governance' may actually 'weaken' the political authority of the government itself. Rosenau (2003) considers such arrangements as potentially a "rival" source of authority.

Processual

The processual argument begins from the assumption, as implied in the critiques of the institutionalist arguments, that 'governance' requires a singular political authority. It endorses the view that political authority should remain vested in the democratically elected (assuming such situations) government of the time. The processual argument to governance suggests that new ways of including the voices and opinions of the experts should be found to improve the effectiveness of various governmental institutions. Inviting experts to serve on various task-forces, committees and decision-making bodies is a common practice in this approach. Typically, the experts come from the academia, business or intermediary NGOs, nationally as well as internationally. Such a process ensures access to high quality information, competence and perspectives by the government. Formal representation is also sought from organized interest groups in order to improve governance from the point-of-view of enhanced commitment to the decisions of governance. Analysing such approaches from the Swedish context, Oberg (2002) concludes that representation of interest groups to boards and policy committees enhances trust towards the system of governance itself.

Its major critique comes from the implied exclusion of ordinary folks, the citizens, from such opportunities. Thus elite perspectives displace or crowd out popular perspectives in this approach (Tandon and Mohanty, 2006; Tandon, 2002).

"Most governments and businesses see themselves as initiators of citizen's involvement or participation, paying scant attention to citizen's concerns or citizen initiated processes. Concerns are expressed about citizens lack of experience, difficulty in understanding the issues or the complexities of policy making. And, increasingly, these doubts are being framed in the context of the additional complexities of a globalized world. There is somehow a sense that experts are needed to negotiate territory, which is complex and complicated, and that Herculean efforts would be required on the part of citizens—which they are unable or unwilling to expend"(Commonwealth Foundation, 2002).

One of the more recently argued forms of 'governance', from the processual point of view, is the deliberative form. 'Deliberation' is seen as an opportunity to discuss, debate and argue for different issues concerning the people. Hunold (2001) has argued that the focus of such deliberation should target rule-making by public officials. His analysis is that modern democracies are characterized by relatively more power of executives over legislatures; this power is more in the arena of drafting rules, procedures and laws by such 'unelected' officials; so, deliberation should counter such undemocratic exercise of administrative power. Hunold suggests that independent impact assessments and publicity are two effective tools for supporting such deliberations. The typical 'town hall' meeting (or Gram Sabha in Panchayats) can be seen as such a deliberative forum. There has been quite a body of literature on deliberative forms of governance, deriving its main conceptual basis from the notion of public sphere as propounded by Habermas (1989).

Another processual approach has been variously called multi-stakeholder one. Such an approach assumes that the issue being addressed is such that its solution cannot be effectively implemented by government alone, or by people themselves, but its complexity requires several parties working together. Various actors who have a stake in the outcomes related to that issue are invited to develop a shared diagnosis and solution to the problem. Such stakeholders include an appropriate government agency as well as people (and their representatives/associations) affected by that issue. Some issues require the involvement of business as a stake-holder as well. Multi-stakeholder approaches tend to develop shared responsibility in the process of diagnosing and solving an issue. The primary focus in these approaches remains on the process of working together by different stakeholders. "Multi-stakeholder dialogue is a process to build a shared understanding on a particular issue, to create a common platform among different stakeholders through dialogue, discussion and debate and to initiate joint action planning"(PRIA, 2004).

These strands of governance, therefore, attempt to expand the institutionalist and processual domain of the authorities and mechanisms of governance. As has been noted above, there remain considerable disagreements towards the veracity and legitimacy of such strands of governance.

Public Good

I would like to argue that the concept of governance, in its differing meanings, can only be seen to be appropriate when explored along with the concept of public good. Thus, governance as a concept, and as an approach, can only make sense when related to 'governance of public goods'.

Economists distinguish between private and public goods. Private goods are those which are consumed by people in private. These are provided for in the market by private businesses and paid for by the consumers. Banana is a private good, and those wanting to eat a banana buy it from the market and consume it. But certain goods are such that they are needed by all people (like roads and drinking water and clean air) to live. Such goods need to be made available for all people, irrespective of their desire to consume them by paying for them. Economists call them public goods, and argue that they cannot be profitably provided for by the businesses. Hence, the government has a responsibility in ensuring their provision for all (Leach, 2004).

Public goods are those which economists identify as having the twin characteristics of non-rivalrous and non-excludable. Non-rivalrous means that consumption of such goods by one set of people does not preclude their consumption by another set of people. Sunshine is one such good, which is consumed by all people without creating any rivalry among them. Pure public goods are also non-excludable, meaning that the providers can not exclude anyone from consuming them. Take for example, radio signals; anyone who has a radio can listen, and radio signal provider cannot exclude anyone. Thus users of such non-excludable public goods cannot be charged for their consumption (Leach, 2004).

In reality, most public goods are not pure; most public goods are 'impure' in different ways. Some public goods are 'impure' because they are partially rivalrous. A park, for example, is partially rivalrous, because its swings and slides may be so limited that they soon get congested over a weekend, as many more children come to use it. The access to such goods can be controlled by charging user fee; so the park could have an entry fee, and a specially higher fee over the weekend. The fee may reduce the use of the park's facilities and thereby reduce congestion.

Many goods and services provided for by the government take the form of public goods. Safety on the streets, traffic lights, roads and bridges, etc are assumed to be such public goods that no private provider can make profit in providing for them. Thus the role of the government, as provider of safety, traffic lights and roads, is assumed. The government exercises its political authority to raise revenue (from various forms of taxation) to pay for the provision of such public goods.

Several difficulties arise in practice. First, the government may run short of resources to pay for all its provisions. It then prioritises which public goods to pay for; so, its decision-makers may decide to build an extension of roads in the capital city as a priority; but then no resources are left over for building roads to connect villages and small towns. Second, its own service delivery machinery may be inefficient and corrupt; so, even though it pays for the extension of the roads in the capital city, it costs much more, and the road develops cracks soon due to its poor quality. Third, the government then decides to use its revenues for building further new roads, and the maintenance of existing roads suffers; a constant flow of heavy machinery on those roads, causing much damage to its surface. Now, who would be responsible for its maintenance? Due to public hue and cry, the government then spends more money on repair of existing roads in the capital city. The residents of the capital city demand better road system in their city since they pay higher taxes. The roads in rural areas get further neglected.

In this scenario, several questions arise. Who decides how much revenue needs to be generated? How are priorities about expenditure set? How can rural roads also be built? How should maintenance be financed? Should users of roads in capital city pay for their use (a sort of toll)?

The underlying issue here is the definition of public good.

Are roads a public good? Are city roads impure public good (so that toll on users can be charged), and rural roads pure public good (so government should pay for it entirely)? Who defines it? How is it defined? Whose voices and arguments are heard? What are the alternatives to direct provision by the government? How to ensure that long-term development of the country is not sacrificed in short-term considerations? A discussion of such questions brings us into the realm of 'governance'.

> "Not only is this true in theory, but in practice no country has achieved significant improvement in child mortality and primary education without governmental involvement. Furthermore, as mentioned earlier, private sector or NGO participation in health, education and infrastructure is not without problems—especially in reaching poor people...
>
> Why? First, these services are replete with market failures—with externalities, as when an infected child spreads a disease to playmates or a farmer benefits from a neighbours ability to read. So, the private sector, left to its devices, will not achieve the level of health and education that society desires. Second, basic health and basic education are considered fundamental human rights...no matter how daunting the problems of delivery, may be, the public sector cannot walk away from health and education. The challenge is how the government—in collaboration with private sector, communities and outside partners—can meet this fundamental responsibility." (WDR, 2004)

Governance Revisited

In light of the above, I would like to define 'governance as structures and processes of public decision-making about mobilisation and use of public resources for common public good'.

In the first instance, I am combining both the institutionalist and processual strands discussed above. In my view, both structural arrangements (their design and mandate) as well as the manner in which they function (processes) have to be simultaneously considered. It is not uncommon to come across brilliant structural designs with chaotic/ineffective operational/ behavioural processes in the functioning of governance systems.

Nye and Donahue (2000) have taken a similar view, and expanded somewhat further, when they define governance as "processes and institutions, both formal and informal, that guide and restrain collective activities".

The second aspect of the above definition is the focus on public decision-making; how and by whom are such decisions made? The notion of transparency becomes included here; transparency is about publicly known criteria and bases by which public decisions are made; it further includes publicly known composition (who are those people) of such decision-making bodies.

Third, the definition clearly focuses on both the mobilisation and use of public resources. Governance does entail mobilizing tax revenues from the public; many a times the criteria and rationale for taxation and revenue raising remain unknown to and hidden from the public view. The basis for charging user fee or fee-for-service decisions remains invisible to the general public, as well as to those asked to pay for those charges. Likewise, the criteria and rationale for revenue allocation and budgetary decisions by public authorities remain unknown to the public.

Fourth, the definition squarely focuses on common public goods. The relationship of decision-making structures and processes is sought to be limited to those related to the common public goods. As argued above, some aspects relate to definition of public goods themselves. There are two theoretical questions here. First relates to the economists' view that all human beings are rational, self-interest seeking actors; therefore, if they want something, they will pay for it. Hence, there is not much scope for public, pure or impure, goods. Several thinkers and philosophers have countered such narrow views of human beings by showing their moral make-up. If human beings are capable of compassion, love, charity and fraternity, then they also have a sense of values, which impel them to consider some things in life as 'public goods' (March & Olsen, 1995).

The second question is how do we know that there exists some elements of commonality in accepting something as public goods. What is included as public good?

These definitions change over time. In the 1970s, ILO argued for the 'basic needs' approach to public provision in developing countries. The ILO (1976) defined "basic needs as, first, minimum family requirements for basic consumption such as adequate food, shelter, clothing, household equipment and furnishings; and second, as essential community services such as potable water, sanitation, health services, educational facilities and public transport". Later Sen (1999) argued that 'freedoms' are public goods. Twenty years ago, actions within the household were generally kept out of the purview of public scrutiny and were considered as private domain. Through the struggles and campaigns of civil society, domestic violence against women and children is now considered a public 'bad'. Historically, many such aspects of rights as public goods evolved through social movements.

The ideals of liberty, equality and fraternity also provide the basis for identifying common public goods. Constitutions of most countries codify many of these rights, and mandate the political authority to protect and advance them. These too may be considered common public goods. In the global context the rights outlined in the Universal Declaration of Human Rights (1948) encompass the domain of public good. The Declaration proclaims "a common standard of achievement for all peoples and all nations, to the end that every individual and every organ of society, keeping this Declaration constantly in mind, shall strive by teaching and education to promote respect for these rights and freedoms and by progressive measures, national and international, to secure their universal and effective recognition and observance, both among the peoples of Member States themselves and among the peoples of territories under their jurisdiction."

The studies by Norris (1999) and the Commonwealth Foundation (1999) tend to confirm that certain public goods can also be common across many countries and societies.

It is my contention that like domestic (local, provincial or national) public goods, the referent constituency for global public goods should be global publics, not nation-states or national governments. Safety for the people, prevalence of peace, absence of violence and prevention of war is a major global public good which was the initial motivation for the establishment of UN. The General Assembly and the Security Council seem to have failed in delivering this public good to millions of people around the world. Palestinian people are still looking for a homeland; Iraqis are facing more insecurity on the streets since the American invasion; the minorities (ethnic, tribal, racial and religious) in many parts of the world have been facing severe persecution by militia groups, para-military and state police (like Bosnia, Rwanda, Timor... and now Darfur). The UN as a political authority has not been able to provide for this public good, and today stands discredited in this regard.

Regulation of currencies, stability in the macro-economic environment and support for economic reconstruction were the public goods for which Bretton Woods Institutions (and their regional counterparts) were initially set up. The IMF has moved away from its mandate of macro-economic regulator in the world to promoter of the neo-liberal economic agenda in developing countries; it has failed to discipline the run-away financial deficit in American economy today; it did not regulate the tax-havens which encouraged flight of capital, money laundering and indebtedness of nations; it did not work to establish, and monitor, transparent standards for the functioning of global stock markets (Scholte, 2002). The World Bank, on the other hand, gave concessional and market-linked credit primarily to developing countries to follow a standard model of development based on economic growth and physical infrastructure—almost 'a one size fits all' approach; it pushed such structural adjustment programmes to its recipient countries that caused more disruption than reconstruction of local economies and human capabilities (NGO Working Group, World Bank, 1994). The mechanisms for regulating markets, capital flows and transnational corporations to assure economic stability and "reasonable" profits just do not exist today.

Over the past thirty years, it has become obvious that ecological destruction is occurring due to over-consumption around the world, much more in western and richer societies. Pollution of air, water, acid rain, ozone depletion, climate change, deforestation, loss of marine life, loss of bio diversity, reducing supply of potable water, etc. the list is long and growing. Availability of basic necessities for survival—air, water, vegetation—is a universally relevant global public good. But the record of treaties and agreements is not very encouraging in ensuring such public goods to future generations. UNEP, CSD and other institutional arrangements are unable to enforce and monitor commitments; Kyoto has been dumped by the largest polluter and consumer of natural resources in the world—America. Formulation and production of environmentally sound technologies and products is not being monitored or enforced, except voluntarily by trans-national corporations themselves.

In recent years, new problems have surfaced at the global level, addressing which is essential for the provision of various global public goods. These are health related trans-border diseases like HIV/AIDS, SAARS, MAD COW etc. There are new problems of human security as exemplified in growing drug-trafficking and its related trend of growing illegal trade in arms and ammunitions (the newly "democratised" Afghanistan produced poppy crop worth nearly half of its GDP this year). Then, there is increasing commodification of human intellect—ideas, music, poetry etc. which were seen as heritage of all humanity, a public good, not a private property, and thus not a public good now under the Intellectual Property Rights regime.

Universal provisions of human rights—rights of women, children, minorities, indigenous groups—are still contested as not global public goods, as their cultural relativity and historical specificity is argued and debated; thus gender equality, violence against women and children within household are seen as cultural conditions of communities, not to be categorised as universally desirable global public goods.

Over time, contestations about the meaning of public goods have been a major source of challenge to governance. In recent years, under the neo-liberal hegemony, many aspects that were taken for granted as public goods (like primary education) in many countries are being pushed to the private domain of consumption. Recent campaigns against privatisation of water like the Peoples World Water Forum, The Campaign Against Privatisation of Water, Bangalore etc. are to be viewed as contestations over the definition of water as a common public good. These campaigns advocate at two levels—one, with the UN "to ensure that water is entered as a fundamental right in the International Covenant of Ecological, Social and Cultural Rights of the United Nations" and second, with national governments "to accept and give water the status of a human right". As Tony Clarke of the Polaris Institute, Canada put it "Water is a public good that needs to be publicly financed and not to be given in private hands" (Article by Rahul Kumar, One World South Asia, 2004).

Therefore, what does 'good' governance mean in light of this definition? As noted above, transparency and accountability are seen as *sine qua non* of good governance. While some elaboration of the meaning of transparency in this definition was made earlier, accountability is a more complex issue. Simply stated, it implies holding the decision-maker to account for his/her decisions. But account for in what manner? I would argue that 'account for' means in terms of the intended, and unintended, consequences of that decision. Take the case of a dam; with full transparency, and a lot of open consultation with those likely to be displaced by the dam, assume that the oustees agreed to voluntary resettlement because the information provided for by the decision-makers convinced them that millions of acres of agricultural land would be irrigated, and they agreed to this common public good. Ten years later, if it is found out that not even one-fifth of the Promised Land has got water for irrigation, then who is accountable for it? Should not those decision-makers be made to account for the 'erroneous' decision made by them, because if it was then known that only such a small land area would be irrigated, perhaps the local people would not have agreed to resettlement. Thus, the accountability issue requires comparison of intended benefits, as common public goods, and unintended benefits and losses, typically after a few years after the decision is made.

Accountability is a big question in the global context as well. A number of inter-governmental agreements on issues of socio-economic development of people in the developing countries of the world are in existence. Poverty in the south, its elimination through provisions of basic education, primary health care, drinking water and livelihood is not even acknowledged as a serious enough global public good. In the face of terrorist attacks, some political leaders make pious statements about generating enough resources to address poverty and discrimination globally, but there is no mechanism to hold these governments accountable for their international commitments. They are elected by domestic publics, and accountability mechanisms for commitments made in global fora are almost non-existent. Rosenau (2003) calls it the crisis of compliance of state authorities.

Other references to good governance include aspects like rule of law, respect for human rights, etc., these aspects, combined with multi-party elections, suggest that good governance is akin to democratic form of government (Tandon & Mohanty, 2002). A more expansive definition of good governance reinforces the elements of multi-stakeholderness, partnerships, and devolution of resources and authority to local levels (Weiss, 2000). Such definitions are based on some of the arguments noted earlier. In particular, the focus on effective devolution to local spheres is in response to the reality of too much centralisation at national and provincial levels of governments, specially in developing countries. Many arguments for greater transparency, relevant use of resources and ease of civil society participation have been advanced in recent years in support of greater devolution to local levels.

"It is increasingly apparent that there are many functions which national governments can effectively decentralize to the local levels and others that are more efficiently and effectively carried out at the regional or even global level" (Nelson, 1996).

"For citizens such local bodies create a 'proximate' opportunity to participate in Governance. Attending meetings, voicing opinions, negotiating differences and monitoring progress of local plans are ways in which such participation in governance is being expressed. The new opportunities for interfacing with elected representatives of local bodies are creating a new democratic dynamic where citizens do not abdicate and representatives do not manipulate" (Tandon, 2003).

Finally, a strong case for direct citizen participation has been made by several commentators. Citizen participation is argued to be the most fundamental building block of grassroots democracy, not merely as voters but also as shapers of policies and rules. In many countries and regions, citizen referendums are regularly used to define priorities for public allocation of resources, extent of taxation, and even formation of administrative jurisdictions. In some cases, direct citizen participation has been occurring in determining budgetary allocations across an array of programme (and public goods) choices. In addition to representative form of democracy, many experiences suggest the need to promote and nurture direct citizen participation in governance. This is what has come to be called 'participatory governance'.

The Fancourt Declaration on Globalisation and People-Centered Development, Durban 1999 reaffirmed that *"If the poor and the vulnerable are to be at the center of development the process must be participatory, in which they have a voice...Good governance requires inclusive participatory processes"* (Commonwealth Foundation, 2004).

Implications

In this paper, I have tried to link the meanings and interpretations of governance to its historical and contemporary manifestations. In doing so, I have argued that the essential core of understanding governance (including good governance) is in relation to an understanding of public goods. Without reference to public goods, governance may remain a hollow concept. Several implications follow from such a formulation.

First, it is important to keep in mind the multiple spheres of governance in society today. National governance sphere is most commonly focused upon. But, provincial and local spheres are becoming increasingly significant; governance at local sphere needs to contend with public goods at local level.

Unless Panchayats and Municipalities manage their own locally relevant priorities and plans, regeneration and nurturance of natural resources will not occur. This will be possible by devolving to local bodies the mandate to manage and control all natural resources within their jurisdiction (Tandon, 2002).

In the increasing discourse on global governance, likewise, governance needs to contend with global public goods (Kaul, *et al*, 2003). This view of governance, then, would imply that similar reference to appropriate public goods and engagement of multiple stakeholders would become operative at all spheres of governance. In this sense, a unitary model of good governance is maintained (Krahmann, 2003).

Second, emphasis on both structures and processes helps to analyse not just institutions of governance, but also people responsible for such institutions. A socio-technical approach to improving governance can then entail a variety of techno-structural and human-processual interventions (Tandon and Serrano, 1996). It then becomes important to get the design of institutions right, but also get the attitudes and competencies of people working in them relevant and appropriate. Improving governance may thus entail a variety of interventions focusing on both structural/institutional and behavioural/processual aspects.

Third, this approach to governance may blur the traditional private-public boundaries across sectors and institutions. Such an approach to governance may then ask voluntary, non-governmental organisations if they serve to provide any public goods; most would readily agree that charitable work is providing public goods (Leach, 2004). Then they are covered in this definition and their own governance becomes a matter of public interest. Extending this argument to for-profit business, do they serve to provide any public goods? No? Really? What about environmental protection, protection of human rights of workers employed by their suppliers? The ISO 14000 certification includes such standards for private businesses. In that case, should private for-profit businesses not be included in this view of good governance?

"Corporations determine far more than any other institution the air we breathe, the quality of the water we drink, even where we live. Yet they are not accountable to anyone... As corporations become globalised, they assume more responsibility, not less. The same forces of world competition that produce higher and increasingly common standards of quality and performance, produce higher and increasingly common standards of ethical behaviour" (Nelson, 1996).

A further extension of the public good argument could then include universities, hospitals, media, etc.

Such an approach to governance may then cover all publicly operating institutions in society today. That is certainly the trend, with greater attention being paid to corporate and NGO governance these days. This author would argue in the same direction, and suggest that a common framework should be made applicable towards improving governance in all types of institutions and sectors of society today.

REFERENCES

Beeson, Mark, (2001), Globalisation, Governance, and the Political Economy of Public Policy Reform in East Asia, *Governance*, Vol. 14, No. 4, October.

Charles, Abugre, ISODEC Ghana, (1999), *Partners, Collaborators or Patron Clients: Defining Relationships in the Aid Industry*: *A Survey of Issues*—Background Document prepared for CIDA/Canadian Partnership Branch.

Cohen, Edward S., (2001), Globalisation and the Boundaries of the State, *Governance*, Vol. 14, No. 1, January.

Commonwealth Foundation, (1999), *Citizens and Governance*, London.

Commonwealth Foundation, (2003), *Multi-Sectoral Partnerships for Democracy and Development: The Kampala Vision*; ; 12-14 August, Kampala, Uganda.

Commonwealth Foundation, (2004), *Citizens and Governance,* Toolkit, London.

Farnham, David, and Sylvia Horton, (ed.) (1996), *Managing the New Public Services,* MacMillan Press Ltd., London.

Giddens, Anthony, (1998), *The Third Way: The Renewal of Social Democracy,* Polity Press, UK.

Habermas, J., (1989), *The Structural Transformation of the Public Sphere: An Inquiry into a Category of Bourgeois Society,* Cambridge, Polity Press.

Human Development Report, (2002), Deepening democracy in a fragmented world, UNDP and Oxford University Press.

Hunold, Christian, (2001), Corporatism, Pluralism, and Democracy, *Governance,* Vol. 14, No. 2, April.

Jreisat, Jamil, (2004), Governance in Globalising World, *Governance,* Vol. 27, Nos. 13 &14.

Kaul, Inge *et al.* (2003), *Providing Global Public Goods,* New York: UNDP.

Krahmann, Elke, (2003), National, Regional & Global Governance: One Phenomenon or Many?, *Global Governance,* Vol. 9, No. 3, July-September.

Leach, John, (2004), *A Course in Public Finance,* Cambridge: Cambridge University Press.

March, James G. & Johan P. Olsen, (1995), *Democratic Governance,* New York: Free Press.

Multi-Stakeholder Dialogue: A Facilitator's Manual, PRIA, November 2004.

Nelson, Jane, (1996), *Business as Partners in Development: Creating Wealth for Countries, Companies and Communities*; The Prince of Wales Business Leaders Forum, World Bank and the UNDP.

NGOs launch campaign against privatisation of water, Article by Rahul Kumar, *One World South Asia,* 14 January, 2004; www.uk.one-world.net

Norris, Pippa, (1999), *Critical Citizens: Global Support for Democratic Governance,* Oxford: Oxford University Press.

Nye, Joseph S. & John D. Donahue, (eds.) (2000), *Governance in a Globalising World,* Washington: Brookings Institute Press.

Oberg, Perola, (2002), Does Administrative Corporatism Promote Trust? *Governance,* Vol. 15, No. 4, October.

Report of the PPP Sub-Group on Social Sector; *Planning Commission,* GOI, 2004.

Rosenau, James N., (2003), *Distant Proximities,* Princeton: Princeton University Press.

Ruddle, Kenneth and Roadinelli, Denais A., (1983), Transforming Natural Resources for Human Development: A Resource Systems Framework for Development Policy, The United Nations University.

Scholte, J.A., (2002), Civil Society and Democracy in Global Governance, *The Global Governance Reader,* R. Wilkinson, London, Routledge.

Sen, Amartya, (1999), *Development as Freedom*, New Delhi: Oxford University Press.

Tandon, Rajesh & Ranjita Mohanty, (2002), *Civil Society and Governance*, New Delhi: Samskriti.

Tandon, Rajesh (ed.), (2002), *Participatory Research: Revisiting the Roots*, Mosaic Books, New Delhi.

Tandon, Rajesh and Isagani R. Serrano, (1996), *Reforming the State: A Citizens Perspective*, PRIA papers.

Tandon, Rajesh and Ranjita Mohanty, (2002), *Civil Society and Governance*, Samskriti, New Delhi.

Tandon, Rajesh and Ranjita Mohanty, (2006), *Participatory Citizenship: Identity, Exclusion, Inclusion*, Sage Publications, New Delhi.

Tandon, Rajesh, (2002), Identity and its challenges for the Voluntary Sector in India—Guest of honour speech delivered at the inaugural session of *VANI's Annual Convention* held at Dehradun, September 27.

The Citizens and Governance Programme: Issues for Debate, Volume 1—Commonwealth Foundation, 2002.

The Democracy-Poverty nexus: Summary on issues of Participation; Simi Kamal paper presented at International IDEA 2000, *Democracy Forum*.

UNDP (1997) *Reconceptualising Governance*, Discussion Paper 2.

Walter, C. Opello Jr.; Stephen J. Rosow, (2005), *The Nation State and the Global Order: A Historical Introduction to Contemporary Policies*, Viva Books Pvt. Ltd.

Weiss, Thomas, (2000), Governance, Good Governance and Global Governance: Conceptual and Actual Challenges, *Third World Quarterly*, Vol. 21, No. 5.

World Development Report, (2004), Making services work for poor people, Oxford University Press and the World Bank.

Wyman, Miriam, (2001), *Thinking about Governance*, Discussion Paper, Commonwealth Foundation, London.

Young, Oran R. (ed.), (1997), *Global Governance*, Cambridge: MIT Press.

3

Rights, Citizenship and State Accountability Contentious Claims of Industry Over Tribal Land[1]

Ranjita Mohanty

Introduction

The history of development in post-independent India is littered with instances where tribal people have lost their agricultural land and habitat to further the cause of industrial enterprises. Even when their ownership over land is backed by legal sanction making it inalienable, the industries, in collusion with the state, are often successful in encroaching upon the tribal land. Through forced compensation, which in most cases remains inadequate, forgery and inducement, the industries grab land in the remote tribal areas thereby turning the owners of land into resource less victims. As poor, illiterate and inhabitants in the backwaters of the country, the tribals, understandably, experience exclusion and

1. The paper draws from the studies on tribal land rights and industry accountability, conducted in the year 2004 in Chhattisgarh, Orissa and Jharkhand. The respective authors of these case studies are : Surajit Mukhopadhyay, Suryanarayan Mishra, Hasrat Arjjumand. The studies were conducted as part of PRIA and IDS collaborative research carried out under the Development Research Center (DRC) on Citizenship, Participation and Accountability. DRC is located and coordinated at the Institute of Development Studies, Sussex. I am thankful to the authors of the Case studies; I am also thankful to Peter Newell and Joanna Wheeler at IDS, and Harsh Jaitly at PRIA for contributing to the studies their ideas and insights.

powerlessness in defending their rights and negotiating with the industries whose might is backed by the state, which, ironically, bestows land rights and is expected to protect them. While in the neo-liberal framework, the market comes across as an important actor in 'governance', and the industry has found an unprecedented respectability in the policy framework, in the backward regions where the tribals live, it remains insensitive to their needs, manipulates their situation to further its own interest, and completely bypasses those, ostensibly for whose development industries are set up. However, in this contentious claim of industry and people over land, the state is the main facilitator for industrial development, and therefore, much of the accountability claim is directed towards the state. In the absence of accountability from the state, land rights remain unrealisable. In the context of inadequacy of rights and continuing negligence by the state bordering to exploitation, the tribal communities' sense of citizenship remains inadequate, often fractured, and merely a legal—constitutional rhetoric which does not get translated into reality in their daily living experiences.

At the heart of this contentious claim on tribal land remains the ill-defined notion of 'public good'. While on the one hand there are legislations that give sovereignty of governance of tribal land to the tribals, the state retains its control over such land in the form of Land Acquisition Act, 1894, that vests immense power in the hands of the state to acquire land for what is euphemistically called 'national interest' and 'public good'. This act has been used unsparingly to facilitate industrial enterprise and usurpation of large chunks of land from the tribals in different parts of the country particularly for mining and power projects. Since the tribals live in the secluded hills which are rich in minerals such as iron ore, bauxite, dolomite etc., the industries have found it attractive to encroach on such land. In facilitating the profit making of the industry in the myth that it will trickle down to the poor people, the state has severely by passed the rights of the tribals. Inadequate compensations, allurement of jobs in the industry which never materialise, large scale displacement, pollution of water sources, degradation of forest land, are a few fallouts of the industrial development in India.

The paper drawing from empirical studies conducted in Chhattisgarh, Orissa and Jharkhand, illuminates how tribal land is manipulated by the industry, albeit in collusion with the state, thus bringing out the larger issues of rights, citizenship and accountability. It will argue that notions of rights and citizenship hinge on the behaviour of the state towards its marginalized citizens. The struggles around mobilisation for rights and claiming accountability while on the one hand are about loss of rights, resources and experiences of marginalisation, they on the other are to be seen as efforts by the tribal communities to re-construct their relationship with the state by acting like 'citizens'.

The paper has three sections: Section I will provide a broad sketch by situating the 'state' and 'industry' in the developmental thought and practice in the post-independent India, and implications for tribal communities; Section II will give a contextual account of specific industry behaviour in the regions where the studies were undertaken, thereby bringing out the questions of rights and accountability, and the experience of the tribal communities in claiming their land rights and making the state accountable; Section III attempts to provide a frame to put the contentious relationships between citizen-state-industry, the interface between the citizen and the state on the one hand, and the citizen and industry on the other, and the implications these have for rights and citizenship.

Situating the State and Industry in the Post-Independent Development Period

The modern democratic state in India was the outcome of the freedom movement against British colonialism. The oppressive colonial rule and the freedom movement, despite considerable variation in opinion among the leaders, had shaped the form of governance and development India would adopt after independence. The colonial regime made people aware of the inadequacies of an alien rule and realise the importance of political sovereignty in a broader sense. The freedom movement since its beginning was inspired by the principles of rights, rationality, justice, freedom and the dignity of the individual. The leaders, particularly those influenced by modern western ethos realised democracy to be the answer to the aspirations of the people who had suffered and struggled against the colonial regime. The Constituent Assembly deliberated for three years (1946-49) and on January 1950 a sovereign democratic state was established. Universal adult franchise, constitutional granting of the rights, rule of law and an impartial judiciary established the *impartiality* of the state and the *sovereignty* of citizens. Democracy implies that the state treats its citizens as equal. But democracy in a divided society also means that equality of opportunity would be denied to the people at the bottom of social hierarchy till they are brought at par with others. Thus right to equality was supplemented with principles of protective discrimination and special welfare provisions. The lower castes who were subjected to social oppression since generations and the tribals living in seclusion in the hills and forests were given the benefits of protective discrimination through reservation of seats in education and employment. The state took special measures to make special provisions for the protection of the tribal communities by safeguarding transfer of tribal land to non-tribals, special welfare programmes for the tribal for education, livelihood, health, shelter etc. Special tribal welfare programmes were launched under successive five year plans to uplift the tribals from poverty, illiteracy, ill health and exploitation by the outsiders.

The low agricultural growth, famine, and oppressive colonial economy had left deep dents in the country's economy. The onus of promoting economic growth naturally fell on the state. The dominant development model prevalent in the west at that time was adopted as the appropriate model to augment economic growth. Thus economic growth through industrialisation and commodity production became the core of Indian economy and industry, mining, and giant irrigation projects took shape in quick succession to change the economic and social landscape. Industrialisation in post-independence area was guided by the Industrial policy resolution of 1948, which set out increased production and equitable distribution as the twin objectives of industrial growth. Along with the production of consumer goods, production of iron, steel, aluminium, and ferro-alloys etc. were given added emphasis in the First Five Year Plan. The state was at the centre of industrial development with a dominant public sector and the private sector had a limited role and was expected to operate under the surveillance of the state. The state thus facilitated the growth of industries with generous grants of land and access to mineral resources. The Industrial Policy Resolution of 1950 guided that industrialisation be pursued to create a socialist pattern of society, with the state assuming the commanding heights of economy.

With a vision and agenda for socio-economic transformation, the state assumed the central role of provider, protector, and regulator. It became the state's responsibility to promote economic growth, eradicate inequality, promote social justice, generate employment, and protect citizens against the violation of their rights.

The state in independent India was expected to remain an independent and autonomous actor that would reform the society, create opportunities, promote growth but would remain above the diversity, complexities and divisiveness of the society. But as the subsequent years revealed, the state could not remain an independent actor. The socio-economic transformation agenda was subverted by the same forces against which it was planned. The dominant landed elite, industrial class and the higher castes, historically placed in a dominant position, wielded pressure on the state to mould the democratic polity and appropriate the developmental benefits, thereby undermining the purpose of democratic institutions and developmental agenda (Kothari 1986; Bardhan 1984, 1988; Kohli 1987, 1988; Dhanagre 1987). Not only did developmental projects not benefit them, but they also added new dimensions of disadvantages to their already disadvantaged position. As the technocentric economic growth took off, and huge irrigation, hydel projects, and heavy industries took shape, thousands of people were displaced from their original habitat and without a comprehensive resettlement and rehabilitation policy, displacement became the inevitable fall out of development. As the natural resources were put into commercial use a large number of people directly dependent on nature for their subsistence lost their access and control over their resources. It is no surprise then that they have resisted the policies formulated to bring benefit to them.

The State and Industry in Post-Liberalisation Era

The facilitation of the entry and growth of foreign capital encouraged the growth of private sector in the years following Narsimha Rao—Manmohan Singh led liberalisation reforms, and this led to the change in the industrial policies and strategies. The Tenth Five Year plan spoke about the new role of private sector: "The industrial development strategy is being re-oriented towards enabling our vibrant private sector to reach its full entrepreneurial potential, to contribute towards production, employment and income generation". The new Industrial Policy adopted in 1991 carved out a much bigger role for industries and capital investment and minimized the role of the state to that of a mere facilitator. The Mines and Minerals Act, 1957 was amended to open mining industry to private investment. The new environment gave rise to competition among states to behave 'investment friendly' and added to their zeal to allow uncritical entry to the private industries. Many states have new industrial policy and vision documents that talk about the state's agenda of promoting economy and progress, no matter how disjoined the former remains from the latter and no matter how contentious the latter remains. Among the efforts to boost the economy, the industry features in a significant way. The vision documents still talk about measures of literacy, employment, livelihood promotion, and health facilities for the tribals and other weaker sections, but as we will see in the subsequent sections this has not only reamed a long forgotten rhetoric, but the situation has worsened for the tribal who cannot interrogate the state and the industry primarily because they have remained far too long at the far end of the boons of the economy. This has not only impoverished them and put them in a much disadvantaged powerless position *vis-à-vis* the powerful industries, but by turning them into wage labourers has put them in an adversarial exploitative relationship with the capital.

The retreat of the state under neo-liberalism and its changing role to a mere facilitator also means that the state while still doing the midwifery role for industrial growth, has lost much of its power to deliver *vis-à-vis* its citizens. It is not merely the question of redistribution of benefits of industrialisation, but also the normative role the state plays in protecting the rights of its citizens. In the post-liberalisation era both have suffered. The citizens are the sufferers as the state either does not respond or responds rather brutally. It is found conniving with industry, indulging in corruption or simply remaining silent and indifferent.

In the shifting discourse on governance, the market, along with the state, is considered as partners in governance. That is, the act of governing is no longer the sole responsibility of the state, the market is also invited to play a critical role. While the new respectability for the market in the policy circle is clearly visible, it is not clear how the market can be made accountable to the citizens in the same manner as the state can. While the state, despite its occasional violent character and its non performance, is still the agency that is looked up by a large number of poor people (Chandhoke 2005), the same argument does not hold ground for the market. The state has a normative grounding in the sense that it is ideally constructed as the agency to bring about social change. The transformative agenda of the state puts it at a different footing than the market, which is governed by profit motives.

This makes the accountability question a tricky one. The state shifting from a patronage and dominance to a position of retreat is still the facilitator of industrial development. While the market can wash off its hands by propaganding the populist corporate social responsibility, turning citizenship into mere corporate philanthropy (Newell), the state as the giver of rights is governed by a different notion of citizenship. And when the state in facilitating the growth of capital, does not protect the rights, it upsets their ideas of citizenship. This explains why even in the event of gross negligence by the industries, many of the movements for mobilisation of rights are taken *vis-à-vis* the state.

Claims and Conflicts Over Tribal Land: Cases from Chhattisgarh, Orissa, Jharkhand

Governance of Tribal Land

The tribal land can broadly be categorized under private land which the families own, and common property which the village communities own. There are strict strictures governing the transfer of tribal land.

Schedule V, article 241(1) of the Constitution of India vests the power with the Governor of the state to 'prohibit or restrict the transfer of land by or among members of the scheduled tribes'. The Panchayat (Extension to Scheduled Areas) Act, 1996, vests the power of decisions of land transfer/acquisition with the gram sabha (village assembly) and gram panchayat, the elected local governance unit. The Act says that the gram sabha and panchayat will have to be consulted before acquisition or transfer of the land for any purpose including, development projects and industrial enterprise, and before plans are made to resettle and rehabilitate the displaced tribal communities whose land is thus acquired. Another legal landmark in the governance of tribal land is the Samta Judgment passed by the Supreme Court in 1997 against GoAP for leasing out tribal land to the private companies in the scheduled areas. The judgement says: "...transfer of mining lease to non-tribals, company, corporation, aggregate or partnership form etc. is unconstitutional, void and imperative".

There are also international conventions securing the right of the indigenous people over their land and habitat. ILO conventions 107, 1975 in the article 11 says that "The rights of ownership, collective or individual of the member of the populations concerned over the lands, which these populations traditionally occupy, shall be recognised". Article 12 of the Convention says, "The population concerned shall not be removed without their free consent from the habitual territories except in accordance with national laws and regulations for reasons relating to national security, in the interest of national development or of health of the said population". Article 13 of the Convention says, "Procedure for the transmission of rights of ownership and use of land which are established by the customs of the populations concerned shall be respected, within the framework of national laws and regulations, in so far as they satisfy the needs of these populations and don't hinder their economic and social development."

If there are laws that protect the land right of the tribals, there are also laws that permit the violation of the right given. The Land Acquisition Act, 1894, amended in 1984 and in 1998, gives absolutes power to the state to acquire land for public purpose, and in this context the state alone has the right to define and decide the nature of public purpose/public interest. The 1994 Supreme Court judgment reinforces this: "The power to acquire private property for public use is an attribute of sovereignty and is essential to the existence of a government. The power of eminent domain was recognised on the principle that the sovereign state can always acquire the property of a citizen for public good, without the owners consent."

Industries on Tribal Land: Chhattisgarh, Orissa, Jharkhand

This section deals with three kinds of industrial activities and the manner in which tribal land is acquired for the purpose. The first case is about the Jindal corporate house, called Jindal Organisation, which is carrying out coal and iron ore mining on a large scale in Chhattisgarh. The second is iron ore mining in Joda Block in Sundergarh district in Orissa. The big industries here are Tata Sponge Iron Ltd., Ferro Manganese Plant managed by the Tata Iron and Steel Company. The Jindal Steel and Power Ltd. is also present in Joda, but compared to the Tatas, its operation is rather small. The third case is slightly different. It concerns small stone mining quarries that are carried out by the contractors in the Santhal Pargana area in Jharkhand. The areas where the industries are set up are populated by tribal communities, whose predominant occupation is agriculture. They are also dependent on forests for various forest produces such as timber, mahua, herbs, berries and fruits.

Chhattisgarh, earlier a part of undivided Madhya Pradesh, became a separate state in 2001. The first wave of industrialisation in the then Madhya Pradesh was dominated by public sector industries such as the Bhilai Steel Plant. The second wave comprises a host of private sector companies engaged in mining, the most prominent among them is Jindal Organisation. A series of MoUs signed between the Government and the Jindals have facilitated the encroachment of the land for mining purposes. The study carried out in the Tamnar block of Raigarh district provides a rather grim picture about the way land was acquired. Mukhopadhay writes: "...no documents for land handover was signed and no receipt was given for the monetary transaction. In other words there are no records with the landless now. However, it seems that the villagers who 'agreed ' to sell their land to the corporate entity put their thumb impression on a register kept with the Jindal Organisation. In other words, since these people do not have any written document to prove that they were the original landlords, all that they say has no legal basis" (Mukhopadhyay 2004). There were also cases where people were hounded by armed men brought by the Jindal managers to force them to part with their land.

The jobs that were promised to the villagers never came up,

and most of them now work as daily wage labour. Here also the Jindals follow their method of not keeping any record. Hence, while the labourers do not sign in any register when they go into the mines, they have to sign on their way out of the mines. This clearly is the strategy to avoid paying any compensation if a labourer meets with an accident. The poor at the far end of the industrial boon have no bargaining power, as having lost their agricultural land to the corporate, the only means of livelihood they have is to work as casual wage labour.

Adding to their woes there is severe environmental pollution as a result of open cast mining and pollution of water bodies. To quote Mukhopadhay again, "One is confronted by the sense of desolation that the locals feel, surrounded as they are by a hostile environment that is totally alien to their traditional life-style. The villagers despair the depletion of forest acreage and cover as intense mining increasingly eats up the source of *tendu* leaves and *mahua*. These were the mainstay for the better part of six months in a year, while for the rest of the time they found employment in the agricultural field as farm labour. But the deterioration of the environment has led to the decline of agriculture as well, with the consequence that farmers no longer hire tribals as labourers as they used to do previously. This has made the villagers completely bereft of any earning avenues, as the promised employment in the industries in lieu of land has not materialised" (*Ibid.*).

In Joda, the displaced families were paid compensation, but the amount of compensation did not match with the value of the land acquired. People also said that they received the amount after several rounds of visits. The factor that affected and delayed the compensation was lack of land records with the families. Many of them were unaware of the legalities of land records and were at a loss when they were asked to produce the land record to establish their claim over the piece of land. However, unlike the Jindal case cited above, people did not express much resentment, as one member from each family was given a job by the industry. Besides the Tatas also follow the Social Service Package which is part of the Periphery Development Programme, under the MoU signed between the Government of Orissa and Tatas. Under the Social Service Package each panchayat is given a fixed amount to meet the requirements of the village people such as construction or repair of approach road, construction of culvert, sanitation, club, water supply etc. Earlier the gram panchayats were given two lac rupees, which was enhanced to four lacs from the financial years 2004–2005. The relatively better off situation in Joda, compared to Chhattisagrah is probably due to the presence of the Tatas, the old private house with a strong sense of social commitment and business ethics that surpasses the industrial houses like Jindal (Mishra 2004).

The third case from Shikaripara Block of Dumka district in Jharkhand is different from the two cases discussed above. Unlike the Tatas and Jindals, for whom land was acquired by the State under 'public purpose' of development, the stone quarries are considered private operations. It is an agreement between the lessor of the land, usually his/her private land, and the lessee which has to be approved by the District Collector. The transfer of land takes place under Bihar Minor Mineral Concession Rule, 1972 (Jharkhand was part of erstwhile Bihar). However, the Santhal Pargana Tenancy Act (SPTA), the legislation that governs the transfer of tribal land and all other legislation, strictly prohibits the *raiyat* (farmer) to transfer the land by lease or any contract or agreement. The Act even instructs the District Collector to recover and restore *raiyati* lands of tribals transferred in contravention of the SPTA.

In the Shikaripara block most of the lease (a total of 196) have been given through manipulation of the middle man/local fixers, which resulted in the landholder getting much less than the value of the land and it took several months to retrieve money from the miners. Taking advantage of the illiteracy of the tribals, the middle men and the miners often cheat them by absorbing more land than the landholder had agreed to, or continuing operation even after the lease period is over. There are also instances where the adjacent land of another raiyat was forcefully taken over either by convincing the *raiyat* that the land would be unsuitable for agriculture after the mining operation or through methods of intimidation and bribe. In continuing mining operations, the miners in some instances have encroached upon the common village land and have also got illegal possession of *khas* land which is the government land given to the landless families. Only the gram panchayat *pradhan* has the power to settle disputes arising on the *khas* land, and in circumstances such land are to be given on lease. The obvious consequences for mining operations are loss of livelihood for the tribals as they give away their agricultural land, and while the mine owners promise jobs to them, such promises never materialise as miners prefer getting labour from outside the mining area so as to keep away from any dispute arising out of discontent over wage or working hours or safety conditions. Besides losing agricultural land and livelihood, people also suffer environment pollution created by mining operations and dumping of stone dust around the villagers. Pollution of the water-bodies is a common problem in villages where stone quarries are in operation.

Struggle for Rights: Making the State Accountable

There have been sporadic resistance to the miners in Santhal Pargana, but an organised and sustained movement against illegal mining is lacking. People in their individual capacity have questioned the miners, and at times there is a collective strength visible at the village level. But such efforts are largely sabotaged by the miners either by hiring the mining supervisor from the same village, who acts both as an informer supplying the miners with information about the brewing of resistance, as well as acting as the peace maker between people and the miners, or by bribing the leaders, or by using force. There are instances where the local struggles were linked to the larger issue of labour right and were taken up by the Jharkhand General Mazdoor Union, affiliated to AICTU, which is the trade union wing of the Communist Party of India (Marxist-Leninist). But faced with coercion by the miners and the right wing nationalist party which rules the state, the struggle has remained localised and suppressed.

In Chhattisgarh no mainstream political party has taken up the tribal cause against the Jindals, but there is a strong wave of people's movement. Partly addressed by the Ekta Parishad which is a Pan Indian (?) movement for the land rights with its head quarters in MP, and Jindal Birodhi Sangharsh Samiti, active in the Tamnar block, issues of oppression and brutality of the industry and failure of the state are raised. However, the resistance to the Jindals have not seen much success as the state does not support the agitation, but much worse, it lends its support to what can be called 'criminalisation of the state', a strategy which the Jindals have used to keep the people silent. The Jindals have used all the state institutions—bureaucracy, police, and court to intimidate the tribals and suppress their voices. There are four ill famous strategies adopted by the Jindals to suppress any resistance—first, buy the bureaucrats and politicians; second, transfer those who are not amenable to be bought; third, implicate the locals who agitate against the Jindals in false legal cases; and fourth, in an extreme case of criminalisation, obliterate those who resist. There are many instances which people cite where the leaders of movements were killed, and as fear spread far and wide no one came up to give evidence against the Jindals.

Between the State and Industry: Whatever Happened to Citizenship and Rights?

The invocation of the language of citizenship and its core associate 'right' to interrogate development has got added momentum in the recent times due to changes that has led to reconfiguration of polity and economy. As the state withdraws under neo-liberalism, making space for the market and as the boundaries of nation states become porous due to influence of globalisation, there is added emphasis on the role of the citizens in the new forms of governance. This calls for new role for citizens not as subjects or mere voters in an electoral democracy, but as 'actors' whose active engagement is desirable for making development and governance equitable and just.

It is clearly at this point that citizenship enters into the developmental thinking for a couple of reasons. First, since citizenship is intrinsically associated with democracy, which turns subjects into citizens by bestowing and recognising certain rights desirable for dignified life, any democracy building agenda can not do away with citizenship practices. One could argue that a fascist state also gives rights, but it is only in a democratic polity the rights can be used to challenge the misconduct of the state. Second, the mobilisation of rights to create demand on the state is not possible without reference to citizenship, for at the heart of all rights lies the way the state positions its people. Third, citizenship offers a perspective to analyse where the universal status of citizens run counter to the particular identities of poor, women, tribal, low castes. That is, citizenship makes it possible to analyse why and how some citizens can be better placed than others and implications of this unequal positioning for the actualisation of rights for the marginalised populace. Fourth, it brings into focus the relationship between the state and its lesser citizen and raises the critical question as to how lesser citizens can be 'actors'. Lastly, but importantly, citizenship touches the normative aspects of development in a much more poignant way, for it evokes the concepts and practices of equity, equality, freedom and justice, which constitute the core of democratic relationships (Mohanty 2006).

While there have been attempts to rescue citizenship from its state-centricity and locate it in the community, or social practices (Turner, Kabeer...), it is argued that citizenship in the ultimate analysis, and despite the shortcomings of its legal foundations, has its central reference point as the state, not so much because the state is the central authority governing people's lives, but because what Chandhoke calls the 'bridging movements' the state performs (Chandhoke 2003). The state comes into picture, she argues, because "it is precisely the state that recognises these rights as moral constraints; it is the state which translates these rights into legal norms, and it is the state which upholds these rights through the constitution and the judiciary. In sum, the state, through a series of bridging movements, connects the possession of rights and the actualisation of rights (ibid: 2958). The state is also the central reference point for it, at least theroetical and shows the willingness to be guided not only by the legal juridical dimensions of citizenship, but also by what Gupta calls the 'moral imperatives of citizenship' (Gupta1998). That is, the state is expected to take action to dismantle the unequal power relationships through a series of legal enactments, positive discriminatory practices, and special welfare programmes so that a basic minimum equality can prevail for people to actualise their rights and to participate as equals. While people, as the history of political struggles suggests, mobilise themselves to redress injustices and seek equality, such practices are established as constitutional/juridical norms only when they are recognised by that state.

While the normative underpinnings of citizenship and rights invoke images of the normative state as both Chandhoke and Gupta point out, the conducts of the actual existing state can at best be trusted to respect these partially and occasionally, and at worst can completely bypass these. The indifference and often brutality of the state lead to the fracture in the normative vision of the state people have—a fracture that colour much of the state-citizen relationship. The character of the state in legislating laws that are expected to benefit the tribals, and then having laws that can be invoked against the former, reveals the duality of the state. And while the legal-juridical dimensions of the right may allow the tribal to fight for their rights, in reality the existence of multiple legal realities, often in contravention to each other, means that only this much can be achieved by invoking the language of rights. The alliance of the state agencies with the industry, whose might people can question only at the risk of their lives as the Jindal case indicates, means that the state in such situations will use its institutions to protect the industrial class against its resource less populace. The command polity of the state which earlier operated under the guise of socialism has now become even more pervasive as the state has dropped the guise and has embraced capitalism under liberalisation reforms.

The question of accountability is a fair question to raise with the state, not only because the notions of citizenship and rights resonate with the state, but also that the state, from time to time, attempts to create conditions for citizens to exercise their choice and decision in matters that affect their life. One such landmark condition was the enactment of 73rd Constitutional Amendment which vests power at the hands of the people to select their representatives at the local level. The gram panchayats, as units of local governance, are to be responsible for all decisions related to governance at the village level and be accountable to the gram sabha, which is the village assembly comprising of all adult members residing in a village. Since the tribals areas have special need in terms of land, livelihood and natural resources such as forest, a Special Extension Act, PESA, was enacted for the tribal areas. As mentioned earlier, PESA vests power in the hands of the panchayat and gram sabha for land decisions regarding the transfer and acquisition of tribal land. However, despite the emphasis on local governance, the panchayats have been either bypassed, or been manipulated through misinformation or bribe to consent for the transfer of large chunks of land to the industries.

In comparison to the state, with whom people, in this case the tribals, have a relationship that has its foundations on the transformative role the state is expected to play, their relationship with industry is characterised by profit based interests, for that is the only logic the market understands, and people who lack the resources to enter the market remain out side its periphery. In the case of tribals whose land the industry requires to further its enterprise, they remain at the receiving end of compensation, of casual wage labour, and as we saw in the previous section, industry does not pay much attention to the dislocation people suffer in their livelihood, habitat, culture. Their weak negotiation power *vis-à-vis* the industry is further weakened when the state withdraws its support and allies itself with the industry rather than with its neglected citizenry.

The language of citizenship cannot be invoked with the industry in the same way as with the state, for the state and not the industry is the giver as well as violator of citizenship and rights. As we see in the cases discussed in the previous section, in Santhal Pargana the state agencies indulge in petty corruption to give the mining lease to the contractors, and in Raigarh, the state simply turns deaf to the miseries caused by the Jindals. And not only that, the industries (mis)use the state provisions to protect their interest. The number of false cases filed against the people who are part of movement against the Jindals brings the sordid alliance between the state and industry against the tribals. All these cases indicate the alliance of the state with and accountability to the resourceful 'classes', much to the chagrin of its marginalized citizenry. In those situations where the state has refused to align with the industry, the concerned officials were transferred to another district, and 'industry friendly' officials were posted at the industry site so that business could go as usual. The Jindals have been particularly apt in using their influence at the higher levels of government to get the unfriendly district officials transferred. The membership of Navin Jindal—the scion of the Jindal family—in the national Parliament has helped the Jindal organisation to access those who are at the highest echelon of political power.

Conclusions

In the contentious claims of tribal and industry over land, the state plays the critical role of the facilitator. However, as the cases of industrial enterprises indicate, the state has often taken side with the industry and neglected its poor citizenry. When it came to transfer of sustenance resources such as land to the industry, negotiation for adequate compensation and resettlement for the people who lost their source of livelihood and habitat, and distribution of benefits of industrialisation to the people whose resources the industries take away, the state remained soft to the industry. The lack of accountability from the state has created a situation where people find their rights non-realizable and their citizenship merely a legal connotation, which does not translate into anything meaningful in their daily lives. The struggles for rights, therefore, are directed at the state in order to make the state accountable and to re-structure the relationship between the state and its neglected citizenry, so that citizenship gets expanded to include their choices and decisions on issues that affect their lives.

It is interesting indeed to find how the language of citizenship is appropriated by the corporate in promoting what is called corporate citizenship—a term that in corporate parlance means promoting corporate responsibility towards society or communities in which they operate. However, such responsibility seldom exceeds beyond a few philanthropic activities, such as education, health care, planting of trees for environment protection etc. Good corporate citizenship is defined as "integral to successful business operations, and of partnership between sectors to meet the challenges of social development." Notwithstanding the appropriation of the term citizenship, their social responsibility of industries at best can be described as philanthropic and service delivery, which in the absence of the state adequately performing these tasks, makes some impact, but does not address the questions of rights. As Guptara writes: "Ultimately, the question is: does corporate responsibility blaze a trail, or is it an alibi for a government declining to do what it ought?" (Guptara, 2002). And ultimately corporate citizenship comes to mean successful business. "Each company is finding its own way to exercise social responsibility and act as good corporate citizen. We are drawing on ancient wisdom, modern management theory, and hard experience to frame concepts which will help shape the way business is done in the 21st century" (preface from IBCPT 1997).

REFERENCES

Arjjumand, Hasrat, (2004), *Tribal Land Rights and Industry Accountability: Case Study of Mining in Dumka District*, Jharkhand, Study Report, PRIA, New Delhi.

Bardhan, Pranab, (1984), *The Political Economy of Development in India,* Oxford University Press, New Delhi.

Bardhan, Pranab, (1988), Dominant Proprietary Classes and India's Democracy, in, Kohli, Atul (ed.), 1988, *India's Democracy: An Analysis of Changing State-Society Relation,* Princeton University Press, NJ.

Chandhoke, Neera, (2003), 'Governance and Pluralisation: Implications for Democratic Citizenship', *Economic and Political Weekly.*

Chandhoke, Neera, (2005), Seeing the State in India, *Economic and Political Weekly.*

Dhanagre, D.N. (1987), Green Revolution and Social Inequalities in Rural India, *Economic and Political Weekly.*

Gupta, Dipanka r, (1998), 'Recasting Reservations in the Language of Rights', in Gurpreet Mahajan (ed.), *Democracy, Difference and Social Justice,* Oxford University Press, Delhi.

Guptara, Prabhu, (2002), *One CSR World, in Corporate Social Responsibility: A View from India,* EU-India CSR Network, Brussels, Belgium.

IBCPT, (1997), *Good Corporate Citizenship: Business and Social Development Perspectives,* Report of seminar held on 7th August 1997, The Indian Business and Community Partnership Trust, New Delhi.

Kabeer, Naila, (2002), Citizenship, Affiliation and Exclusion: Perspectives from the South, *IDS Bulletin,* Vol. 33, No. 2, April.

Kohli, Atul, (1987), *The State and Poverty in India: The Politics of Reform,* Cambridge University Press, Cambridge.

Kohli, Atul (ed.), (1988), *India's Democracy: An Analysis of Changing State-Society Relation,* Princeton University Press, NJ.

Kothari, Rajni, (1986), Masses, Classes and the State, *Economic and Political Weekly of India,* Vol. 21.

Misra, Suryanarayan, (2004), *Tribal Land Rights and Industry Accountability: Case of Joda and Kumarmunda Blocks,* Orissa, Study Report, PRIA, New Delhi.

Mohanty, Ranjita and Rajesh Tandon (eds.), *Participatory Citizenship: Identity, Inclusion, Exclusion,* Sage Publications, Delhi.

Mukhopadhyay, Surajit, (2004), *Tribal Land Rights and Industry Accountability: Case Study of Raigarh District,* Chhattisgarh, Study Report, PRIA, New Delhi.

Turner, Bryan, (1993), 'Contemporary Problems in the Theory of Citizenship', in Bryan Turner (ed.) *Citizenship and Social Theory,* London: Sage Publications.

4

Challenging Institutional Reforms for Democratic Decentralization in India
Trinity of Institutions to Strengthen Local Self Government

Manoj Rai

Democracy (literally "rule by the people", from the Greek demos, "people," and kratos, "rule") is a form of government. Arguments in favour of democratic decentralization are based on the belief that the democratization and empowerment of local political bodies will create institutions that are more accountable to local citizens and more appropriate to local needs and preferences. One of the well-known proponents of this view, John Stuart Mill provided two important arguments for democratic decentralization: (i) local political institutions are 'a school of political capacity', making citizen capable of genuine and informed participation, and (ii) such institutions would be more efficient if informed by local interests and local knowledge.

Decentralization is thought to create the conditions for a more pluralist political arrangement, in which competing groups can voice and institutionalize their interests in local democratic forums (Crook and Manor, 1998). It is also argued that states (based on principles of command and control) are qualitatively different from markets (based on competition and exchange) and voluntary organisations (based on some measure of altruistic motivation) (on this, see Robinson *et al.*, 2000). Viewed in this way, states lack the flexibility and reach to provide certain types of goods and services, particularly ones with large information requirements. Decentralization, it is argued, creates institutions that are more amenable to local needs and preferences (Ostrom *et al.*, 1993). These, of course, imply a system of indirect representation, whereby candidates engage in competitive elections for public office.

Another view argues that unchecked authority and inadequate incentives (reflected in salaries, rules of promotion and so on) encourage 'rent seeking behaviour' among government officials (Ostrom *et al.*, 1993). In theory, decentralization would undermine these opportunities by creating institutional arrangements that formalize the relationship between citizens and public servants, giving the former the authority to impose sanctions (such as voting, recourse to higher level authorities) on the latter (Blair, 2000; Crook and Manor, 1998).

The case for democratic decentralization is also predicated upon the notion that greater participation in local political affairs will improve the quality and reach of government services, particularly ones aimed at improving the lives of poor and politically marginal groups in society. For proponents of democratic decentralization, a central challenge of improving the delivery of public services becomes one of 'crafting' (Ostrom, 1990) institutions, which can maximise participation in political life.

Studies of decentralization have shown that devolution of authority can enhance systems of local governance in a number of ways. First, the establishment and empowerment of local resource user groups (delegation or privatisation) can improve the ways in which local people manage and use natural resources, thereby improving the resource base on which poor people are often disproportionately dependent (Ostrom, 1990). Such arguments are generally made in relation to the provision of local public goods, such as common pool resources or local credit organisations (e.g. Agrawal and Gibson, 1999). Second, and related to this, collaboration between public agencies and local resource users can produce 'synergistic' outcomes (Ostrom, 1996), in which citizens and civil servants cooperate to provide goods that would be unobtainable were they acting alone. Third, and most important in Indian context, the democratization and empowerment of local administrative bodies can enhance participation in decision-making fora, particularly among groups that have traditionally been marginalised by local political processes (Blair, 2000; Crook and Manor, 1998). Studies from Africa, Asia and Latin America have shown that the introduction of elections, systems of transparency and rights of association can empower poor people, enhancing their ability to participate in local decision making and (crucially) encouraging them to hold public officials to account (Blair, 2000; Crook and Manor, 1998; Drèze and Sen, 1996; Manor, 1999). As Blair (2000: 25) points out, 'increased representation offers significant benefits in itself.' Framed in this way, participation in local, democratically elected bodies can lead to improvements in self-identity and worth, which can help to break down customs of inequality and discrimination. Second, membership of local administrative bodies can provide important skills (e.g. bookkeeping, leadership, etc.) that can be transferred to other walks of life.

However, ideals of local democracy in India, as inserted by Constitutional Amendments, include most of the views and evidences. It goes beyond Gandhian vision of constellation of village republics and village self-sufficiency and Ambedkar's rival vision of Indian village as a sink of localism, den of ignorance and narrow mindedness. Domestic political imperatives coupled with global contexts of enhanced participation and greater efficiency and accountability in governance shaped constitutional sanctity to the local governments in India.

While 73rd Constitutional Amendment Act, 1993 gave Constitutional Status to Panchayats at the District, Intermediate and Village levels, through the insertion of Part IX in the Constitution, the 74th Amendment Act provided constitutional status and provisions for vibrancy of municipalities in urban areas. In the thirteen years following the enactment of the Amendments, the objective of creating a strong base of political empowerment of people through Panchayati Raj and Urban local bodies has been broadly achieved. Elections to Panchayats and Municipalities have been held in all States, except in the case of Jharkhand and Pondicherry. The Panchayats and Municipalities today provide the strongest possible political base in favour of inclusive growth. More than 3 million elected representatives (out of them more than two-third belong to marginalised sections: women and *dalits*) of Panchayats and Municipalities provide new dimension to participatory and democratic governance at grassroots. In fact, Panchayati Raj Institutions offer possibilities to catalyze, mobilise and sustain people's participation in countering the problems of poverty. Panchayats across the States have been constitutionally mandated to prepare and implement a holistic village plan based on the needs and aspirations of the villagers. These institutions (with mandatory reservation of seats for women and *dalits*) also provide political space to more vulnerable sections of the society. There are provisions to ensure that these institutions function as vibrant and accountable institutions of local self-governance. Panchayats can exchange information and interface with other social and political institutions including markets, trade and commerce. Being constitutionally elected bodies, Panchayats are capable of negotiating with the people and governments for efficient delivery of services and accountability. And with the provision for elections every 5 years, there are conditions for choice and change.

The spirit of the Constitution is essentially that elected Panchayats and municipalities function as institutions of self-government in rural and urban areas respectively. They are to be empowered with clear functional mandates, given a significant degree of autonomy, and imparted an element of self-reliance and self-sufficiency through fiscal transfers, taxation powers and tax assignments. However, actual devolutions of functions, functionaries and finance have yet not materialised in most parts of the country. The Constitution has visualised institutional arrangements to energize and sustain vibrancy in local governments by creating a Trinity of Institutions: (1) State Election Commission, (2) State Finance Commission, and (3) District Planning Committee. But these institutions themselves require strengthening before they could fulfil their constitutional obligations to respectively promote (i) periodically free, fair and regular elections, (ii) devolution of functions, finance and functionaries, and (iii) bottom up planning process, beginning at Gram Sabha level to preparation of draft district plan.

The present paper looks into institutional mechanisms to strengthen the trinity of institutions. The first section of the paper provides an overview of recent progress (rhetoric and realities) made in terms of efforts to devolve genuine powers and authorities. The second section deals with empirical and legal constraints in vibrancy of those institutions of local government, which have been created to strengthen the systems of local self-governance. Finally, an attempt has been made to suggest reforms required in the institutional framework of local governments in Rural and Urban areas. It may be mentioned here that the focus of the present paper is Panchayati Raj Institutions.

2. Rhetoric and Realities of Devolution: Round-tables, Activity Mapping and Memoranda of Understanding

Meenakshisundaram (1999: 66-67), on the basis of Chinese and

Nigerian experiences argues that effective decentralization was dependent on the existence of three necessary conditions:

- Strong political commitment from higher level authorities within government;
- Relative autonomy of the local body in decision making and implementation of local schemes; and
- The availability of internally generated resources at the local level.

Crook and Manor (1998) conclude that effective decentralization requires:

- Elected bodies at local levels have adequate funds;
- They enjoy substantive autonomy; and
- Lines of accountability to exist between elected representatives and citizens, and between non-elected bureaucrats and elected representatives.

If we take into account these conditions to analyze current situation in different states of India, it seems that Panchayats in most parts of the country have yet to experience sincere initiatives for devolution. In constitutional terms, Panchayat is a 'subject' under jurisdiction of state governments (state list). So, even though the Indian Parliament has amended the Constitution to provide constitutional sanctity to the Panchayati Raj Institutions, states were left to decide on appropriate measures to strengthen the institutions of Panchayats. Accordingly real powers and authorities with Panchayats vary from state to state. All State Panchayati Raj Acts describe legislatively what roles Panchayats have to play and how. However, these legislative ambiguities (regarding which tier of Panchayat would exclusively do what and how) were never addressed systematically. Union and State governments emphasised on agency function of Panchayats and governance function for Panchayats, which is the soul of the constitutional amendment, remained knowingly or unknowingly neglected. Panchayats are forced to act as contractors of governmental schemes.

It is no longer surprising that the State governments, who keep raising issues of participation and devolution when it comes to Union and States relations, have deliberately not devolved appropriate functions, functionaries and finances to the three tiers of Panchayats. Perhaps demand for decentralization stops at one's own level. Union Government's enabling roles to energize local governments have not been very visible during the first decade (1994-2004) of constitutional local governments. Though some efforts were made and unmade during the first decade of constitutional Panchayats. These efforts (Year of Gram Sabha, 1999; Constitutional Review with special panel on PRIs-NCRWC and various dialogues at various levels to reiterate needs to further strengthen Panchayats) were not systematic and sustainable.

After a decade of indifferent and uneven devolution of governance to Panchayati Raj Institutions in India, there appeared new hope for the realization of the Constitutional mandate approved in Part IX of Constitution of India. A new Ministry of Panchayati Raj, Government of India was constituted in May 2004. Following a meeting of state Chief Ministers convened by the Prime Minister of India towards the end of June 2004, it was agreed that all Poverty Eradication and Rural Development programmes in future would be governed through Panchayati Raj Institutions. As a result of this meeting, seven Round-Table Conferences were convened by the Ministry of Panchayati Raj where all the governments of States and Union Territories actively participated (see Table-1 in Annexure). Covering a wide range of subjects, the resolutions developed during these Round-Table Conferences presented a possible Roadmap for further strengthening of Panchayati Raj Institutions in India. This agreement between Ministries of Panchayati Raj of Central and State governments has been communicated to the respective cabinets as well. Civil Society Organisations in different states took initiatives to educate people and Panchayats on the need for urgent implementation of the resolutions of these round-tables.

As a follow-up of Round-table conferences, it was resolved that devolution of functions to three tiers of Panchayati Raj would be the first step in devolution of genuine powers and authorities to enable Panchayats to function as vibrant institution of local self-governance. Each state government agreed to first complete activity mapping for three tiers of Panchayats on the basis of principle of subsidiarity. Then these activities were needed to be devolved irreversibly to PRIs. In order to perform these activities, necessary funds and related functionaries were also to be devolved.

Ministry of Panchayati Raj Institutions (Union Minister of Panchayati Raj, Shri Mani Shankar Aiyar, *vide* his letter no.

D.O.No.R-12011/5/2004-PR dated September 20, 2004 wrote to all Chief Ministers) requested state governments to expedite completion of Activity Mapping on the basis of principle of subsidiarity and with a holistic and integrative perspective. The Minister also offered to provide expert assistance to State governments through two organisations: Society for Participatory Research in Asia (PRIA), New Delhi, and Institute for Social and Economic Change (ISEC), Banglore. On the request of Union Ministry, PRIA provided technical assistance to some of the state governments in facilitating Activity Mapping for three tiers of Panchayats. However, current review of states (see Table-2 in Annexure) suggests that barring very few states, most states have not devolved the 3Fs to Panchayats on the basis of Activity mapping.

In the meantime Union Minister of Panchayati Raj proactively visited different states between May 2005 till date and signed Memorandums of Understanding with Chief Minister of that state for time bound strengthening of Panchayati Raj Institutions in the state. Till now such MOU's have been signed with 14 states, namely Karnataka, West Bengal, Rajasthan, Orissa, Arunachal Pradesh, Chhattisgarh, Haryana, Uttaranchal, Himachal Pradesh, Punjab, Andhra Pradesh, Goa, Sikkim and Lakshadweep. These MoUs are in addition to consensus resolutions of round-table conferences. Repeated political statements have been made by Union and State Governments to devolve genuine powers and authorities to three tiers of Panchayati Raj (see, MOPR website www.panchayat.nic.in). Unfortunately, experiences from different states in the field and also on papers (Factsheets prepared by the Ministry of Panchayati Raj, Government of India for a conference of Secretaries and Ministers of States and Union Government during 13-16 June 2006 at Bhubaneshwar) do not suggest that even some parts of this political rhetoric have been translated into realities in most states.

3. Status of Institutions Mandated to Strengthen Panchayati Raj Institutions

73rd and 74th Constitutional Amendments have created 'Trinity of Institutions' to support and strengthen democratic continuity, financial autonomy and grassroots participation in planning and implementation. These institutions are respectively State Election

Commission, State Finance Commission and District Planning Committee.

3.1 State Election Commission

Article 243K of the Constitution delineates that (1) the superintendence, direction and control of the preparation of electoral rolls for, and the conduct of all electors to the Panchayats shall be vested in a State Election Commission consisting of a State Election Commissioner to be appointed by the Governor, (2) Subject to the provisions of any law made by the legislatures of a state, the conditions of service and tenure of office of the State Election Commissioner shall be such as the Governor may by rule determine. Provided that the State Election Commissioner shall not be removed from his office except in like manner and on the like grounds as a Judge of a High Court and the conditions of service of the State Election Commissioner shall not be varied to his disadvantage after his appointment, (3) The Governor of a State shall, when so requested by the State Election Commission, make available to the State Election Commission such staff as may be necessary for the discharge of the functions conferred on the State Election Commission by clause (1), (4) Subject to the provisions of this Constitution, the Legislature of a State may, by law, make provisions with respect to all matters relating to, or in connection with, elections to the Panchayats.

1. The experiences in the functioning of State Election Commissions and conduct of elections so far seem to indicate that the system is now working in a reasonable manner. However, several discrepancies and infirmities have been noted in the manner in which some states have operationalised their constitutional obligations. In this regard, several consultations among State Election Commissions and their conferences have brought out these specific difficulties very clearly (Conference of SECs, October 12, 2004, IHC, New Delhi).
2. One of the common difficulties is in relation to splitting up the overall responsibility of State Election Commissions in a manner that the executive wing of the government in some states is responsible for delimitation of seats, reservation of seats and notification of elections. As a

result, elections have been delayed in some states (notably Jharkhand); partisan considerations influence delimitation of seats, causing delays and confusions in the nomination process; likewise, decisions about rotation and reservation of seats become contested and cause further delays.

3. It is, therefore, recommended that all state governments amend their legislations to align complete responsibilities with the State Election Commission, as is being done in Maharashtra and West Bengal. This will ensure compliance with the spirit of the Constitution as well as the highest standards of conduct already established by the Election Commission of India. "To this end, it would be desirable to vest all responsibilities for the election process in State Election Commissions rather than splitting these up, including:
   (a) preparation of electoral rolls;
   (b) delimitation of constituencies;
   (c) reservations and rotations;
   (d) qualifications of candidates;
   (e) conduct of elections; and
   (f) functioning as the first stage of adjudication in election disputes".
   (Sixth Round Table Conference of Ministers-in-charge of Panchayati Raj, Guwahati, November 27-28, 2004.)
4. The present situation with respect to the constitution of District Planning Committees is rather unsatisfactory. One approach towards ensuring timely constitution of District Planning Committees is to bring them under the purview of State Election Commissions. "Elections to District Planning Committees provided for in Article 243ZD of the Constitution might also be brought within the purview of State Election Commissions to ensure full conformity with Constitutional provisions, which has not always been the case" (Sixth Round Table Conference of Ministers-in-charge of Panchayati Raj, Guwahati, November 27-28, 2004).
5. Another major problem experienced by State Election Commissions in conduct of panchayat elections is the preparation of electoral rolls. In many states, two different sets of electoral rolls are being prepared—one by Election Commission of India for assembly and parliamentary

elections, and another by State Election Commission for panchayat and municipality elections. It is essential that the two systems be aligned and a common set of electoral rolls be prepared to reduce ambiguities and reduce costs. This may entail changes in the legislative provisions of some states as well as the system of defining wards by Election Commission of India.

"With a view to evolving a common electoral roll for all levels of elections, consultations between the Chief Election Commissioner and the State Election Commissioners might be encouraged with a view to resolving practical problems that might arise in the preparation, maintenance and updating of such electoral rolls for elections to be held at different times for different levels of Governments. The Panchayat and nagarpalika wards should be regarded as the building blocks for electoral rolls for all levels of election"

(Sixth Round Table Conference of Ministers-in-charge of Panchayati Raj, Guwahati, November 27-28, 2004.)

6. One of the perpetual irritants in the constitution of State Election Commissions is the status and resources accorded to the State Election Commission. Different states have formulated different modalities. The tenure and conditions of service of State Election Commissions vary greatly across states. The National Commission to Review the Working of the Constitution (NCRWC) had recommended in 2002 that State Election Commissions should be accorded the status of the Judge of High Court in the same manner as the Commissioners in Election Commission of India are accorded the status of Judge of the Supreme Court. It is imperative that all state governments amend their provisions to ensure that State Election Commissions are accorded the status and privileges equivalent to the Judge of the High Court in all manners of appointment, service conditions and separation.

"States may consider according the same salary and emoluments to State Election Commissioners as High Court Judges are entitled to".

(Sixth Round Table Conference of Ministers-in-charge of Panchayati Raj, Guwahati, November 27-28, 2004).

3.2 State Finance Commission

To review financial position of the state, Article 243-I of the Constitution ask for creation of Finance Commission in each state. It says that:

1. The Governor of a State shall, as soon as may be within one year from the commencement of the Constitution (Seventy-third Amendment) Act, 1993, and thereafter at the expiration of every fifth year, constitute a Finance Commission to review the financial position of the Panchayats and to make recommendations to the Governor as to:
   (a) the principles which should govern:
      (i) the distribution between the State and the Panchayats of the net proceeds of the taxes, duties, tolls and fees leviable by the State, which may be divided between them under this Part and the allocation between the Panchayats at all levels of their respective shares of such proceeds,
      (ii) the determination of the taxes, duties, tolls and fees which may be assigned to, or appropriated by the Panchayats,
      (iii) the grants-in-aid to the Panchayats from the Consolidated Fund of the State;
   (b) the measures needed to improve the financial position of the Panchayats;
   (c) any other matter referred to the Finance Commission by the Governor in the interests of sound finance of the Panchayats.
2. The Legislature of a State may, by law, provide for the composition of the Commission, the qualifications, which shall be requisite for appointment as members thereof, and the manner in which they shall be selected.
3. The Commission shall determine their procedure and shall have such powers in the performance of their functions as the legislature of the State may, by law, confer on them. The Governor shall cause every recommendation made by the Commission under this article together with as explanatory memorandum as to the action taken thereon to be laid before the Legislature of the State.

Most of the states have constituted two State Finance Commissions so far and some of them have also constituted third State Finance Commission. However, experiences (PRIA, RGICS; 2005) and also findings of different studies and reports, including Twelfth Finance Commission report, find serious gaps in the functioning of SFCs across almost all states of India. It has been observed that SFCs are not constituted in one go. Their reports are not available to Central Finance Commissions in desired time-frame. It has also been found that secretary level officials of state governments are assigned 'additional' charge of SFC-secretariat. SFCs in some states are given extension and they do not submit their reports on time. These reports are usually not based on exhaustive, systematic and update data. In the absence of human and financial resources and lack of continuous supports from state governments, most SFCs have to rely on limited data, which are available in different places. Moreover, delays and adhocism by State Governments in taking decisions on recommendations of SFCs are very common.

3.3 District Planning Committee

Article 243-ZD of the Constitution states that:

1. There shall be constituted in every State at the district level a District Planning Committee to consolidate the plans prepared by the Panchayats and the Municipalities in the district and to prepare a draft development plan for the district as a whole.
2. The Legislature of a State may by law, make provision with respect to the composition of the District Planning Committees; the manner in which the seats in such Committees shall be filled: Provided that not less than two-thirds of the members of such committee shall be elected by, and from amongst, the elected members of the Municipalities and Chairpersons of the Panchayats in the Metropolitan area in proportion to the ratio between the population of the Municipalities and of the Panchayats in that area.

Though DPCs are very important bodies, most of the states have not even constituted these bodies. A report of Expert Group in the Ministry of Panchayati Raj (Report of Expert Group, 2006) finds that only 16 states have so far constituted the District Planning Committees in all districts. Those who have constituted, many of those states have either made them 'dysfunctional' by hijacking real powers from Local Governments or have not done anything to encourage horizontal and vertical planning linkages for vibrancy of these bodies. Perhaps Kerala is the only exception where DPCs are functioning and bottom up planning processes take place regularly. In all other states, wide gaps exist on what DPCs have been defined on paper and what actually they are doing. The Group has suggested concrete steps that could be taken to establish and strengthen participatory planning during 2006-07, the last year of Tenth Five Year Plan and period for the Eleventh Plan from 2007 to 2012, keeping in the mind the provisions of Article 243G of the Constitution, which envisages Panchayats as local self-governments planning for economic development and social justice. It has also suggested to reform guidelines for important Centrally Sponsored Schemes to link them with plans of DPCs.

But all these things can happen only when Panchayats at all levels and Municipalities become vibrant units of local self-governance. So, this Group reiterated for

(i) A clear and unambiguous activity mapping
(ii) Engagement of all stakeholders (specially women and *dalits*) in participatory planning and implementation,
(iii) Devolution of adequate funds in an untied manner,
(iv) Streamlining and consolidation of schemes to ensure flexibility and measure of autonomy,
(v) Assignment of significant revenue raising powers and building capacity of local governments to arise revenue from sources assigned to them, and
(vi) Maintenance of proper Management Information System (MIS) for local governments.

4. Reforming the Institutional Framework and Ways Forward

The Trinity of Institutions has potential and constitutional mandate to strengthen Panchayats and Municipalities as institutions of Local Self-Governance. There is an urgent need to 'institutionalize' the efforts related to strengthening of Local Governments. Constitution of India has already created these three institutions to institutionalize the system of local self-governance in the country. However, unfortunately these institutions have not received the type of attention, which they deserve. Unless these institutions are provided sufficient capacities and ample autonomy in transparent and accountable ways, it may not be possible to sustain institutionalization of local democracy at grassroots. Institutional capacity building of SECs, SFCs, and DPCs on one hand, and devolution to local governments on the other hand, should go hand in hand. Ultimately these constitutional institutions would become custodians of constitutional democracy at local levels.

The first Round-table held in Kolkata resolved that the Union and State Governments would endeavour to promote healthy conventions with respect to: how State Finance Commissions are constituted and staffed; and the processing of the recommendations of State Finance Commissions by State Governments so that they reflect, as far as possible, the practice followed in respect of the Central Finance Commission's functioning and recommendations. Similarly Mysore Round-table agreed that

- There shall be constituted in every State, at the district level, a District Planning Committee (DPC) by the end of the current financial year wherever such DPCs do not already exists.
- All DPCs should be constituted according to the procedure laid down in the Constitution in Article 243ZD (2).
- All States must make provision, by law, for the functions relating to District Planning Committees.
- District planning must take into account resource endowment of the area; felt needs of the people; and relative absorptive capacity.

As provided for in the Constitution, each tier of the Panchayati Raj system—Village, Intermediate and District—must prepare the perspective Five Year Plan and Annual Plans for its respective jurisdiction. The same exercise should be undertaken in the Municipalities of each district. The DPC should "consolidate" the plans prepared by the Panchayats and Municipalities, provided for in the Constitution, rather than prepare the District Plan of its own accord or of its own volition. To fine-tune the plans prepared at different levels, as also to undertake the consolidation of plans in the DPC in a technically acceptable sense, State Governments, in accordance with the provisions of Article 243ZD(3)(b) may specify institutions, organisations and individuals, who may assist the Panchayats, Municipalities and DPCs in preparing plans of a technically acceptable nature. To facilitate such planning, the State Government, in accordance with the provisions of Article 243ZD, may indicate to each level of the Panchayats and Municipalities, "the extent and type of available resources, whether financial or otherwise".

These resolutions along with Guwahati round table resolution for strengthening of SECs could become roadmap for immediate reforms of these institutions. Guwahati Round-table Conference expressed that,

While all matters relating to Panchayat elections have been vested by the Constitution in State legislatures/governments, there is a need to work towards commonality, if not uniformity, in election procedures and provisions. To this end, it would be desirable to vest all responsibilities for the election process in State Election Commissions rather than splitting these up, including:

- preparation of electoral rolls;
- delimitation of constituencies;
- reservations and rotations;
- qualifications of candidates;
- conduct of elections; and
- functioning as the first stage of adjudication in election disputes.

Civil Society organisations have to play a very important role in enabling these processes through: (i) local mobilisation for participation and accountability of local governments, (ii) empowering the poor and marginalised, and (iii) monitoring/complementing the efforts for genuine devolution and institutional strengthening of the Trinity of Institutions. These efforts would go a long way in the institutionalization of Local Self Governments at all levels.

ANNEXURE

Table 1: Overview of Round-table Conferences

Round-table	*Theme*	*Date*	*Place*	*No. of Resolutions*
1.	"Panchayati Raj: Effective Devolution", comprising Functions, Functionaries and Finances, as well as Empowerment of Gram Sabhas	Sat – Sun, 24-25, July 04	Kolkata	18
2.	"Panchayati Raj: Planning, Implementation and Rural Business Hubs", including the question of Parallel Bodies	Sat-Sun 28-29, Aug. 04	Mysore	26
3.	"Reservations in Panchayati Raj", comprising Scheduled Tribes (including implementation of PESA), Scheduled Caste and Women	Thu-Fri 23-24 Sept.04	Raipur	10
4.	"Panchayati Raj in Union Territories and Panchayati Raj Jurisprudence"	Sat-Sun 7-8 Oct 04	Chandigarh	14
5.	"Annual Reports on State of the Panchayats" (including preparations of Devolution Index)	Sat-Sun 28-29 Oct. 04	Srinagar	6
6.	"Election and Audit of Panchayati Raj Institutions"	Sat-Sun 27-28 Nov. 04	Guwahati	26
7.	IT Enabled e-governance and Capacity Building and Training for Panchayati Raj Institutions	Sat-Sun 17-19 Dec. 04	Jaipur	50

Table 2: Status of Activity Mapping in Different States

S. No.	*State*	*Transfer of Subjects transferred through legislation*	*Details of activity mapping undertaken*	*Latest position*
1	2	3	4	5
1.	Andhra Pradesh	17 Subjects	9 Subjects	Committee constituted under Special Chief Secretary has held 3 meetings and submitted its formulation. This is being considered by a Group of Ministers.
2.	Assam	29 Subjects	29 Subjects	Assam claims that it has done activity mapping more than 3 years back. However, this Activity mapping was in the form of a consolidated executive order, not in the matrix that we have prepared. The order is also quite vague in respect of certain subjects as it has remained on paper and individual departments have not operationalised this order through executive orders transferring funds and functionaries. After the 7 RTs, Activity Mapping is being monitored by Additional Chief Secretary. He has reviewed the earlier order and stated that whatever has been transferred, even if faulty has to be first implemented through issuance of orders. He has passed orders fixing time limits for departments to issue executive orders for transfer of funds and functionaries. It is reported by the Secretary, PR, that about 8 departments have passed partial orders. Copies will be sent to MoPR.
3.	Arunachal Pradesh		29 Subjects	An officer of the State government, Mr. Otem Dai has been engaged by the State Government to prepare the final Activity Mapping. PRIA has provided its inputs to the State in this regard.

(*Contd.*)

(*Contd.*)

1	2	3	4	5
4.	Bihar	25 subjects		Discussions towards activity mapping between PRIA and Government of Bihar have been held. Work is in progress, though, it is not proceeding fast enough.
5.	Chhattisgarh	29 subjects	27 subjects. All except forest and drinking water supply	Activity Mapping for 27 items has been prepared. However, in spite of several workshops conducted by the PR department to discuss Activity Mapping, no progress has been made to issue the necessary executive orders in this regard.
6.	Goa	6 subjects	18 subjects	Eighteen functions have been devolved to village Panchayats and 6 to ZPs. However, these are not in terms of the items listed in the Eleventh Schedule, but in terms of actual civic functions. Goa needs to place its Activity Mapping in the matrix suggested.
7.	Gujarat	15 subjects	14 subjects	Activity mapping has been done for 14 subjects. 5 subjects have been partially devolved. With respect to 10 functions, activities are yet to be devolved. The matter has been taken to the State Cabinet for policy decisions on identification of funds, functions and functionaries. An action taken report on the Round Table resolutions has been submitted by Gujarat. However, this information is incomplete.
8.	Haryana		10 subjects	Activity Mapping in respect of 10 subjects was released on 17-2-2006 in the joint presence of the Chief Minister, Haryana and MPR.
9.	Himachal Pradesh	26 subjects		15 departments had issued delegation orders delegating powers to Panchayats in respect of their schemes. However, no activity mapping has been attempted in the matrix as suggested by MoPR. Secretary Panchayati Raj states that recently, Panchayat elections have been held and Panchayat members have taken their oath on 23rd January. A new impetus is required on Activity

(*Contd.*)

1	2	3	4	5
10.	Karnataka	29 subjects	29 subjects	Activity Mapping completed in respect of all 29 items in August, 2003. This was followed by another exercise of devolution of funds through the State Budget. A 'GO' was issued in October, 2005. The Activity Mapping has been given full effect through Fiscal devolution in the budget pertaining to 26 subjects completed with effect from 2005-06.
11.	Kerala	26 subjects	26 subjects	119 activities relating to 19 functions have been devolved earlier. Kerala is revisiting this responsibility mapping currently. In this respect a new Activity Mapping matrix has been prepared, which is very detailed and unique, in the sense that it also covers Municipalities, as well as lists out the Activities in respect of each function that ought to be performed. This has been forwarded to the Ministry of Panchayati Raj, and orders are under issue by Kerala Government. Untied funds are being devolved to Panchayats in respect of devolved functions.
12.	Madhya Pradesh	23 subjects	7 subjects	For 7 or 8 activities, Activity Mapping was prepared by PRIA/Samarthan. The same NGO, has been requested to undertake this, for all 23 subjects to be devolved. This report has not yet been considered, by the government.
13.	Maharashtra	18 subjects		There has been no move on Activity Mapping after the Round Table. Chief Secretary took two meetings, but nothing has progressed since then. Principal Secretary, PR, Maharashtra states that saturation has been reached in respect of devolution of powers and it is not intended to devolve more than 18 subjects. He states that in respect of these 18, orders were issued in 2003.
14.	Manipur	22 functions	22 subjects	Activity Mapping of 22 subjects completed.
15.	Orissa	25 subjects	7 Subjects	Activity Mapping has been issued in October in respect of 9 subjects, in the presence of the Minister and the Chief Minister.

(*Contd.*)

(*Contd.*)

1	2	3	4	5
16.	Punjab	7 subjects		Draft Activity Mapping has been prepared for all departments in a detailed fashion. This was circulated to all Ministries. However, only Social Security department, Public Health and Health departments have responded. Though meetings have been held at the level of Chief Secretary with all departments, nothing much has happened. In certain sectors such as Health and Education, significant work has been undertaken. 1300 doctors and rural dispensaries have been handed over to ZPs. Existing doctors have been shifted to city hospitals and new recruitments will be at the ZP level. 4000 primary schools are being transferred to the Panchayat Samiti and 10000 teachers being recruited at that level.
17.	Rajasthan	29 subjects	12 subjects: Agriculture, Soil Conservation, PHED, Elementary and Secondary Education, Health and Family Welfare, Irrigation, Forest, Industry, Food, Tourism, PWD, Energy and Technical Education.	The Activity Mapping exercise was started for 18 departments and has now been completed for 12. An interesting aspect of activity mapping undertaken is in respect of tourism. A Cabinet sub-committee chaired by the Home Minister, Mr. Gulab Chand Kataria was constituted in August 2004 to recommend measures to strengthen PRIs. The sub-committee has had detailed discussions and visited Kerala, Karnataka and AP. The report is ready, but not yet submitted to Cabinet for consideration. It is informally learnt that the report recommends full devolution by 2007, when the 11th Plan starts. It has made several far reaching suggestions regarding fiscal devolution.
18.	Sikkim	28 functions		Activity mapping has just started and is expected to be completed in a few months.

(*Contd.*)

(Contd.)

1	2	3	4	5
19.	Tamil Nadu	29 subjects		Tamil Nadu claims to have issued instructions for devolving all subjects to Panchayati Raj. GOs have been issued to devolve certain activities relating to the functions devolved, but these remain on paper. In January 2006 meetings were held with Panchayat presidents. Work has since stopped due to election notification. Rural Roads, Water Supply, Sanitation and Rural Housing Schemes have been taken up for discussion. 3rd State Finance Commission is also addressing this issue.
20.	Tripura	29 subjects	21 subjects	In 1994 orders were issued for devolving 21 subjects. With respect to 8 subjects orders are awaited because of operational problems related to 6th Schedule. Activity Mapping exercise is on and it is also looking at administrative powers to the PRIs. Earlier only functions and financial devolution was there. Current exercise is aiming administrative control to PRIs. This is for 10 departments. The matrix for Activity Mapping has been prepared last year itself and is pending for decision at cabinet level. The matter is getting postponed due to conduct of different elections.
21.	U.P.	12 subjects		Activity Mapping was completed in respect of 32 departments as part of the recommendations of a committee (Bholanath Tiwari report). However, this report has not been implemented. Currently the effort is to take steps to implement the same. A meeting was held under the APC, seeking to identify at least 5 schemes per department to transfer to Panchayats. However, not much headway has been made in this regard.

(Contd.)

(Contd.)

1	2	3	4	5
				On devolution of functionaries, the Multipurpose workers at Gram Panchayat level were progressively taken back to the State departments concerned. However, as per a recent judgement of the Allahabad High Court (8th February), these workers have been restored to the Panchayats. State government is examining the implications of the same.
23.	Uttaranchal	14 subjects	9 subjects	Activity Mapping in respect of 9 departments has been completed and is under consideration of the Government. GOs for devolution of 3 departments issued.
24.	West Bengal	29 subjects	15 subjects	Activity Mapping has been completed and orders issued in respect of 15 subjects on 7-11-2005.

Source: MOPR and States Concerned.

REFERENCES

Agrawal, A. and Gibson, C.C., (1999), 'Enchantment and Disenchantment: The Role of Community in Natural Resource Conservation,' *World Development*, 27 (6): 629–49.

Blair, H., (2000), 'Participation and Accountability at the Periphery: Democratic Local Governance in Six Countries,' *World Development* 28(1): 21–39.

Crook, R.C. and Manor, J., (1998), *Democracy and Decentralisation in South Asia and West Africa*, Cambridge: Cambridge University Press.

Drèze, J. and Sen, A., (1996), *India: Economic Development and Social Opportunity*, Delhi: Oxford University Press.

Meenakshisundaram, S.S., (1999) 'Decentralization in Developing Countries,' S.N. Jha and P.C. Mathur (Eds.) *Decentralisation and Local Politics: Readings in Indian Government and Politics* (2). London: Sage, pp. 54–69.

NCRWC, (March 2002), *Report of National Commission to Review the Working of the Constitution*, Ministry of Law, Justice and Company Affairs, Government of India.

Ostrom, E., (1996), 'Crossing the Great Divide: Co-production, Synergy and Development,' *World Development* 24(6): 1073–87.

Ostrom, E., (1990), *Governing the Commons: The Evolution of Institutions for Collective Action*, Cambridge: Cambridge University Press.

Ostrom, E., Schroeder, L. and Wynne, S., (1993), *Institutional Incentives and Sustainable Development: Infrastructure Policies in Perspective*, Oxford: Westview Press.

PRIA, (2004), *Report on Role of State Election Commissions and Proceedings of Conference of State Election Commissioners*, 12th October 2004 at India Habitat Centre, New Delhi.

PRIA, (2005), *Report on Status of State Finance Commissions, shared in a national conference organised jointly by PRIA and RGICS at Rajiv Gandhi Foundation*, New Delhi on 2nd December 2005.

Report of Twelfth Finance Commission (2005-10), November 2004, Government of India, Chapter 8, Local Bodies.

Report of Expert Group: Planning at the Grassroots Level: An Action Programme for the Eleventh Five Year Plan, (2006) Ministry of Panchayati Raj, Government of India, March 2006, New Delhi.

Robinson, D., Hewitt, T. and Harriss, J. (eds.) (2000), *Managing Development: Understanding Inter-Organisational Relationships*, London: Sage for the Open University.

www.panchayat.nic.in: Official Website of Ministry of Panchayati Raj, Government of India.

5

Mobilising Civil Society

Campaigning at the Grassroots

Shailendra Dwivedi

In the recent past, concerns about increasing apathy of ordinary citizens to the institutions of governance, and growing non-accountability of state to citizens have been shared, variously. Simultaneously, importance of a strong civil society for enhancing citizen participation, and ensuring democratic stability and performance has also been advocated, vigorously.

Civil society conceptualized as a public sphere comprising individuals and collective initiatives for common public good[1] has taken many varied forms. They include struggles for freedom and independence, people's movements and organisations, campaigns for social, economic and environmental improvement, and for human rights, establishing community organisations engaged in a wide range of activities, including, tackling poverty, employment creation and advancing education; preserving indigenous cultures, working for human security and peace. These and many other actions are the basis on which democracy, pluralism, respect for human rights, good governance, and the cohesiveness of the society rest. According to some scholars, civil society in India consists of very fluid social groupings which are found on primordial identities of caste, ethnicity, kinship lineages, religions; though most theorists regard voluntary social associations as prime component of civil society (Commonwealth Foundation, 1999; Dhanagare, 2005).

Civil society in these varied forms, broadly, performs two key functions. First, it ensures distribution of power in society, and in political life. This demands that organisations are autonomous in terms of decisional competence, selection of leaders, and financial and administrative resource necessary for continued operations. Second, civil society enhances democratic culture and practices. Both as a sector of associations in public space, as well as norms and values, it is considered to be a source of virtues that sustain democratic interaction, trust, tolerance, cooperation and equality. For societies to sustain these values, the educative functions of civil society are critically important (Hadenius, 1996).

While performing these functions, civil society adopts a wide range of strategies, and follows different routes varying from charity and welfare, to development and mobilisation. Grassroot struggles and campaigns, however, have emerged as a thriving, and growing force in civil society. The grassroot action groups illustrate the best forum, both for deepening democracy as well as for the educational process. The report of Commonwealth Foundation (1999) highlights the significance of acknowledging, encouraging, and supporting the wide variety of citizens' action carried out in small, local, informal and invisible ways to promote common public good in all societies.

Mobilisation carried out by civil society, however, have been largely, posited as anti state. These mobilisation processes at the grassroots have been visualized as a potent source of accountability of the state to citizens. According to Tandon & Mohanty (2002), in the backdrop of the gap between what is Constitutionally provided, and its frequent violations, the way the poor and subaltern relate to the state and to the society, civil society initiatives illustrates collective action in the public sphere against the dominant interests, and an unresponsive state. Oommen (1996), however, argues that elements of civil society are not always, and necessarily antistate. Sometimes they are neutral, and occasionally they are even prostate. Also, the state is not always against all the elements of civil society. An alternative perspective, therefore, visualizes civil society mobilisation occupying the social space created by decline of the conventional mainstream politics of legislature, election, political parties, trade unions etc (Kothari, 1990; Sethi, 1998). There efforts are, basically, aiming at deepening democracy at the grassroots, and promoting a strong state which can demonstrate efficient and effective performance. This perspective visualizes an enlarged role for citizens in realizing the dreams of 'good society'.

Interestingly, the recent past has also witnessed a parallel phenomenon of growing mandates for decentralized governance. In many countries devolution of power and resources from national authorities to institutions of local governance has been Constitutionally mandated over the past decade. The opening up of new democratic space created opportunities for participation in governance at the local level. It provided a platform through which citizens can begin to engage at the local level in the process of governance.

In the Indian context, the 73rd CAA promoted Panchayati Raj Institutions (PRIs) as constitutionally sanctioned institution of local self governance to establish 'democracy' at the grassroots level. In the backdrop of evident limitations of existing structures of governance to deliver economic development and social justice at the grassroots, PRIs were visualized as political initiative of the state to resolve existing governmental crisis. Lack of political will associated with the existing complexity of sociopolitical reality at the grassroots, however, posed serious challenge to flourish them as institutions promoting inclusive governance. Amidst an increasing and clear deficiency of governance, civil society started addressing the growing concern of transparency, accountability, self management and self governance in PRIs (Rai, *et al.* 2001).

The efforts of civil society in this backdrop grappled with not only the issue of promoting citizens' participation in PRIs, but also to ensure effective voices of new citizen leaderships, particularly, from the marginalized sections like women, dalits, tribals, and youths. Imbibing democratic norms and values in social sphere also emerged as a serious challenge to promote people's participation in governance.

While understanding the dynamics of civil society mobilisation, it is necessary to ask and answer the question — why a collectivity resorts to this particular route to change, and what are the factors which facilitates the mobilisation process. This paper, while trying to understand this dynamics in the context of small scale grassroots campaigns also provides insights into the opportunities and constraints within which they operate.

Conceptualising civil society as public space constituted by associations raises questions concerning how a shared understanding about the purpose of the mobilisation is developed among various collectives, and also about the relationship with the mainstream political parties. The paper highlights some of the challenges that emerged during the campaign. For illustrations, the paper dwells upon the participatory experiences drawn from Pre Election Voters' Awareness Campaigns (PEVAC) carried out in the context of PRIs, and Gram Sabha campaigns[2] that have been carried out in India by hundreds of civil society organisations during the past one decade.

Setting the Agenda

Civil society is a deeply fragmented, highly segmented, and largely localized sphere of social associations. Attempts to develop a shared understanding about the broad perspective, and objective of grassroot mobilisation face a great deal of variations in terms of political lineage, size, geographical level of operation, importance attached to some issues over others, and their mode of intervention. This poses challenges of building public sphere for dialogue and consensus, as well as, developing a mechanism of vigilance, self policing, and modulation (Chandoke, 2003; Dhanagare, 2005; Walzer 2003).

The process of developing a shared understanding among various constituents of civil society about the purpose of mobilisation confronts two inter-related issues. First, about who sets the agenda, and second about how the agenda/issues are formulated. In this context, civil society organisations engaged in grassroots mobilisation may be broadly categorized as either community based action groups like SHGs, Mahila Mandals, youth clubs etc., or intermediary organisations like voluntary development organisations (VDOs). The internal and external environment in which they operate, vary. While, community based organisations (CBOs) confine the purpose with the local realities, VDOs tend to visualize the mobilisation more from the larger perspective of policy advocacy. CBOs are rather informal, membership based, and comparatively less susceptible to legal or procedural formalities. VDOs on the other hand, are more formal, structured, and bounded by formal rules and procedures. Even within CBOs, and VDOs there are variations in terms of ideological shades, sizes, level of work, and linkage. They may also differ in the mode and approach of their intervention. Developing a coherent perspective in this highly complex framework demands a lot of negotiations at various levels. The consensus building process must safeguard the autonomy, identity, and territory of individual organisations.

Usually, the process of negotiations, and discussions are facilitated by intermediary VDOs. The challenge before VDOs in this process of formulating shared perspective is to demonstrate its sensitivity to the local, specific, and contingent needs of the grassroots. While facilitating this process, if VDOs define a more media centric, and structured role for themselves, then in the latter phase of the mobilisation it creates avoidable cleavage between VDOs, and CBOs. During PEVAC, and Gram Sabha mobilisation campaign it was observed that whenever VDOs allocated a role for themselves at the grassroots levels, the agenda setting process became comparatively smoother. Similarly, CBOs playing an active role in steering committees, formulating the outline of the campaign, laying down the focus and coverage of the campaign, identifying roles and responsibilities of members of *the alliance,* and developing a code of conduct for civil society organisations involved in mobilisation; greatly helped in developing their ownership of the campaign. Building a consensus, therefore, demands creative methods of accommodation as well as inclusive strategies.

The process of striking a synergy in the roles and responsibilities of grassroot action groups, and VDOs, however, need to be clearly distinguished from their key role, which these two categories of organisations are conceptually supposed to play in a mobilisation process. While community based action groups provide spaces, and grassroots local experiences, VDOs can effectively provide direction and support (Pandey, 1991). Whaites (2000) visualizes small grassroots based groups, which use 'small issues; like provision of credit, health care etc. playing *empowering roles,* and NGOs facing the challenge of strengthening local civil associations. Thus there possibilities, and space for these two categories of organisations mutually reinforcing each other.

Another challenge faced by organisations in developing a collective stake is to establish an organic linkage between the 'mobilisation programme' and 'other' ongoing activities of individual organisations. Ensuring this continuum is crucial from the point of eliciting popular participation, as well as sustaining the campaign. Otherwise event based, episodic, media centric approach limits the conscientisation process at the grassroots. Both PEVAC and Gram Sabha mobilisation have successfully linked the campaign with local developmental issues like water, ration cards, education and health. Grassroot mobilisation, thus provides opportunities for breaking unfortunate cleavages that continue to divide NGOs and grassroot action groups, and bring together diverse grassroot efforts into a common political struggle (Kothari, 1990).

Eliciting Participation

The focus of these grassroot campaigns is on the new social political formations of the marginalized and poor, rather than any particular social category of caste, ethnicity, and gender. Participation or non-participation in grassroot mobilisation by these marginalized sections is, largely, looked upon as a political issue. Questions about who is involved, how, and on whose terms are seen in terms of existing power relations. Interests in participation, politics of participation, dynamics in participation are some of the important issues to explore while understanding any grassroot mobilisation process (White, 2000).

Agenda of promoting local governance, from the point-of-view of citizens' *participation,* and not merely as an electoral legitimation, creates opportunities and spaces for significant learning and mobilisation around issues of democratic governance. Quality of participation of grassroot groups to a great extent, depends on power, capacity and information. Local governance provides a formal and legal space to institutionalize participation. Participation of the grassroot community as the main actor in the campaign with the focus on 'development' agenda should be visualized as a long term process. Their *participation* in the process of strengthening political space, and deepening democracy, facilitates meeting the real needs of people. It generates pressure on PRIs to ensure better allocation of limited resources according to priorities set by the common masses.

Quality participation of civil society formations in grassroot mobilisation enhances participation of ordinary citizens, especially of women and dalits. Wherever Gram Sabha mobilisation campaigns have been undertaken, it has been found that their participation levels have increased both in quantitative and qualitative terms. This increase varies from marginal to significant proportions. Women prefer to participate in groups. So, wherever formal or informal women associations are vibrant, women participation has increased significantly. For example women SHGs in Andhra Pradesh, Nari Networks in Haryana and Mahila Mandals in H.P. played significant roles in enhancing women participation in 'mobilizing' Gram Sabha meetings. Though it is difficult to generalize but a sense of gender solidarity and comfort has been observed in many places in the sense that women headed Panchayats attract more women participation in their Gram Sabha meetings.

The same trend has been noticed in case of dalit participation. For example, in Sabarkantha region where Samajik Nyay Manch (an association of dalit civil society organisations) is active, participation of dalits is higher and more effective in comparison to the Gram Sabha meetings in other places. With support from PRIA, Khap (caste) Panchayats of dalits in Mahendragarh district of Haryana helped its members to effectively participate in updating the voter list.

Social exclusion, and economic dependency, however, poses a serious challenge to ensure quality participation of women and dalits in grassroot mobilisation. In actual practice, the Gram Sabha has not risen to the expectations of the lawmakers and spirit of the Constitution of India. The socio-economic and political realities of Indian villages are not so conducive that just the passing of a legislation will bring desired change. Even today almost two-third villagers are functionally illiterate. Their illiteracy, crippled with prevailing caste and gender biases, excluded dalits and other backward castes from the realm of political decision-making. The powerful patriarchic norms still restrict women to participate in public arena. That is, on an average, almost three quarter of the population in every village had been traditionally excluded from socio-political decision-making at local levels.

In normal circumstances if a Gram Sabha meeting is organized, women and lower caste men will not come to the meeting unless they are prompted to come. Even if they come, they will sit in one corner and will not raise their voice unless supported to do so. So, the legislative order (progressive provisions of the Seventy-Third Amendment Act) cannot be realized unless social prompting, and social support is provided to marginalized sections. Unfortunately, except some civil society initiatives, no institutional support mechanism exists to encourage and support dalits and women to effectively participate in the Gram Sabha meetings.

Another constraint to strengthen civil society mobilisation at the grassroots is the history of dependency syndrome, and ignorance about importance of participation in Gram Sabha meetings which in turn makes citizens apathetic. The natural question asked by an ordinary citizen is, "What benefit will I receive if I participate in Gram Sabha Meetings?". If Gram Sabha can not deliver the basic needs of its citizens, why should one spend time and energy in its meeting?

It has been found in almost all states that just after Panchayat elections when the first Gram Sabha takes place more people participate in the Gram Sabha with new expectations. However, with the passage of time, when they realize that the Gram Sabha is unable to deliver, the participation level dwindles down. It connotes that any grassroot level mobilisation should make Gram Sabha a genuinely effective forum for people to influence decisions related to local economic development and social justice. Similarly, in the context of PEVAC, the mobilisation should promote effective leadership who can groom PRIs as an institution of participative democracy in its real sense.

In the long run, effective participation promotes effective Community Based Monitoring and Social Monitoring system to ensure the follow up of the decisions taken in Gram Sabha meetings, or promises made by candidates during elections. In the implementation of different schemes and programs, quality is assured, and the domination of the officials reduced. Despite all odds, it has been experienced that people do want to participate once they know 'whys' and 'hows' of participation. And when they participate, Gram Sabha discusses real issues ranging from social justice to economic development of the village.

Nonetheless, mobilisation of the rural poor is a serious challenge which contemporary community based action groups face. Any mobilisation strategy must analyse the factors that inhibits the conversion of what Omega (1994) calls 'action preparedness' into 'action participation'. The non-conversion and erosion of participation also vary across sub-population. Although these small participatory bodies provide avenues for greater participation, Mahajan (2003) feels that they may be appropriated to sanction majority practices and unequeal structures of power. She therefore advocates for the 'right based' conception of civility.

Educating Citizens

Any organisation process that works towards conscientisation of people is a highly educational process in which leaders and people together experience true authority and freedom, which they then seek to establish in society by transforming the reality which mediates them (Freire, 1972). Grassroot mobilisation, in this framework, provides an informal but effective forum for civil society to demonstrate its educative functions. According to Hamelink (1999), empowerment potential of the methods, and tools used for communication should be of primary concern to civil society organisations.

In the context of mobilisation for deepening democracy at the grassroots, there has been a growing demand for involving civil society organisations (CSOs) by means of public education for building awareness and social audit. Campaigns provide scope for using a variety of methods for public education that help in mobilisation. Gaps in information and understanding about PRIs pervades from ordinary citizens to people in powerful positions. Lack of appreciation about importance and implications of the 73rd Constitutional Amendment Act is common in government officials who are supposed to play a very important role in the success of Panchayati Raj Institutions. Because of affirmative reservations, almost one million women and more than half million from lower castes have been elected to Panchayats. They do not know about their roles and responsibilities as elected representatives. Citizens find it difficult to distinguish between Gram Sabha and Gram Panchayat. And past track records of governmental initiatives provide very bleak statistics. The most optimistic estimates suggest that less than one percent of elected representatives are provided basic orientation during the first year of their election.[3]

Many of these issues can be effectively disseminated, and discussed in campaign mode. Broadly, there are two modes of information dissemination and public education. First, aimed at core constituencies of the mobilisation, like key functionaries of CSOs, potential candidates for panchayat elections, citizen leaders, volunteers, and select people from media, academia, and administration. For them, special orientation programs are organized where information related to functions, powers, responsibilities, legal entitlements, decision making, importance of participation of women and dalits etc. are disseminated to the participants. This is done through structured workshops, followed by periodical sensitisation. During the PEVAC carried out by PRIA and its partners in the year 2005 around 51,242 Village Panchayats (out of total 10,2447 Village Panchayats) in seven states were covered by state level partnerships with 1455 CSOs and their networks.

The second mode of public education targets common masses through a variety of methods listed below:

(a) *Wall Writing*: The salient features of the issues of campaign are displayed on the walls in common places of the villages. In this method the letters used are large in size (font) and is attractive colours. Messages are also conveyed pictographically.
(b) *Kalajathas*: Cultural programs with the focal theme of importance of popular participation in Gram Sabha or election process are covered. This is conducted in the form of Nukkad Nataks, Pad-dangal, Folk Songs, Puppet shows etc.
(c) *Posters and Pamphlets*: The information dissemination on critical issues, primarily, for illiterate citizens is done pictorially, through fixing of posters in common places, and also distribution of pamphlets.
(d) *Yatra*: Rathyatras and Pad-yatras are organized in order to sensitize people, and disseminate information related to the campaign. It generates lot of spontaneous discussions, and deliberations.
(e) *Meetings*: Small group and informal meetings with the members of the women groups, citizen collectives, youth clubs are also done.
(f) *Audio/Video Cassettes*: Short duration video films are also shown in the villages. Songs are also played through public address system, which exclusively covers gram sabha. Use of state context, local issues, and local language in these films and songs leads to household discussions on issues highlighted through the film and songs.

In this mode, volunteers are engaged in large numbers to meet ordinary citizens, personally, and mobilise them to participate in the meetings of Gram Sabha, as well as in the election process. The target groups are mainly women and *dalits* who have been historically kept away from the mainstream of participation. According to one estimate, PRIA and its 1500 key partners were able to cover more than 100 million voters during PEVACs in seven states in 2005.

An increasing number of individuals and groups around the world are beginning to express concerns about the quality of media performance vis-à-vis highlighting issues pertaining to grassroot mobilisation. Involving media, both print and electronic, as an integral part of education and awareness building strategy helps in generating mass mobilisation. Linkages with media at various levels were maintained by inviting them in the campaign related activities, as well as providing regular information and briefs about the campaign. However, it was observed, that the preference of the media is more towards highlighting negative, and sensational aspects of the 'issues' raised during the campaign. Despite a concerted efforts by the lead VDOs towards orientation and sensitisation of media people, core issues related to the status of institutions of local self governance, efforts of civil society, participation of women and dalits did not receive the deserved coverage.

The concerted efforts aimed at educating common masses contributed to enhancing the quality of deliberations in Gram Sabhas. It also exerted pressure on the potential candidates of panchayat election to come up with their ideas, opinions, and commitments on 'development' agenda for their constituency. It may be noted that most of the time government imposes agenda for Gram Sabha meetings, and so discussions in such meetings are restricted to selection of beneficiaries for certain schemes. But it has been found that an effective strategy of educating masses in the mobilisation mode helps people raising, and discussing issues related to their daily lives. Women often raise social issues and issues related to women. However, the major issues that are addressed in the Gram Sabha meetings are mainly the livelihood issues or development issues or issues associated with basic needs and facilities. Gram Sabha meetings also discuss slightly technical issues like voters' list update (MP, Rajasthan, Chhattisgarh and

Haryana) for Panchayat elections, Birth-Death Registration and Sanitation (Bihar), Alcoholism (Haryana), Widow pension (Uttaranchal).

Taking Political Stance

Discourse on civil society in contemporary social sciences started in the backdrop of mass mobilisation witnessed during political upheavals in the new nation states during the second half of the 20th century. Amidst declining public esteem of mainstream political parties, civil society mobilisation emerged as an alternative social phenomenon occupying central place in some of the current conceptions of civil society (Beteille, 2005).

Decentralisation provides new political space, marked by freedom to struggle for deepening democracy at the local level. Panchayats cannot be genuinely strengthened till political will exists to empower them. The issue of taking into account political perspective, engaging with political actors, and creating a political space should be part of any grassroot mobilisation process on decentralisation. In this context, it is important that CSOs associated with the campaign are thoroughly acquainted with key features of legal and procedural nuances. It is important that these nuances are communicated to ordinary citizens in a simplified mode. Tracking and highlighting the gaps between the intended objectives of government policies and programmes, and their actual status need to be vigorously taken up by the civil society.

For instance, the laws in most of the states prescribe that at least two meetings of the Gram Sabha should be held in a year. Unfortunately, the minimum has been interpreted as maximum. The provisions related to quorum are confusing and prone to manipulations by persons in powerful positions. It may be surprising to know that the people or their representatives practically do not decide the agenda of meetings of Gram Sabhas. The state government often fixes these agendas in advance. Some state acts do provide for powers to the Gram Sabhas to identify beneficiaries to be covered under different development schemes. This provision though expresses faith in the Gram Sabha but at the same time it also restricts and undermines the role of Gram Sabha. Gram Sabhas has been converted into Beneficiaries Sabhas[4]. The functional relationship between Gram Sabha and Gram

Panchayat has not been clearly spelt out in most of the states. Moreover, Gram Sabha decisions may or may not be binding to the Gram Panchayat. Similarly, in most of the states the territorial jurisdictions of Gram Sabhas are fairly large. It is impossible to convene a single Gram Sabha for many revenue villages. Even if a meeting of such a large Gram Sabha takes place, quality and levels of participation get affected, where almost thousands of citizens are required to sit together and discuss the developmental issues for their fairly large Village Panchayat. Though some states like Orissa, Rajasthan, West Bengal and HP have legally divided Gram Sabhas into smaller units[5], namely Palli/Ward/Up Gram Sabhas; many states have yet to realize this gap. The grassroot mobilisation process must translate the popular sentiments against such lapses into a strong political demand from the grassroots.

Simultaneously, the campaign should also have a strategy to regularly communicate these gaps to the concerned state machinery. For example, during PEVAC, interaction with the State Election Commission (SEC), and the department of Development and Panchayat started from the time when the delimitation process began. District wise list of Gram Panchayats with number of reserved wards etc. were collected from the department of Development and Panchayat, and posted to all the CSOs associated with the campaign. The list provided inputs about the status of reserved wards, as well as about the total number of wards after the delimitation process. Post-delimitation — close and regular interactions with the SEC were maintained throughout the phases of voters' list updation, nomination filing, polling, and post-poll. The State Election Commissioner endorsed the brochures, and CD, which were used during PEVAC. He appealed to all the concerned officials to cooperate in this unique effort of civil society, and encouraged the voters to participate in the election process in a fair and peaceful manner.

Even at the grassroot level, local administrations were regularly informed about all the campaign related activities, which the concerned partners were organising at the district level. Whenever required, prior permission was secured to organise rallies, or to use public address system. Important documents like voters' list, application forms for voter registration, forms of filing nomination etc. were procured from the block development and Panchayat office.

Then there is a social dimension involved in grassroot campaign – schallenging old and new power structures. Constitutional compulsions have coerced men of higher caste to strategically align with their lower caste counterparts and women. This strategic, unholy and unequal alliance has resulted into proxy women and dalit panches/sarpanches. Traditional power structures, with the support from Panchayat Secretaries and other government officials, manipulate the constitutional mandate and rule by proxy. The elected women and dalit candidates work according to the whims and fancies of those who 'sponsor' them.

But, when Gram Sabha mobilisations ensure regular and systematic meetings of Gram Sabha, automatic checks and balances take place. Such mobilisations have not only enhanced participation and systematized Gram Sabha meetings, but have also facilitated building of new leaderships of women and dalits. These Gram Sabha meetings start silently challenging unjust behaviour (untouchabilities, atrocities on women) of Caste and Patriarchal systems. Gram Sabha mobilisations have helped establishing Gram Sabha as a political forum of people in the village to meet and discuss their common problems, and consequently, understand the needs and aspirations of the community. It empowers panchs to play their responsible roles as people's representatives. They start questioning the conduct of Sarpanchs. That is why many times many Sarpanchs perceive that Gram Sabha mobilisations are threats to their own monopolies and hegemonies.

In the backdrop of the challenges posed from the political perspective, it is important for any grassroot mobilisation process to decide about two things. One, the breadth and depth of networking among CSOs, and its sustenance. This is important, since to make any impact at the political level the issue of critical mass needs to be addressed. For example, during the PEVAC undertaken by PRIA and its partners in 2005 it was decided that to make a significant impact at the state level, efforts would be made to cover at least 50 percent of Village Panchayats in the state. Second, the mobilisation strategy should clearly articulate the nature of engagement with the mainstream political parties. Quite often, political parties make covert or overt attempts to hijack the agenda as well as momentum generated by the campaign at the grassroots.

Sustaining the Mobilisation

Challenges which civil society mobilisation faces are many. While on the one hand, there is the huge challenge of fulfilling varied expectations emerging from different levels, there is also an expectation to maintain and sustain its basic normative and value driven identity by devising some mechanisms for internal self policing, and modulation. Elliott (2003) is, however, skeptical against the optimism that a strengthened civil society would bring or sustain democracy. Associational groupings, according to her, may be self interested and unavailable to the poor. Nor are they necessarily internally democratic or respectful of individual autonomy and choice. A modest expectation from the mobilisation, therefore, should be that it increases opportunities for citizens to engage in critical discourse about the goals and values of governance, and attempts to solve problems locally. Sethi (1998), also supports the arguments against labeling grassroots struggle as reformist or revolutionary, or even as success or failure. He basically visualizes these micro struggles as an evolving and ongoing process towards a deeper democratisation of state and society. Even if these grassroot struggles fail to acquire a significant presence, these activities, according to Sethi, provide a basis for hope.

Particular challenges are faced in terms of sustaining campaigns through programmatic interventions, and sustaining alliances. Issue of financial resources, and institutional support are some of the difficult questions that any grassroot mobilisation process needs to respond in this regard. Sustaining alliances that emerged during the mobilisation face impediments of institutionalisation. Sustaining and expanding the alliances made during the mobilisation process demand simultaneous efforts at various levels. Some of the key questions to be explored by the alliances are about the nature of long term engagement with the state; the rationale for this engagement; and the ways and means of building knowledge, and developing ownership to that knowledge by all the associated organisations. Oommen (1977) figures out the inevitable tension between mobilisation and institutionalisation. Regarding mobilisation programmes, he opines that an organic linkage between the ideology and programmes, reinforces the mobilisation. For example, civil society platforms evolved during PEVAC in 2005 remained intact even after the election but, their engagements during other campaigns like Panchayti Raj Jagrukta Abhiyan, and Gram Sabha Mobilisation could not mobilise citizens at the same scale as it was during PEVAC. The reasons behind this are institutional impediments. In states like Haryana, Chhattisgarh and Rajasthan where resources were made available, Civil Society groups and citizen leaders provided wholehearted supports for Panchayti Raj Jagrukta Abhiyan (PRJA). But in case of Gram Sabha the basic question is still there. Unless Gram Sabhas are empowered to move beyond their present role of Beneficiary Sabha, it is difficult to sustain CSOs and citizens engagements for strengthening peoples' participation in Gram Sabha.

Importance of intermediary organisations like VDOs, which play a crucial role in the grassroot mobilisation also needs to be acknowledged. Sharing their concerns about under acknowledgement of the role of intermediary organisations, Tandon & Mohanty (2002) highlight the crucial role of intermediary organisations as an anchor to many such coalitions which provide institutional resources, linkages with different tiers of government, partnerships with media and academia as well as access to international fora.

In the absence of long term commitment of efforts, resources, and partnerships civil society mobilisation appear to be no more than a sporadic intervention. It is, therefore, important that during the initial phase of mobilisation, citizens and citizens' collectives develop a greater understanding of each others' views. The process according to Hadenius (1996) helps in promoting broader common interests. The alliances developed in this process helps them gain collective power and skills to negotiate with the state. This process of building and expanding alliances ensures that discourse initiated by mobilisation does not end at the grassroot level. Rather, it goes atleast upto the national level, and also generates scope for engagement with the mainstream political parties. This provides the alliances a legitimacy to negotiate on behalf of a majority of people rather than a few.

NOTES

1. For meaning and forms of Civil Society, Refer, Tandon (2002).

2. Gram Sabha is a Constitutional body consisting of all persons registered in the electoral rolls of a village Panchayat in India.
3. PRIA and Partners experiences and crude data available with State Institutes of Rural Development, nodal training institutes for Panchayats.
4. PRIA (2000): Panchayati Raj Institutions: A Balance Sheet.
5. PRIA (2004): State Thematic Reports on PRI Programme.

REFERENCES

Beteille, A., (2005), "Civil Society and the Good Society", in N. Jayaram (ed.) *On Civil Society — Issues and Perspective* editor, Sage Publications, New Delhi, p. 280.

Chandoke, N., (2003), " 'Civil' and the 'Political' in Civil Society", in Carolyn M. Elliot (ed.) *Civil Society and Democracy — A Reader*, Oxford University Press, pp. 238-61.

Commonwealth Foundation, 1999, Citizens and Governance — Civil Society in New Millennium, A report prepared by Commonwealth Foundation in partnership with CIVICUS, p. 10.

Dhanagare D.N., (2005), Civil Society, State and Democracy: Contextualising a Discourse, in "On Civil Society — Issues and Perspective" editor N. Jayaram, Sage Publications, New Delhi, Thosnds Oaks, London, p. 43-63.

Elliott, C.M., (2003), "Civil Society and Democracy — A comparative review Essay", in Carolyn M. Elliot (ed) *Civil Society and Democracy — A Reader*, Oxford University Press, pp. 38-39.

Freire, P., (1972), *Pedagogy of the Oppressed*, Penguin Books, Harmondsworth, Middlesex, England, pp. 145-46.

Hadenius, Axel & Fredrik Uggla, (1996), "Making Civil Society Work, Promoting Democratic Development: What Can states and Donors Do?", *World Development*, Vol. 24 (10), pp. 1621-39.

Hamelink, C.J., (1999), "The People's Communication Charter", in Deborah Eade (ed.) *Development and Social Action*, Oxfam GB, pp. 171-72.

Kothari, R., (1990), *State against Democracy: In Search of Humane Governance*, Aspect Publication Limited, Delhi, pp. 72-87.

Mahajan, G., (2003), "Civil Society and its Avtars — What happened to Freedom and Democracy" in Carolyn M. Elliot (ed) *Civil Society and Democracy — A Reader*, Oxford University Press, pp. 167-90.

Omega, D. and B. Klandermans, (1994), "Why Social Movement Sympathizers don't participate: Erosion and non conversion of support", *American Sociological Review*, Vol. 59, pp. 703-22.

Oomen, T.K., (1977), "Sociological Issues in the Analysis of Social

Movements in Independent India", *Sociological Bulletin*, Vol. 26 No. 1, pp. 14-35.

Oommen, T.K., (1996), "State, civil society and market in India: The Context of Mobilisation", *Mobilisation*, Vol. 1 (2) pp. 191-202.

Pandey, S.R., (1991), *Community Action for social Justice: Grassroots Organisations in India*, Sage Publications, New Delhi, pp. 221-48.

Rai, Manoj, et al. (2001), *The State of Panchayats — A Participatory Perspective*, Samskriti Publication, New Delhi, pp. 234-36.

Sethi, H., (1998), "Micro Struggle, NGOs, and the State" in Manoranjan Mohanty *et al.* (eds.) *People's Rights — Social Movements and the State in the Third World*, Sage Publication, New Delhi, pp. 405-18.

Tandon, R., (2002), *Voluntary action, Civil Society and the State*, Mosaic Books, New Delhi, p. 32-45.

Tandon R. and R. Mohanty, (2002),*Civil Society and Governance*, Samskriti, New Delhi, pp. 19-21, 131-37.

Walzer, M., (2003), "The Idea of Civil Society — A Path of Social Reconstruction" in Carolyn M. Elliot (ed.) *Civil Society and Democracy — A Reader*, Oxford University Press, pp. 63-82.

Whaites, A., (2000), "Let's Get Civil Society Straight: NGOs, the State, and Political Theory" in Deborah Eade (ed.) *Development, NGOs, and Civil Society*, Oxfam GB, p. 127.

White, S.C., (2000), "Depoliticising Development: The Uses and Abuses of Participation" in Deborah Eade (ed.) *Development, NGOs, and Civil Society*, Oxfam GB, p. 154.

6

Gender and Governance
Empowering Women's Leadership

Mandakini Pant and *Martha Farrell*

Context

The current discourse on 'Governance' follows a broad understanding of the goals of sustainable human development. Premised on a *rights-based approach* to the development process, the sustainable human development paradigm sets upon enlarging choices of each person in a society to be an active and productive participant in the development process. *The Human Development Report* describes governance as "the exercise of power or authority —political, economic, administrative or otherwise—to manage a country's resources and affairs. It comprises the mechanisms, processes and institutions through which citizens and groups articulate their interests, exercise their legal rights, meet their obligations and mediate their differences" (UNDP: 1997).

Three underlying assumptions are clearly evident. Firstly, governance is about the structures and processes of public decision-making on mobilisation and use of public resources for common public good (Mohanty & Tandon: 2002). Secondly, governance recognizes plurality of domains and actors, viz., the state, markets and the corporate and civil society, in influencing the participation of citizens in the systems and processes of deliberation and decision-making at all levels and also to build their capacities for sustaining human development. State creates conducive politico-legal environment for all citizens. Private sector generates jobs and income. Civil society facilitates political and social interactions through mobilisations of groups to participate in economic, social and political activities (UNDP: 1997). Thirdly, governance is intricately woven around the active agency and participation of citizens in their social, economic and political development. Governance, therefore, entails not only the efficient and cost effective public agencies for responsive public services but also an active and meaningful participation of all citizens including the poor, marginalized and the under-represented people.

Gender equality is built-in governance. Both women and men have equality of rights under the law, equality of opportunity, including equality in access to capabilities and other productive resources that enable opportunity, and equality of voice to influence and contribute to development process (World Bank: 2001). Equal participation by both men and women in governance is essential for a number of reasons, viz.,

- Influence the allocation of scarce resources;
- Improve living conditions and promote the interests of women;
- Shift the political focus towards issues affecting the quality of life of both men and women by ensuring equitable distribution of productive resources and opportunities for growth, giving visibility to reproductive roles of women in policy making and increasing women's participation in the political process (Commonwealth Foundation: 2004).

Beijing Platform for Action (1995) clearly mentions that without the active participation of women and incorporation of the perspectives of women in all levels of decision-making, the goals of equality and development cannot be achieved (Panda: 2004). The affirmative action within India in terms of one-third reservations of seats for them in local level governance processes is one such process. The rationale underlying this affirmative action is to build a critical mass of women leadership in the decision-making in order to make meaningful difference to the outcomes of governance.

The 73rd and 74th Constitutional Amendments of 1992 enabled 33 per cent representation of women in Panchayats and Municipalities. An unprecedented number of women occupying leadership positions in local bodies and participating actively in the local political process is a reality now. Beginning with the first round of elections to Panchayats after the states passed conformity legislations in 1994, nearly one million elected women are occupying constitutionally mandated public offices. In most states, with the third round of Panchayat elections, approximately three million elected women would acquire a leadership position in local bodies (Tandon: 2004).

This paper addresses the issues in engendering governance institutionally. The paper has four sections. The first section looks at the issues in gender and governance; draws attention to the factors responsible for non-participation of women in the decision-making; tracks the efforts to mainstream gender and highlights the practices of engendering governance institutionally in the domains of state and civil society. The second section highlights the key findings of the study by PRIA on *Women's leadership: Towards Gender Mainstreaming in Governance*. The research was conducted before the third round of local body elections. It studied women elected representatives (WERs) in the States of Andhra Pradesh, Chhattisgarh, Haryana, Rajasthan, and Uttaranchal. The third section analyses the issues in the agency of women leadership in governance of local self-institutions. The concluding section reflects on the ways to institutionally mainstreaming gender.

SECTION I

Gender and Governance: Issues

Like race, ethnicity and class, gender as a social category shapes and establishes one's life chances in society and development. The term *gender* refers to a set of roles, attributes, behaviours expected from women and men by their societies. *Gender relations* represent the ways in which the *socially constructed* categories of women and men relate over a wide range of social interactions within family, community as well as in all economic and political relations in a given society. Gender relations are institutionally constructed. It creates and reproduces systemic differences in the positioning of women and men in the society. Rules, norms and practices of gender relations have a strong ideological content as it reflects the normative or prescriptive version of female and male roles. Gender relations are constituted in terms of relations of power and dominance; therefore, the nature of gender relations is one of opposition and conflict and often takes the form of male dominance and female subordination.

Gender is a salient factor in participation and representation in public decision-making. Both women and men need to participate and be active in decision-making and policy formulation. The nation-states, world over, guarantee all its citizens the right to political equality. The criteria of equality between sexes afford women the right to participate and represent in formal political decision-making without any discrimination. But do women really participate equally with men in policy and decision-making bodies?

The discourses, procedures, structures and functions of governance are, in general, heavily skewed in favour of men. Women and men do not have equal social, economic and legal rights. Women still lack independent rights to own land, manage property, conduct business or even travel without their husband's consent. Women continue to have poor command over a range of productive resources including education, land, information and financial resources. Limited access to resources and weaker capabilities constrain women's power to influence resource allocation and investment decisions at home, in their community and at national level. Women remain vastly underrepresented in national and local government (World Bank: 2001).

A close look at the recent gender development indicators in India, for instance, reveals disadvantaged positions of women:

- There are fewer women than men. The sex ratio is 933 women per 1000 men.
- 53.67 per cent women are literate as compared to 75.26 men.
- Fewer girls go to school. Fewer girls are in school for more than ten years. Drop out rate amongst girls is high.
- Work participation rate of women is 25.6 per cent as compared to 57.9 per cent men. Only 4.83 per cent of them, compared to 23.20 per cent men, are in organised sector. Women generally work in unorganised informal sector, in piece rate and subcontracting work. They earn a far lower wage than men doing the same work.

- They are under represented in governance and decision-making positions. For instance, there are about 72 women in Parliament as against 712 men. (GOI: 2001).

Factors Constraining Participation of Women in Governance

A noteworthy factor responsible for non-participation of women in decision-making and governance is *unequal gender relations*. Gender relations and power distribution between the sexes in both the private (personal) and public spheres create gender inequalities. Unequal gender relations, reproduced across the range of inter-related institutions as household, community, market and state, mediate the construction of gender identities and synergistically determine the capacities to exercise independent agency. Such relationships determine and influence the way resources, roles and responsibilities are allocated; values are assigned and power is mobilised. Without any sense of power whatsoever, their participation in decision-making is generally minimal not only in the political sphere but also at home and within the community.

Private-public divide associated with women and men have always hindered women to negotiate in the public domain. The private domain is associated with household, reproductive work and femininity, whereas, the public domain is associated with political authority, public decision-making, productive work and masculinity. Women are either being criticized for their inadequacies or patronized by men.

Autonomy of women in family/household, also influences their status and ability to participate in governance. Development policies often conceptualize altruist, conflict free, harmonious households where production, income, consumption are equally shared. Empirical studies, on the contrary, have shown that far from being a unit where all resources and benefits are pooled and shared equitably, the use of resources and labour, distribution and output have to be constantly negotiated within the households. Intra-household relations are often conflictive. The bargaining power is derived from options available to household members, the perceptions of contributions by members to the household prosperity and the degree to which members identify their self-interests within their personal well-being. Although, the private domain of the household is typically associated with women, men are held responsible for the welfare and safety of all members. Women's bargaining power in the household is restricted typically due to lack of access and control over resources, no autonomy in decision making, low self-esteem, low skills and education, restricted physical mobility and eventually less power as compared to men.

Other intersecting hierarchies such as *class, caste, ethnicity, religion,* and *rural/urban locations* further complicate gender inequality in governance. In India, for example, women face hurdles posed by patriarchy, caste and class when they enter the political domain. Women from lower caste groups, despite reservations, seldom wielded any real political power due to the strongly entrenched notions of caste and gender hierarchy (Anandhi, S., 2002). Studies have also shown that women elected representatives with no economic entitlements were often under the control of those who owned and controlled resources (usually males). Consequently, dependency curbed their independent decision-making powers (Niranjana, 2002).

The existence of persistent discrimination against women and inequality between women and men requires that engendering governance strategies be by and large complemented with targeted interventions on women's empowerment. Definition of empowerment ranges from increasing choices available to and capacities of women to transforming the power structures of society. It is assumed that by increasing women's choices, capacities, decision-making power, women's right and gender equality can be realized at all levels of decision-making.

Missing women in development processes clearly indicates that public decision-making processes have not actually addressed the strategic needs of women in the context of gender relations. Amartya Sen urges to look at women as agents of change and not as passive beneficiaries. Agency is the ability to define and articulate needs and priorities and to act upon them. Female agency implies the role of women as a member of the public and participant in economic, social and political action (Sen: 1999). A paper presented by Commonwealth Foundation to the meeting of Commonwealth Ministers Responsible for Women's Affairs in 2000 notes:

> *If the desired outcome of good governance is distributional equity then gender equality should stand high on the agenda of any government* (Commonwealth Foundation: 2004).

The Ministry of Foreign Affairs, Netherlands in 2000 explicitly stated that a gender sensitive governance means: (a) increased participation of women in governance institutions and decision-making processes, (b) freedom of association and space for an active women's movement, (c) transparent and accountable gender equity in the allocation of resources and power, (d) legislation of gender equality and the promotion and protection of women's rights and (e) gender sensitive policies and institutional structures (Commonwealth Foundation: 2004).

Gender Mainstreaming

The concept of bringing gender issues into the mainstream of society has been clearly established as a global strategy for promoting gender equality in the development agenda. Mainstreaming is not just about adding a 'women's' component into an existing activity.

"Mainstreaming goes beyond increasing women's participation... bringing together the experience, knowledge and interests of men and women to build upon the development agenda. Gender mainstreaming requires that all policy, planning, implementation and resource allocation reflect the interests and the views of both women as well as men" (Alkazi *et al.*, 2004).

Several efforts have been made across the world to ensure that development policy makers take note of the existing gender inequalities and proactively act towards addressing them.

Before the Decade for Women, development essentially had a *welfare* approach, addressing the practical needs of women surrounding their reproductive role through delivery of food, family planning, health care, etc. The *Women in Development* (WID) approach, ushered in during the Decade for Women, was initially conceived as an equity approach. This approach recognised women's active role in the 'development process as reproductive, productive and community workers, and emphasised the fulfilment of their strategic needs through direct state intervention. However, due to its political nature, this approach was not very acceptable to governments, and was soon replaced by an *anti-*

poverty approach. The *efficiency* approach sought to enhance women's contribution to the development process in order to ensure the efficiency and effectiveness of project interventions, albeit it tended to assume that women's time and energy are elastic. The *empowerment* approach considered women's improved condition and position to be the end in themselves. It focused on meeting women's strategic needs focusing on a bottom-up, self-reliant approach. The equity and empowerment approaches together labelled as *Gender and Development* (GAD) approaches, because of their emphasis on strategic needs, changed the focus and interventions from women as a target group to "gender analysis of women and men's roles and relations as part of all development interventions, and to gender equality as a goal of development" (Alkazi *et al.*, 2004). More recently, a *rights-based approach* sets the achievement of human rights and the creation of an enabling environment in which human rights can be enjoyed as the main objectives of people-centred sustainable development, as well as the means to achieve it. In this way, a rights-based approach transcends sectoral concerns, and encompasses the concepts of *welfare, anti-poverty, equity* and *empowerment* as facets of the rights of all people (Mahbub ul Haq Human Development Centre, 2000).

The UN summits on environment, social development, human rights and population brought the issue of women's rights to the forefront of international development debates. A major breakthrough was in getting women's rights on to the mainstream human rights agenda. Women's movements across the world mobilised and organised in the build up to the Vienna Human Rights Conference in 1993. The recommendations made by women's rights groups were included in the Vienna declaration and Programme of Action. The mobilisation on rights continued in Cairo's conference on Population and Development in 1994. The Beijing conference saw major advances in pursuing women's rights commitment. It took forward the Cairo agenda and crystallised the core rights issues: equal rights in law, entitlement to productive resources, right to education and health, equal right to representation in decision making, security and freedom from violence. The Beijing Platform for Action, 1995 (BFPA) provides a comprehensive mandate for governments to ensure that gender equality and women's empowerment are actively addressed as core development concerns. It clearly mentions that without the active participation of women and incorporation of the perspectives of women at all levels of decision-making, the goals of equality and development cannot be achieved. The BFPA became the basis for civil society advocacy. Many NGOs and civil society groups used the policy recommendations and agreements to lobby their own governments.

Complementing the BFPA is the Convention on the Elimination of Discrimination against Women (CEDAW). It is one of the most important international human rights instruments having a legal binding. These two mandates have informed the most recently proposed Millennium Development Goal (MDGs) that resolves to promote gender equality and women's empowerment to combat poverty, hunger, disease and to stimulate sustainable development.

Achieving equal participation in decision-making and governance is a high priority according to the recommendations of the World Summit on Social Development. Addressing gender in governance requires states to create spaces for women to participate at all levels. Its recommendations are consistent with other International agreements such as Agenda 21. Agenda 21 is a comprehensive plan of action to be taken globally, nationally and locally by organisations of the United Nations System, Governments, and Major Groups in every area in which human impacts on the environment. It represents a *global consensus and political commitment at the highest level* on socio-economic development and environmental cooperation. One of its commitments is allowing people to participate in decision making at all levels; particularly empowering women and increasing their participation in decision-making (Commonwealth Foundation: 2004).

Gender mainstreaming in India emerged in the early 80s as a concern of the women's movement to move women's issues from the periphery to the centre of development decision-making. The Eighth Plan (1992-97) spoke of the need to ensure a definite flow of funds from the general development sectors to women. The Ninth Plan introduced the Women's Component Plan to ensure that 30 per cent of funds and benefits under various welfare and developmental schemes were to be earmarked for women. The Tenth Plan reaffirmed the major strategy of mainstreaming gender perspectives in all sectoral policies, programmes and plans of action.

India's commitment to gender equality is further evidenced by the fact that it is a signatory to Convention on the Elimination of All Forms of Discrimination against Women (CEDAW), which was ratified on the 25th of June, 1993. The aim of the National Policy for the Empowerment of Women (2001) and the Tenth Plan has been to bring about social change—changes in attitudes towards women, and women's empowerment. The effort is to bring gender justice and make de jure equality into *de facto* equality.

Among the most significant achievements of the decade has been the reservation of one-third seats for women elected as representatives in panchayats and urban local bodies through the 73rd and 74th Constitutional Amendments. This has brought about a million women into positions of decision-making and has contributed significantly to the political empowerment of women. (GOI: 2001).

Gender and Institutional Change

The basis of gender sensitive governance institutions is sensitivity to the principles of gender equality, entitlement and justice. The rights or entitlement based approach to engendering governance places commitment to protect and promote the realisation of equal rights and justice. States and civil society organisations (CSOs) across the world are committed to address gender inequities in their various programmes and operations. The task of facilitating women's involvement in political processes at the local level requires a strong state and a strong civil society.

A gender equality policy in these institutions defines the norms and states how the institutions would guarantee equal treatment and spaces to women and men. Spaces created for equal participation are, however, not necessarily gender neutral. Theories of organisational culture point that people within the institutions and the foundational structure of the institutions, albeit autonomous, are actually complimentary forces that either challenge or maintain the gendered *status quo*. Institutions, as gendered sites reflect, shape and maintain the values of the larger society. Organisations are not gender-neutral entities; they are inextricably linked. Gendered power relations and dominant ideologies as regards gender roles and relations within and surrounding these institutions often shape the nature and extent of women's participation in governance. Their gender belief systems not only affect the manner in which the programmes are delivered in the field, but also the functioning of their internal processes. There is a link between the inner workings and outer impacts (Tandon & Farrell: 2006). It is by deconstructing these institutions through a gendered lens; in terms of processes and outcomes that one can understand to what extent the institutions are engendered.

State, Gender and Governance

In India, if one were to examine the measures that have been undertaken by the state to engender governance, quotas or reservations are the most prominent. The 73rd and 74th Constitutional Amendment Acts (CAA) of 1992 enabled 33 per cent representation of women in Panchayats and Municipalities and ensured their entry in the domain of politics. While the Article 243G and 243W of the Constitution empowered the State Legislatures to endow Panchayats and Municipalities with such powers and authority as may be necessary to enable them to function as institutions of self-government, the provision of reservation for Scheduled Castes, Scheduled Tribes and women (Article 243D and 243T) gave an opportunity to them to hold formal positions of power and, in turn, participate in the decision making process. The political restructuring and affirmative action have given the rural women an opportunity for participation in the political decision-making. Women not only have one-third membership, they also head as chairpersons in one third of the Panchayats.

The impetus for empowerment came from the State to 'enable women to make strategic life choices, organise and participate in and influence the process of decision-making as per their needs and priorities' (Deshmukh-Ranadive, 2005). Since Indian rural women by and large experience marginalisation, deprivation and oppression *vis-à-vis* the existing power structures, it is assumed that affirmative action will build a critical mass of local leadership who will be active participants in the strategic decision-making process. The political representation will give them the voice and a solidarity base to change initial gender-biased preferences and help in formulating democratic policies. The constitutionally mandated Panchayats and constitutionally mandated participation of women will change the power concentration.

The case studies on women elected representatives in the post 73rd and 74th CAA phase have reported mixed impacts. On the positive side we find that women despite their low level of literacy became articulate. They began asserting control over resources. They regularly attended local body meetings. In many instances they have even used their elected authority to address several critical issues such as children's education, drinking water facilities, family planning facilities, hygiene and health, quality of health care and village development such as pucca road and electricity in their areas. They have also brought alcohol abuse and domestic violence on to the agenda of political campaigns (Nambiar and Bandyopadhyay: 2004).

These profiles of active participation also co-exist with reverse stories of inert participation. Some of the factors such as intra-household gender relations, caste and livelihood issues, the masculinity of political processes, construing men as the only real political actors, the public and private forms of violence exercised by men against women and mandatory rotation of reserved seats have curbed and controlled their self-determining and risk-taking behaviours in the political process. According to PRIA's study on PRIs, the male family members who previously were elected representatives of the Panchayats often pushed women to contest elections so that the seat and the power could be retained within the family. As a result, women behaved as mere token representatives (dummy candidates) (PRIA: 1999). There are evidences of women elected representatives becoming the targets of character assassination. Their male colleagues in the meetings still treat them with indifference. The bureaucracy does not hold them in the same esteem as would give to the male elected representatives. It is clearly evident that numerical presence of women in leadership positions in the local bodies does not necessarily mean enhanced participation of women in governance.

It is clear that decentralisation as initiated by the state has not actually guaranteed equality of voice, access or influences in the decision-making within local governance. The gap between formal recognition of the right to participate and its actualisation remains large. Gendered identities and practices have often acted as forces for exclusion of women from leadership positions by limiting their capacities to articulate and act upon their claims and concerns. The authority structures of the governance institutions are not gender-neutral. They are essentially built on conventionally male ideals.

SECTION II

Key Findings: Women's Leadership in Local Self Governance

Individual Profiles

- The majority were married and above 35 years of age. Experienced older women with less household responsibilities could devote more time to public activities.
- A substantial section of them were engaged in productive work, working either in their own fields or as agricultural labourers.
- There were a few higher educated women elected representatives. Poor educational qualifications by and large affected the quality of performance. Elected representatives did not really understand any official documents. They signed when their husband/children asked them to sign or read out the document to them.
- Most of them were serving for the first time.
- Majority contested from the reserved seats. In Haryana, however, a little more than one-fourth, and in Andhra Pradesh, less than one-tenth, contested from general seats too.
- A substantial section of Women Elected Representatives (WERs) in Haryana and Rajasthan did not receive any training related to their roles and responsibilities as elected representatives. In Chhattisgarh one-fourth of them were trained mostly by government agencies. In Uttaranchal nearly half of them received training by an NGO (PRIA and its partners). In Andhra Pradesh 65 per cent of the WERs attended trainings organised by an NGO (PRIA) as well as by the political parties and the Government of Andhra Pradesh.
- WERs contested elections primarily to fulfil their family's

wishes. The husband and other family members such as father-in-law; brother-in-law, by and large, decided the candidature of women elected representatives. Political parties, previous elected representatives and NGOs also determined the candidature of WERs. In Andhra Pradesh, for instance, political parties and NGOs determined the candidature of around one-third of WERs. An interesting trend in Andhra Pradesh could be seen. Previous elected representatives, the Vice-Sarpanch, nominated about one-fifth of WERs to take their place officially but themselves continued to exercise power. Community members influenced the candidature of about one-third of WERs in Chhattisgarh, one-tenth WERs in Rajasthan, and a little more than one-tenth of WERs in Uttaranchal. It is interesting to note that the decision taken by women's groups on the candidature of WERs was very low (less than one-tenth in Andhra Pradesh and Uttaranchal and a little more than one-tenth in Chhattisgarh).

Table I: Decisions on the Candidature

Household Members	*Andhra Pradesh*	*Chhattis-garh*	*Haryana*	*Rajas-than*	*Uttaran-chal*
Husband/other family members	25.7	20.97	80.35	83.3	54.83
Political parties	29.03	4.84			6.45
Women's groups	8.8	12.90			6.45
Community members		33.87		10	12.90
Self	12.09	24.19	19.64	6.6	19.35
Previously elected representatives	19.3	3.23			
Others (NGOs)	4.8				
Total	100	100	100	100	100

Note: 1. Figures in percentage. 2. Indicates multiple responses of WERs.

Participation in Local Body Meetings

- The local body meetings were overwhelmingly male dominated events. The sheer presence of men intimidated WERs. They participated only to sign registers. Often their spouse or male relatives attended the meetings on their behalf. The limited attendance of elected representatives was juxtaposed with the ambiguous nature of the meetings themselves. On most occasions meetings were just formalities to be completed and marked only in records without their actual occurrences. Often proxy meetings were held and the proceedings were recorded even without the knowledge of those who attended them. However, such proceedings bore the signature of all the members, including those who happened to be absent from the meetings.

- Women elected representatives were primarily concerned with the issues related to infrastructure (roads, water, electricity, housing facility, drains, and toilets), education, health and sanitation, and employment. They could not transcend the agenda of infrastructure development. A significant section of them remained a mute spectator by proposing nothing in the meeting. However, with the support of community-based organisations (CBOs) such as self-help groups, some of them have been successfully raising their issues of concern in the gram sabha meetings and implementing several schemes. In Andhra Pradesh for instance, they took initiative in the implementation of the schemes such as *Janmabhoomi, Shramdan,* old age pensions, financial assistance during childbirth and girl child protection schemes. They raised issues relating to the streetlights, schools, low-cost sanitation, micro credit, drainage facilities, shopping complexes, flyover bridges etc. WERs in urban areas were relatively more active in taking up special assistance schemes for urban slum areas and for women. They also did a follow-up of government schemes sanctioned for the development of their ward/ village people.
- The attributes of self-confidence, ability to speak out in public, education, organizing skills and personal behaviour facilitated some elected representatives to function effectively. Absence of these hindered the ability of many to perform. While significant, others (Male Elected Representatives, other functionaries and officials) felt that WERs were, by and large, not capable

of conducting meetings and keeping the records. While WERs believed that training could enable them to overcome their constraints particularly those related to low education, low levels of awareness, and inability to speak in public.

Table II: Areas of Concern

Areas of Concern	*Andhra Pradesh*	*Chhattis-garh*	*Haryana*	*Rajas-than*	*Uttaran-chal*
Education	24.3	6.67	19.16	25.53	20.00
Infrastructure	18.9	82.22	56.28	30.83	34.00
Health	30.3	8.89	20.95	29.78	12.00
Women		2.22			2.00
Employment	19.5		3.59	13.82	28.00
No response	6.7				
Total	100	100	100	100	100

Note: 1. Figures in percentage. 2. Indicates multiple responses of WERs.

Intra-household Relations

- Joint family background facilitated their participation in local bodies. Shared and fewer household responsibilities gave women more time for leadership roles.
- The presence and involvement of family members in political parties, village/community based groups, caste groups and cultural groups eased their entry into local decision-making bodies.
- Family members (mostly husband, father-in-law, and brother-in-law) of WERs were also involved in governance as elected representatives, largely sarpanches, panches and councillors. The prestige of family within society due to the involvement of family members in socio-political activities and in governance eased their entry and participation despite the fact that they were first timers and untrained.
- The provision of mandatory participation of women in governance prompted households with strong socio-

political involvement to promote their wives/women members of their households in the sphere of politics. Findings showed that the husband and other family members such as father-in-law, brother-in-law largely decided the candidature of women elected representatives. One of the reasons behind this was the inherent interest of the household in politics. The male members/husband could not contest as the seat was reserved for women. Such ERs merely acted as 'rubber stamps' while their families took decisions on their behalf.

- Mobility is an essential factor for participating effectively in governance. Elected representatives need to interact with agents of the administration or state institutions, all of which are located outside the private spaces of their home. The capacity for mobility plays a key role in determining women's location in politics because it determines their access to resources and opportunities and the actual ability to engage in mobilisation. For women, the meanings and valences assigned to mobility are linked with the perimeters of domestication (Tambiah: 2003).
- The WERs faced mobility constraints in terms of household chores, economic constraints, and family interference. All these constraints restricted their mobility. WERs in the study opined that they should be either called in groups or persons. Those accompanying them should also be given transport allowance when they are attending meetings or training camps at a distance. These facilities would help them to face problems related to mobility (Table III).
- Work such as the maintenance of household, working in the field or engaging in income generating activities influenced the extent of women's political engagements. Women ERs felt that their work burden was incompatible with their public role performance. Daily pressures of occupation as well as household often prevented them from taking on additional governance related responsibilities. Hence, they did not mind their husbands or adult

family members taking interest in their activities and even acting on their behalf. They depended on them for day-to-day advice and support on governance related matters.

Table III: Mobility Constraints

Mobility Constraints	*Andhra Pradesh*	*Haryana*	*Rajasthan*	*Uttaranchal*
Household chores	38.8	20.53	32.35	52.13
Economic	32.2	17.85	58.82	11.42
Family Interference (dependency)	23.4	61.60	5.88	27.85
No social standing	5.6		2.94	8.57
Total	100	100	100	100

Note: 1. Figures in percentage. 2. Indicates multiple responses of WERs.

- Lack of mobility emanating from household responsibilities and dependency on male relatives constrained women's performance as ERs. Besides their family members interfered and often misused their authority.

Relations with Community (Civil Society)

- Culture and community played influential role in determining the authority, power, resources, time and spaces of women. The study findings (Table IV) reveal that the WERs faced constraints of traditions and customs, caste discrimination and safety issues. WERs could not take independent initiatives.
- The study findings (Table V) also demonstrate that caste associations played an important role in facilitating the leadership of WERs. CBOs as women collectives supported one-third WERs in Uttaranchal, and nearly one-sixth of WERs in Rajasthan and Andhra Pradesh. Political parties too played a decisive role. They supported a little less than one-half of WERs in Andhra Pradesh, nearly one-fourth WERs in Rajasthan and one-sixth WERs in Uttaranchal.

Table IV: Constraints within Community

Constraints	*Andhra Pradesh*	*Haryana*	*Rajas-than*	*Uttaran-chal*
Caste discrimination	18.07	28.84	16.66	9.67
Traditions and customs	21.08	64.41	78.57	29.03
Safety issues	24.09	2.88	4.76	12.90
Sexual harassment	22.2	3.84		
No interaction with CBOs/NGOs	14.4			9.67
No response				38.70
Total	100	100	100	100

Note: 1. Figures in percentage. 2. Indicates multiple responses of WERs.

Table V: Support of Institutions Within Community

Facilitating factors	*Andhra Pradesh*	*Haryana*	*Rajasthan*	*Uttaranchal*
Affiliation with political parties	47.75		26.31	16.12
Affiliation with CBOs/NGOs	17.5		15.78	32.25
Caste Association	27.5	100	57.89	12.90
Community support				32.25
Not Answered	7.5			6.45
Total	100	100	100	100

Note: 1. Figures in percentage. 2. Indicates multiple responses of WERs.

Relations within the Institutions of Local Self-Governance

- WERs, being undereducated and inexperienced, were often not allowed to carry out their mandate. Their efficacy was always under scrutiny; their views were not considered significant, and they were not included in the meetings. Male elected representatives (MERs) and government officials had reservations about the potentials of WERs to govern, as they were, by and large, ignorant of administrative proceedings. They felt that illiteracy, lack of communication skills and dependency on male relatives inhibited their regular participation in the local bodies. Consequently, development in their areas suffered. According to them, WERs could effectively participate in the service delivery monitoring such as pulse polio programme and in promoting associational groups like Mahila Mandals and SHGs. They encouraged WERs (Uttaranchal 87.1%, Andhra Pradesh 77.5%) to carry out their function, albeit in a very patronising manner by showing interest in their ideas, informing them about the various rules/clauses, upcoming schemes and new government grants. They also provided support in getting the tasks done.

- Indifference, vested interests, abusive language and non-cooperation of many MERs constrained the ability of many to perform better (Table VI). Due to these factors, they deliberately did not attend the meetings. These constraints have led to their being less informed on the issues related to governance.
- A substantial section of WERs found government functionaries such as panchayat secretaries, supportive and encouraging. Their support included action on the proposals, bringing projects and grants, solving/listening to their problems. Lack of experience and awareness made them fully dependent on the Panchayat Secretaries. This, however, many a times constrained their performance to act independently.

Table VI: Relational Constraints: MERs

Constraints	*Andhra Pradesh*	*Chhattis-garh*	*Haryana*	*Rajas-than*	*Uttaran-chal*
Lack of support	15	36.36	22.36	38.29	11.76
Indifference	40	18.18	18.01	14.89	8.82
Individual Interests	27.5	45.45	21.11	38.29	20.58
Abusive language	7.5		16.77	8.51	5.88
Corruption			21.73		
Do not attend meeting	10				42.94
Total	100	100	100	100	100

Note: 1. Figures in percentage. 2. Indicates multiple responses of WERs.

- Insensitivity, indifference, abusive language towards women and corruption of government officials constrained many WERs. For instance, Government officials' insensitivity towards women inhibited three fourths of WERs in Andhra Pradesh, about one-third in Rajasthan and about one-sixth of WERs in Uttaranchal to perform. For more than one-third of WERs in Rajasthan and about one-fifth of WERs in Uttaranchal the corruption of government officials was a deterrent factor (Table VII).

Table VII: Relational Constraints: Government Officials

Constraints	*Andhra Pradesh*	*Haryana*	*Rajasthan*	*Uttaranchal*
Indifference	12.5	20	24.59	6.25
Corruption		30.43	40.98	21.87
Disregard for women	75	24.34	34.42	15.62
Abusive language	7.5	25.21		3.12
No Interaction at all	5			53.12
Total	100	100	100	100

Note: 1. Figures in percentage. 2. Indicates multiple responses of WERs.

- While suggesting changes in making functionaries/state officials to respond more positively, the WERs emphasised on appointment of women functionaries/officials. This, according to them, would encourage WERs to actively participate in programmes, events and meetings. They also suggested training for attitudinal change in the male functionaries/officials in order to sensitise them about their specific problems.
- Some of the policy imperatives such as rotation of seats and two-child norm, constrain their participation. In our study, the WERs have identified honorarium, rotation of seats, no confidence motion and two-child norm as major barriers to their effective participation.
- Most of the WERs felt that honorarium for elected representatives is very important as they put in a major amount of time in the work. They wanted a policy to

compensate for the loss of the wages while they were participating in activities of Panchayats/Municipalities. They added that this would make them financially independent, and in turn their status within family would get enhanced.

- Rotation policy de-motivated WERs. They opined that by the time they would understand their roles and duties, their term would get over and they would not be given a second chance to implement the lessons they learnt. An interesting fact emerged during the course of our study. that women and men within community, by and large, believed that general seats were only for men. That is why perhaps most WERs in our study felt that they could not contest the general or unreserved seats. Political parties also did not nominate women for the unreserved seats.
- Political constraints, like party memberships, also hampered the WERs. With the increasing power of political parties in India, women's reserved seats are used as a way to gain an edge over a competing political party. WERs feel powerless, intimidated or forced by parties to contest elections, and then are caught in the crossfire between parties. WERs have not been able to overcome such policy related constraints (Table VIII).

Table VIII: Policy Constraints

Constraints	*Andhra Pradesh*	*Chhattis-garh*	*Haryana*	*Rajasthan*	*Uttaranchal*
Honorarium	43.6	56.25	22.4	46.55	47.05
Rotation of seats	14	25.00	24.8	25.86	11.76
No confidence motion	12.6	6.25		25.86	5.88
Two child norm	26.7		24	1.72	2.94
Political factionalism		12.50			
Training			28.8		
No response	2.8				32.35
Total	100	100.00	100	100	100

Note: 1. Figures in percentage. 2. Indicates multiple responses of WERs.

SECTION III

Agency of Women Elected Representatives: Discussions

Women in Panchayats and ULBs are getting exposed to the process of governance and consequently getting a sense of intimacy with and control over governance processes. Exposure to the ways of governance has instilled in them a sense of power. To be called a sarpanch, panch or councillor is an exhilarating experience, promoting an independent identity. This may be seen as gains in terms of the consolidation of gender equality, though the gain has not expanded over the years. A careful reading of the data, however, alerts us to the limitations of the gender mainstreaming in governance.

Equality of opportunity to women in local self-governance has not actually transformed the prevailing institutional practices (relations), which still emphasise male dominance. Gender mainstreaming has not gone beyond the level of rhetoric. An analysis of emerging issues not only explains ways in which women are constrained from exercising their leadership but also suggests ways to overcome the constraints.

Feminisation of Leadership

Mandatory one-third reservation for women has increased their presence in governance but their voices are silent. The study result shows that most of the WERs did not have previous experience in politics. They lacked technical expertise, organisational and communication skills. Only a small minority received training and most of them had little awareness about rural and urban development and administrative affairs. New entrants faced an unfriendly environment in carrying out the duties attached to their office. Vice-presidents, husbands, sons and male family members or others dominated them for planning and executing the powers of local self-governance.

The constitutional mandate has not adequately addressed the needs and rights of WERs. The realities of gender inequality restrict WERs ability to exercise their agency. The responsibilities to meet the household subsistence requirements, mobility restrictions and limited support structures limit their social interaction and participation in local self-governance. Domestication and seclusion ethics also undermine their potential for holding public office. Having no formal educational qualifications, being deficient in information, skills and experience, they are dependent on men both within the household and the institutions of local self-governance in matters relating to governance. Men exploit their naivety to their naiveté. The social image of women as housewives renders the work of many WERs invisible. Organisational resources are steered towards quantitative targets i.e. increasing the number of women in leadership positions. The engendering process has become an 'add women' process without questioning the basic assumptions, strategic objectives, or ways of working towards institutional change for gender equality.

Limits of Policy Imperatives

The Affirmative Policy in the form of reservation of seats for women has both enhanced their participation as well as obstructed it. The study findings show that while women have gained entry mainly because of the number of seats reserved for them, the very provision has been manipulated by men, either the family members, or those currently serving in office. Political parties too have divised ways of capturing women seats. As they need a namesake representative, they sponsor compliant women. The family members and political parties who sponsor them do not really invest in developing their capacities or potential because their usefulness does not extend beyond the immediate term of office. The study findings also show that WERs are first timers. Male relatives generally officiate on their behalf. Women as proxy representatives have reduced affirmative action to mere tokenism.

Policies of rotation, two-child norm and the absence of honorarium policy constrained the agency of WERs. For instance, rotation policy de-motivated them. WERs in the study contested only from reserved seats. They were not sure whether they would get a second chance to implement the lessons learnt from the general unreserved seats. Absence of honorarium policy inhibited their participation. WERs were mostly poor engaged in household subsistence activities, either in the field or in some income generating work. Attending meetings, visiting block level officials or taking training meant loss of a day's wage. Honorarium policy could help them as they were putting in a major amount of time in the activities of Panchayats/Municipalities. WERs, as the study findings have indicated, did not attend meetings or training camps organised because they were being organised at a distant place. They had to depend on family members to escort them. Provision of honorarium could also address problems related to mobility. Policy of two-child norm violated their right to participate as elected representatives. Several states had passed a provision prohibiting contestants to PRIs if they had more than two children. Women bore the brunt of it. Thus, many women (20-40 age group) were barred from contesting. There is an urgent need to seek a review of judgments of High Courts/Supreme Court in this regard. Now some state governments are thinking of keeping basic literacy as minimum qualification for contesting elections to PRIs, which besides being unconstitutional, will further discriminate against women.

Internalised Self-Image

Women's cognitive experiences about themselves and their role as elected representatives reflect a given structural situation. Internalisation of dominating ideologies and stereotypes about gender roles, values and behaviour, deterred women from taking up active leadership roles. Many WERs described themselves as housewives with no sense of independent identity. Low self-esteem has made them passive, dependent on men in matters relating to governance.

Interlocking of Private and Public Patriarchy

WERs are not looked upon as independent political agents. Their participation is tokenistic. Study findings clearly indicate that systemic patriarchy perpetuated the gender bias and powerlessness in WERs. Constraints within households directly influenced their capacity for public engagements. The mobility constraints have prompted the men in their lives (husbands, brothers, fathers, and fathers-in-law) to take up their job such as visiting Panchayat Samiti offices at block headquarters. They became *de facto* head or members of panchayats and municipalities when "their" women got elected. Ambivalence about their public role as elected representatives and dependency on male family members rendered their participation in governance meaningless. They functioned as 'add on' who came to politics only because of policy imperatives.

Everyday practices of MERs, Government officials, as the study findings have indicated, construe men as the only real political actors, thereby excluding WERs from actual exercise of power. When women make an effort to assert themselves, local government functionaries (like panchayat secretary) prefer to deal with the men-folk, instead of women elected representatives. The patriarchal nature of local administration reinforces a sense of worthlessness among these women. The masculinity of political processes, the adversarial proceedings, subtle forms of coercion to conform to the central interests of MERs, the timing of meetings and sessions, the pervasiveness of patronage etc. curb and control women leaders' self-determining behaviour.

One common expression of 'significant others' in the study has been that *women are unfit for public life because it is essentially male in character*. Public-private divide perpetuated by local governance bodies prevents women from being full participants in these organisations. The relegation of women to the private world of the household is so deeply embedded in the institutions of local self-governance that even though they have become elected representatives, political office continues to be the preserve of men. Deeply ingrained gender relations construct women as those whose voices are unreliable. Mostly cast as wives, daughters and sisters under the care of men, they are not taken seriously as political agents.

Civil Society as Political Learning Ground

Though caste associations, membership to various groups and political parties eased their entry into politics, such forms of civil society, however, did not actually support their independent agency. They co-opted WERs for their vested interests and created in them the feelings of being obliged to them for their positions. Pro-active engagement of CBOs like women collectives, on the contrary, enabled WERs to work confidently. As the study findings have revealed, WERs associated with them were more confident and articulate about their concerns and constraints. Continuous interaction with them enabled them to deal with issues of women's empowerment, corruption and generate unity amongst people.

Institutional Inadequacies

Women's representation in local government structures does not automatically result in their informed and effective participation in these structures. The simplistic appeals for increased participation of women generally overlook the institutional inadequacies such as the timings of meetings, problems of quorum and procedures adopted for finalizing development plans and projects, articulations of their priorities and issues in the meetings, the quality of deliberations and manipulation of discussions by dominant groups, rules for filing nominations and travel allowances, etc. Consequently, women including the elected representatives rarely attend local body meetings and hardly ever articulate their priorities.

Knowledge, training, and education as resources enable women to act as their agency. Empowerment as the processes of learning and action strengthens the self-esteem, analytical skills, competencies and political consciousness. The marginalized and excluded citizens gain a sense of their rights and join together to transform inequitable power relations and develop more democratic societies. WERs need to be politically enlightened, not only about their rights and duties but also about the nature of our constitution, democratic process and values, working of democratic institutions, concept and relevance of local body administration, particularly the message of the present 73rd and 74th CAAs and, and various poverty alleviation programmes and policies for women and weaker sections. Our findings reveal that those who received training were able to exercise their leadership effectively. However, systematic orientation and capacity enhancement of elected women has been largely ignored.

SECTION IV

Engendering Governance Institutionally: An Alternative

The lessons from the study point to the challenge of addressing difficulties of attitudinal and behavioural changes of actors in key institutions—the household, community (civil society) and the institutions of local self-governance. The construction of public and private spheres profoundly affects women's ability to exercise power. Engendering strategies, therefore, need to address the history of exclusion, marginalisation and invisibility of women's voices, which prevent them from exercising power actually; and also initiate processes of change by which women are enabled to make informed choices and exercise power.

Civil society intermediation, has enabled women to transcend the narrow identities of beneficiaries to become citizens with voices and rights. For instance, grassroot women's movements, community based organisations at the local level have been actively providing the poor and marginalized women, in particular, the intangible resources like information, social networks and associations; strengthening their ability to exercise agency for collective action around both community and gender issues in panchayats. They have been actively advocating and lobbying for women's interests in local bodies. CSOs generally have a gender unit which deals with programmes concerning women and governance. The governance concerns may include gender sensitising, providing support and training for elected representatives in local governments. They are sensitising women as an organised constituency and active agents, making them aware of their entitlements and enabling them to take decisions on their own developmental needs. Some CSOs are integrating gender concerns in all the projects undertaken. They have been addressing issues of gender discrimination, undertaking systematic gender analysis of locations and designing projects/programmes, which address conditions and interests of women from a gender perspective. The question here is whether the staff is sensitised to ensure that gender is mainstreamed in all its activities.

CSOs have been, by and large, actively promoting gender equality in society, paying little attention to the means—the instruments of their own organisations—in achieving those normative ends. Consequently, they typically remain 'outward-focused', and rarely make the link between their inner workings and outer impacts. (Tandon and Farrell: 2006). CSOs without practicing gender equality are unlikely to act as watchdogs on behalf of the people. It is in this context that the issue of engendering civil society institutions and its contribution to gender sensitive governance assumes importance.

Transforming power or gender relations mandates the organisations to discover their own reality of structures and practices. Engendering requires an approach that begins with collaborative research on the nature of gender dynamics and analysis of gender fair organisational practices. Such collaborative modes of documentation and enquiry can then generate organisational specific diagnosis for actions (as opposed to universal prescriptions of gender equality). For instance, preventing sexual harassment at work place is only possible when both women and men analyse the existing realities and develop norms of behaviour and organisational standards which are enforceable. The leadership is then able to take some responsibility for bringing about relevant and meaningful changes that address the underlying dynamics of power relations based on gender, both within and outside the organisations (Tandon & Farrell: 2006).

In recent years some interesting and positive experiences of engendering organisations have been reported where organisational change was introduced by uncovering roots of gender inequality within organisations. The example of PRIA gives an idea how development organisations are engaged in engendering governance both programmatically and institutionally.

Institutionally, PRIA is committed to address gender-based inequality. Its core values include mainstreaming gender-justice and equity through analysis of social reality, organisational policies, systems and structures, and programme priorities and plans as integral to its vision. Gender mainstreaming, driven by its long-standing concern about gender equity at workplace, has become an explicit Governing Board Policy. Taking recognition of these and adhering to its commitment to gender-justice, PRIA formed a Committee against Sexual Harassment (CASH) in December 1998. This decision was also in response to the Supreme Court guidelines to constitute CASH, which was in existence for two years (till 2001). It eventually evolved into the Committee on Gender Awareness and Mainstreaming in PRIA (CGAMP). The Committee has well defined Terms of Reference which act as guidelines to its functioning. In an attempt to address and integrate issues of gender equity within the organisation, the CGAMP plays a key role in the mainstreaming of gender within the organisation.

- *Staff Policies*: All staff policies, service rules and regulations of the organisation are gender sensitive. Periodic reviews of the same are done through a gender lens to ensure that gender sensitivity is maintained. These policies are in line with the government provisions.
- *Recruitment and Induction*: All interviews for staff recruitment in the organisation have women equally represented on the interview panel. PRIA has a gender sensitive recruitment policy where preference is given to women candidates in appointments. All new staff members joining the organisation are oriented on PRIA's gender policy and the role and functions of CGAMP within the organisation.
- *Personnel Systems*: Women with young children are allowed to take them to the field. Focused attention is given to HRD of women staff to take up leadership positions. Provision of paternity leave enables men to take on their household responsibilities.
- *Performance Reviews*: All performance reviews of individuals by self or supervisors/peers/subordinates have indicators to assess gender sensitivity in the overall performance.
- *Commitment to Creating and Promoting a Gender Sensitive Work Environment within the Organisation and its Various Branch/Field Offices*: Towards achieving this goal, it organises regular workshops/seminars and exposure to a variety of inputs. All PRIA organised events/programmes, both internal and external, have a gender component and address gender specific needs of the participants.
- *Sexual Harassment*: Through CGAMP, PRIA also acts as a CASH and addresses complaints relating to sexual harassment made by staff members, guests, and participants to workshops etc. The organisation is responsible to set up structures where staff members may feel free to seek redressal of their complaints.
- *Capacity Enhancement*: One way of sustaining the process of enquiry and change is to invest in the capacity of individuals and groups. Gender focal points in each partner organisation and field location is mandated with this role, and provides proper orientation on gender,

grievance handling, facilitating reflections and change, etc.

- *Documentation of Processes and Dissemination*: PRIA also ensures a detailed documentation of all the processes related to activities on the issues of gender within the organisation. These are accessible to all those who wish to use the same to promote and strengthen gender equality within their work spheres. These are also reported in the PRIA Newsletter and Website regularly.

Programmatically, in PRIA's framework of *'Governance Where People Matter'*, reforming governance is particularly accomplished through an engendered perspective. Emphasis on women's empowerment and strengthening their leadership in public roles as elected representatives of PRIs and municipalities has been particularly focused on. Likewise, women as leaders and agents of change are at the core of strategy of civil society building. Gender equity forms an essential element of all project planning, implementation and monitoring. All reports and evaluations include a specific focus on gender. Gender audits and gender analysis form part of PRIA's gender mainstreaming efforts. All staff policies, service rules and regulations of PRIA are gender sensitive. All new staff members joining the organisation are oriented on PRIA's gender policy and the role and functions of the Committee for Gender Awareness and Mainstreaming (CGAMP) within the organisation.

Rearrangement of relations and changes in attitudes and behaviour within an institution is necessary to sustain and take forward the steps towards changing the structure and system, which creates gender inequality.

REFERENCES

Alkazi, F. *et al.* (2004), Gender on the Agenda, *A Training Manual*, New Delhi. PRIA.

Anandhi, S., (2002), "Interlocking Patriarchies and Women in Governance: A Case Study of Panchayati Raj Institutions in Tamil Nadu", in Karin Kapadia, (ed.) *The Violence of Development*, London, Zed Books.

Brooke, West, (2004), *Women's Leadership: Towards Gender Mainstreaming in Governance*, Unpublished Document.

Commonwealth Foundation, (2004), *Citizens and Governance Toolkit*, London, Commonwealth Foundation.

Deshmukh Joy-Ranadive, (2005), *Women in Self-Help Groups and Panchayati Raj Institutions: Suggesting Synergistic Linkages*, Occasional paper no. 40, New Delhi, CWDS.

Government of India, (2001), *Platform for Action: 10 Years After, India Country Report*, New Delhi, Department of Women and Child Development, Ministry of Human Resource Development.

Mahbub-ul-Haq, Human Development Centre, (2000), *Human Development in South Asia*, Oxford, Oxford University Press.

Mishra, Panda Smita, (2004), *Gender Issues in Governance*, Paper presented in the workshop on Gender & Governance at Institute of Rural Management, Anand on 15-16 December.

Nambiar, Malini and Bandyopadhyay Kaustuv Kanti, (2004), "Self-Help Groups: Engagement with Governance Institutions" in *Participation and Governance*, Vol. 10, No. 29, March.

Niranjana, Seemanthini, (2002), "Exploring gender Rnflections within Panchayati Raj Institutions: Women's Politicisation in Andhra Pradesh", in Karin Kapadia, ed., *The Violence of Development*, London. Zed Books.

PRIA, (1999), *Women Leadership in Panchayati Raj Institutions: An Analysis of Six States*, New Delhi, PRIA.

Sen, Amartya, (1999), *Development as Freedom*, Oxford. Oxford University Press.

Tambiah, Yasmin, (2003), "The Impact of Gender Inequality on Governance" in Martha Nussbaum *et al. Essays on Gender and Governance*, New Delhi, UNDP.

Tandon, Rajesh, (2004), "Women's Panchayati Raj" *Ministerial Round Table Conference on Devolution to Panchayats, Draft Resolution*, New Delhi, PRIA.

Tandon and Farrell, (2006), *Collaborative Research in Gender Mainstreaming in Organisations*, Unpublished draft, PRIA. New Delhi.

Tandon, Rajesh and Mohanty, Ranjita, (2002), *Civil Society in Governance*, New Delhi, Samskriti.

UNDP, (1997), *Governance for Sustainable Human Development*, A UNDP Policy Document, magnet.undp.org/policy.

World Bank, (2001), *Engendering Development through Gender Equality in Rights, Resources and Voice*, New York, Oxford University Press.

7

Municipal Solid Waste Management Through Civic Engagement

Issues and Challenges

Nilanjan Ghose

Introduction

Urbanization is an irreversible trend. It is a response to economic, social and political forces, but the specific ways in which urban settlements develop and grow, in different countries, change under the influence of new factors. Globalization, democratization, new information and communication technology, economic transformation, social and cultural changes—all of these are strongly influencing the pattern of urbanization in the 21st century (UN Habitat, 2002).

Almost half of the world's present population lives in towns and cities. The world's urban population is likely to reach 4.2 billion by 2020. As per the "State of the World Cities 2006-07" report released by UN Habitat at the recently concluded (June 2006) World Urban Forum III at Vancouver, it has been estimated that there will be 1.4 billion slum dwellers by 2020 comprising roughly 80 per cent of the world's population. Majority of this growth is expected in the developing countries across the world. In developing regions, urbanization has become virtually synonymous with slum growth, especially in Sub-Saharan Africa, Western and Southern Asia where annual slum growth rate and urban growth rate are almost identical.

India's urban population as per the 2001 Census of the country was 285.35 million which was 27.8 per cent of the total population of 1.027 billion. Projected estimates indicate that the population would be around 550 million by 2021 increasing the level of urbanization to about 41 per cent. Presently there are three mega cities, with a population in excess of ten million in the country, but by the year 2021, with 6 mega-cities (Kolkata, Mumbai, Delhi, Chennai, Bangalore and Hyderabad), India will have greatest concentration of mega-cities in the Asian region (Tiwari, 2004). India alone has a slum population of 170 million.

Rapid unplanned urbanization poses a threat to the achievement of sustainable development in particular because of the environmental and other adverse effects of intensive resource consumption and poor management. The potential conflict between economic growth and environmental sustainability poses the greatest challenge for sustainable urbanization.

Sustainable urbanization is a dynamic, multi-dimensional process covering environmental as well as social, economic and political institutional sustainability. It embraces the relationship between all human settlements, from small urban centres to metropolises, and between towns and cities and their surrounding rural areas (UN Habitat, 2002). Reducing poverty is a pre-condition to achieving sustainable urban development. The key responsibility for achieving sustainable urbanization lies with local governments and their partners at the local level by making governance more inclusive.

Governance invokes more than just a political strategy; it also demands attention to social circumstances on the ground and to cultural values, to our understanding of multiculturalism and diversity. An inclusive approach to governing cities requires a deepening awareness of the intersection between civil society and government and the creation of new institutions and paths necessary for fostering inclusiveness, empowerment and engagement (World Urban Forum III, 2006).

Ensuring inclusion of the excluded is an important challenge for governance in general and urban governance in particular. The 74th Constitutional Amendment Act in India is the most important step taken to bring governance closer to the citizens. Civic engagement in the sphere of urban service delivery system ensures a better management and monitoring mechanism. Efforts are on both by the government and civil society organisations to create space for civic engagements. Creation of neighbourhood groups, self-help groups are some examples of civil societies endeavour to ensure civic engagement. Constitutional provision to develop ward sabhas for municipalities with more than three lakh population and the provision for preparation of Community Participation Law by the state government as a conditionality to avail funds from the recently launched *Jawaharlal Nehru National Urban Renewal Mission* are just some of the initiatives taken by the Government to ensure people's participation.

Solid Waste Management is one of the essential and obligatory functions of the Urban Local Bodies in India. Solid Waste Management is a part of public health and sanitation and according to the Constitution of India, falls within the purview of the State List. The activity being local in nature is entrusted to the urban local bodies. This paper looks at the scope of citizen's participation regarding the service delivery mechanism of solid waste management in two different circumstances and in two different locations.

This paper looks at two scenarios:

(a) where state through an act or a government order has created space for civic engagement;
(b) where civil society has spearheaded initiatives for civic engagement irrespective of state creating the space for it.

In Madhubani Municipal Council (Bihar), the civic engagement is driven by civil society while in Pithoragarh Municipal Council (Uttaranchal), it is driven by a government order. The paper analyses these two models and the impact it has on civic engagement. It looks at their similarities and dissimilarities and also takes note of the changing roles and nature of a set of stakeholders in these two models. Nature, intensity, level of community dynamics and outcome of civic engagement differ depending on a complex set of factors within the two models. In order to make governance inclusive, special effort needs to be made by the government to ensure participation of civil society.

Civil Society Driven Civic Engagement Model: A Case Study of Madhubani

Madhubani is a medium sized town with a burgeoning population of 70,000 spread across 24 municipal wards. The municipal council, like any other municipality of a small and medium town, has a fragile revenue collection system, with steadily declining resources for ensuring a quality service delivery system. Participatory Research in Asia (PRIA), New Delhi and Centre for Communication Resource Development (CENCORD), Bihar have been working with the issue of urban governance for quite sometime in Madhubani.

Initial meetings were conducted in different wards to have an understanding of the felt needs of the community. In course of the meetings it was realised that absenteeism of the municipal sweeper is one of the major concerns for a large section of the population. Due to irregular solid waste collection, most of the wards remain dirty and unclean. In course of the consultations with community, solid waste management emerged as a major issue. The positive and encouraging response from the residents of ward number 10 made interventions stronger in this particular ward. The ward consists of Yadavs, Swarnkars, Telis, Mahatos and Harijans. While the Yadavs are in majority, there are also a good number of Harijan households located in the southwestern part of the ward.

Mohalla Swachhata Samiti (MSS) in Madhubani: The Genesis

Initial curiosity to understand what's going on, drew a large section of the ward members to the meetings organised by PRIA and CENCORD. After a few meetings the participants decided to hire a private sweeper to regularize household waste collection. In order to monitor the activities of the private sweeper, it was felt that there should be a citizen's collective. Therefore, community residents prepared a group and developed their own mechanism for waste management. Mohalla Swachhata Samiti primarily refers to a citizen's collective developed informally through civil society organisations.

Composition of the Samiti

Initially the group was formed with interested members who participated in all the community meetings that were organised by PRIA and CENCORD. But later to make Mohalla Swachhata Samiti more functional special attention was given to select interested members from different locations of the ward. Incidentally different castes/groups of the community resided in different parts of the ward. Therefore, in case of group formation, care was taken to make use of these existing groups. However, it would be unjustified to say that a particular member represents that particular community. The group consisted of 8 members spread across different areas of the ward.

Process for Selection of the Sweepers

In more or less all the wards there are a few households belonging to the lower caste commonly known as "Dom" community. Information for the need of a private sweeper is primarily spread through word of mouth. The sweeper generally belongs to a backward community and is also a resident of the same ward. Her/His job is primarily to collect the wastes from the households and to clean the road and remove the wastes from the adjacent drains.

The sweeper is generally selected from a group of interested persons. The interested persons are shown the area that needs to be covered including the work that needs to be done. After that they are asked to quote their remuneration. The members of the Mohalla Swachhata Samiti take the final decision regarding selection and remuneration of the sweeper.

The present sweeper has been selected from a group of three persons and his salary is fifteen hundred rupees.

Process of Collection of Money

The mohalla samiti members divide themselves in two teams and visit the different households to collect money for the payment of the sweeper. Approximately Rs. 10-15 is collected from each household as a cost for availing the service. However, the elected representative ensures access to basic municipal resources like broomstick, spade, basket and trolley for waste collection.

Dynamics within the Madhubani Model: A Closer Look

The greatest challenge with the Madhubani model was to develop authenticity of the group and to ensure its sustainability. When the civil society organisation (Participatory Research in Asia and it's Partner CENCORD) started its operation to develop citizen's collectives at the ward level, some youth came forward and showed interest in bringing about a change within their community. Their enthusiasm encouraged the civil society organisations to organise more meetings with a larger section of the community. Successive meetings at the ward level were organised and the uninterrupted presence of some common people obviously marked them as the most enthusiastic members of the group. The common members by dint of their sincere interest and enthusiasm obviously became the core group of the swachhata samiti. It was expected that the enthusiasm of the community would rise once the system was in place. Things did change by attracting more participation from the community. With the passage of time it was observed that the local elected councillor started taking a lot of interest in the work of the Mohalla Swachhata Samiti.

Reflections reveal that there was a need to regulate and monitor the nature and flow of participation. The particular ward in which the activities were undertaken had the elected representative from the opposition party. Since he was from the opposition party, he was marginalised within the municipal council and had serious reservations about the activities sanctioned by the municipal chairperson.

The elected representative looked upon the apolitical space created by the civil society for civic engagement as an opportunity to take forward his personal/political agenda. The youth taking active part in the formation of the mohalla samiti were closely related to the local elected representative. Later on, informal discussions revealed that the interested youth involved in the samitis were not well accepted by the community because of their political activities. What looked as an apolitical forum for civic engagement to the members of the civil society was already converted into a political platform by the presence of these members, thus reducing acceptability and authenticity of the group within the community at large.

Government Order Driven Civic Engagement Model: A Case Study of Uttaranchal

Pithoragarh Municipal Council in Uttaranchal has a population of 40,000 spread across in 11 municipal wards. Solid Waste management is a major problem especially in the hilly regions. Littering of waste damages the beauty and ecology of the hills. A considerable amount of the waste is carried downstream polluting the valley. Hilly terrain and heavy rush of tourists make solid waste management not only difficult but also complicated.

The State Government has taken initiative to seek the help and co-operation of the citizens in ensuring a proper waste management system. Therefore, a government order has been passed by the Uttaranchal State Government in 2004 to ensure engagement of citizens for municipal waste management. But in order to develop these groups, they required the support of civil society organisations. Therefore Mohalla Swachhata Samitis were developed in close collaboration with the municipality and civil society organisations (Participatory Research in Asia and its partner Himalayan Study Circle) to monitor and manage solid waste management delivery system.

Mohalla Swachhata Samitis are formed covering approximately 200-250 households.

Composition of the Samiti

All the households existing within the particular area (demarcated by the urban local body) are members of the Mohalla Swachhata Samiti. But in order to ensure smooth functioning of the work, an executive committee is formed with selected members from the community. The executive committee generally consists of a president, a secretary and a treasurer. The members of the executive committee are generally selected through a community meeting. In some cases, because of lack of community participation in the initial stages, the officials of the municipality along with civil society organisations form an executive committee by selecting the most respectable and acceptable persons of the community/ locality.

These members are selected for a time period of one to two years depending on the willingness of the ward members. These are honorary posts and the major role of the committee is to ensure smooth functioning of the Mohalla Swachhata Samiti.

Functions of the MSS

The prime function of the Mohalla Swachhata Samiti is to have an effective municipal solid waste management system. The major responsibilities can be clubbed in the following heads:

Selection of the Sweeper

Mohalla Swachhata Samiti has the right to select the sweeper responsible for cleaning the particular area. Generally a local person is selected for the particular work. The portion of the salary that is to be provided by the municipality remains fixed (i.e. rupees one thousand five hundred). But the rate for door-to-door collection of household waste is decided in course of the negotiation. By transferring the power to select the sweeper to MSS, the urban local bodies have shifted a considerable power to these citizens' collectively.

Monitoring the Activities of the Safai Karmachari (Sweeper)

The members of the Mohalla Swachhata Samiti have the prime responsibility of monitoring the activities of the *safai karmi*. The entire area is divided into different sub-divisions (beats) and a particular member of the mohalla samiti is responsible to take note of the activities undertaken by the *safai karmis*.

Organizing different community meetings and discussing different issues related to solid waste management is one of the primary activities undertaken by MSS.

Mode of Payment

The payment of the sweeper is shared both by the community and the municipality. As per the Government Order the Municipality is supposed to provide an amount of Rs. 1500 as salary of the concerned *safai karmachari*. The sweeper collects a fixed amount from the households located within the area.

The amount to be collected from the households is mutually decided by the swachhata samiti members and the sweeper. The household basically pays for the door-to-door collection of the waste while the municipality pays for waste collection from the public places. Generally, the amount of money collected from each household varies between ten-fifteen rupees per household per month. The process for collection of the money varies. It is either collected by the sweepers from the households or is collected by the swachhta samiti members. Therefore, the sweeper is able to collect approximately two thousand five hundred (10 × 250) rupees from the households.

As mentioned earlier, the sweeper carries a small notebook along with him and the swachhata samiti members in each of the sub-divisions mark his attendance everyday. The payment of the *safai karmachari* is released only after checking his attendance from the notebook. If the member of the MSS makes a negative comment, the municipal official often gets back for further clarification from Mohalla Swachhata Samiti before payment. Thus the sweeper is not only accountable to the municipality but also equally accountable to the community.

The municipality of Pithoragarh is working jointly with civil society organisations to ensure the growth and development of Mohalla Swachhata Samitis to ensure proper solid waste management. The municipality does not have the required reach within the community and needs the support of civil society organisations (PRIA & HSC). Civil society organisations have the required reach within the community and organise community meetings for the municipality. Thus in Pithoragarh municipality a symbiotic relation has been developed between civil society and the urban local body.

Analyzing the Role and Nature of Stakeholder's Involvement in These Two Models

In order to have a comprehensive understanding of these two models it is important and necessary to analyse the role and nature of involvement of the same set of stakeholders. By the term stakeholders, we mean all the individuals and/or groups who are or can be directly or indirectly affected by the above-mentioned models. Citizens, civil society organisations, municipal officials and elected representatives are the primary stakeholders in these two models.

In both the models, civil society organisations play the most pertinent role in facilitating and developing citizen's collectives.

The role of civil society is much more challenging in case of the Madhubani model. Making the community agree to the fact that the problem of solid waste management can be addressed by citizen's collectives and then developing the authenticity of MSS by building trust of the community are the two primary challenges of the civil society driven civic engagement model.

In municipal wards, it is difficult to work with the community without building relations with the elected representatives. Any community mobilisation programme driven by a civil society organisation engaging ward members, is looked at with an eye of suspicion and skepticism by the elected representatives. Fear of the fact that any efficient citizen's collective can be in a position to negotiate for basic service delivery with the municipality, bypassing the elected representative remains uppermost in their mind. Therefore, generally, the civil society organisation has to make sure to take the elected members into confidence before intervening in any community mobilisation programme. But at the same time, the possibility of hijacking an apolitical civic platform by the elected representative and utilizing it for his/her vested political interest also remains a major concern. Therefore, the civil society organisation has to have a very delicate and fine balance of consulting and at the same time monitoring and if necessary regulating the role of the elected representative. Clarity of purpose and a clear understanding of the different motives of the various stakeholders becomes a critical and essential aspect for civil society organisations in this particular model.

A government order driven civic engagement is primarily free from most of these challenges. The government order provides the required authenticity for the entire exercise. It ensures a level playing field for all the stakeholders. Therefore the role of the civil society organisation, in this model, becomes that of a facilitator and a partner of municipality for ensuring community participation. Most importantly there is a clarity regarding the composition, roles and responsibilities of the respective members within the samiti.

The role of the municipal officials in the two models also varies to a considerable extent. In case of the civil society driven model, role of the municipal officials remained neutral. Madhubani municipal officials knew that with the existing resources it was not possible for them to provide for daily door-to-door waste collection. But, however, the ward councillor could make provisions for accessing materials like broomstick and waste collection trolley for the private sweeper from the municipality.

In case of the government order driven model, the civil society is seen as a partner in development. The officials know that civil society organisations have greater access to the community. So in order to implement the government order relating to civic engagement, the civil society organisations are in a position to mobilise the community. Therefore, the urban local body shares a very forthcoming attitude towards civil society organisations.

Comparison Between the Two Models of Civic Engagement (Civil Society Driven *vs* Government Order Driven)

The two models discussed above have a number of things in common. Most importantly the objective of both models is to involve citizens in the monitoring and management of the municipal service delivery system. The basic function of civil society in both the models is to facilitate the community mobilisation process. Mohalla Swachhata Samiti, in both the models, is formed to monitor the activities of the sweeper. The function of the MSS revolved, in both the models around selecting the sweeper, monitoring his/her activities, collecting money for his/her salary and organizing community meetings to get feedback from the community. It is interesting to note that in both the cases, the community is willing to pay for a service delivery system, which is accountable.

However, the two models are also different in more ways than one. The state sponsored civic engagement derives its authenticity from the government order that legalizes its composition and interactions with different stakeholders. It removes the suspicion and doubts to a considerable extent from the minds of elected representatives and of the community about the motives and intentions of the entire programme. The institutional support provided by the municipality ensures better sustainability of the intervention.

The civil society driven civic engagement model is primarily a bottom-up approach towards planning, engaging people's collective based on their own funds. Since the community feels that the ULB is collecting taxes, therefore it is their responsibility to provide necessary support for regular collection of municipal wastes. Changing the mindset of the community and making them believe that they can make a difference through their engagement takes away a major chunk of time and resources from civil society organisations. Therefore, developing the trust of the community regarding the purpose and importance of the group is itself a primary challenge for the civil society organisation.

In a civil society driven civic engagement model, community mobilisation surrounding an issue becomes the primary and elementary aspect. Once the community is mobilised, the civil society organisation then tries to develop systems/mechanisms for effectively addressing the particular issue. But in a government order driven civic engagement model, community mobilisation is an outcome of the government order/law.

A government order driven civic engagement model is applicable for all the wards within the municipality. Replicability becomes a key aspect for the government order driven model. But the civil society driven civic engagement model is undertaken only in a few wards within the municipality. Replicability of a model depends on a complex set of factors. Integrating the civil society driven civic engagement model with the existing municipal system depends a lot on the attitude and openness of the urban local body.

The role of a particular civil society organisation is limited in case of a government driven civic engagement model. The basic function of a civil society organisation is to facilitate the urban local bodies to develop a Mohalla Swachhata Samiti. But once the samiti is formed the role of the civil society becomes limited and it is taken care of by the urban local body.

In the other model, the role of the civil society organisation goes much beyond just the formation of the Mohalla Swachhata Samiti. Understanding the community dynamics and the stake of the different stakeholders becomes a very crucial aspect of civil society. The sustainability of a Mohalla Swachhata Samiti depends to a large extent on the vision and leadership of the civil society organisation.

Sustainability becomes an important aspect for both the

models. In case of the Madhubani model, financing the entire campaign through citizen contribution is a major concern. Besides, developing unanimous decision regarding the amount of money to be collected from different households is also a difficult task. In Madhubani, it was not possible to collect money from all the households as a reasonable section agreed but later refused to pay. In some cases, the households paid for the initial months but stopped later. In the Madhubani model the sweeper was selected and paid by the community. But they had to depend on the municipality for supply of the basic tools (trolleys to carry the waste to the disposal ground). The elected representative acted as a bridge between the municipality and the Mohalla Swachhata Samiti. Therefore, the civil society also had to maintain a good rapport with the elected representatives. Any confrontation with the elected representative could lead to denial of access to the above stated municipal resources making its sustainability more fragile.

But in case of the Pithoragarh model, the financial cost is shared between the community and the municipality. The citizen's only pay for their household waste collection. The selection of the sweeper and monitoring of his activities are being done through Swachhata Samitis. Even before making the payment of the sweeper, community feedback is taken. The *safai karmacharis* in Pithoragarh Municipality are accountable not only to the municipality but also to the community. But in case of Madhubani the accountability of the *safai karmachari* was limited to the members of Mohalla Swachhata Samiti.

Conclusion

Cities worldwide, whether rich or poor, confront the challenge of civic engagement and how to foster an inclusive governance process in their local political environment. Engaging people within a city, through an inclusive political process that involves long-term residents, international migrants, the poor, marginalised groups, national minorities, and indigenous people is the critical base for building safe, livable and sustainable cities in our shared future. Inclusiveness is the key for deepening democracy and promoting citizen's involvement and social cohesion. When citizens are effectively engaged in a city's development, engagement in the everyday decisions and in longer-term planning and policy development, they develop a sense of ownership and loyalty to the city.

Civic engagement in municipal service delivery system ensures better management and accountability of the service provider. Problem of solid waste management cannot be tackled just by upgradation of technology. Developing citizen's stake in the entire system of waste management is not only necessary but also essential. In both the above discussed models, civil society plays a vital role in mobilising the community to ensure civic engagement. However, the scope of civil society engagement is limited to a considerable extent in the government order driven civic engagement model. Civil society driven model is a bottom-up approach towards addressing issues affecting a large section of the community. Replicability of such a model and integrating this model with the existing municipal system of waste management depends to a large extent on the attitude of the state government. Therefore, the role of civil society to facilitate and encourage citizen's participation is necessary but not a sufficient condition for ensuring community participation. The nature and intensity of citizen's participation and the outcome of civic engagement becomes more meaningful and sustainable in cases where the state provides adequate institutional space for civil society organisations to mobilise citizen's collectives.

In case of a civil society driven civic engagement model, the role of civil society organisations is much more challenging than that of its counterparts in the other model. Ensuring sustainability and diluting the suspicion from the minds of the community and the elected representatives becomes the greatest challenge for civil society organisations as it has to negotiate for its created space. Protecting civic engagement from the vested interest of politicians takes away a major chunk of civil society resources. Often the uninvited entry of biased political workers mars the focus and nature of civic engagement. Successful civic engagement in both the models depends on a combination of complex factors. Thus it can be said that in order to make governance more inclusive, the urban local bodies need to develop a more meaningful civic engagement by creating more formal spaces for civil society organisations.

Glossary of terms used in the text

74th Constitutional Amendment Act	A constitutional act to ensure devolution of powers from the state governments to urban local bodies.
Jawaharlal Nehru National Urban Renewal Mission	A reform based infrastructure investment project for urban renewal in India launched in December 2005.
Ward sabhas	A citizen's collective at the ward level to ensure citizen's participation at local level.
Municipal wards	Lowest political unit for urban governance.
Yadavs, Swarnkars, Telis, Harijans	Different castes within Indian society.
Safai karmachari	Sweeper.
Dom	A particular caste, which is engaged in undertaking activities like scavenging, collection of wastes etc.
Mohalla	Community/Neighbourhood.
Swachata	Cleanliness.
Samiti.	Collective/group.

REFERENCES

UNHABITAT, (August 2002), *Sustainable Urbanization: Achieving Agenda 21.*

World Urban Forum III, (June 2006), *Our Future: Sustainable Cities: Turning Ideas into Action,* Background paper.

Tiwari, Vinod, (February 2004), *Municipal Reforms for Sustainable Urban Infrastructure Development in India.*

8

Strengthening Citizen Leadership

Kaustuv Kanti Bandyopadhyay

Introduction

The present reality of Indian society is characterised by increasing inequality, discrimination and conflict. The problems of poverty and marginalisation have got intertwined with issues of conflict and security. As voices of hitherto excluded groups of people begin to get articulated, society lacks the mechanisms to channelize them into constructive and transformative engagements. Visionary citizen leadership at the grassroots can play a meaningful and constructive role in this context.

In India, as in much of the developing world, the promotion of collective conscientisation and organisation building among women, *dalits,* tribals (and similar marginalised groups) over the past three decades has resulted in new stirrings of community-based groups and associations. Many of these collectives have come about as a result of the development programmes like promoting Self Help Groups (SHGs) or Sectoral User Committees (e.g. Forest Protection Committees, Water User Association, Watershed Committees etc.). Many more have been promoted by intermediary Civil Society Organisations as new collectives (*sangam, mandal, sangathan, samiti, andolan,* etc.). Many of these have attempted to transform traditional associations like youth groups, *ghotul, baisi,* etc. into contemporary actors.

The growing demands of local governance through a variety of legislative and constitutional provisions for devolution and decentralisation have also drawn many of these local, informal groups and associations into active roles. These community-based associations have been playing a key role in supporting the new leadership of women, *dalits* and tribals in Panchayati Raj Institutions and Urban Local Bodies in India. Their contribution enhances the accountability of the local elected representatives as well as supports a more transparent and participatory democratic functioning by the new leadership.

In recent years, there is an increasing realisation of the role of civil society in promoting socio-economic development. Small, local and informal associations and their alliances are playing a key role in policy reform and implementation from the vantage point of the poor and marginalised. However, the interests of underprivileged groups remain unarticulated unless and until initiatives are taken to organise them and empower them to question the government agencies as well as to engage with them. The interests of the subaltern groups were articulated only when an organisation intervened to address them as a collective and raised their concern *vis-à-vis* the state (Tandon and Mohanty, 2002).

Citizens are able to act more often when they are part of a collective. A neighbourhood organisation, a local union, a youth group, a village committee are all examples of various types of collectives. Individuals who get associated with such collectives, who have access to such formations, who have experience of participation in organisations are able to sustain their engagement and activism (The Commonwealth Foundation, 1999).

Institutions at any level involve more than purely individual efforts. They embody some kind of 'collective action' in which the interests, resources, ideas, and ideals of many persons are brought together. Similarly the benefit from the institutions tend to be 'public goods', things of value to persons besides those immediately engaged in the activity (Uphoff, 1986).

The growing democratisation of traditional power relations in civil society and the failure to create a rational basis for generating new leadership through formal political institutions are at the heart of the increasing authority vacuum in Indian politics. This is where the leadership of visible citizens can make a significant difference. Citizen activists can build the bridge—between citizens and the state. Leadership of citizens is exercised when they act to build society and improve governance. Recognition, visibility and promotion of such citizen leadership are the keys to this. Citizen leadership is also exercised when they enable other citizens to act—when they promote citizen activism in society and polity (Kohli, 1991).

Yet, many of these informal local leaders, their associations and networks remain fragile and weak. Sustained capacity building support in the form of information sharing, exposure, networking, handholding and training is not easily accessible and available to them. Recent trends in linking capacity building merely to project delivery and financing through demand ('user pays' principle) has resulted in higher order, supply-side, structured, expert-based approaches to capacity building, largely confined to intermediary associations (Tandon and Bandyopadhyay, 2001).

The citizens' assessment of the present reality is that of dissatisfaction. Basic needs remain unfulfilled. The need for associations is not being met either. Citizens find growing individualism and self-centredness in communities and families. Narrowly and newly defined identities are creating tensions and conflicts in societies. There are growing disconnections between citizens within a community and hostility towards other communities. Citizens also find that their own connection with and participation in the governance of their communities and societies is limited or absent. This further increases their sense of alienation in society and dissatisfaction with the present reality (The Commonwealth Foundation, 1999).

This article is based on PRIA's experience to reach to hitherto excluded local informal community based initiatives and citizens associations to enable their access, their entitlements and rights through a process of collective engagement. The initiative to strengthen citizen leadership came at a time when strengthening the coalitions of citizens' leadership at the grassroots could significantly alter the balance of power and resources in favour of the marginalised.

Understanding Citizenship and Citizen Leadership

The term 'citizenship' has been discussed, defined and understood at different points of time in the political history. One can find different traditions in citizenship thoughts through out the discourse. While some of these thoughts have supplemented the existing thoughts, others have given rise to inherent polarity. These polarities are many a time competing with each other, which needs to be considered while defining citizenship. This is especially true in the Indian context.

In the Western context, citizenship emphasises individual choices. It is considered that individuals act 'rationally' to advance their interests in the society. This emphasis on individual choice is based on the faith that the state will provide necessary protection and welfare provisions in exercising the individual choices. However, it does not recognise the fact that individual choices are restricted by the inherent structural inequalities in the society. In the Indian context, individual choices are also conditioned by collective choices of the community. In a hierarchical society, the choice and interest of the powerful is often projected as collective community choice. It is a fallacy of 'community'. In Indian context the community and the individual have to be considered together. Collective communitarian living is part of individual living. Being part of the society, a person should create conditions and opportunities for self-development as well as for the common good and welfare of the entire community with a particular focus on the poor and marginalised.

Rights and obligations are at the core of citizenship. Citizenship as 'rights' is understood as formal status granted by the state. Individuals are entitled to specific universalised rights enshrined in the law. Citizenship as 'obligations' is understood as political participation of all citizens as duty.

Rights are conceived as *political* (e.g. right to vote, right to form association), *civil* (freedom of speech, liberty of the person), *social* (not to be discriminated against on the basis of caste, class, religion or gender and equal access to basic services like health, education etc.), *economic* (protection of private property, equal access to employment and sources of livelihood) and *cultural* (protection and preservation of traditional culture). It is a matter of choice for the individual to claim and exercise rights. Some of them are formalised in law while others are not. The role of state is to protect citizens in exercising their rights. Many argue that it is not enough. Exercising choice or claiming rights requires resources, power and knowledge. Rights to the protection of property and livelihood mean little if claiming such rights requires sufficient resources, power and knowledge to fight against powerful interests in formal political arenas. This is particularly so when powerful interests are portrayed as 'common interest' against the 'individual interests' of landowners and community members (Jones and Gaventa, 2002).

The institution or the person against whom the claims are made influences the outcomes of claiming rights. Thus the other side of the coin is an obligation to respond and be held accountable. Since the processes of claiming rights are inherently political and are played out as struggles between the interests, power and knowledge of differently positioned actors, the poor and marginalised citizen who are most disadvantaged in relations of power and resources are those less likely to be conscious of and able to assert their claims to rights (Jones and Gaventa, 2002).

While citizenship is bestowed on a person by the state, in a democratic set up state derives its legitimacy from the citizens who voluntarily allow themselves to be governed by their elected representatives and if citizens collectively refuse to offer the legitimacy the state loses its identity. So there is a relationship between a citizen and state.

The state could be defined as people organised for governance within a definite geographical territory. A nation is a body of people who possess some sense of a single communal identity, with a shared historical tradition, with major elements of common culture, and with a substantial proportion of them inhabiting an identifiable geographical unit. Nation-state describes a context in which the whole of a geographical area, that is the homeland for people who identify themselves as a community because of shared culture, history and probably language and ethnic character, is governed by one political system (David, 1993). The modern state is limited by national frontiers. We are members of the state within whose frontiers we are born and we can change our state allegiance or nationality only with the specific permission of the state to which we wish to belong.

To summarise, it can be said that citizenship means 'full membership of a community'. The membership entails participation by individuals in the determination of the conditions of their own association without any discrimination on the basis of caste, ethnicity, religion or gender. Citizenship is an over-arching civic identity produced by, and productive of a sense of belonging to a particular nation-state. Citizenship is a status, which bestows upon individuals equal rights and obligations, liberties and constraints, powers and responsibilities.

Citizenship is always a matter of belonging to a community. In this sense, the citizen is always a co-citizen, somebody who lives with others... The citizen in a democratic society is a person who has rights and duties. The first right is that of establishing the law; the first duty is that of respecting the law (Korsgaard, 2001).

A citizen may be regarded as a person who enjoys social, political, civil, economic and cultural rights, who is part of a nation-state and society and who has certain rights and obligations. An active citizen should be aware about the reality, be willing to work to change the reality, strive for common public good and promote collective efforts in their own community.

Leadership in the community context could be understood as a process of influencing and motivating people for bringing positive social change in favour of the marginalised sections of society. Leadership is that humanistic quality through which a person tries to fulfil the needs of the community by securing its cooperation and by establishing credibility. A citizen leader is an individual who has the ability to represent, to provide direction and to seek acceptance of a particular section or group. Furthermore, a leader has a direction, necessary energy and ability to influence for achieving common public good (desired social change). Therefore, in the process of promoting citizen leaders, the attributes of citizenship and leadership should be considered together. A good citizen leader should be an active citizen and should have the ability to shoulder responsibility.

The relationship between individual leadership and the collective is a dialectical one rather than hierarchical. The collective enables the nurturing of and provides grounds for ensuring the public accountability of leadership. It implies transparent and democratic decision-making within the collective, nurturing inter-personal and inter-associational relationships, honest sharing of how resources are mobilised and utilised and an appraisal of performance in relation to the stated objectives of the collective. The leadership is viewed as an interactive process with emphasis on intermediation capacity. It implies that the leadership would be able to play key roles bringing additional resources (information, material, expertise, fund etc.) from 'outside' agencies and ensuring the effective use of internal resources. It also means ensuring informed participation of individuals and different interest groups within the collective.

Citizen leaders are expected to play a variety of roles. However, the following two sets of roles are of prime importance.

Society Building

The first important function of a citizen leader is to contribute towards building a society, which promotes norms and values, related to associative and inclusive life. Citizen leaders must aspire for a society, which promotes equal justice to all the citizens, and does not allow any person to be discriminated against based on caste, class, ethnicity, religion, gender or age. Such a society can be achieved if citizen leaders play three important functions:

(*a*) *Facilitating Social Mobilisation*

It includes mobilisation of the poor and marginalised for collective action. Individual action is important in society, however, it may feel powerless in the face of powerful interests of advantaged sections in the society. Collective action and collective empowerment are powerful tools to change fundamental structural differences, injustice and discrimination in the society. The purpose of social mobilisation and collective action may range from engaging in self help construction work in a village or neighbourhood (like building a road or cleaning of ponds) to exercising rights over natural resources (like protecting forest or common property resources) to large-scale protest activities (like protest against acquisition of agricultural lands).

(*b*) *Overcoming Social Exclusion*

The society in its present form is deeply stratified and hierarchical. The structural and other forms of inequalities based on caste, class, ethnicity, religion, gender and age reinforce social exclusion. The resources, knowledge and opportunities in mainstream society are denied to the poor and marginalised. One of the functions of citizen leaders is to facilitate the poor and marginalised in accessing resources, knowledge and opportunities.

(c) *Managing Differences/Divisions*

In a democratic society plurality should be seen as an asset. However, when society is fragmented across hierarchical stratification it may lead to discrimination against and exploitation of the poor and marginalised that are at the bottom of the hierarchy. In both cases conflicts around interest and priority are inevitable. One of the functions of citizen leaders is to manage and resolve these conflicts within the community through negotiation and consensus. Citizen leaders must be sensitive enough to understand that the poor and marginalised feel powerless in such conflict situations unless an external facilitation process helps their interest to surface.

Engaging Governance Institutions

Governance is defined as the structures and processes of public decision making for mobilising public resources for the common public good like health, education, drinking water and other service provisions. Several public institutions are responsible for decision making related to the governance functions of a society. The citizen leaders must be aware about those public institutions and how their decisions related to common public good affect the lives of citizens. They should not only become aware about these structures and processes but also actively engage in decision making so as to espouse the interest of the poor and marginalised. The citizen leaders can engage governance institutions in the following three ways:

(a) *Amplifying Voice*

For generations the powerful people in society suppressed the voices of the poor and marginalised. In order to make governance institutions responsive to the needs and aspirations of *dalits*, tribals, women, children, persons with disabilities, their voices must be mobilised so that the decision makers can hear them. The citizen leaders should be able to amplify the collective voices of the poor and marginalised to get access to and control over resources, which support their livelihood; to get access to justice and social services.

(b) Engaging in Negotiation

In order to bring about changes in society, changes in the fundamental power relationship are absolutely necessary. The desired development outcomes cannot be achieved without altering the power differentials between dalit and non-dalit, tribal and non-tribal or women and men. The development outcomes cannot be sustainable with a massive power gulf between 'haves' and 'have nots'. Any alteration in the existing power relationship would require a process of negotiation between the two parties. Experience shows that external facilitation always helps the poor and marginalised in such negotiations with a view to changing the power relationships. The citizen leaders should act as external facilitators in such negotiations. They should encourage, mobilise, educate and build capacities of the poor and marginalised to negotiate with the powerful. The citizen leaders must understand that such political negotiations may involve conflicts. Therefore, these conflicts must be resolved by engaging in dialogue with the powerful.

(c) Enhancing Credibility

Years of exploitation, deceit and discrimination have made the poor and marginalised sceptical and frustrated about political leadership and governance institutions. In order to win the hearts of these citizens, the citizen leaders must earn credibility in the community. This credibility can only be earned when citizen leaders actively support the struggle of the poor and marginalised; amplifying their voices, negotiating with the powerful, overcoming social exclusion, fighting discrimination and mobilising their views in decision making processes and structures. The citizen leaders must earn a reputation in the community as "whatever this person says, she/he also does."

The citizen leaders should also earn a good reputation in the eyes of the representatives from governance institutions. It can be earned through personal attributes like honesty, punctuality, seriousness, understanding and sensitivity. The citizen leaders must be taken seriously by the political leadership and officials and seen as individuals dedicated to the cause of social change.

Society building and engaging governance institutions are

cyclic in process and are based on knowledge, attitude and the skill of citizen leaders. So in order to perform these roles we require different individuals or even one person who can perform multiple roles. In addition to this a leader should have clear vision/direction, for example, what is the basic purpose of organising regular SHGs meetings? Are they meant for economic development only or are they also providing a forum for discussion on other social issues emerging within the society? Further, how can these meetings be organised so that the excluded sections of society like the disabled, the disadvantaged (widows, *dalits*, tribals, old aged, minorities etc.) find a space to voice their views, along with the process of society building.

Active citizenship not only involves rights but also engaging with public institutions and reforming society. With some exceptions, very few citizens are participating in society building or interfacing with governance institutions. Citizens are by and large sceptical about participating in development efforts or claiming their rightful place in governance institutions. It is true that there are numerous barriers, which inhibit participation of citizens. Many citizens are grappling with everyday problems—poverty, livelihood, or lack of awareness and information. Active citizenship can overcome these barriers. Practicing active citizenship, especially by extremely disadvantaged and marginalised groups, requires systematic learning opportunities to create the confidence and the necessary capacities required to play this role effectively.

The Intervention

PRIA in association with other partners started the intervention on strengthening citizen leadership with the expectation that a cadre of enlightened leadership and their networks would facilitate meaningful interface between citizen associations and various governance institutions to articulate their demands and access their rights and entitlements. The programme although initiated as a stand-alone intervention (in 2002), became a cornerstone approach in the overall strategic and programmatic framework of PRIA from the beginning of 2003. According to the programmatic framework of PRIA "Governance where People Matter" strengthening citizen collectives and citizen leadership was seen as instrument to strengthen the bottom-up demand for accountable and transparent local governance institutions, including Panchayati Raj Institutions and Urban Local Bodies. PRIA and partners took a considered decision for not creating new local level institutions. Efforts were made as a first step, to identify existing local community based organisations and their leadership. Therefore, women SHGs, Mahila Mandals, Youth Organisations, various project initiated committees like Watershed Committees, Water User Associations, Village Education Committees, Community Development Societies (formed under the Central Government sponsored programme on Swarna Jayanti Saheri Rozgar Yojana), organisation of Ex-Servicemen and many others were trained and mobilised. The existing community leaders were given training and educational input to act as citizen leaders; to make interface with various other community based institutions as well as various state agencies and local governance institutions.

The interventions in the first two years (2002-2004) specifically encouraged and targeted women leadership. As a result, a large number of SHGs and Mahila Mandals were included in the intervention. However, in the later years leadership of men particularly that of youth was also targeted while a consistent focus remained on developing women leadership.

A multi-track approach to capacity building for the citizen leaders and citizen collectives was undertaken to achieve the objectives. The following is a brief description of capacity building approaches.

(*a*) *Preparing Profiles of Citizen Collectives*: As a prerequisite to engage, efforts were made to map the existing community based organisations to identify potential citizen leaders. A comprehensive database was prepared for all the Blocks and Municipalities where PRIA and partners were working. It was quickly realised that there are several active citizens in a given community who take part in a variety of collective actions or become helpful to other fellow members in a variety of ways. The community members recognise their contributions. Efforts were made to contact these citizens to weave the programme around their existing capacities.

(*b*) *Training for Citizen Collectives and Citizen Leaderships*: Series of short duration (one day to three days) training programmes for a variety of citizen collectives and citizen leadership were organised in most of the locations. The purpose of these training programmes ranged from building perspective on local governance and citizenship to enhancing skills on group management, local level planning, Gram Sabha and Ward Sabha mobilisation, gender justice etc. In many places film shows were organised as a learning tool. The purpose was to share stories of struggles by various other groups and to initiate discussion within the collective and community.

(c) *Regular Meetings and Ongoing Support*: The intervention required regular meetings and ongoing support to the collectives and their leadership. In many places counselling, guidance and support to individual leaders proved to be useful. The members of the citizen collectives were provided support generally related to their daily needs. Since the collectives were in a nascent stage in almost all locations, the collectives and leadership often demanded handholding support.

(d) *Exposure Visits*: The purpose of organising the exposure visit was to facilitate learning for the citizen leaders on various development initiatives, which could be replicated by them. Since only select individuals could participate in those exposure visits, efforts were made that the learning acquired by the citizen leaders could be shared with other members of the collectives and community at large.

(e) *Citizen Centred Interface Workshop/Meeting*: One of the expected outcomes of strengthening citizen collectives and citizen leadership intervention was to enable effective interface between citizens and governance institutions. In many locations various interface meetings and workshops were facilitated to initiate dialogues. The purposes of these interface meetings ranged from initiating dialogues on specific development problems to disseminating information among citizen collectives.

(f) *Organising Campaigns*: Series of campaigns have been organised on Pre-Election Voters' Awareness, Citizens' Participation in Birth and Death Registration and Solid Waste Management. Folk medium like songs, dances and street plays were extensively used in these campaigns. Efforts were made to build ownership through involving citizen collectives and leadership, right from planning to implementation of these campaigns.

(g) *Facilitating Networks of Citizen Collectives*: Facilitating and catalysing networks of citizen collectives with specific focus on women, *dalits* and tribals were the explicit objectives of civil society building interventions at the district and lower levels. The initiatives have started showing favourable results in many locations while posing deeper challenges—to further strengthen these collectives.

Implications of Capacity Building

The pursuit of multi-track capacity building approaches and numerous interventions paid dividend to engage citizen leaders in initiating range of collective as well as individual actions at the community level. They not only undertook these tasks voluntarily but also led the collectives in social and political action from the front. Though engagements varied in nature, context and intensity a common thread could be found.

(*i*) *Initiating Self-Help Actions*: The citizen leaders themselves realised as well as caused the realisation among the community that they were not dependent on the state for each and every development activity. They became instrumental in mobilising the citizens to undertake activities like renovating school buildings, contributing labour to build roads, cleaning of ponds etc. In many locations the citizens acted first by taking developmental initiatives and then the state authorities extended their support.

(*ii*) *Engaging in Bottom-up Local Level Planning*: Despite decades of rhetoric on participatory bottom-up planning process, the Indian planning system remained by and large top-down. The 73rd and 74th Constitutional Amendment Act created opportunities for elected local governance institutions like Panchayats and Municipalities to initiate bottom-up planning. However, denial of resources and capacities to these institutions by higher tiers of governance institutions has been perpetuating the old traditions and power relationships. Notwithstanding these denials, in a number of locations the citizen leaders mobilised fellow citizens to prepare local level development plans at the Ward and Gram Panchayat level in collaboration with the Panchayats or Municipalities. They organised extensive consultations at the village and Mohalla level with other citizen groups and identified development priorities of the citizens. Detailed plans have been prepared and shared with the local governance institutions to incorporate the development priorities in the annual plans. In some of these locations many citizen leaders not only ensured that the development priorities were incorporated in the plans of Panchayats and Municipalities but also actively remained engaged with these institutions till the actual work was initiated or completed. The perseverance of the citizen leaders paid off to the communities and the entire experience of engaging instilled lots of confidence into them to prepare for further engagements in the future.

(iii) Mobilising Gram Sabhas and Ward Sabhas: Despite Constitutional provisions for mandatory Gram Sabhas at the Gram Panchayat level, much needs to be desired in terms of convening them as per provisions. A variety of reasons adversely affected the effectiveness of Gram Sabhas which have been discussed in detail elsewhere (PRIA, 2001). Prominent among them are lack of information and apathy from the elected representatives as well as citizenry. Many citizen leaders after equipping themselves with relevant information and understanding acted as change agents by disseminating relevant information related to Gram Sabha dates, venue etc. to other Gram Sabha members. They articulated different development issues in the Gram Sabha and tried to improve the conduct of Gram Sabhas. Many of them have successfully chased the Block or District level authorities to announce the dates and venues in advance so that they could pass on the information to other citizens.

The urban citizens of small and medium size towns of India are still deprived by any Constitutional Amendment of similar participatory mechanisms like Gram Sabha in the urban locations. Notwithstanding such a disadvantage the citizens from many urban locations have formed Mohalla Samitis or Ward Sabhas with the active facilitation from PRIA and Partners. The citizen leaders after being trained and armed with information took the initiative to convene Ward Sabhas. They collectively identified the local development priorities and interacted with the elected councillors to incorporate these priorities in the plans and programmes of Municipalities. The elected councillors have also found new citizen platforms in the form of Ward Sabhas or Mohalla Samitis to garner political support for the development of work in their respective Wards.

(iv) Engaging with Line Departments for Accessing Services: Despite making the elected Panchayats and Municipalities

Constitutionally responsible for provisioning basic services to the citizens, the sectoral line departments like drinking water, health, education etc. have remained the main service providers. They have also largely remained unaccountable to the elected local governance institutions and citizens. This left citizens with no options other than to engage with these sectoral service provisioning departments to demand for services that they require on a daily basis. There were numerous occasions where citizen leaders collectively in collaboration with the elected representatives demanded basic services from these departments. The issues they addressed ranged from drinking water to the functioning of primary schools, provisions of anganwadi centres in the villages, to roads and so on. These numerous interfaces have not always resulted into successful service provisioning due to deep-rooted unequal power relationships and unaccountable and non-responsive behaviour of the government officials. However, the engagements made for a modest beginning of exercising and articulating the basis rights of the citizens, particularly of the poor and the marginalised.

(*v*) *Engaging with Governance Institutions to Address the Issues of Social Injustice or Social Discrimination*: The issues related to injustice and discrimination were not new in the society. However, the situation got exacerbated when the institutions of governance became instrumental for their perpetuity. In many situations, the women, dalits and tribals became subjected to atrocities by the powerful. On numerous occasions the citizen leaders from women, *dalit* and tribal groups after being enlightened through training, exposure and collectivisation, refused to accept this sub-human subordination. They got mobilised and protested against discrimination as well as against the inaction of public authorities. The issue of domestic violence was taken up to the higher level authorities by many women's groups in many locations. The issue of land rights to dalits have been addressed through their own organisations.

(*vi*) *Participating in Panchayat and Municipality Elections*: PRIA and partners in many states have launched massive campaigns prior to the elections to Panchayati Raj Institutions and Municipalities. The purpose of these campaigns has been to educate the citizens and contestants of local governance elections on free and fair electoral processes. The citizen groups and leaders trained through this intervention participated in huge numbers in these Pre-Election Voters' Awareness Campaigns both in urban and rural locations. They participated in the enumeration of voters' list, distribution of informational materials, organising "kala jathas" and also in door-to-door educational campaigns. A good number of citizen leaders either supported other credible citizen leaders to contest elections or they themselves contested the elections. These campaigns proved to be an excellent learning ground for the citizen leaders to participate in the local political processes and to gain visibility in the community.

Conclusion

Recent trends in the socio-political arena characterised by local level decentralisation and mechanisms for the political participation of the hitherto marginalised and poor have provided a new climate to foster citizen leadership and citizen associations. Largely untapped both by the governance institutions and civil society, very little input in the form of structured educational and mobilisational interventions has been provided to strengthen and encourage these leadership initiatives. The intervention of PRIA and partners on strengthening citizen leadership proved to be an exception in this regard.

By and large, most of the development initiatives by the governments, bilateral and multilateral donors and intermediary civil society organisations have resulted in the formation of community groups or associations to ensure the responsibility for delivering specific programmes. The community level user groups thus created were mostly treated as an alternative vehicle of service delivery and cost sharing. Although these initiatives have created a good amount of "social capital" at the community level, the process of conscientisation—the mantra of the voluntary actions in the 70s—has not been adequately addressed through these community formations. The intervention to foster citizen leadership has helped to bring back the process of conscientisation of a large number of groups and individuals by collective reflection of the reality and taking appropriate actions.

Till date, the perspectives on individual rights have, by and large, guided the capacity building interventions. Although a necessity, it was not sufficient to enable citizens to assert and interface with other intermediary development agencies including intermediary civil society organisations and government institutions. The perspective of collectivisation and engagement of the citizens in collective action has not been addressed in a systematic manner. Strong leadership at the grassroots level fostered through this intervention has made significant headway to effectively interface with other institutions, access information and other resources from government, local bodies, civil society organisations and market institutions.

A critical balance between developing perspective on citizenship and governance and honing up "social skills" (e.g. communication, mobilisation, managing the collectives etc.) became the basis of designing and nurturing capacity building support to these citizen leaders and collectives. This approach paid considerable dividend as evidenced from the key results achieved through these interventions.

A wide range of capacity building interventions, including structured educational interventions like trainings, workshops, conferences, regular hand holding support, exposure visits and networking provided to nourish, develop and strengthen citizen leadership, proved to be very useful. A multi-track approach to capacity building has been far more effective than a single-track approach, like only training or only campaign. The challenge, however, was to make all the approaches relevant for the learning of a large number of semi-literate or illiterate women and men.

REFERENCES

Jones, Emma and John Gaventa, (2002), *Concepts of Citizenship: A Review*, IDS Development Bibliography 19, IDS, UK.

Kohli, Atul, (1991), *Democracy and Discontent: India's Growing Crisis of Governability*, Cambridge, Cambridge University Press.

Korsgaard, Ove, (2001), Why Has Citizenship Become Such A Vogue Word? in *Learning for Democratic Citizenship* edited by Ove Korsgaard, Shirley Walters, Randi Andersen. The Danish University of Education, The University of Western Cape and The Association for World Education.

Rai, Manoj, *et al.* (2001), *The State of Panchayat: A Participatory Perspective*, Samskriti Prakashan, New Delhi.

Robertson, David, (1993), *The Penguin Dictionary of Politics*, London, UK.

Tandon, Rajesh and Kaustuv Kanti Bandyopadhyay, (2001), *Capacity Building of Southern NGOs: Lessons from International Forum on Capacity Building*, PRIA, New Delhi.

Tandon, Rajesh and Ranjita Mohanty, (2002), *Civil Society and Governance*, Samskriti Publication, New Delhi.

The Commonwealth Foundation, (1999), *Citizens and Governance: Civil Society in the New Millennium*, The Commonwealth Foundation, UK.

Uphoff, Norman, (1986), *Local Institutional Development: An Analytical Sourcebook with Cases*, Kumararian Press, USA.

9

Innovations in Participation

Anju Dwivedi and *Namrata Jaitli*

Participation: Taking a Walk Down History

Within development debates and discourses one concept which has gained significance since the last four decades is "participation" or "popular participation". In the initial years, the contribution of people's participation towards equitable and sustainable development was supported by the work of a number of social activists, field workers, community based organisations and social scientists.

The government controlled, growth oriented development model of sixties failed to effectively address needs of the poor and marginalized. This paved way for an alternative people centric development model, wherein the marginalized and poor participate in defining their goal of development and in being active agents of change. Recognition by facilitators of participatory research that popular knowledge and collective action are important vehicles for empowerment, made important contribution to the practice of participation (Tandon, 1996). Number of social movements on livelihood, social justice and women's rights brought forward the issue of citizen's and community rights. They, along with key national and international conferences, helped bring community participation as an important component in development initiatives of government and Voluntary Development Organisations (FAO, 1979).

Participatory methodologies like participatory rural appraisal and participatory monitoring gained significance in the eighties, assisting the incorporation of participatory philosophy to project cycles. The eighties was home to the ecological movement, which introduced the need for environmentally sustainable development and women's movement which highlighted the need to mainstream gender in development.

The nineties witnessed growing recognition, by number of international aid agencies and the national government, that community participation is important for effective and efficient development (Oakely, 1994). In India, development projects and policies, cutting across sectors, had participation as an essential component. Democratic decentralisation, in India, gained impetus in the nineties, with the 73rd and 74th Constitutional Amendment Act, 1993. These Acts laid the basis for Panchayati Raj Institutions and Muncipalities as institutions of self-governance in the country, thus bringing to focus the importance of participation in the sphere of governance. Late nineties and early 21st century's approaches to participation began to stress upon the need to treat citizens not as mere users or choosers of services, rather makers and shapers of policies. This involved citizens' active engagement with the state and policy makers to develop policies which were pro-poor (PRIA, 1999).

The Many Forms of Participation

Tracing Conceptual Growth

In keeping with the historical context, we can state that in the seventies the focus of participation was more on mobilisation and conscientisation (Friere, 1972). Emphasis was on strengthening popular knowledge, popular movements and people's organisations, and working towards social transformation (Hall, 1982). Participation was seen as an end in itself, as a process which unfolds over time, and its purpose was to develop and strengthen the capabilities of rural people to intervene more directly in development initiatives and control their own development.

In the eighties and nineties, the focus of participation, however, became more *instrumental in nature*. Its role was carved more within the development projects and programme framework (Rahnema, 1997). Focus was more on participation in projects, with participation taken as means to an end, to enable harnessing of existing physical, economic and social resources of the rural people to achieve the previously established objectives of the development programme more efficiently and effectively (Oakley and Marsden, 1984).

A critical assessment of the trends will show that by late nineties and early 2000 the nature of participation, along with its mobilisational and instrumental role, has become more *political*. From a development perspective, participation has slowly entered the *arena of governance* (Tandon, 2002). *Participation* now includes action by citizens and citizen collectives to influence decisions of the state and make it more accountable. Moving beyond representative democracy, wherein citizens influence the representatives of the state, participation also includes direct ways by which citizen's influence and exercise control in governance (Gaventa and Camilo, 1999). There is growing emphasis on citizens demanding policy reform and accountability, and transparency of institutions of governance (PRIA, 1999). Participation and accountability thus can no more be seen in isolation.

Tracking Methodological Progress

The conceptual growth of *participation* has had some very significant methodological implications. Historically, different methods have evolved to ensure instrumental and political functions of effective participation. Most popular and effective among them are those facilitated by the tradition of participatory research and participatory rural appraisal (now called Participatory Learning and Action).

Participatory Research (PR) is actively rooted in the history of people's struggle for survival and growth. As a concept it, however, evolved as a critique to the dominant system of knowledge production, as perpetuated by the social science research methodologies and various disciplines which were used extensively in the development policies of the state (Hall, 1982). Participatory research with grassroot groups ensures legitimisation of their knowledge system and facilitates their involvement in creating new knowledge to improve their reality. This process is 'empowering' as it facilitates a process of learning among the poor; organises and mobilises them to take action to improve their lives (Tandon, 1997). PR methods include group discussions, community seminars, dialogue, enumeration, popular theatre, role plays, educational camps, learning circles (PRIA, 1995).

Participatory Rural Appraisal (PRA) emerged in mid 1980s as "a family of approaches and methods to enable rural people to share, enhance and analyse their knowledge of life and conditions, to plan and to act"(Chambers, 1992). PRA methods are distinguished by shared visual representation and analysis by local people. Some common methods and approaches are mapping and modeling, time line, trend and change analysis, Venn diagramming, well-being ranking, matrix scoring and ranking.

The following trends best describe some of the methodological progress and innovations in the practice of participation:

From Micro to Macro Influence

In the eighties and nineties, the influence of participatory methods (i.e. PRA) was more "micro" in nature: i.e. enhancing participation in development projects; ensuring collective take up of issues at the community level. Demand for "upscaling" participation and ensuring participation in development policies became evident in the nineties. We saw emergence of processes like community's participation in developing Country Assistance Strategy (CAS); monitoring participation in development institutions like World Bank etc. PR, PRA and other participatory approaches thus were adapted to address these macro demands i.e. as seen in emergence of Participatory Poverty Analysis (PPA) and Multi-stakeholder dialogues (MSD).

From Development to Governance

As participatory approaches are scaled from projects to policies, they inevitably enter the arena of governance. There is now a growing recognition that participation can only become effective as it engages with issues of institutional change. It is interesting to note that the early use of methods of participation (i.e. popular theatre) was more for conscientisation and mobilisation; it then shifted to facilitating development intervention (i.e. PRA methods); and in recent years it has increasingly focused on addressing issues of governance (i.e. community monitoring, multistakeholder dialogues). The roles of the primary stakeholder, thus, progressed from being a "participant" to a "beneficiary", and more recently to a "citizen".

From Primary to Multi-stakeholders

The earlier methodological thrust was on facilitating participation of the poor and marginalized. Upscaling participation generated the need to also involve other key stakeholders, without affecting the interest of the primary stakeholder. In recent years there is growing focus on participation of multi-stakeholders to ensure effective development and good governance (i.e. Multi-stakeholder dialogues).

Facilitating Innovations in Participatory Methodology: PRIA's Experience

Since last 25 years, PRIA has evolved its programmatic focus in responding to changing contexts as well as in anticipating emerging trends. At the core of PRIA's work has been the promotion of participation and empowerment of the poor, the oppressed especially of women, dalits and tribals. PRIA's work has spanned micro-action in local settings at the grassroot level to national and international initiatives on the same issues.

PRIA's philosophy and its history are closely linked to the inception of the philosophy and approach of PR. In response to emerging trends, as mentioned above, in recent years we have actively facilitated practice of two innovations in participatory methodologies: they are *Community Monitoring* and *Multi-Stakeholder Dialogue*. Both these methodologies are build on the principles of participatory research

Community Monitoring

The term Community Monitoring gained wide recognition in nineties when it was recognized that under the *garb* of participation. The actual control of management of development projects remained with the project officials. It became evident that for development projects to be truly effective and sustainable community's participation was important not only in planning and implementation, but also in monitoring and evaluating the projects.

Monitoring is defined as the checking, collecting and analysis of information about current project developments to improving implementation, performance and results. In essence it means comparing the actual situation and then taking action to bring reality and expectations together (Shordt, 2000). The term Community Monitoring signifies involvement of the community in the monitoring process. It is a way of learning from and with community members and other stakeholders, to investigate, analyse and evaluate constraints and opportunities and make informed and timely decisions on issues of common community concern. It has an inbuilt problem solving and action component.

Key steps involved in facilitating Community Monitoring would broadly include: identification of key issues and problems; identification of key stakeholders who are interested in and influenced by the particular issue at hand; building indicators to track progress on addressal of those issues; collection of data against the indicators; analysis of the data and to disseminate the findings and use the findings for corrective action to address the issue at hand. As the name suggests, the community should be involved in all the steps as active participants. Recent arguments in support of monitoring brings to focus that action is an integral part of monitoring, without action monitoring becomes reporting only.

Key Principles of Community Monitoring include:

- People readily monitor those issues which concern them the most. All issues related to the project, thus may not be considered relevant for the community to monitor.
- Community Monitoring is an important means for facilitating community empowerment and collective action. People possess the ability to engage in investigation of issues related to them, reflect on those issues and think of possible actions. Monitoring should lead to problem solving and if it remains confined to serving only decision-making needs of a small management group, the purpose gets defeated.
- People have enormous capacity to improve their community based systems and practices. Those capacities have to be recognized and properly utilised.
- Capacity building required at each step is the key to

monitoring. It is an ongoing process rather than a one time activity. This helps the marginalized groups to develop confidence in their ability to improve the situation through meaningful action as also to take corrective action or innovate, wherever needed.

- Facilitators of community monitoring also need to build their own capacity to facilitate a process, which empowers the people to improve situations and effectively manage the resources.
- Community Monitoring systems are built up gradually, beginning with limited number of concerns or issues.

Key Approaches in Community Monitoring

Various approaches began to be used from nineties where people are engaged to monitor the development interventions and public services.

(a) *Report Cards*: Report Cards are a means of collecting feedback from users of public services. They are an "aggregate" of public ratings on different aspects of service quality, built on scientific random-sample surveys of users. Report Cards can be used in many sectors and themes, such as the quality of health care services in public hospitals, service delivery of education in government schools, public distribution system, impact of information technology, impact of economic liberalisation on small and medium industries, irrigation systems in the farm sector, etc.

The Report Cards approach is based on the assumption that the citizens already have access to the information they need for assessing their degree of satisfaction with services or government. It provides a means of ensuring accountability in contexts where people do not want or cannot commit themselves to full "participation", but are happy to provide this sort of market research response and have it mediated and fed back to service providers or local government on their behalf (Citizen's Monitoring: Report cards).

The use of Report Cards enhances performance management and accountability in public service delivery. The experience in India has demonstrated that after having used Report Cards twice in one city with an interval of a few years, there was a greater awareness among both the citizens (users) and the government agencies (service providers), dialogues with service providers for reform had been established and service delivery had partially been improved.

The process requires the involvement of experts for the design of the survey, to monitor its implementation and to draft the report at the end of the exercise. The basic critique of this approach from Community Monitoring lens is that engagement of community remains that of respondents and voicing out concerns through surveyors to the government officials or project authorities. In this way, community participates indirectly in the whole process but gets benefited if the social audits lead to improvement in the quality of services.

(b) *Social Audit*: Social Audit is a direct engagement of people with the government and other stakeholders as opposed to the Report Card method.

> "Social Audit is a process in which, details of the resource, both financial and non-financial, used by public agencies for development initiatives are shared with the people, often through a public platform. Social Audits allow people to enforce accountability and transparency, providing the ultimate users an opportunity to scrutinize development initiatives" (Vision Foundation, 2005).

Social Audit focuses on people's audit of development initiatives, builds the capacity of people, encourages local democracy and community participation, benefits the disadvantaged groups, promotes collective decision-making and sharing responsibilities and ensures accountability.

For any Social Audit, it is important that people have access to information on development interventions that are taking place in their communities. Therefore, information dissemination and awareness of people on issues is very important. Only then can people use Right to Information to obtain details of the works carried out by a Government Department or the manner in which the money is spent by that Department.

Various Civil Society Organisations have undertaken campaigns to engage people in monitoring processes and conduct Social Audits. MKSS (Mazdoor Kisan Sangarsh Samiti), an NGO working in Tilonia, Ajmer, in Rajasthan spearheaded the campaign,

"Hamara Paisa, Hamara Hisaab" and organised people to secure minimum wages and get the muster rolls. Similarly, Parivartan too engaged people in monitoring the development interventions by using Right to Information.

Strengthening Citizen's Monitoring in Jamtara (Jharkhand)

PRIA undertook a process of engagement of citizens in monitoring the development interventions. A project was identified which was on providing non-formal education (NFE) to working children in the three blocks of Jarmundi, Saraiyahat and Jamtara (Jamtara attained the status of district in 2001). All these blocks had high incidence of child labour in *bidi*-making, restaurants, brick-kilns, rag-picking and other trades/industries. These NFE schools purported to educate working children up to class III and then mainstream them into government-run primary schools. It was perceived that participation of parents as stakeholders was practically non-existent to the extent that they had little or no idea about the basic provisions of the project. Citizens monitoring was clearly viewed as a mode of enhancing citizen participation in this project and generating valuable learning experiences that could also be utilised by other civil society organisations in Jharkhand.

The exploration of the Bal Shramik Vidyalayas yielded some useful insights into the actual working of the schools and it allowed an opportunity to understand the various concerns of the stakeholders.

A series of block and village level meetings with parents were followed by meetings with local civil society groups/activists and school teachers and generated a lot of optimism. PRIA built the capacity of teachers and facilitated workshops. A committee of parents was formed to monitor the quality of education. The workshop helped the participants to build indicators and modalities of monitoring the role and responsibilities of monitors. Indicators identified were: the presence or absence of teachers; serving of midday meals to the children; and routine health checks for children by the local health department. It was also agreed to devise a suitable format to record data, keeping in view the limited ability of parents in recording detailed observations. Data was to be recorded on simply designed but ingenious worksheets with suitable pictures/drawings depicting the three broad indicators.

Parents collected data on the indicators regularly and met the circle officer and apprised him of their findings, concerns and suggestions for improved school functioning, such as slackness on the part of doctors in conducting routine health checks, difficulties in the running of one school due to a vacant teacher's post, need for

(*Contd.*)

(*Contd.*)

roof construction/repair in another school and sports equipment for all schools. The process of engaging themselves in monitoring the working of schools itself acted as a mechanism that not only built the confidence of the parents, but also imparted the necessary rudimentary skills of negotiating with government officials. The committee members met the First Medical Officer and the Circle Officer armed with reliable data, and apprised them of the working of the schools along with their concerns and suggestions.

Enthused by a constructive dialogue with government officials and to share their experiences, the parents' committee decided to organise some structured events. On the request of parents, one such meeting was presided over by the CO of Jamtara. The parents apprised him of their findings, concerns and suggestions for the improved functioning of the schools. For example, slackness on the part of doctors in conducting routine medical check-ups of students, difficulties in the running of the Pandemic centre due to a teacher's post being vacant, construction of the roof at the Amlachatar centre, making sports goods available to all schools, and admitting students against vacant seats etc., were put before him.

The parents put up a number of demands before him. They demanded that since they are recognised as BPL families, they be provided loans against the Self-employment Guarantee programme for small earning opportunities, like mat/basket making or preparing puffed rice. They also demanded that they be given priority under *Rashtriya Parivar Labh Yojana* (RPLY), *Vriddha Pension Yojana* and *Indira Awas Yojana*. Besides, they also demanded that drinking water facilities should be provided in all school centres through wells or hand pumps. Responding to these, the CO not only acceded to some of the demands but also focused on some other opportunities under government programmes available to the parents. He also utilised the event to take follow-up action on some of the concerns of the parents and the teachers.

Viewed from a broader angle, this and other such meetings can help citizens to understand the way government business is conducted and also the skills of negotiating with officials.

Source: Anand, 2002.

Emerging Issues

Practice has shown that by and large the participation of community in monitoring is inadequate and ambigious. Many development practitioners are finding it difficult to include Participatory Monitoring in their projects. Some are of the opinion that only PRA tools can facilitate community monitoring, as they feel that other techniques and formats like LFA and RBM are too rigid to allow space for participatory monitoring.

It has also been observed that though community is being engaged in the collection of data and in preliminary analysis, but their contribution is restricted in taking corrective action. It has thus, become important for practitioners to see that all the stakeholders (community, NGOs, Government agencies) engage themselves in the process and take efforts to improve the current situation. This also ensures process of accountability and transparency of each actor.

Multi-Stakeholder Dialogue

As concerns about good governance and state responsiveness grow, questions about how citizens engage and make demands on the state also comes to the fore. Multi-Stakeholder Dialogue (MSD) has become an important vehicle to facilitate the same. As an approach, it is inclusive in nature and includes people/citizens/ local governance institutions/state and national governments and CSOs, including donors to think and act. In this process, all the parties engage in a facilitative process to make changes possible. Powerless negotiate for getting legitimate space for participation while powerful (decision makers) attempt to create space and institutionalize structures for them to participate (Tandon, 2002).

Multi-Stakeholder Dialogues (MSDs) are being used as part of many international policy-making efforts. Officials and unofficial representatives are being brought together to build relationships, set agendas for future official and unofficial dialogues and even to generate packages of proposals or recommendations. MSDs provide a forum in which official and unofficial stakeholders can talk face-to-face. Many MSDs are convened to generate specific proposals for responding to pressing problems.

There are a number of reasons that multilateral organisations have organised MSDs over the past decade. The objectives tend to fall under five headings: relationship building, gathering and exchanging information, agenda setting, brainstorming and problem solving, and consensus building (Susskind E., Lawrence *et al.* 2003).

Rational for MSD

Relationship Building: Improve relationships among conflicting parties—many holding fundamentally different values—and improving the public legitimacy of the process, its products, and its conveners. MSDs that are undertaken solely for public relations, however, often have difficulty in maintaining their legitimacy under stakeholder scrutiny.

Information Sharing: Gathering existing, and creating new information relevant to the issues being considered—including factual analyses as well as analysis on the spectrum of stakeholder values. Clarifying areas of disagreement and agreement.

Agenda Setting: Identifying key problems, framing future deliberations, planning future actions and deliberations. The participants plan together what problems need to be explored in future deliberations and may make a plan on how to address those issues using more collaborative dialogues that they plan and perhaps implement, collectively.

Brainstorming and Problem Solving: Jointly analyzing problems with the purpose of recommending possible options. The participants seek to identify viable policy options for the consideration of decision makers, without seeking to agree on which options are best.

Consensus Building: Brainstorming and problem solving for the purpose of developing a joint recommendation or a "package" that meets the needs of all key stakeholders.

The intention is that a consensus among the participants will exert a strong influence on "official" decision-making.

Source: Multi-Stakeholder at the Global Scale by Lawrence E. Susskind *et al.*, Netherlands.

MSD creates a common platform among different stakeholders through dialogue, discussion and debate and to initiate joint action planning. It is based on the principles of mutual accountability and equity in communication amongst stakeholders. An open communication and a level of transparency, basic trust is desired for the people who come together on a common platform to participate meaningfully. Development problems cannot be solved by a single actor, as already specified earlier in this chapter. The problems are multilayered and multifaceted and need solutions of those kinds which is possible only when diverse actors can get engaged together to solve the problems.This approach imposes trust on the perspective of participation involving civil society and community to address policies which affect them directly.

Key Features of MSD

- The MSD can take place effectively when different stakeholders coming together have a common issue of concern on the type of dialogue and suitable action to be undertaken to address the issue.
- As a first step, it requires identification of stakeholders and the issue on which an MSD would take place; idea of possible action points which can lead to future effort and joint action wherever possible.
- Issues of common concerns can emerge when all the stakeholders have some basic understanding of the issue on which everyone has joined hands.
- Sometimes it is desirable to facilitate processes of capacity building of less powerful groups before MSD to make them participate effectively in the process.
- As a process, MSD also witnesses imbalance of power equations which can be detrimental if not dealt with right from the beginning. Partially powerlessness can be addressed by having effective strategies of capacity building and information dissemination so that actors who are important but may have lesser influence can speak out and be listened.
- There could be different types of MSDs. It covers a wide range of structures and levels of engagements. MSDs can be undertaken in big forums, at the macro level with policy makers and international donors, and it can also be contexualised in the field, and at the grassroots. Within the project cycle framework this method can be applied either at the beginning—in the planning, implementation and monitoring phase, or in each of the above, depending upon the exact purpose of the MSD.

Gearing Up for Newer Challenges

Having reviewed the history and current practice of participation and participatory methodologies, it becomes imperative to assess the impact of this concept on issues of development and governance.The result is not so heartening. Despite a history of participation in development and policy, poverty, discrimination,

MSD on Girl Child Education

PRIA conducted an action based study to assess the status of girl child education in Mewada Kala Gram Panchayat of Kekri Panchayat Samiti (Ajmer) and to take corrective action. The study brought out the fact that admissions take place but the retention of children remains a problem and that is significant in the case of girls. The study also pointed out towards lack of sufficient teachers in the school, toilet and drinking water facilities the condition of school building and unavailability of proper classrooms. The provision of mid day meal was also explored and it was found that there was no definite place for cooking the meal. As it was cooked in open it invited dust and dirt on the cooked food, in affecting children's health. The study was able to assess the role of committees (SDMC) formed under the project and pointed towards the inactive participation of the members of the committee. The study highlighted the following issues:

1. Due to responsibility of domestic chores, girl children drop out more than boys.
2. Teachers are compelled to show 100 per cent enrolment despite the drop outs.
3. Toilets are closed in the school, therefore, students (especially girls) prefer not to come.
4. Unavailability of female teachers in the school also discourage girl children from going to school.
5. Lack of drinking water facilities, improper fencing of the boundary forces children to be in dangerous situations, since they go to far off places to drink water and cross the roads which increase the risk of accidents.
6. Even though the schools remain understaffed, they are engaged in arranging the mid-day meals in the school. They are also engaged in various kinds of surveys which also takes away their time and thus, education suffers.

A multi-stakeholder dialogue was planned on the day of Gram Sabha (February 2006) meeting in Mewadakala Panchayat where the study findings were presented before 225 people. The participants included elected representatives, parents, teachers, other community members, government officials including SDM, Assistant Engineer.

The following action points emerged in the Gram Sabha meeting:

1. Education Committee of Panchayats to take responsibility of monitoring and developing commitment for increasing enrolment of girl children and checking the dropout.
2. The drinking water facilities to be arranged in the school by installing handpumps and taps by PHED.

(*Contd.*)

(*Contd.*)

3. Unutilised funds of TSC to be used for construction of more toilets.
4. Toilets of the school to be open throughout and for cleaning it regularly, funds (Rs. 5) to be generated from the community.
5. To extend the school building under SSA.

One of the Panchayat Samiti members, who was also the member of SDMC in a school at Surimata took the initiative by meeting with BEO (Block Education Officer) to appoint teachers. The Pradhan of Panchayat Samiti ensured that she would follow up seriously and work with other members to ensure to quality education to students.

Source: Dwivedi, 2006.

social exclusion, marginalisation still exists. People continue to be treated as voters and beneficiaries and not as "citizens".

Some emerging concerns and challenges for participation and related methodologies thus, include:

- Growing danger that the "instrumental" role of participation will override its "social transformational" and "political" role. There is thus a need to balance both the roles which would include ensuring that community and citizens participate effectively in development interventions and also have effective voice on issues of governance. The instrumental role of participation also has its own challenges. In large number of cases participation of the poor in large scale, as well as micro projects, has not been effectively ascertained. Assurance and commitment to ensure quality of participation in these interventions thus, becomes a challenge for the future.
- Growing incidence of the growth of participatory techniques, at the cost of the underlying philosophy. Misuse and manipulation of these techniques, with pursuit for "right" and "quick" tools and methods of participation by some practitioners, educators, policy makers is also on the rise.The challenge thus, is to demystify participatory processes and methods; to innovate and use the methods without undermining the underlined philosophy.

Capacity building of practitioners of participatory methodologies thus becomes important.

- Inadequate emphasis on strengthening the capacities of the poor and marginalized to effectively participate in issues of development and governance. In the absence of the same, the impact of participatory methodologies gets diluted. The deep rooted attitude of dependency of the poor frustrates efforts of promoting participation and accountability through community monitoring and multi-stakeholder dialogue. It is, therefore, important that along with the spread of participatory methodologies, due effort to strengthen capacities of poor need to be made. External agencies can be facilitators in strengthening engagement at the local level.
- A compartmentalised view of social change, wherein participation is seen within the limited context of given programme and project. For participatory methodologies to yield the desired results, there is also a need to be sensitive to and if possible to address the wider structural, administrative, organisational and socio-cultural factors which are influencing the community's and citizen's participation.

Addressal of some of these issues, we feel, would assist participation and its methodologies to effectively address the developmental and existential challenges facing the society and its citizens today.

REFERENCES

Anand, Pankaj, (2002), *Experiences and Lessons of Strengthening Citizen's Monitoring in Jharkhand: A Citizenship Perspective*, Delhi:, PRIA.

Bandhyopadhay, Kaustuv K., (2004), *Multistakeholder Dialogue: Guide Book*, Delhi: PRIA.

Capsian, Richards *et al.* (2004), *Practical Approaches to Participation, Socio-Economic Research Programme (SERP)*, UK: The Macaulay Institute.

Chambers, Robert, (1992), Rural Appraisal: Rapid, Relaxed and Participatory in *IDS Discussion* Paper 311, October.

Chambers, Robert, (1995), Rural Appraisal: Rapid, Relaxed and Participatory, in Amitava Mukherjee (ed). *Participatory Rural*

Appraisal: Methods and Applications in Rural Planning. Vikas Publishing House Pvt. Ltd.

Citizen Monitoring: Report Cards (http://www.pacindia.org/rcrc/03Report % 20 cards).

Cornwall, Andrea (2002), Making Spaces, Changing Places, Situating Participation in Development, *IDS Working Paper Series 27*, IDS, Sussex, UK.

Dwivedi, Anju, (2002), *Community Monitoring in Water and Sanitation Projects, A Facilitators Manual*, Delhi: PRIA.

Dwivedi, Anju, (2006), *Social Development Monitoring, Way to Ensure Accountability*, PRIA (presented the paper on International Conference on Governance and Citizenship organised by PRIA and HCM RIPA in Jaipur).

FAO, (1983), "People's Participation in Rural Development. Report on the Expert Consultation on People's Participation in Rural Development", Rome, Italy, 8-10 December, 1982. FAO of the UN, Rome, March.

FAO, (1989), "Participation of the Poor in Rural Organisations—A Consolidated Report of the studies in selected countries of Asia, the Near East and Africa," FAO.

Friere, Paulo, (1972), *Pedagogy of the Oppressed*, Herder and Herder, New York.

Gaventa, J., (2004), *Participatory Development or Participatory Democracy? Linking Participatory Approaches to Policy and Governance*, IDS, Sussex, UK.

Gaventa, John and Camilo, Valderrama, (1999), *Participation, Citizenship and Local Governance*, June.

Hall, Budd, (1982), Breaking the Monopoly of Knowledge: Research Methods, Participation and Development, in Hall, Budd, Arthur Gillette and Rajesh Tandon, *Creating Knowledge: A Monopoly? Participatory Research in Development*, PRIA, New Delhi, pp. 13-26.

IDS Policy Briefing, (2006), *Making Spaces for Citizens, Broadening the New Democratic Spaces for Citizen Participation*, IDS Sussex, UK.

IFCB, (2001), *Synthesis of Multistakeholder Dialogue Process*, IFCB.

Jaitli, Namrata, (1999), *Participation: Building Perspectives*, PRIA.

Lisa, *et al.* (2004), *Right Based Approaches and Beyond; Linking Rights and Participation: Challenges of Current Thinking and Action*; Just Associates, Washington DC.

McGee, Rosemary and Norton, Andy, (2000), *Participation in Poverty Reduction Strategies: A Synthesis of Experience with Participatory Approaches to Policy Design, Implementation and Monitoring*, Working Paper 109, IDS. December.

Oakely, Peter, (1991), Understanding Participation in Projects with People, *The Practice of Participation in Rural Development*, Geneva: ILO.

Oakely, Peter, (1994), *People's Participation in Development: Reviewing the Balance Sheet,* June, Manuscript.

Oakely, Peter and David, Marsden, (1984), *Approaches to Participation in Rural Development,* ILO, Geneva.

PRIA, (1995), *Participatory Research: An Introduction,* Participatory Research Network Series No 3, Delhi: PRIA.

PRIA, (2006), *Report on Status of Primary Education in Mevadkala in Panchayat Samiti Kekri,* Ajmer, PRIA DRC, Ajmer, Rajasthan.

PRIA, (1999), 'Citizens and Governance: Civil Society in the New Millennium', November. A report prepared by PRIA and its partners.

Rahnema, Masjid, (1997), Participation in Masjid Rahnema *Development Dictionary. A Guide to Knowledge as Power,* Orient Longman Int. New Delhi. pp. 155-75.

Shordt, Kathleen, (2000), *Action Monitoring for Effectiveness, Improving Water, Hygiene and Environmental Sanitation Programmes (Part 1),* Technical paper series, IRC International Water and Sanitation Centre, Netherlands.

Susskind E., Lawrence *et al.,* (2003), *Multi-Stakeholder at the Global Scale,* Kluwer Law International, The Netherlands.

Tandon, Rajesh, (1996), The Historical Roots and Contemporary Tendencies in Participatory Research: Implications for Health Care, in Koning, Korrie De Koning and Marin Martin, *Participatory Research in Health: Issues and Experiences,* Zed Books Ltd., London and New Jersey and NPPHCN, Johannesburg, 1996. pp. 19-39.

Tandon, Rajesh, (1997), *Civil Society and Construction of Knowledge Systems 1997* (Paper presented at Fourth World Conference on Action Research, Action Learning and Process Management and Eighth on Participatory Action Research, June 1-5, 1997).

Tandon, Rajesh, (2002), Linking Citizenship, Participation and Accountability: A Perspective from PRIA: *IDS Bulletin,* Vol. 33, No. 20, Sussex, UK.

Vision Foundation, (2005), *Social Audit, Gram Sabha and Panchayati Raj, Assessment of Present Status and Recommendations of Methods for Making Social Audit a Viable Instrument for Sustainable Programmme Delivery,* Final Report Submitted to Planning Commission.

10

In Search of a Conclusion

Rajesh Tandon

The chapters in this collection represent a set of themes during a period of PRIA's interventions between its 20th and 25th Anniversaries. Yet, in some fundamental sense, they represent the original inspirations and moral commitments that were the foundations of PRIA.

A brief review of those perspectives, interventions and results seem to ask specific questions: Where are we now?
What does it mean to posit citizen participation and democratic governance in India, and elsewhere, today?

Several trajectories of understanding emerge which may have a bearing on possible future courses of action. First, democracy in its institutional and historical sense needs to be re-energized and reconstructed. This implies that representative forms of governance, through periodic election of representatives every 4-5 years, is inadequate to address the core problems of governance facing humanity today. Some ways have to be discovered to promote participatory democracy parallel to, in continuation with, and periodically challenging to, the representative forms of democracy. Thus, in a specific sense, citizen participation can bring new life to the practice of democracy.

The second trajectory is where the meaning of governance requires explicit reference to citizen participation. In this reference, the process of taking decisions about the use of public resources to be applied towards common public goods needs to be built around active citizen participation. Governance cannot be merely by the professional politicians, bureaucrats and experts; for it to have the expanded meaning relevant to contemporary context, it must have citizen participation at its core.

A third trajectory refers to the notions of active citizenship. In this trajectory, citizenship is not merely legally conferred by a state institution; it is citizenship actively practiced and learnt in the struggle for daily survival. Meanings and expressions of citizenship from the perspective of the excluded and the marginalised provide particular challenge for citizen participation. In this perspective, citizen participation goes beyond the formal and the mandated to the spontaneous and self-initiated.

Given the above three trajectories, what are the places of action and sites of intervention? Making the state account for its democratic proclamations and participatory policies is clearly one way of deepening citizen participation in democratic governance. Different regions, provinces and countries may require different range of interventions in this regard. But the role of civil society is not limited to pressurizing the state. As many elements of the above trajectories indicate, a substantial site for intervention has to be the society itself. Discrimination, intimidation and violence within the society has made a mockery of citizen participation, specially for women, dalits, tribals and minorities. Therefore, another profound manner of intervention could well be the various sites of society where citizens are born and acquire identity, values and meanings. In some significant way, therefore, the circle may be getting completed as the focus of societal transformation may be a necessary preparation of citizens as future actors, once again.

Can we then conclude? But is it really a conclusion? Or a new introduction? The duality of conclusion–introduction, in the perspective of Participatory Research, is similar to the dynamics of action-reflection-action. Thus searching for conclusions may well be preparing for a new introduction.

In the world that surrounds us today and tomorrow, discourse on poverty and exploitation has been displaced by celebrations of Growth and Inclusion (the buzzwords in the Approach paper to the Eleventh Five Year Plan, Government of India, September 2006). So, we need citizen participation in Growth and Inclusion—the only logical way to inclusive growth.

Viewed with this lens, the scope of interventions, with respect to all those three trajectories mentioned above, in fact, expands enormously. A larger number of countries in the world, many different societies in Asia-Pacific, various communities, cities, towns, neighbourhoods, hamlets, households and individuals—are all searching for opportunities to participate in *inclusive growth*. This thus opens up a new vista of opportunities since the canvas for the paintbrush has increased manifold.

Citizens in search of inclusive growth—are many, all around, everywhere. Society as a whole becomes the canvas for intervention—preparing its 'civil' culture. 'Civility' in societies needs to be redrafted and refurnished. Civic energy, civic action, active citizenships in societies is the vehicle for restoring and reinventing its civility. Civilising society is, therefore, a new mission. Inclusivity must then be practiced in rebuilding a society that is 'civil'—characterised by humanitarian values of justice, equity, love, care and peace.

This may well appear to be the last conclusion we drew a quarter of a century ago; is not it a full circle? Another introduction? Possibly yes; because the primal site of social transformation is society itself. Possibly no; because local, national and global states have become manipulation instruments, regulating society and its institutions. So, civilizing society means civilizing the state and its instruments. This is the challenge of balancing society and state—for inclusive growth—citizens— all citizens—in the centre.

In some interesting ways, it means reexamination of the recent proclivities to only focus on rights. Inclusive, participatory citizenship entails rebalancing rights with responsibilities; rights alone are not just state-conferred; so are obligations. Obligations and responsibilities of citizens—as citizens for inclusive growth - need to be more sharply focused upon in future.

Civilizing society lens may also begin to bring into our vision other institutions of society—private business, media, academia. The respect, legitimacy and acknowledgement gained by for profit private business in the past decade has been phenomenal worldwide (even in the parties, regimes and households of the 'comrades'). What is the relationship between inclusive growth and corporate citizenship? Where are the opportunities for profit private business supporting movements towards civilizing societies? Honest, transparent and sustained profit-making economic activity as an element of inclusive growth? Is it conceivable? Does it make sense?

Many others may consider this line of search for conclusion as archaic, myopic and repulsive; but should we not bury the dead properly first, before we seek ghosts?

"I have known, you too may have known, those slightly odd families who continue to keep a place at the table for someone who has died. They deny the irreparable. And I have never believed that this act of defiance comforts them. The dead should be treated as dead. As such, they can then regain a different kind of presence. But the families I am speaking of prevent this return. They make the dead into missing persons for eternity, into guests who will for ever be late. They barter mourning for a hollow expectation" (De Saint-Exupery, 1995: 98).

Moving beyond this prism, it becomes obvious that future opportunities for inclusive growth exist everywhere—countries, societies, communities, institutions, workplaces, neighbourhoods and families. Therefore, sites for action needed to facilitate and support *inclusive growth* are myriad; sites are spatial and temporal junctions—located in time and space that acquire specificity and concreteness. Such time and space determined sites for actions open many possibilities for engagement for PRIA, its allies and partners, and many others. 'Desire to make a difference' is the only prerequisite.

"Our intention in writing this book is to connect with people who desire to make a difference. We can act only in time and space, we can act only from who we are. This apparent limitation is actually our greatest strength. In connecting to the world, even in the smallest ways, we engage its complexity and we begin to shift the pattern around us as we ourselves begin to shift. Social innovation begins where the individual and the system meet. It takes courage to engage and stay engaged; it takes courage to act in the absence of certainty and clarity" (Westley *et al.*, 2006:19).

This collection of essays, therefore, indicates a major conclusion—that citizen's participation is *sine qua non* of inclusive growth. Recharging that civic spirit, energy and action can happen around any thematic, at any time and space determined site. Thus, catalytic actions of a few are enough to start the chain reactions of civic engagements to make a difference in our own lives and those that cohabitate with us. PRIA, and several other civil society actors, can periodically summarise their lessons and draw some conclusions (as is being attempted in this collection). But a few others can start with new introductions.

Gurudev Rabindranath Tagore's (2002:120) poem said it succinctly:

"The world knows that the few are more than the many".

REFERENCES

De Saint-Exupery, A., (1995), *The Little Prince*, Penguin Books.
Tagore, Rabindranath, (2002), *Fireflies*, Rupa & Co., New Delhi.
Westley, F., B. Zimmerman and M. Quinn Patton, (2006), *Getting to Maybe*, Randon House Canada.

11

History of an Ideal
Journey of an Institution

It is never easy to record, analyse and present history as it is unfolding. Therefore, this chronicle is as much a record, as a travelogue, as an overview of not just the ideals of Participatory Research and institutional achievements of PRIA, but a commentary on the changing contexts and development discourses, nationally and globally.

The roots of PRIA are enshrined in the philosophy of Participatory Research. In its first strategic review, 'In search of Relevance (February 1986:2)', it was so described:

"Participatory Research now implies an effort on the part of the deprived and the powerless to:

- understand the role of knowledge as one of the significant instruments of power and control,
- value their own individual and collective experiences and existing popular knowledge as legitimate,
- acquire ability to appropriate knowledge produced by others,
- acquire confidence and the tools to produce their own knowledge, and
- to utilise this knowledge to further their common interests through collective action."

Application of this perspective locally, nationally and globally was the next challenge faced by PRIA. This challenge implied

PRIA becoming a Support Organisation (as enumerated in its second strategic review 'Exploring New Horizons', August 1989:61):

> "PRIA believes that as a support institution, it works with other activists, individuals, groups or organisations in ways that:
>
> - respond to the needs of the groups and individuals it works with;
> - encourage and motivate them continuously in their work;
> - cajole and push them;
> - inform them about rules, regulations, happenings which have some bearing on their work;
> - explore options with them;
> - question them to enable them to clarify their work to themselves; and
> - PRIA stands by them at moments of crisis or need".

In the changed context of early 1990s, both at national and global levels, PRIA had to expand its repertoire of interventions and its outreach to different constituencies and stakeholders, specially governments and donors. PRIA's 10th Anniversary celebrations (February 1992) deliberated upon 'Liberating the Mind, Democratising Societies'.

The third strategic review of PRIA 'The Future We Are In' (April 1994) emphasized its purposes in this manner:

"Mission and Strategy

To promote people-centred, holistic and comprehensive evaluation of society characterized by Freedom, Justice, Equity and Sustainability, by

(a) creating opportunities of sharing, analyzing and learning among formations of the Civil Society (in particular, people's organisations and NGOs);
(b) engaging in independent and critical analysis of societal trends and issues, development policies and programmes; and

(c) enabling dialogue across diverse perspectives, sectors and institutions".

The progress of its new interventions and engagements with new constituencies resulted in simultaneous extension of PRIA to local and global levels in mid 1990s.

Fourth strategic review 'Enter the New Millennium' (April 1999:23) pointed out PRIA's new identity:

"PRIA is an international center for learning and promotion of participation and democratic governance.

- It learns about challenges of promoting participation and democratic governance through local grassroots action,
- It undertakes systematic documentation and study of grassroots experiences and societal trends to build knowledge,
- It promotes learning of others through dissemination of knowledge and capacity building,
- It encourages promotion of enabling environment and public policies towards this end, and
- PRIA operates locally, nationally, regionally and globally."

Deepening its efforts at grassroots engagements with panchayats and municipalities reduced PRIA's global roles over the next period. But its 20th Anniversary celebrations on the theme "Governance Where People Matter" (February 2002) generated broader set of demands.

Fifth strategic plan of PRIA "Governance Where People Matter" (April 2003) enhanced its direct role in reforming governance from the vantage part of ordinary citizens.

"Mission

To work towards promotion of policies, institutions and capacities that strengthen the voice and participation of the poor and the marginalized in improving their socio-economic status through democratic governance in society.

PRIA's analysis of existing situation of discrimination in society provides the basis for identifying the poor and the marginalized.

- Gender discrimination necessitates focusing upon changing women's roles and status, as agents and leaders of change.
- Economic discrimination requires addressing issues of poverty and powerlessness.
- Social exclusion entails mainstreaming participation by children, youth, tribals, *dalits*, minorities, elderly and others.
- Discrimination of rights focus on workers (particularly women in the informal sector) and ordinary citizens."

Now, PRIA's strategic interventions combine Knowledge Building, Capacity Building and Policy Advocacy in an organic and interactive manner.

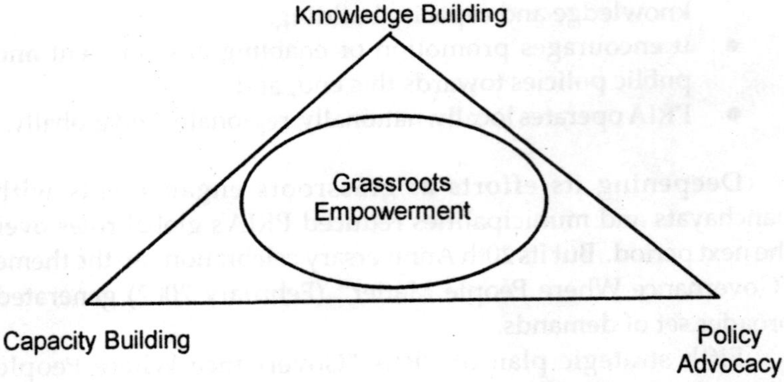

Box 1: A Short Reference to PRIA's Knowledge Building Interventions

Year	*Themes*	*Resarch Sudies and Pblications*
1982	Participatory Research	• Creating Knowledge: A Monopoly?
1984	Adult Learning and Primary Health	• Participatory Research: An Introduction • Learning for Health
1985	Participatory Training Methodology	• Manual on Participatory Training Methodology
1986	Enabling Environment for VDOs	• GO-NGO Relations: A Source of life or a Kiss of Death?
1987	Management of VDOs	• Forms of Organisations : Square Pegs in Round Holes • Manual on Financial Management • Management of VOs
1988 (onwards)	Occupational Health and Safety	• Diseases at Work (3 Vol.) • Struggle for Justice (5 Vol.) • Diagnosis of Occupational Diseases • Impairment, Disability and their Assessment
1990	Nature and function of VDOs	• Voluntary Development Organisations in India
1990	Women's Economic Empowerment	• Work and Empowerment
1991	Support Functions and Organisations	• Strengthening the Grassroots : Nature and Function of Support Organisations
1992	Collaboration and Partnership	• Holding Together
1993	Women's Leadership and Learning	• Videos and Booklets
1994 (onwards)	Institutional Development	• Journal of Institutional Development
1995 (onwards)	Participation and Governance	• Participation and Governance Bulletins, Manuals, Videos

(*Contd.*)

(*Contd.*)

1995 (onwards)	Civil Society, its meaning, roles and problematique	• A number of papers: CITIZENS (published by CIVICUS)
1995 (onwards)	Strengthening Panchayati Raj Institutions	• A number of booklets, videos, study reports
1997	Social Policy	• Shaping Policy: Do NGOs matter?
1998	Capacity Building of Civil Society	• A number of study reports on Capacity building initiatives of Southern NGOs with IFBC
1999	Collective Initiatives	• Journal on Environmentally Sustainable Industrial Development.
	Innovations in Civil Society	• Journal on Civil society initiatives.
2000	Citizens and Governance	• India and Commonwealth study on Civil society in the new millennium.
2001	Strengthening Panchayati Raj Institutions	• Various reports have emerged on studies conducted on the status of PRIs, Parallel bodies and Panchayats, Primary Education and Panchayats and Dalit Leadership
		• National Commission to review the Working of the Constitutions: Suggestions and Recommendations
	Civil society and Governance	• A book, which traces the history of the concept and elaborates the various initiatives civil society has made in improving governance in India.
2002	Occupational Health,	• Compilation of study reports into a CD-ROM
	Governance where People matter	• Compilation of speeches that take stock of PRIA and its partners' intervention and revisioning the future
	Strengthening Municipalities	• Reports on Urbanization trends, Municipal Finances, and Gender Paradigm in Urban Governance
	Voluntary Action, Civil society and State	• A Book which seeks to clarify concepts, roles and future relationships

(*Contd.*)

(Contd.)

2003	Scale and Status of Non-Profit Sector in India	• Invisible, yet widespread: The non-profit sector in India and statewide reports on Giving and Volunteering
	Local Self Governance	• Series of studies on Municipal Finance • Series of booklets on Local Self Governance Globally
	Rights and Citizenship	• Study Reports—Development Research Centre
2004	Pre-Election Voters Awareness Campaign (PEVAC)	• CDs, posters, pamphlets on PEVAC
	Citizen Engagement:	• Series of manuals on innovative practice promoting citizen participation
2005	Gender Mainstreaming	• Gender on the Agenda—A trainer's manual
	Continuing Education for Social Change	• Certificate courses on Participatory Research and Evaluation; Management of Projects; Occupational Health and Safety
2006	Citizenship and Governance	• Participatory Citizenship

Box 2: Chronicling Capacity Building Programmes of PRIA

Year	*Theme*	*Constituency*
1981	Group Building, Leadership, Experiential Learning, Participatory Planning	Grassroots Groups (Mahila Mandals, Youth Groups, Tribals)
1984	Participatory Training (TOT), Participatory Monitoring and Evaluation, Promoting Participatory Research and Community Participation	VDOs (Government Agencies, UN Agencies)
1985	Management of VDOs, Statutory Requirements, Financial Management	VDOs
1985	Occupational Health and Safety	Workers (VDOs, Trade Unions)
1986	Management of Women's Livelihood and Income-Generation Programmes (Production, Marketing, Financing etc.)	VDOs (Women's groups, Government Agencies)
1988	Vision-Mission-Strategy	VDOs
1988	Participation in Literacy Programmes	Government Agencies
1990	Support Organisation Functions, Organizational Management, Human Resource Management	Regional Support Organisations, South Asian Support Organisations
1994	Development Management	VDOs in South Asia
1995	Participatory Development	Schools of Social Work, Government Agencies
1995	Leadership Building	Women in PRIs
1996	Organizational development Participatory development	VDOs, Donors
1997	Occupational Health	ESI Doctors

(*Contd.*)

(Contd.)

1998	Governance, Policy Monitoring and Advocacy, Strategic Planning, Advocacy	VDOs, Civil Society Actors
1999	WELLD (women empowerment through literacy and livelihood development)	Women
	Monitoring environmental pollution	CBOs and VDOs
2000	Leadership Development and Policy Advocacy, Coalition Building	VDOs at South Asian level
2001	Social Development Monitoring (Citizens, monitoring)	Women's Groups. CBOs
2002	Citizen leadership	Women informal workers, tribals, dalits.
	Multi-stakeholder Dialogue	VDOs GO, media, Academia
2003	Gender mainstreaming	Partners in the voluntary sector
2004	Participation in Governance: Local Self Governance	ERs, CBOs, CSOs, citizen leaders, women's networks.
2005	Organisational Development	Voluntary Development Organisations
2006	Right to information	ERs, government officials, CBOs, CSOs, citizen leaders, women's networks

Box 3: An Overview of PRIA's Policy Advocacy Interventions

Year	*Issues*	*Partnership*
1982	Protecting Tribals' access to forest resources in wake of Forest Bill	Convening loose network of VDOs with ISI
1984	Right to Information and Policy on industrial hazard in wake of Bhopal Gas Disaster at Union Carbide Plant	Campaigning with CSE, TUs, VDOs, Highlander Centre (Tennessee)
1985	Ecological Destruction and Human Displacement due to Large Dams	Convening with CSE, XISS, ISI (later a network 'Assertion of Collective Will Against Large Dams')
1985	National Campaign of Construction workers	Informational support to TUs
1986	Protection of space and autonomy of Voluntary Action (GO-NGO Relations)	Convening loose coalition of VDOs
1987	Land Alienation due to industrialization	Information support to local struggles
1988	Workers' Take-over of Sick Industry (Kamani Tubes Ltd.)	Informational support to TUs
1990	Campaign against Dust related Lung Diseases	Convened a coalition of TUs, VDOs, Doctors, Professionals, Media, etc.
1992	Voluntary Action in support of Secularism	Active participation and information support to a coalition convened by VANI
1995	Monitoring World Bank Participation Policy	Chaired the Sub-Group of NGO Working Group on World Bank
1997	Strengthening Panchayati Raj Institutions (Women's Leadership, Strong Gram Sabha, Micro-planning, Panchayat Finance, etc.)	Mobilizing and convening

(Contd.)

(*Contd.*)

1998	Enabling Policies for Capacity Building	Convening International Forum on Capacity Building of Southern NGOs with other southern NGOs and northern donors
1999	Strengthening democracy and deepening citizens' participation	Platform facilitated to initiate multi-stakeholder dialogue with GO, Donors, Social Activists, tribal youth and women leaders
2000	Pre-Election Voters' Awareness Campaign (PEVAC)	Building civil society platforms in different states for voter's awareness on Panchayats and Municipal elections
2001	Round table on state of Panchayats, Parallel bodies and panchayats	Sharing Field realities with GO, Donors, NGOs, media and academia
	Towards Capacity Building Agenda	Reforming Technical Co-operation for Capacity Development–UNDP
2002	Status of Non-profit Sector in India: Need for enabling policies	Sharing of finding with GO, Donors, NGOs, Academicians, Media
	Round table on Primary Education and Panchayati Raj	
2003	Citizens and Governance	Pan-Commonwealth Platform of civil society to promote citizens' engagement with governance
2004	Election Reforms–local self-government	Ministry of Panchayati Raj, State Election Commissions, VDOs
2005	Devolution of Finances to Panchayats	Ministry of Panchayati Raj, State Finance Commissions, VDOs
2006	Urban Governance Reform	Platforms for civil society, Ministry of Urban Development (JNNURM) and State Governments
	National Rural Employment Guarantee Scheme	Platform of civil society organizations, Ministry of Panchayati Raj and Ministry of Rural Development

Thematics

With a variety of stakeholders in a diversity of spaces over a quarter century, PRIA has worked on a wide spectrum of issues, problems and themes. As our 'Journey towards Empowerment' suggests, some of these themes stand out as being most persistent, pervasive and pronounced. These are enumerated below in further detail.

Land, Water, Forests, Minerals—Control over Natural Resources

PRIA began its journey by joining peoples' struggles in the fight for 'Right over Forests'. Natural Resources have been a bone of contention between governments, industries and the people ever since society created formal institutions of governance. For centuries, village communities managed and nurtured natural resources in their surroundings as their main means of survival. Major conflicts over control and use of natural resources began with the colonial era as colonial masters transformed these natural and vital resources into commodities for generating profits. This not only meant their systematic exploitation but also through their packaging as 'commodities' placed them outside the purview of rural and tribal communities, who were traditionally both the users and the protectors of these resources.

With the creation of the nation-state and India's independence, this control shifted from the colonial masters to the democratically elected ones and their functionaries. Forests belonged to the forest department, water-bodies to the water and irrigation department, minerals to the excise and mining departments and land to the revenue department. This capturing of ownership in the name of 'common public good' often threatened the survival of the rural and tribal communities, whose resource requirements were minimal and who depended on them for their survival. Policies often failed to recognize their existence and their role in conserving the environment which kept them alive.

It was towards this right of the marginalized that PRIA directed its work from the very beginning. Its first participatory research study on the 'Impact of the Forest Policy on Forest Dwellers in Himachal Pradesh' in 1982 aimed at creating a demand for protecting access of forest dwellers to forest resources in the wake of the new Forest Bill.

The 1980s was a time of unrest with increasing conflicts around big development projects. The issue of alienation of land and forests was brought to the forefront. It was during this period that PRIA undertook a number of studies on the issues of land alienation and the lack of control of tribals over water and forest resources. Participatory Research was seen as a tool for empowering the marginalized and as a tool for advocacy. It was also used as a means of bringing people together.

The power of peoples' knowledge and its strength in bringing together people with common problems and concerns was visible in PRIA's attempts at mobilising various civil society actors on the issue of environmental protection and natural resource management. Along with other civil society actors like ISI, XISS and CSE, it was instrumental in creating an informal network of organisations around displacement and environmental issues (Assertion of Collective Will Against Large Dams) that threatened the lives of millions of poor and marginalized citizens across the country. Later, in collaboration with this network, PRIA launched a major study on the 'Impact of Large Development Projects' in 1989.

PRIA's work on issues of control over natural resources gained prominence during the period 1990-1995 with a large number of studies being conducted on forest, water, irrigation, and issues related to the coastal poor. Major studies by PRIA during this period were 'Land Alienation in Bihar' (1991) and the 'Impact of National Parks and Sanctuaries on Local Populations' (1993).

PRIA's focused work on such issues comprising research, alliance-building and advocacy had achieved sporadic successes by the mid-1990s with the inclusion of the peoples' participation in almost all policies related to natural resource management. Formation of village user committees to monitor forests, water etc. was being promoted as a means of mobilizing citizen participation. Tribal rights over *Jal, Jangal, Jamin* were being given relevance through such programmes.

In this changing scenario, PRIA's focus and strategy on 'peoples' ownership over natural resources' shifted to 'peoples' ownership of natural resources through institutions of local governance'. Therefore, all efforts since then (1995) have focused on strengthening institutions of local self-governance (Panchayats) to ably address issues related to conservation and use of natural resources. Attempts at creating 'parallel bodies' separate from the Panchayats like watershed committees, forest committees etc. were resisted. Being elected bodies, Panchayats were accountable to the people through constitutional forums like the Gram Sabha whereas the only accountability that the parallel bodies had was to the government functionaries at the Block and District levels.

Today, twenty-five years later, PRIA's struggle for the rights of the people over natural resources remains as focused as it was when it started in 1982. The direction has changed with the changing context, but the vibrancy in efforts has not decreased. Efforts at strengthening Van Panchayats, enabling the role of Panchayats to undertake watershed management, advocacy efforts at ensuring the implementation of PESA etc. are in full swing.

Safe Workplace

Twenty-five years ago, industries operated in a highly labour surplus economy without much domestic or international competition. They, therefore, operated in a largely unrestrained and informal manner. The government and ministries dealing with industries and labour issues focused on wages, service conditions and regulation of employment while trade union movements in the country, as elsewhere in the developing world, largely expressed concerns over jobs and wages. Fighting for formalisation of wages of the informal sector, especially in the agricultural sector, fell within the purview of the non-governmental organisations. However, twenty-five years ago, in 1982, when PRIA began its interventions, issues related to occupational health and safety did not find any place in either the agenda of the government or the trade unions.

PRIA began its programmatic work on health and safety in 1983 with efforts at conscientisation and leadership building of worker activists and trade unionists. Applying its *participatory research* perspective to workplace health and safety issues, it encouraged workers' knowledge. As in all fields, popular knowledge finds no credence with experts and institutions. PRIA sought to break this barrier by giving legitimacy to the worker's own popular knowledge, using it to sensitize practitioners, experts and institutions for better health and safety measures for workers. In February 1984 after a National Workshop in Mumbai, reflecting on its work and experiences in the field, PRIA embarked on a major study on 'Workers Awareness and Occupational Health'.

With the Bhopal Gas Disaster in December 1984, concerns over occupational hazards grew in strength, and initiatives in this direction gained momentum among all stakeholders. There was a flurry of activities by the Government, trade unions, scientific establishments and NGOs, both regionally and nationally. Throughout all this activity, PRIA maintained its focus on worker awareness and education in the informal and formal sector through facilitation of workshops, studies, diagnostic camps and dialogues with various stakeholders.

A host of diverse workplaces and occupational health and safety issues in diverse occupations were studied and documented. These included issues of occupational health for cotton and farm labourers, women workers in *'bidi'* and *'agarbathi'* industries, mineworkers in coal, silica, agate and uranium mines, tannery workers, workers in stone crushers, workers in chemical estates and plantations, health hazards of hospital and municipal workers, child workers in fireworks and metal polishing industry, textile workers etc. Knowledge and understanding developed from these studies were used to enhance the capacities of trade union leaders and workers as well as for policy advocacy.

By 1989, PRIA shifted its emphasis to integrate the twin concerns of workplace health and safety with community health and safety issues. The attempt was to bring about an integration of the environment movement and the workers movement for better impacts. It aimed at supporting educational activities of workers, in general, and occupational health and safety issues in particular, attempting to bridge the gap between the environment within and outside the factory premises. In 1993 this integration was formalized with establishment of the Centre for Occupational and Environmental Health (COEH) in PRIA. One of the major areas of policy advocacy during this period was ESIC (Employees State Insurance Corporation); its systems of diagnosis and treatment of work-related illness have improved as a consequence.

A strategic shift for an expanded and more comprehensive focus on the issue took place in 1998 when PRIA renamed its occupational health and environment programme as Centre for Environmentally Sustainable Industrial Development (ESID). In its expanded existence, the ESID focused both on workers' initiatives and on citizens' initiatives. Worker Resource Centres were operationalised in Mumbai, Aurangabad (Maharashtra), Ahmedabad (Gujarat) and Amritsar (Punjab), with the main objective of broadening and deepening workers' awareness. Meanwhile, citizens' initiatives were aimed at promoting innovation in engagement with the local community, industry and the government for sustainable industrial development.

Two decades of capacity building, awareness campaigns, studies and policy advocacy have seen positive results. Today, most trade unions are addressing worker health and safety issues seriously. There is greater awareness among managements that glossing over such issues will not be beneficial to their productivity and profits. Government agencies and research institutes have begun to focus on health and safety aspects in informal and unorganized work places.

However, the challenges seem never ending and change with time. Economic liberalisation and greater encouragement to private sector has resulted in new levels of growth. With the growth of service sector and the changing nature of workplace practices, issues of occupational health and safety have crossed new boundaries. Issues related to the IT industry, the hotel and tourism industry, and even the agriculture industry with the emergence of biotechnology are areas yet to be explored and understood. The gap between environmentalists and labour unionists – those concerned with pollution of air, water, land etc. and those concerned with jobs and benefits – has narrowed, but differences in perspectives and priorities continue.

In the context of globalisation and rapid economic growth in the country and the Asian region, there is a growing opportunity to engage with such issues once again.

Accountable Local Self-Governance

From its conception, PRIA's vision has been to develop a democratic society based on the values of equity and justice. It has been working towards the empowerment of the poor and marginalized, promoting peoples' participation in knowledge generation and in using their knowledge to play an active and aware role in their own development.

The first ten years of PRIA's work largely focused on pushing for the inclusion of people's participation in various developmental programmes and schemes being implemented by the Government. With the growth of globalisation and the increase in the activities and interest of multilateral institutions like the World Bank, came the focus on 'good governance'. Experiences with largely centralized state institutions had resulted in unsatisfactory development with rampant corruption, inefficiency and untargeted planning causing global funding institutions to stress on the need for decentralized planning and implementation. With this came the thrust on local governance for ensuring effective and sustainable use of development resources.

In India, as in many other developing countries across the world, the 1990s was an era of restructuring. The 73rd and 74th Constitutional Amendments passed by the Indian Parliament in 1992 redefined the meaning of democracy in India. From a mere 5000 people representing a population of over a billion, the number increased to approximately 3.2 million. There was a governance institution in place in almost every village, with the people having the right to govern themselves through their representatives and through the constitutional body of Gram Sabha. It was a giant step towards creating democracy of the people, by the people, and for the people.

For PRIA, this landmark Act provided an opportunity to push the participation agenda further. Anticipating the resistance of those in power, both in the political and official machinery of national and state governments, to actually devolve substantial powers to the local bodies, PRIA adopted a quad-layered strategy to make this possible.

Firstly, working directly with institutions of local self-governance to strengthen them through capacity building of elected representatives and government functionaries.

Secondly, working with the people to enable them to participate actively in the governance process through awareness generation, mobilisation and capacity building initiatives. These initiatives focused specifically on marginalized groups like women, *dalits* and tribals.

Thirdly, working to empower civil society organisations at the local level to ensure their sustainability and improved efficiency and effectiveness in the field. This entailed capacity building of staff and field workers of civil society organisations and support for engagement with multiple stakeholders at the Block, District and State levels.

Fourthly, pushing for policy change through advocacy efforts at the State and National levels using experiences gained from working at the grassroot level. Systematized through research and documentation, these experiences strengthen advocacy initiatives, enabling the process of change.

PRIA began its efforts at strengthening local self-government in Haryana and Himachal Pradesh in 1994. In this first phase (1994-1999) the focus largely remained restricted to research studies, capacity building of newly elected representatives and institutional support to local and regional civil society organisations for facilitating awareness and educational campaigns aimed at strengthening peoples' participation. A major study during this period was the study on Women's Leadership in Panchayats (1999) covering six states of the country.

The new millennium brought with it the realisation that sporadic efforts through partners would not yield the results required for creating models for advocating changes in the system. Strengthening Panchayats required more focused efforts at educating and enhancing the capacities of the poor and marginalized, enabling them to participate in decision-making forums like the Gram Sabha. It also required strong advocacy efforts to strengthen the institutions themselves which largely remained autonomous only on paper, with inadequate finances and functionaries to fulfil the responsibilities devolved to them. Their identity was limited to that of being 'implementation arms' of the state and national governments. The real powers remained with the various development departments.

Thus, 2000–2005 saw the deepening of efforts for enabling governance reform. Gram Sabha Mobilisation Campaigns were initiated in October 2000 and PEVAC (Pre-Election Voters Awareness Campaign) began to be organized as a massive campaign facilitated by a forum of multiple civil society organisations. By 2003 PEVAC had acquired the status of a model campaign supported by the State and National Governments.

By 2003, the success achieved in strengthening PRI's also brought with it the need to further deepen efforts to cross the more difficult hurdles of advocating for clear devolution of functions and greater devolution of finances. A strategic decision to deepen interventions was taken and the Panchayat Resource Centres (PRCs) instituted by PRIA in many States in 2000 were reinforced by the opening up of District Resource Centres by 2003.

PRIA thus truly became an organisation with linkages from the grassroot to the national level. Armed with direct field experience, PRIA's State Resource Centres strengthened advocacy efforts resulting in successes like PRIA partnering with the Ministry of Panchayati Raj (MoPR), Government of India in facilitating Seven Round Table Conferences on Devolutions in 1994. Providing the Government with field based data, these conferences were instrumental in the drafting of the Memorandum of Understanding to be signed by State Governments committing them to serious decentralisation and devolution.

At the State level, advocacy and mobilisation efforts saw successes like the incorporation of the concept of PRC by the Rajasthan State Government in December 2004 and the involvement of civil society organisations in facilitating Activity Mapping to streamline devolutions in 14 states.

Another strategic decision taken in the new millennium was the need for PRIA to focus on the largely ignored sister amendment, i.e. the 74th CAA. Urban Local Bodies were not only more inept than their rural counterparts at addressing local issues (as they lacked both functions and finances) but they also lacked the provision of a constitutional forum enabling people's participation. PRIA focused on small and medium towns in its intervention areas to begin the process of reforming urban governance. Direct interventions began in 2001 to mobilise communities to engage with urban governance institutions by forming informal 'mohalla committees' as an interface forum with their local elected representatives. Taking into account the weakness of the municipalities as institutions of local self-governance, studies on the financial status of municipalities for effective service delivery were initiated in 2006. Along with the advocacy for greater devolution of powers to ULBs, there was an equally strong demand for the inclusion of people's participation in urban planning. Today, with the introduction of the JNNURM and the UIDSSMT scheme, PRIA's efforts at facilitating participatory town planning has gained strength.

Twenty-five years later PRIA's long journey for promoting peoples' participation and rights continues; voicing the theme and the vision of creating a system of 'Governance where People Matter'. Its efforts are now directed towards consolidating lessons of the past few years by focusing on specific issues within the governance framework. Major studies on the role of Panchayats in delivery and monitoring of primary education and the role of Panchayats in delivery of NREGA (National Rural Employment Guarantee Act) are underway with the aim of facilitating and advocating for 'adequate and enabling devolution' to institutions of local self-governance. There is still a long road ahead but every step is a step forward.

Responsive Civil Society

The roots of PRIA are the principles of *participatory research,* which focus on the role of knowledge as one of the significant instruments of power and control. Democratizing this source of power has been the driving agenda of PRIA since its inception in 1982. It was this agenda that led to the growth of PRIA as a support organisation.

Civil society had started re-emerging in India during the 1980s with increasing poverty and marginalisation despite campaigns like *'Garibi Hatao'* and attempts at liberalizing the economy. Centralized planning and decision making with token involvement of people was the bane of all development planning in the country. People continued to be treated as beneficiaries rather than primary stakeholders in the development process. In this context, the role of civil society in voicing the needs and opinions of the poor and marginalized increased in relevance.

Challenging the largely centralized governance system required a capacity that not only increased the efficiency of civil society organisations in empowering the powerless but also increased their credibility *vis-à-vis* other sectors. Using the principles of *participatory research*, PRIA attempted to address this need through training and evaluation studies. It undertook its first participatory evaluation studies in 1982-83 of Sewa Mandir in Rajasthan, Gram Vikas in Orissa, Ankur in Delhi and Shramik Sangathan in Maharashtra. PRIA's, now renowned, Training of Trainers (ToT) programme was also initiated during this period.

Aimed at both assessing the needs as well as strengthening the capacities of civil society organisations, PRIA's civil society building efforts moulded itself as per the demands of the times. Never deviating from its value base of 'participation', by 1986 PRIA had expanded its mandate in its support role. Along with trainings and evaluations it started focusing on:

- Providing informational material to civil society groups and activists and dissemination of knowledge through popular publications and videos;
- Facilitating exchange programmes and creating opportunities for mutual sharing of experiences and analysis;
- Promoting formation of informal and formal networks of civil society organisations to come together on issues of mutual concern, especially for strengthening the voice of the voluntary sector,

It was during this period that PRIA facilitated the formation of a network of voluntary organisations, VANI, to act as a nodal agency for taking up the issues of voluntary sector in India.

With the increase in the number of civil society organisations in the 90s, PRIA strengthened its focus on creating a resource pool of trainers and organisations to continue capacity building efforts on a wider, deeper and regional scale. Regional Support Organisations were promoted and intensive ToT programmes were run from 1995-1998 to create a rich resource pool of trainers in the country.

Efforts at strengthening regional and local civil society organisations were aimed at strengthening efforts at policy advocacy. The changing socio-economic and political context of the country and the world in the face of globalisation and liberalisation meant a concerted effort at carving out a legitimate space for civil society in the new development paradigm. Civil society was being recognized as the third sector; however, its role and capacities were still being defined and were still in a formative state. Thus, there was a need for unified civil society voices defining their own agenda instead of having the government define them. PRIA played a major role in the birth and evolution of a global civil society network – CIVICUS.

The early 1990s, therefore, saw PRIA facilitating national level consultations on the role of voluntary sector in support of secularism, natural resource management and other related issues. In 1995, PRIA entered the global advocacy arena in support of the voluntary sector when it chaired the Sub–Group of NGO Working Group of the World Bank on 'Monitoring World Bank Participation Policy'. As a follow-up, a global multi-stakeholder forum IFCB (International Forum for Capacity Building) was Chaired by PRIA to advance the agenda of capacity building of civil society in southern countries. These successes both represented and deepened PRIA's efforts at facilitating a vibrant and strong civil society in India and around the world.

As with all its themes, the introduction of the 73rd and 74th constitutional amendments in India caused a strategic shift in PRIA's focus at strengthening civil society. The Act had deepened democracy to the lowest level and so too did the focus of PRIA's civil society strengthening program. Moving beyond supporting regional organisations, PRIA extended its outreach to small local civil society groups. With the aim of strengthening their capacities and thereby their sustainability, PRIA also extended handholding support to enable them to work towards motivating and mobilizing the participation of people in local self-governance. The MIND fellowship program introduced in 1994 too aimed at providing support and enhancing the skills of individuals and leaders of small civil society organisations, facilitating their sustainability.

By 2004, the focus of capacity building efforts deepened and community based organisations, especially Mahila Mandals and youth groups, became the target of the civil society strengthening programme. Efforts were made at creating informal and formal networks of community based organisations within the same block so as to promote both mutual exchange and learning as well as initiate a collectivisation process to give them strength.

Thus, the efforts at facilitating the creation of a vibrant and responsive civil society reached its very depth, without loosing its expanse, by the new millennium. Working on the principles of *Participatory Research*, the key to these efforts was sustainability. Without generating sustainability these efforts remained futile and therefore, in all its endeavours PRIA focused on developing local capacities and playing a support role rather than an implementing one.

It carried out a series of studies, documenting and analyzing the role of civil society in national development and democratic governance. The success of these efforts are visible in the recognition of civil society organisations at all policy making and implementation levels with civil society members being invited to participate in all deliberations and discussions on policy formation and reform. PRIA itself is a member of a number of advisory committees with both the state and national governments.

Success is also visible through the huge network of civil society groups that came together to facilitate campaigns like the PEVAC (Pre-Election Voters Awareness Campaign) in numerous states of the country. Today, the greatest recognition of the responsiveness of Civil Society is the creation of the National Policy on Voluntary Sector formed through active participation of voluntary organisations from across the country.

PRIA remains committed to its support role even today, expanding its role as an organisation for promoting learning to an organisation that promotes education and learning. It recently introduced educational courses for practitioners and young students providing a practical perspective to learning as opposed to a mere theoretical approach. Such efforts and more continue to define PRIA's role as a facilitator of a strong civil society locally, nationally and globally.

Citizen Leadership

At the heart of democracy is citizen. Unfortunately, democracy is being increasingly narrowly defined in terms of multi-party elections. Therefore, people are treated as mere voters—persuaded, cajoled, induced or threatened to cast their votes every 4-5 years. After that, people become mere spectators in the 'sport of democracy', being played by professional politicians, career bureaucrats and permanent judges.

In welfare states, another identity for the ordinary folks, specially the poor and the marginalized, is a beneficiary—for whose benefits governments implement a number of welfare schemes. In the modern world of a global marketplace, ordinary folks are treated as consumers – of goods and services. They are voters, beneficiaries or/and consumers—but not citizens.

It is this gap that PRIA tried to respond to by focusing on conscientisation and awareness raising of people—marginalized, exploited and poor—about their rights; it attempted to facilitate their collectivisation to demand, acquire and use rights and resources meant for them. Women's leadership, tribals' collectives, youth activists, Kishori Panchayats (of adolescent girls), *dalit* organizers—are all illustrations of this stream of work that began in the early 1980s.

Civic engagement and citizen participation got another opportunity in Ward and Gram Sabhas under panchayats and municipalities in mid 1990s. Preparing, supporting, informing, enabling, motivating and facilitating ordinary folks to voice their views on issues of their concerns became a widespread intervention of PRIA then.

Several studies conducted during late 1990s began to identify the distinction between legal, juridical notion of citizenship ('all citizens are equal') and lived-in, real experiences and meanings of citizenship for nomads, *dalits*, women, tribals, slum-dwellers, etc. PRIA utilised this understanding to promote active and participatory citizenship as a focused programme of intervention.

Thus, citizens' leadership efforts have since early 21st century been widely undertaken in both rural and urban areas; unemployed youth, high school students, retired defence personnel, teachers, women educators, former elected representatives, shop-keepers, farmers, shopfloor workers, labourers and community elders—a wide range of ordinary folks are feeling empowered to engage with processes, spaces and institutions of governance on an ongoing basis—to solve problems of their neighbourhoods, communities, villages and workplaces.

A billion citizens—active, proactive and engaged—in India, and six times more around the world—that's PRIA's dream for strengthening citizens leaderships!

Gender Mainstreaming

Historically, through culture, societal, legal and juridical norms and practices, women have always been relegated to a position of the disadvantaged. Whether it is politics, economics or culture, the contribution of women far surpasses men, yet it remains largely unrecognized. It is women who constitute the vast majority of the informal and the agricultural sectors, the heart of our economy; it is women who as voters and leaders define the political shape of the country; and it is women who in their designated role as nurturers of the future generation preserve the richness and continuity of culture.

Yet, while fulfilling all these recognized and unrecognized roles, the question that arises is who defines these roles and who determines? It is the male patron who defines cultural norms; it is the patriarch who dons the mantle of political leadership; and it is the male expert who decides the value of labour. In other words, it is the male perspective that rules and makes invisible the voices of women in society.

It was to help women find their voice, believe in their capacities and create an equal space for themselves that PRIA directed its *participatory research* principles and practice in the 80s. It began its work with the belief that "gender discrimination necessitates focusing upon changing women's roles and status as agents and leaders of change". Women were organized and encouraged to articulate their agenda within projects like the Development of Women and Children in Rural Areas (DWCRA) etc. Attention was given to the distinct ways of women's learning—what's different and unique as well as problematic.

Gender inequality in the industrial sector was stark—women faced both unsafe working conditions and unfair wage and welfare policies based on their being 'women'. To challenge these perceptions, participatory studies on occupational health and safety were conducted focusing on women workers – textile workers, *bidi* workers, construction workers, etc. The consistent pressure through mobilisation and voicing of women specific issues resulted in the successful implementation of policies and norms for better working conditions for women.

Towards the latter part of the 80s, concerns around women's economic empowerment came to the fore and PRIA undertook a number of studies examining income generation possibilities for women. A multi-pronged approach was taken with workshops on women's access to credit and income generation, trainings for economic empowerment like the Mini Social MBA for strengthening the organisational and managerial capacity of women and handbooks on legal procedures, practices, and forms for setting up economic programmes.

By the early 90s, PRIA's programmatic focus on local self-governance brought with it increased emphasis on the social and political empowerment of women. Capacity building and mobilisation of women at the local level was initiated with specific focus on motivating and enabling them, specially from marginalized communities, to play an active role in the political arena and to participate in the decision-making process of development planning and implementation.

A rich knowledge base on gender issues through years of practice and participatory research created a favourable environment for setting up a Committee Against Sexual Harassment (CASH) in 1998, in consonance with the Supreme Court judgement. Moving beyond the narrow mandate of sexual harassment, the Committee broadened its mandate to include gender mainstreaming as its core agenda and evolved into the Committee on Gender Awareness and Mainstreaming in PRIA (CGAMP) in 2001. In its new role, the Committee spearheaded pioneering efforts at gender mainstreaming of institutions. Gender audit of itself and its partners led to the development of more comprehensive gender sensitive policies, supported by a series of gender sensitisation workshops for staff members.

With the increasing role of women in all sectors in the 21st century, the need is to make 'gender the agenda' for all sectors – civil society, government, and the corporate sector. Today gender mainstreaming is the core strength of PRIA...and the dream is to make gender equity the core strength of the country.

Table 1: PRIA's History

Phase	*Key Achievements*	*Lessons*
First Phase (1981-1985)	• Facilitation of Participatory Research with grassroots groups, organizing sensitizing and building partnerships with them around issues related to land alienation and displacement, forest, occupational health and safety. • Capacity enhancement of Voluntary Development Organisations (VDOs) and Training of Trainers (TOT) on Participatory methodologies. This enabled the development of various participatory learning opportunities as shown in Box 2 as well as contributed to knowledge building that can be perused through Box 1.	• Participatory Research methodology, when applied through Participatory Training and Participatory Evaluation, addressed real issues of the marginalised. • Working with both grassroots and intermediary organisations (voluntary agencies and trade unions) helped to build partnership, with like-minded organisations, that enabled outreach of innovations and greater visibility to advocacy issues.
Second Phase (1986-1988)	• Institutional capacity building support to VDOs, on Organisational management and Participatory planning and monitoring. • Capacity building support on literacy and management of women's economic activities to voluntary organizations and semi-government agencies. • Building local and international networks of Participatory Research and Adult Education helped to share and disseminate lessons across different contexts.	• Management of VDOs requires new perspectives and methods given the mission-oriented nature of their organizations. • Supportive government policies and laws are crucial for the effective contribution of voluntary organizations in people-centred development. • Experiential learning methodology is a valuable contribution in further empowering of field activists and community leaders.

(*Contd.*)

(*Contd.*)

	• Influencing State policies on issue of protection of space and autonomy of voluntary action, workers' take over of sick industry, and against land alienation due to industrialization. The history of advocacy efforts is listed in Box 3.	• Ongoing support to field based voluntary organizations necessitates a networking approach around common issues.
Third Phase (1989-1993)	• A number of Support Organisations in different states of India were promoted to provide context specific support to local groups.	• Building capacity of Support Organizations at national and South Asian level is a crucial ongoing requirement for their effectiveness.
	• Promoting participatory development in large-scale government programmes (like literacy, women's development, etc.) was supported.	• Concrete efforts need to be made to overcome schisms within civil society in the country (e.g. between trade unions focusing on occupational health and safety, and environmentalists focusing on pollution and degradation).
	• Campaign on Dust-related Lung Diseases built a broad coalition of workers, trade unions, medical doctors and government institutions.	• Global networking and linkage building is essential for supporting national level interventions.
	• Emergence of VANI as a national platform to advance autonomous space for value-driven voluntary action was supported.	• Professional development of staff of voluntary organizations requires a long-term HRD strategy.
Fourth Phase (1994-1998)	• Initiation of direct work on strengthening Panchayati Raj Institutions as institutions of local self-governance.	• Large-scale, in-depth intervention is needed in ensuring Panchayati Raj Institutions to become institutions of local self-governance in real sense.

(*Contd.*)

(*Contd.*)

	• Sensitization of the Trade Unions, NGOs and doctors on issues of occupational and environmental health, as a unitary focus.	• Promoting new citizen leadership among women, dalits, adivasis and other marginalized communities requires innovations in participatory methodologies.
	• As the Chair of the sub group on Participation of the Non-Governmental Organisation Working Group on the World Bank (NGOWG-WB), PRIA coordinated monitoring of World Bank's policy of participation at the national and international levels, and used the findings to influence the Bank and the government.	• Civil society formations, other than Voluntary Development Organisations, lack information and capacity to address developmental issues.
	• Formal collaboration with Schools of Social Work was carried out to promote academic engagement with issues of Participatory Research and Local Governance. • Network of Collaborating Regional Support Organisations (NCRSOs) was formalized as a vehicle for undertaking joint programmes.	• Democratic governance is not merely relevant for government departments and agencies, but also for civil society organizations.
Fifth Phase (1999-2003)	• Multi-stakeholder approaches attempted to bring trade unions, doctors and local bodies to ensure participation of workers and community in assuring environmentally sustainable industrial development.	• Strengthening civil society requires working with local community based organisations and informal groups, as well as intermediary voluntary organizations. Linking various levels of civil society action to achieve common goal is increasingly crucial.

(*Contd.*)

(*Contd.*)

	• As active members of global foras like International Forum on Capacity Building (IFCB), SAARC Forum of support organisations, NGO Working Group on the World Bank, CIVICUS: World Alliance for Citizen Participation, Development Research Centre, etc., PRIA got a unique opportunity to bring the voices and perspectives of the grassroots to influence global policies.	• Based on the lessons from the intensive sites, extensive approach enlarges the outreach and influence to other civil society groups, donors, academia and government. State Resource Centres play an important role in this regard.
	• Systematic research on civil society and the scale of the nonprofit sector was carried out for the first time in the country.	• Campaign approach to social mobilization (Pre-election Voter Awareness Campaign and Gram Sabha mobilization) and capacity building (orientation of newly elected representatives of PRIs and municipalities and bottom-up participatory planning) helps build a broad-based platform for civil society as well as serves larger public education function.
	• Direct interventions at grassroots aimed at strengthening PRIs as institutions of local self-governance became nationwide with multiple partners. Interventions in urban municipalities were also piloted.	• Integrating efforts in rural areas in PRIs with urban areas in Nagarpalika/municipalities can bring greater synergy.
	• Meaningful dialogue with Governments (Central, State and District) on shared goals in respect of service delivery, participation in development and creating space for the marginalized in decision making.	

(*Contd.*)

(*Contd.*)

	• Government support used systematically to build civil society platforms for voter awareness and orientation of newly elected representatives.	• "PRIA's network of RSOs and other partners is unique in the world of civil society" (Dr. James Manor, Institute for Development Studies, UK). This strength can be harnessed to widen the outreach and impact on these issues.
	• Linkages with Academia were broadened to enhance greater synergy in Practice-Research Engagement on issues of priority for PRIA.	• Improved processes and systems of documentation are needed to capture lessons from intensive, micro sites for effective sharing with broader constituencies. Better linkage between information sharing and practical actions at local and policy levels may require use of multiple media in dissemination of lessons. Use of new Information Technology can greatly enhance this task.
	• Explicit and sustained engagement with Media to promote public education and policy advocacy was operationalised.	
Sixth Phase (2003-2006)	• Deepening of micro-level initiatives, with direct presence of PRIA at the District Level through the model of Panchayat Resource Centres/Urban Resource Centres and District Resource Centres, has led to significant progress in strengthening the participation of people, especially the marginalized in local governance. Networks of elected representatives in many areas initiated.	• Intensifying programme activities in districts and blocks where there is a higher percentage of marginalised groups in the population, and where there are higher indicators of economic backwardness. This will ensure the best use of resources.

(*Contd.*)

(*Contd.*)

	• Civil society engagements at the state and local levels moved beyond NGOs to include community based organizations of women, dalits, retired servicemen and youth groups as well as urban-based associations representing professionals and traders associations. Focused capacity building of citizen leaders and the facilitation of networks of women collectives increased civil society activity at the local level.	• For understanding the constraints and strengthening the linkages between the three tiers of Panchayati Raj Institutions, specific focus on priority issues (like girl child education, NREGS, water and sanitation) at the block and district level is necessary
	• Pre Election Voters' Awareness Campaign (PEVAC) for Panchayat elections significantly scaled up, covering more than half the Panchayats in intervened states - Uttaranchal, Chhattisgarh, Rajasthan, Haryana, Kerala, Himachal Pradesh, Uttar Pradesh and Madhya Pradesh. Extensive PEVAC for Municipal elections undertaken for the first time, encouraging civil society actors to engage with urban governance. PEVAC institutionalized, with other actors adopting the campaign.	• At the meso-level, sustained engagement with state governments across all aspects of the devolution agenda essential for generating pressure. Specific focus on strengthening the awareness and capacities of elected representatives and officials at the district level for planning and implementing of development programmes through District Planning Committees may prove helpful.
		• Extending outreach to civil society organizations, community based organizations and youth groups (NYK, NSS) by facilitating capacity building, networking and learning exchange programs would help nurture and encourage active citizenship, thereby ensuring sustainability of initiatives.

(*Contd.*)

(*Contd.*)

	• Pilot initiatives at participatory town planning for small and medium towns gain recognition with the introduction of JNNURM and UIDSSMT. PRIA's expertise and experience in promoting people's participation in development planning has led to the successful involvement of PRIA as advisory member and consultant for governments and municipalities at the State and District levels.	• Deepening macro-level initiatives through facilitation of a national platform on decentralisation with other like-minded organisations working on Panchayati Raj and Urban Governance. This would intensify the impact of civil society over the reform and devolution agenda.
	• Linkages with academia deepened to the meso and micro-levels with students and teachers becoming ongoing stakeholders in campaigns for reforming governance.	• The RTI Act presents an opportunity to strengthen efforts at ensuring the transparency and accountability of local governance institutions through mobilization, awareness campaigns and capacity building of civil society and community based organizations
	• Media linkage strengthened at the meso and micro-levels with sensitization efforts deepening the quality of coverage from event based to issue based coverage.	• Recent focus on Urban Development and launching of schemes like the JNNURM provides an enabling environment for deepening PRIA's ongoing efforts at promoting people's participation in Urban Governance and advocating for greater devolution.
	• Government linkages reinforced with active collaborations with State Election Commissions (SECs) and the Ministry of Panchayati Raj for PEVAC, resulting in massive scale up of operations. Engagement with State Finance Commissions and the Planning Commission strengthened.	• There is a need for more sustained focus on gender not only programmatically and institutionally within PRIA and its partners but through influencing program and policy in other institutions—including other civil society, government and corporate actors.

(*Contd.*)

(*Contd.*)

	• PRIA's Continuing Education Program initiated, building and developing capacities of professionals for work in the development sector. It is currently successfully running 5 distance education courses. • PRIA Consultancy initiated, providing social and economic development solutions and advisory support to national and international civil society organizations, government and business organizations.	• A more concerted media and communication strategy is required to enhance the efficacy of PRIA's advocacy work as well as promote its academic linkage and learning programme. • PRIA Continuing Education to develop courses in other languages to reach out to field workers and developmental professionals in different locations.

REFERENCES

The Future We are In, April, 1994, PRIA, New Delhi.

Enter the New Millenium: Strategic Plan of PRIA, April 1999, PRIA, New Delhi.

Exploring New Horizons: A Report of PRIA's Evaluation, August 1989, PRIA, New Delhi.

In Search of Relevance; February 1986, PRIA, New Delhi.

Governance Where People Matter: Strategic Plan of PRIA, April 2003, PRIA, New Delhi.

Occupational Health in India: Making a Difference, March 2004, PRIA, New Delhi.

Index